musical form

musical form

HUGO LEICHTENTRITT

musical form

HARVARD UNIVERSITY PRESS · CAMBRIDGE · 1965

FIFTH PRINTING

preface

This book is intended for all those who are interested in the problem of musical structure. It is based on the aesthetic premise that a mass of sound gains artistic value primarily by a sensible, rational form, a certain method of construction, which is closely allied to what we call style in art and which in fact is the main element of style. But the book is not meant to make prescriptions to the creative artist: it does not state any rules. Its purpose is merely to demonstrate what the great masters of the art have done, how they have treated the problem of form, how sensibly and practically they have understood the demands of the art of construction.

Thus, for example, a new rondo must not inevitably be written in the manner seen in this or that masterpiece. It is necessary, however, to see why such a masterpiece must inevitably be shaped as it is. The student will then come to recognize that "form" in the artistic sense is never a final pattern, but the logical application of a certain formal principle to a particular case. He will learn that "shaping" in an artistic sense means to further the natural tendency of any musical idea and, as it were, to divine in what direction this natural growth of a particular idea is likely to lead. The author hopes that students of this treatise will gain a technical insight into the structural laws of music which will not only clarify their understanding of music but will also stimulate and advance their own creative powers by revealing to them the soul and beauty of the masterpieces.

The fundamental theoretical treatment of the first two chapters owes much to the illuminating studies of Hugo Riemann on the rhythm, meter, and structure of the musical work of art. Several chapters are devoted to

v

an inspection of mainly aesthetic problems. The greater part of the book deals with the analysis of selected masterpieces. The analyses might have been extended to the works of contemporary masters, but such a critical inspection of modern works is better reserved for a special investigation in another volume. The closing paragraphs of the last chapter of the book give an additional explanation of the aim and organization of the book and are therefore recommended to the reader's attention.

Musical Form had its germination in 1909 when Professor Xaver Scharwenka, then internationally famous as pianist and teacher, asked me to contribute a book to the series of textbooks, *Handbücher der Musiklehre,* which he edited. I chose to prepare a book on musical form, not treating my topic with startling novelty, but rather striving to surpass my predecessors and competitors in clarity and conciseness. This first edition, published in Berlin in 1911, was equivalent to Part One of the present volume.

When, ten years later, the second edition was prepared, I added a second part in which my own ideas and observations took the book beyond the status of an elementary textbook. The new chapters on "Logic and Coherence," "The Accompaniment in Its Formal and Stylistic Significance," "The Forms of Unison Music," touched new ground, not adequately tilled in any older book. I also added detailed analyses of the Gregorian chant, oriental and exotic music, renaissance and baroque music, works of Bach, Beethoven, the romantic masters, Wagner and Brahms, César Franck and Debussy. Diagrams helped to translate certain musical constructions into visual terms, thus strengthening the reader's insight into the structure of the composition.

For the third edition of 1927, the main new additions were the chapter on Bruckner's Eighth Symphony and a detailed critical inspection of Schönberg's piano pieces, Opus 11. This present edition, the first in English, enriches the book by the inclusion of many smaller sections, by the analysis of Schönberg's Opus 19, and by two new chapters at the beginning and close of the second part.

The material on Schönberg's Opus 19 was published in *Modern Music* (New York) in May–June 1928. The substance of Chapter X was published in the *Journal of Aesthetics and Art Criticism* in December 1945, and is used here by permission of the editor, Dr. Thomas Munro.

Hugo Leichtentritt

Cambridge, Massachusetts
April 1951

contents

VIII the sonata   **121**

IX the vocal forms   **178**

contents

XIV additional remarks on song form   298

XV the contrapuntal forms   302

XVI variation form   322

XVII sonata form   326

XVIII free forms   355

PART ONE

PART ONE

the regular construction
of musical phrases

Form in music may be conceived in two different aspects. First, in a general sense, a composition possesses form when it is so constructed that it is consistent with musical sensibility, containing neither a measure too much nor too little, exhibiting in all its parts the right balance and the right symmetry. In its second and more special sense, form may mean a musical structure conforming to a particular traditional type, such as a simple song, a march, waltz, polonaise, rondo, sonata, or fugue.

Form in its general sense cannot be the subject of a systematic study. It is a matter of musical instinct, of taste, and of artistic intuition. In its second, special sense, however, form can be clearly demonstrated by examples. This distinction can also be expressed in other words: form cannot be the object of systematic study, but only the forms themselves. Form is something abstract, comparable to the Platonic Idea, whereas forms are concrete examples of the idea. As idea, form is unchangeable in every style and age, an element and guiding principle of all creative endeavor. In contrast with this immutability of form, the various forms are changeable and pliable. Abstract form is related to the concrete forms as the species is to individuals.

3

The species remains, the individuals change. Similarly, the forms in every period alter with every new style, while the idea of form is not affected by these passing phases. The idea of form is the subject matter of a philosophy of art, of aesthetic speculation; forms are the subject matter of practical technical study. It is the study of form in this sense that will concern us here. On the one hand it gives the student a clear insight into the construction of masterpieces by enlightening his understanding and judgment; on the other hand, it serves as a support and guide for the beginner in his own attempts at composition.

To form and forms can be added the forming, the manipulation of the laws of form by the creative artist. Comparison with a work of literature will render the nature of forming in its most primitive aspects more easily comprehensible. In this fundamental sense, forming means division; it signifies organization, perspicuity, clarity of perception. A great novel, for instance, is divided into chapters, these again into sections, the sections are built of sentences, and these in turn of smaller subdivisions through the use of various punctuation marks such as semicolons and commas. The smaller sections are composed of single words, and these in themselves consist of letters.

In the same way, a symphony is constructed in various movements (allegro, adagio, scherzo, and finale), the separate movements are subdivided into larger sections (principal or main section, middle, and final section) and these in turn into shorter ones, indicated by cadences. These shorter sections are composed of still smaller groups of notes, the motifs; the latter, finally, of several separate notes.

The single note, like a single letter of the alphabet, has no expressive value by itself, but it is comparable only to a building stone. In very special cases it may have the importance of an ejaculation, of an "Oh" or an "Ah," but no more.

At least two notes are needed in music to produce something intelligible, something comparable to a word. Barring exceptional cases when a motif is constructed of simply a single note and a rest, it must, in general, have at least two notes. The motif alone is of no more value than a single word. Only a sentence can be said to convey a full meaning. Many proverbs, for instance, consist of but a single sentence. Similarly, in music there are small structures such as folk songs and dances which within the narrow compass of eight measures give an impression of completeness and roundness.

The teaching of musical form, therefore, must proceed from the motif, and pass on to the examination of the eight-measure phrase and its development into still larger groups, into an entire movement. Finally, the still larger cyclical forms will have to be considered, forms composed of several movements, like the suite and sonata.

4

Musical literature is extraordinarily rich in its many different formal types and styles. Practically every epoch of musical history has its own characteristic forms. For the beginner, however, it is especially important to know those forms which are still actively functioning. It is these, therefore, that will be chiefly under discussion here. The forms of the past will naturally also be mentioned, in so far as they still relate to the music of our own day.

the motif

The motion, the progression, from one note to another or to several notes, constitutes the motif. Just as in walking one must first raise the foot before putting it down, so too the motif normally begins on an upbeat (upbeat: lifting, *arsis;* downbeat: descending, *thesis*). Of course there are many motifs which begin with the downbeat, but they are exceptions involving an artificial foreshortening of the normal upbeat motif, as will be more explicitly shown later.[1]

The first problem in composition consists in the proper continuation of the chosen motif. The impression of coherence is not produced by any irregular series of tones, but only where a definite order controls their placement. The easiest method would be simply to repeat a motif starting either on the same note of the scale, or on other degrees of the scale, higher or lower. In the latter case, one speaks of sequences which must be distinguished from exact repetitions. A motif permits a diversified number of changes in both the melody and the rhythm. In spite of such changes, it will be easy to recognize the motif if the distribution of its notes on the accented and unaccented beats of the measure remains unchanged.

The following examples will illustrate:

Der lieb-ste Buh-le, den ich han, der liegt beim Wirt im Kel-ler

| First | Second | Third | Fourth |
| measure | measure | measure | measure |

This little four-measure phrase from an old folk song, "Der Muskateller," is divided into four single measures, which are unified by the same rhythm. The rhythm of the first bar motif

is exactly retained in all four measures. The melodic order, however, is different in each measure: there is in the first, for example, the leap of a fourth,

---

[1] For discussion of the difference between motif and theme, see Chapter XI.

then unison, and a second upwards; in the second measure, a second upwards, unison, a second downwards; in measure three, a descending third, another descending third, an ascending second. Nevertheless, the ear recognizes the original motif in all these changes. This would not be the case if the original rhythm (with the accent on the long note) had been altered. Write the melody in 4/4 time, without changing a note, and it immediately becomes apparent that, through the shifting of the accents, the original coherence has been completely lost; from the simple, natural rhythm something entirely different and more complicated has been evolved:

Every bar motif in the first example was made up of two rhythmically equal subdivisions:

$$♩ \mid ♩$$

This, however, is not always the case. Frequently the subdivisions of the motif are rhythmically unequal. For example, in the well known German folk song, "Der Jäger aus Kurpfalz," the melody consists of two different motifs, *a* and *b,* which together make up the larger bar motif:

In the course of the melody *a* and *b* are used irregularly, *a* appearing five times, *b* only three. Motif *a* alters its melodic guise, appearing in measure one with an upward leap and reversed in measure two. Yet the ear quickly recognizes it because the characteristic accents and the particularly significant repetitions on the third and fourth notes are always retained. The cheerful onward surge, the vivid character of the melody, is attained by the preponderance of motif *a* and the lesser prominence of the retarding motif *b*.

strong and weak measures

In normally built melodies, the measures do not have the same weight. Just as one speaks of an accented and unaccented beat, a strong and weak beat in a single measure, so also are there strong and weak measures as part of the entire melodic line. One can observe in countless simple folk songs such as "Der Mai ist gekommen," shown here, that the second measure is,

in relation to the first, the one which usually has the greater stress. Without further comment, the musical instinct perceives that here each of the even-numbered measures (2, 4, 6, 8) has a particular stress in contrast to the odd measures. This is because in each case the second measure terminates the little phrase, leading to a cadence. We come here to the foundation of musical structure, to the two-measure group. This is the unit by which musical form is measured. As one measures the length of an object by inches, so one measures the extension of a melody by two-measure groups.

The next grouping in size is the four-measure group which consists of two two-measure groups. Here, too, the second group, namely the third and fourth measures, has greater weight than the first one. This stressing of the final group is found in the smaller groups of two to four measures, as well as in the larger groups of eight or sixteen measures. The construction of a four-measure group can be manifold. The last two measures may repeat the motif of the first two, or they may introduce a new motif. Naturally, within each two-measure group there may again be many differences of construction, of which a few have already been indicated.

There is the continuation of motif *a* in the third and fourth measures of the folk song "Es waren zwei Königskinder."

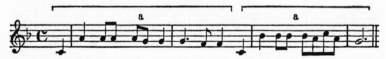

There is the introduction of a new motif *b* in the third and fourth measures in "Die drei Röselein," also a folk song.

7

The possibilities in the construction of four-measure groups are so numerous that an exhaustive treatment would require much space. Therefore only the most common types will be discussed in detail, but they will provide a basis for easily understanding other varieties as well. The above types *a a* and *b b* have many variants, as may be seen if one takes into account the subdivisions of the single bar motif, such as that from Handel's *Aria,* "Lascia ch'io pianga":

The construction is 1 + 1 + 1 + 1 measure. The bar motif *a* appears four times. This is an instructive example because of the apparent difference of motif *a* in each single measure. But the characteristic of the motif, the accent on the second beat, appears in every measure. The entrance on the first beat (measures 1 and 3) is really only an artificial variant of the original type with an upbeat. This original type, of which Handel's melody appears as a polished, stylized variation, would be as follows:

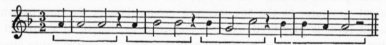

The order is *a, a, a, a.*

Mozart. Quartet in C major

Construction: 1 + 1 + 2 measures. Two different motifs, *a* twice, *b* twice: *a, a; b, b.*

Mozart. Quartet in D major

Construction: 1/2 + 1/2 + 1 + 2 measures. Three motifs, *a* three times, *b* once, *c* once: *a, a, a; b; c.*

Mozart. Quartet in B flat

Construction: 2 + 2 measures. Two motifs. The order: *a, b, a, b.*

This is a very common type, from which one can derive the following type:

Here the same motifs appear in a somewhat less usual order: *a, b, b, a.*

Beethoven. Op. 22

Construction: 1 + 1 + 2 measures. Four different motifs, *a, b, c, d,* with *b* and *c* related to each other. At first glance the variation theme of Beethoven's Op. 26 seems similar in construction:

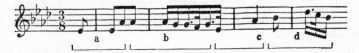

Of the four motifs *a, b, c, d, a* and *c* are related. But the melody might be reduced to the following simpler prototype:

with *a* used four times in melodic transformations. This, too, is an instructive example, in that it shows how a simple theme may be changed by melodic ornamentation into something entirely new. The technique is of great importance in writing variations.

As illustration of several other types, a short and simple melody is given below and its structure varied by changing the order of its motifs:

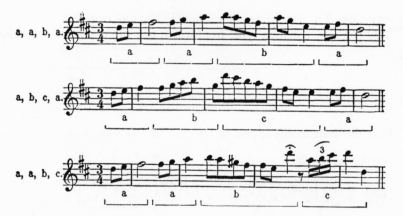

a, a, b, a.

a, b, c, a.

a, a, b, c.

Although the four-measure group has a certain conclusiveness and coherence, it still demands continuation. It is like the beginning of a sentence up to the comma or semicolon. A second four-measure group, connected with the first, brings the phrase to the normal end, the cadence.

For the four-measure group a great diversity of possible constructions has been pointed out. A still greater variety exists in the construction of the eight-measure group.

In the study of eight-measure groups it is even more advisable to confine oneself to the main types if one is to avoid too extended a theoretical discussion. Two main types are to be distinguished:

(1) Eight-measure phrases built in the manner of a "period."

(2) Eight-measure phrases not built in the manner of a "period."

period, antecedent, and consequent

One speaks of a period when an evident correspondence, a resemblance (not repetition), exists between the two four-measure groups, the fifth measure corresponding to the first, the sixth to the second measure. The degree of resemblance may be more or less marked. Sometimes the character of a period is sufficiently established if only the fifth measure corresponds to the first. But even when both sections are identical, one speaks of a period and not of a repetition if the cadences of both sections are different. The first phrase of a period is called the antecedent; the second, the consequent.

Periods are classified according to the kind of cadence or close used in the antecedent and consequent phrases. The types of period most frequently used are:

(1) Antecedent with a half-close (chord progression I, V): consequent with full close (V, I).

10

(2) Antecedent modulating to the dominant with full close; consequent has full close in the tonic.

(3) Antecedent, full close in the tonic; consequent modulates to the dominant.

(4) Antecedent, half-close; consequent modulates to the dominant.

The following examples may illustrate these four types:

(1) Beethoven, Ninth Symphony:

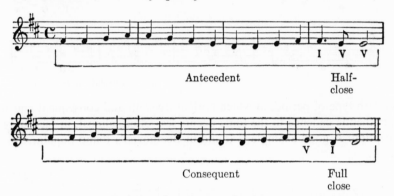

Antecedent   Half-close

Consequent   Full close

Here both sections are identical, with the exception of the cadences.

(2) Beethoven, Op. 27, No. 2:

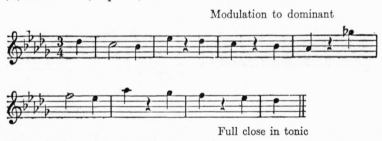

Modulation to dominant

Full close in tonic

(3) Beethoven, Op. 28, Scherzo:

Full close in tonic

Modulation to dominant

Though antecedent and consequent each have eight instead of four measures, this is a good example of the third type. Two measures in 3/4 time
may be thought of as one measure in 6/4 time.

(4) Beethoven, Op. 14, No. 2:

Half-close

Modulation to dominant

The fifth type of period, in which both antecedent and consequent end with
an authentic cadence in the tonic occurs less often, almost, in fact, only by
exception. A good example is found in Beethoven's Piano Sonata, Op. 27,
No. 1:

Full close in tonic

Full close in tonic

Periodic construction makes the structure of a short sentence easily discernible, the symmetry and similarity of the two phrases producing an effect
comparable to that of verse and rhyme. It impresses the ear at once and
gives a feeling of simplicity. Folk songs in particular, and all music of a
popular character make intensive use of periodic construction.

eight-bar melodies without periodic construction

There exist, however, constructions of a more complex nature, which,
in the eight-measure phrase, do not make use of the popular periodic structure with its easily grasped symmetry. They aim rather at a broader curve
of the melodic line, making possible a longer melodic breath and more interesting rhythmic effects. The higher art forms which show a special predilection for these patterns require a finer, more developed musical understand-

ing for their appreciation. The characteristic features of this type of structure are pointed out in the illustrations below.

Two main types are to be distinguished:

(1) Antecedent and consequent develop the same motif.

(2) Antecedent and consequent develop different motifs.

Beethoven's Op. 10, No. 2 exemplifies the first type:

The theme of the slow movement of Beethoven's C Minor Symphony also falls into this category. This theme is particularly instructive, as it shows how one may retain firm coherence by the continued use of the same motif and at the same time avoid the monotony, the cut-and-dried regularity which may occur so easily in this type of melody. Compare Beethoven's setting *a,* with the regular symmetrical form *b* in order to see how the rather monotonous melody *b,* has been refined in Beethoven's version by a few slight changes and thereby really raised to artistic stature. Observe especially in *a,* the gain in expression achieved by the fusion of two measures into one broad plane, instead of the short-breathed, separated, one-measure phrases found in the *b* version.

The second type which uses different motifs for antecedent and consequent, is well illustrated by the main theme of Beethoven's Sonata Pathetique:

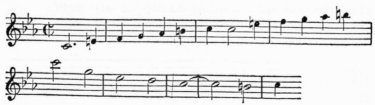

free structure of the period by rhythmical variation

Many of these freely constructed melodic patterns perceptibly approach the structures of the period to which their origin can usually be traced. In the following example from Beethoven's Quartet, Op. 59, No. 1, compare the composer's rather free version with the second, simplified version, which has been reduced to a regular period. Notice how much more expressive and melodically interesting Beethoven's melody is; especially how much more effectively the melodic climax (the long-held f in the seventh measure) stands out:

Simplified version:

Such an example may invite the student of composition to practice trying the reverse method; that is, to evolve through rhythmic variation a freely built melody from a simple period. In practice of composition there will be occasion to employ such a method whenever one wishes to shape and polish a melodic line in order to gain greater intensity of expression. This type of melodic transformation is often useful in variation technique.

Beethoven constructed the cavatina theme in his B-flat major Quartet, Op. 130, with much greater freedom. Here it is hardly possible to reduce the melody to the plain periodic construction without doing serious violence to the melodic structure.

The following transformation would of course be possible:

but in sentiment and expression it has practically nothing in common with Beethoven's melody, as it really represents an entirely new theme built from the original material. Beethoven's composition *a* is a perfect model of the adagio type of melody, in which an extremely broad and slow tempo is not only usual, but even categorically essential. The *b* version represents, through the regular repetition of almost dancelike rhythms, a sample of the andantino or allegretto type to which the slow tempo of version *a* would be a contradiction. Version *b* is therefore an untrue, aesthetically objectionable expression of its emotional content.

Finally, there are the eight-measure phrases constructed with still greater freedom, melodies in which scarcely one measure rhythmically coincides with another. The Adagio in Beethoven's Fourth Symphony is of this type:

the one-part form

The smallest unit in musical structure, complete in itself, is the one-part form. It is built of a single eight-measure phrase. Examples of this type are not frequent. German popular songs like "Fuchs, du hast die Gans gestohlen," or the melody of Mendelssohn's "Leise zieht durch mein Gemüt" (with a small extension in the last measure), or the theme of Beethoven's thirty-two Variations in C minor, as well as some tunes in Schumann's "Kinderlieder," Op. 79, would illustrate this type.

the twelve-measure phrase

Following the eight-measure phrase (2 × 4 measures), the next higher unit in the order of grouping would be the twelve-measure phrase (3 × 4 measures). As a three-part period, one finds it occasionally, though not very often, in old German folk songs, such as "Stille Nacht," "Der Mai ist gekommen," or in the following old Christmas song: "Zu Bethlehem geboren ist uns ein Kindelein."

Zu Beth - le - hem ge - bo - ren ist   uns ein Kin - de - lein

Compare also the twelve-measure construction of the principal theme in the second movement of Beethoven's F-sharp major Sonata, Op. 78.

The easily accessible *Oxford Book of Carols* (London, 1928) containing some two hundred fine tunes—English, Scotch, Irish, German, French, and Dutch melodies—provides rich material for the study of folk song, its melodic structure and form, as do also the American Negro spirituals, the Stephen Foster songs, American hymn tunes, and popular ballads. As regards structure, the Foster songs are quite simple and primitive, making use almost exclusively of eight-bar phrases and multiples of eight, sixteen, and thirty-two measures. The somewhat more advanced 4 + 4 + 3 and 5 × 4 bar structures are found in the "Sussex Mummers' Carol" (No. 45 of the Oxford collection):

16

and in the beautiful spiritual, "Deep River":

Many samples of refined and interesting melodic structure may be found in the numerous Italian canzonette of the early seventeenth century, a number of which are published in my new edition of volume IV of Ambros' *Geschichte der Musik*.[2] Also the English madrigalists of the seventeenth century have written, besides their elaborate madrigals, many simple, popular tunes, in the manner of the Italian canzonette and balletti or dance songs. A song by the great melodist John Dowland shows the interesting combination of four-bar and six-bar phrases:

the sixteen-measure phrase

Very often a freely constructed eight-measure phrase will serve as the antecedent of a larger, sixteen-measure period. All that has been said with references to the eight-measure phrase applies equally to the sixteen-measure

[2] Leipzig, 1909, pp. 788, 806, 809, 824, 826, 885, 886.

phrase, which, in many cases, is to be regarded as a doubling of the eight-measure phrase. There are sixteen-measure periods of the same types as the eight-measure periods, except that the antecedent and consequent phrases are twice as long. Melodies of sixteen measures constructed freely, not periodically, can be found, but they are harder to recognize than eight-measure constructions of the same type. Very often the sixteen-measure phrase is only an inexact version of the eight-measure one, since frequently (without apparent reason, or through carelessness) the real measure is divided into two measures. For example, two 3/4 measures may be written instead of one 6/4 measure. A few examples will suffice:

Beethoven. Op. 2, No. 3

This is a sixteen-measure period; a half-close at measure eight (in the dominant, g—b—d); at the sixteenth measure a modulation to the dominant, G major, corresponding to type four of the eight-measure period.[3] Strictly speaking, two measures in 3/4 should here be taken as one in 6/4, and the first notes of measures two, four, and six should not have as strong an accent as the corresponding notes in measures one, three, and five.

normal treatment of the period in the minor

Beethoven. Symphony No. 7

[3] See page 11.

This is an illustration of the normal treatment of an eight- or sixteen-measure phrase in the minor mode. Instead of modulating to the dominant the progression, in the minor, rather modulates to the third above the relative major key. Here in the eighth measure there is a modulation from A minor to C major; at measure sixteen, a return to the tonic, A minor.

Beethoven uses the reverse order in the theme of the Funeral March of the "Eroica" Symphony. Here the cadences occur at the eighth measure in the tonic, C minor, and at the sixteenth measure in the relative major key, E flat.

larger periodic groups

Corresponding to the aforementioned three-part periods of twelve measures (3 × 4), larger groups of twenty-four measures (3 × 8) occur even more frequently.

In our later study of the song, dance (minuet), and march forms, these constructions will receive more detailed treatment. Here follows but one example of this construction of 3 × 8 measures. It is not, however, a piece complete in itself, but simply a part of a still larger whole: the principal theme of the first movement of Beethoven's piano sonata, Op. 90:

large melodic lines

Freely constructed sixteen-measure phrases, when well built, give the melodic line sweep, amplitude, and the effect of a long breath. But they are difficult to construct, since these same qualities are essential in their invention. If the composer is not gifted with this feeling for the sweep of the large line, he will never be able to do much with it. Elementary teaching has not much to do with the construction of such melodies—they require a master's hand.

Johann Sebastian Bach particularly is unrivaled for the bold expanse, the power, beauty, and elegance of his long melodic line. From the arias in his cantatas, oratorios, and masses, one may cull many an example. In the cantata No. 61, for instance, "Nun komm, der Heiden Heiland," the solo tenor aria begins with the following sixteen-measure ritornello:

One will look in vain for a caesura in the eighth measure. By the signs ||
the completely irregular scansion is indicated. There is no trace of periodic construction. The numerous one-measure phrases are a characteristic of this melodic line. Its structure is: $2 + 2 + 1 + 1 + 2 + 1 + 1 + 1 + 1 + 2 + 2$ = a total of sixteen measures. An arrangement in larger groups seems hardly possible. Nevertheless, the melody has extraordinary flow, great roundness and compactness, close cohesion from measure to measure. The use of only a few rhythmic motifs and the frequent employment of sequences do much towards this end.

rhapsodic melodies

There exist even more freely constructed entirely rhapsodic melodies, which, at first glance, seem to be entirely disconnected, yet they acquire roundness and coherence when supported by an accompaniment in a regular rhythm. Bach presents a simple, but good example in the above-mentioned cantata, immediately after the tenor aria, in an arioso for bass voice. Although the arioso is only ten measures in length, it nevertheless affords a perfect model for this extremely interesting type of melodic structure. Such melodies, because of their irregularity, obviously have less need of the typical eight- or sixteen-measure phrases:

dem wer-de ich ein - ge - hen und das A-bend-mahl mit ihm

hal - ten, und er mit mir.

the song form

Eight- and sixteen-measure phrases of various types can appear as smaller sections of larger works, or as independent, complete pieces. The latter will be discussed first, because works in this form present a complete unit. Such small forms are usually found in the folk dances, and in themes for variation. In most cases it may be classified as a song form of one type or another. One distinguishes between two-part and three-part song form, also called binary and ternary form, and under these classifications, small and large song form.

THE SMALL TWO-PART SONG FORM

The small two-part song form generally has eight or sixteen measures, less often two groups of sixteen measures, which are usually divided into two equal sections. The most frequent variants are built on the pattern of *a b* (8 + 8, or 4 + 4), and *a b a* (8 + 4 + 4), the last four measures being identical with the first four.

Type *a b,* an old folk song of the seventeenth century:

Das Maid - lein wollt' 'nen Lieb-sten han, Bi - re - baum,

22

Type *a b a* is illustrated by the following folk song, "Gute Nacht, mein feines Lieb":

THE LARGE TWO-PART SONG FORM

This form differs from the small one only in that all the proportions are larger. Whereas the smaller one normally has 8 + 8 measures, the larger is extended to 16 + 16. Now and then one may be in doubt whether a melody belongs to the smaller or the larger type, as not uncommonly a phrase of sixteen measures may consist of only eight "real" measures (cf. page 12f.). If the single sections are lengthened by repetitions, the entire two-part form may be enlarged to sixty-four measures, and possible insertions and expansions can increase the number of measures still further. An excellent example is provided by the theme of the Beethoven Sonata in A flat, Op. 26. The construction is: *a,* sixteen measures; *b,* eight measures plus two measures of expansion; *c,* eight measures. The theme of Beethoven's F major Variations, Op. 34, is similarly built.

The middle section, part *b,* plays an important role here. In all larger song form constructions, in dances, in marches, this middle section with its numerous variants is of real importance. Later on, it will be discussed as a "trio." The characteristic feature of a middle section is its tendency to leave the chief tonality, then to modulate more or less freely, and finally to return to the original key. The third part, with its repetition of the first section, gains its justification and its effectiveness through the contrasting middle section. Before the chief tonality can be brought back artistically, it is obviously necessary first to depart from it. In larger structures the middle section often contains new thematic material, while in the smaller forms its melodic line is often related to the main section.

The two-part song form predominates both in folk songs and art songs, in small instrumental pieces of various types, in dance and march tunes, and in the form of theme and variations. In the later discussion of these different forms, the two-part song form will often be considered.

THE SMALL THREE-PART SONG FORM

The small three-part song form is built of three sections of about the same size. The first and third sections correspond to each other. They are either alike or resemble each other closely, while the middle section is more or less different. Here, too, the formula *a b a* predominates, as in the two-part song form.

The difference between the two-part and three-part forms consists in the fact that in the latter *b* is not half the length of *a,* but at least equally long. Occasionally the pattern *a, a, a,* occurs; that is, the same melodic phrase three times in succession, naturally with such changes and treatment as will avoid monotony. A good example is found in the trio from Beethoven's Sonata Op. 2, No. 2:

The first section has eight measures in A minor, with a modulation to the dominant, E minor. The second section, eight measures in G major, with a modulation through D minor back to A minor. Third section, eight measures in A minor.

The pattern *a b a* is illustrated by the minuet from Beethoven's Sonata, Op. 22, shown at the top of the next page.

24

There follows after this a coda of seven measures.

THE LARGE THREE-PART SONG FORM

This form doubles the proportions of the small three-part song form, containing under normal circumstances forty-eight measures (3 × 6) instead of the twenty-four measures (3 × 8) of the smaller form. By virtue of its greater extension, this form is preferred for smaller dance and march forms, which it completely suits. When we consider such compositions, we will refer again to the three-part song form.

In recent years, new elements of formal construction have become known through Alfred Lorenz's fundamental study of the Wagnerian technique of form.[4] This work provides new insight not only into Wagner's art, but the art of music generally. Lorenz coins the term arch-form designating by it not only the traditional *a b a* pattern of the three-part song form, but also applying it to the da capo aria, the sonata form, and even to larger complexes. He also enriches the terminology of music by what he calls the bar-form. This term, by analogy to the older German poetry, he applies to the structures built on the pattern *a a b,* the *a a* signifying two stanzas

[4] A. Lorenz, *Das Geheimnis der Form bei Richard Wagner,* 4 vols., (Berlin, 1924–33).

(*Stollen*), more or less alike, and *b,* a different, closing stanza (*Abgesang*). In the *Meistersinger* numerous examples of bar-form *Stollen* and *Abgesang* are found. Since Wagner, this melodic structure, seldom found in classical music, but common in older music and also in many Protestant chorales, has been restored to honor.

irregularities in the construction of musical phrases

The eight- or sixteen-measure phrase underlies all musical structure. More extended pieces are simply composed of a series of such phrases. The longer the piece of music, the greater the care which must be taken to prevent the monotonous, regular succession of single phrases.

irregularities in the four- and eight-measure structure

The symmetry peculiar to the structure of four- and eight-measure phrases quite frequently therefore demands interruption of a too regular progression. Such interrupting irregularities, extensions, contractions, or elisions act as enlivening, interesting details. Their ingenious use often gives an elegant sweep to the melodic line, in other cases one can produce an effect of capriciousness, or give to the melodic line an otherwise unattainable, widely curved arch, often winning striking rhythmical effects thereby. A few examples will serve to illustrate this point.

The four-bar phrase is sometimes replaced by one of three or of five bars: the three-bar phrase is often a contraction, the five-bar phrase an expansion of the four-bar phrase.

THREE–BAR AND FIVE–BAR PHRASES

The folk music of the sixteenth and seventeenth centuries made extended use of three-bar phrases. The following example, a peasant dance of the seventeenth century, shows the effect of interspersing three- and two-measure phrases:

Tanz mir nicht mit mei-ner Jung-fer Kä-then! Sonst scherz ich mit dei-ner Jung-fer Gre-ten. Laß mir, was mir wer-den soll, lie-ber Bru-der, hörst du wohl! Tanz mir nicht mit mei-ner Jung-fer Kä-then, tanz mir nicht mit mei-ner Jung-fer Kä-then.

The tune is built according to the pattern: *a*, 3 + 3 measures; *b*, 2 + 2 measures; *a*, 3 + 3 measures, representing a small three-part song form. The three-measure phrase

is a contraction of the four measures

or

An effective application of a five-measure phrase is shown in the following folk melody of the sixteenth century:

Frisch auf, gut G'sell,—— laß rummer gahn, tummel, tummel dich,

28

tummel, tummel dich, tummel, tummel dich, tummel, tummel, tummel

dich   gut's Wein - lein.

The fourth measure can clearly be recognized as an insertion and could be omitted without damage to the context. The melody gains its unusual charm, however, precisely by this superfluous fourth measure, which takes care of the "tumbling" in such humorous fashion.

Brahms too, in the theme of the *Chorale of Saint Anthony* taken over from Haydn (theme of the Brahms orchestral variations, Op. 56), furnishes a fine example.

The third and eighth measure could be omitted. Extensions of an eight-measure phrase may arise in three ways:

(1) The beginning may be given twice for greater emphasis.
(2) The end may be underlined by repetition.
(3) The middle may be enlarged by interpolation, by repetition of motifs at places where in the normal structure no repetition is demanded, or through the addition of entirely new motifs.

Characteristic examples of all three cases are given below:

Repetitions at the beginning are not frequent. An excellent example is found in Beethoven's Op. 111:

where he enhances the opening of the piano sonata through echo-like repetition and emphasis. In the older music of the seventeenth and eighteenth centuries, extension by means of the echo is a common effect. The beginning

29

of an aria from Pergolesi's *Stabat Mater* may serve as an example of extension to a six-measure phrase by means of a slightly varied echo:

The same proceeding is found in the Pastoral Sinfonia in Handel's *Messiah:*

The music continues similarly in three-measure phrases. The three-measure phrase is the rule for such echo effects: generally, the second heavy measure is repeated in echo. The echo repetition of a light measure occurs much less frequently. These echo repetitions are not confined to the beginnings of the phrase, but may also enter in the middle or at the end.

The most common extension is brought about by a very convenient method of making the ending particularly expressive. Here one must distinguish between mere appendage at the close and an interpolation somewhere in the middle. The appendage does not affect the structure of the phrase at all, as it only adds a final flourish to an already complete phrase. Such final flourishes, for example, are the rapid little interludes and postludes in the chansons of the operettas, or dance songs, after every stanza or right at the final cadence.

Harder to grasp, but much more interesting, are the interpolations just before the final cadence, which have the purpose of delaying the final ending, and therefore increasing the tension. For this purpose the deceptive cadence is often useful. It brings about a prolongation of the final cadence, somewhat in the following manner: IV V VI / IV V I. In the cadence pattern, IV V I (subdominant, dominant, and tonic) the relative VI is used in place of I. The pattern is then immediately repeated and leads this time to the ending. A well known, very old folk song will illustrate this procedure:

In the eighth measure there is a two-measure extension, through the repetition of the cadence, broken by the deceptive cadence of V VI. In this case the sixth degree chord of A minor might be replaced by the first inversion of the tonic triad I, making the succession V I.

There are so many possibilities for both extensions and elisions that it is hardly possible to enumerate all of them. Whoever wishes to observe the elegant effect of these refinements in greater detail should turn to the minuets in the quartets and symphonies of Haydn, Mozart, and Beethoven, which by deliberately striving for charm, finesse, and surprising curve of the melodic line, offer abundant and most interesting material for study. As but one instance, the minuet from Haydn's "Emperor" quartet (Op. 76, No. 3) may be cited here to illustrate the third kind of extension in the above list:

Here is an eight-measure phrase, extended to twelve. The brackets indicate the interpolations. If one omits these interpolations, one perceives the simple eight-bar melody. The structure is: 5 + 2 + 1 + 2 + 2, instead of 4 + 2 + 2 measures. The basic form of the melody is as follows:

How much finer an impression is produced by Haydn's irregular version is immediately made manifest. The first insertion humorously points up a

31

witty exaggeration of the leap of a sixth, amplified into a skip of a seventh
and then of a ninth. Through the two extensions the entire melody is raised
an octave at the ending.

Beethoven begins the finale of his Op. 26 with a six-bar phrase, which
can be explained as the extension of a four-bar phrase:

The extension becomes more evident when the melodic line is simplified as
follows:

Not infrequently extensions arise from small introductions or preludes.
Sometimes even a single chord answers the purpose. In other cases, one or
more measures are needed:

Schubert. Impromptu

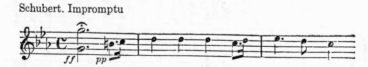

The long-held G with fermata is not counted in the construction of the
phrase.

Beethoven. Quartet, Op. 132

This opening contains a two-measure introduction, establishing the rhythmic pattern of the accompaniment. The melody begins only in the third measure.

Cases like these are easily understandable at first glance, since one can see where the musical phrase begins. But this is not always so clearly seen when the introduction is less definitely delineated. There are musical phrases which do not exactly start with the first measure, but usher in the latter with an introduction, which begins somewhere in the middle of an incomplete eight-bar phrase. Thus the opening of Beethoven's quartet, Op. 59, No. 2, may be explained as follows:

The true first measure of the phrase begins only at the third measure. The previous two measures are but remnants of an incomplete eight-measure phrase. The piece starts out very energetically, setting the listener immediately *in medias res*. The beginning of Beethoven's Sonata Op. 7 shows a similar treatment:

The actual beginning of the theme is in the fourth measure. The same explanation serves for the six-measure beginning of the finale of Beethoven's Second symphony:

Here is an eight-bar phrase, which does not begin with its first, but with its third measure. These six, instead of eight, measures represent of course not an extension, but rather a contraction of the eight-measure phrase.

33

Irregular constructions are sometimes caused by an unusual grouping in the eight-bar phrase, as, for instance, 3 + 5 or 5 + 3, instead of the usual 4 + 4 measures. The following minuet theme will serve as a case in point:

A slight alteration is enough to give this little melody its regular structure. It is only necessary to place the sixth measure after the third and a perfectly symmetrical theme will result (4 + 4 measures):

An attractive example is found in Berlioz' "Minuet of the Will-of-the-Wisp" from his *Damnation of Faust:*

The eight-bar phrase obtains piquant, unexpected effectiveness through the irregular structure of its second half. The structure is: $2 + 2 + 1 + 1 + 2$ measures. The normal continuation could be, after the fifth measure, something like this:

For Berlioz the deviations from the above version are the following: measure 6, a reversal of the order of the first two quarter-note groups: measure 7, introduction of motif *b* instead of the regular motif; measure 8, continuation of motif *b* throughout the measure.

Notice also in this melody the remarkable force of the appendage motifs, of which more will be said in the course of this chapter.

Very quaint irregular effects are sometimes obtained by the piling up and shifting of accents. Thus in 3/4 time, a 2/4 or 4/4 measure may be forcibly superimposed by means of sforzati or syncopation. This effect was known in older music as "hemioles" (hemihole, half-whole, or one and a half). In modern instrumental music, Beethoven has made very ingenious use of such rhythmical effects. Observe, for example, how charmingly capricious a quite regular, well built phrase of sixteen measures becomes through his use of scattered sforzati:

Beethoven. Op. 120. Variation Five

Similar effects can be obtained through syncopation.[1]

the treatment of accents in irregular constructions

The composer in search of irregular effects will find that there are three ways of treating the rhythmical centers of gravity in an eight-bar phrase:

(1) By retaining the four strong measures, in spite of extensions or contractions.

(2) By increasing the number of strong measures.

(3) By reducing the number of strong measures.

The first case has already had detailed comment in the examination of extensions and contractions. The essential fact is that here the extensions do not bring about an increase in the number of strong measures. Such extensions appear as if set in brackets, as if brought in only parenthetically without special stress. Thus a twelve-measure phrase of this sort would have only four strong measures. Compare the Haydn minuet demonstrated above and the Beethoven minuet in Op. 7. An increase in the number of strong beats may be artificially effected through clusters of sforzati. This case is illustrated by variation five in Beethoven's Op. 120 above. A reduction in the number of strong beats by artificial means occurs rarely and seems appropriate only under exceptional circumstances.

Contractions, elisions, or omissions in the eight-measure phrase are just as important as their opposite, the extensions, but are harder to understand.

In elision, either the weak or the strong measures may be omitted. Thus

---

[1] See Hermann Wetzel's study on syncopation in *Music*, May 1910.

a six-bar phrase, shortened from eight, will have two instead of four normal strong accents, if the second and sixth measures are omitted. The following eight-bar phrase may, through omission of the second and sixth measures, be made to lose two strong measures:

This omission of the strong measure occurs often at the end of an eight-bar phrase, when, at the same time, a new phrase begins with a weak measure. The terminating strong measure then loses its meaning as a strong measure, and by permutation becomes a weak measure. Examples of this contraction will be cited later.

More common still is another type of elision in which a weak measure is omitted so that two strong measures succeed each other, producing a redundance of beats. A most interesting example of this simultaneous contraction and extension is found in Mozart's *Abduction from the Seraglio*. The first aria of Act I begins with the following nine-measure phrase:

The phrase appears strikingly irregular. At *a* one measure is missing, at *b* there are two redundant measures. The normal eight-bar phrase could be extracted from Mozart's melody as follows:

In the Mozart version two strong measures follow each other in measures two and four while the weak third measure is left out. Four *a* and four *b* are interpolated as an echo of measures three and four. Thus the phrase is extended to nine measures, with five strong measures instead of four.

In determining the construction of a phrase, one need not pay as much attention to the number of the written measures as to the number of strong beats. Normally, there is one strong beat, one rhythmical center of gravity for every two measures. One may also define a bar motif as a succession of tones which group themselves around a strong accent. A phrase with two strong beats is a four-bar phrase; one with four strong beats is an eight-bar phrase, even though through extensions or contractions a four-bar phrase may have been changed into a three- or five-bar phrase, an eight-bar phrase into a seven-, nine-, or ten-bar phrase. Also the three- and five-bar phrase has, like the four-bar phrase, two strong measures. The seven-, nine-, or ten-bar phrase has four strong measures, like the eight-bar phrase. Exceptions to this rule are rare. More complicated constructions are created by the shifting of the strong measures, the overlapping of phrases through canonic imitation. This case may be illustrated by a few measures from the coda of the first movement of Mozart's C minor piano sonata:

This eight-bar period has in the right and left hands two different groupings of measures: in the right hand, 1 + 2 + 3 + 2; in the left hand, the regular grouping of 2 + 2 + 2 + 2 measures. The imitation is effected so that the weak measure in the left hand coincides with the strong one in the right. As one can well imagine, this divergence of rhythmical structure between the right hand and the left hand presents a definite technical difficulty for the performer.

Such complications occur especially in pieces of a fugal and canonic style, particularly in the stretta sections. The following quotation from Bach's *Well-Tempered Clavier* (F minor fugue of the second book) will show clearly how in such cases the melodic lines are intertwined, how the different parts have their strong accents at different places. In the upper voice, one should note the two-measure insertion at *a*. The middle voice enters with a weak measure simultaneously with the strong measure of the upper voice. In the lower voice, the accents are shifted by a one-measure extension at *b:*

Structural relations become more complicated when the leading of the melodic line is not limited to a single voice, but demands several voices in polyphonic writing. Two main cases are to be distinguished:

(1) When the melodic line passes from one voice to another.
(2) When the imitations weave their patterns below or above a melodic line.

The first case is the simpler one. Almost everywhere in somewhat ambitious orchestral and chamber music it is customary not to retain a single melodic line constantly in the same voice, but to make the melody pass over from one voice to another one.

Considerations of tone color are often decisive: Beethoven, for example, in the "Eroica" symphony distributes a single coherent melodic phrase between four different instruments:

Oboe   Clarinet   Flute   Violin

In this case we are in reality confronted with homophonic writing disguised as polyphony. There are also, however, real polyphonic constructions, where two or more voices not only alternate with each other, but also maintain a more or less intricate dialogue. The example at the top of page 41, from a trio sonata for organ by Bach, will illustrate the point. It is most clearly demonstrated here how the voices interlock: the second voice enters before the first one has come to an end.

Even more complicated are those cases where, either above or below a continuous melody, the other voices are intertwined in canonic imitations.

Variation four in Beethoven's great cycle of variations, Op. 120, illustrates this case well:

The upper voice moves quite regularly in an eight-bar phrase with four strong accents in the second, fourth, sixth, and eighth measures. Because of the limitations, the strong beats in the lower voices are heard in the third and fourth measures, so that three strong measures follow each other directly, namely, in the second, third, and fourth measures (the held G). In the last four measures, the strong beats occur regularly again, because the imitations enter at two-measure intervals instead of one.

It may sometimes happen, however, that several voices in complicated contrapuntal texture are not kept together by a normally built principal melody. In this case, the consequences of the polyphonic style make themselves felt still more brusquely. Two or more melodies may be opposed to each other simultaneously, either of them being intent on establishing its structure without regard for its neighbor. In the old Flemish counterpoint it often happens that several voices are combined which are not measurable by the same unit of time, simply because they have no such common unit. In such cases, an entirely irregular change of double and triple time may take place; two measures in 3/4 time may clash against three measures in 2/4 time, resulting in the following rhythmical scheme:

or the imitation of a phrase in 4/4 time may enter at a half-measure's distance, so that the rhythms are intertwined, as follows:

Frequently an accented beat in one voice is heard simultaneously with an unaccented beat in the other voice, producing a fascinating interplay of accents which distinguishes this old music with its free, barless rhythms from modern music with its regular bar lines.[2]

The accompanying harmonies are also very important for the comprehension of structure: normally the change of harmony will take place in the strong measures, that is, in the second, fourth, sixth, and eighth measures. Especially the fourth and eighth measures, the rhythmical centers of gravity, will be underlined by sharply marked change of harmony. The principal theme of Beethoven's sonatina, Op. 79, may serve as an illustration:

[2] Numerous specimens of this type may be found in my collection of old German part-songs (Breitkopf and Härtel), of Monteverdi's madrigals (Peters Edition), and German House Music of Four Centuries (Berlin: Max Hesse).

In the second, fourth, sixth, and eighth measures, the cadential chords are sharply delineated. But these cadential chords are not the only possible harmonies. Many others might be employed. As a matter of fact, the symmetry of structure in an eight- or sixteen-measure period will generally be balanced by a symmetrically planned harmonic scheme. Wherever a well-rounded impression is desired, the harmonization will also contribute its share towards this end. If the above-mentioned Beethoven melody were harmonized as follows, the impression of roundness, of finish and conclusiveness would be utterly lost because the cadences, having no evident relation to each other, would move capriciously from key to key without orderly plan:

43

It would be wrong, however, to conclude that such a harmonization would be out of place under all circumstances. Wherever the impression of roundness and finality are not important, such a harmonization might be effective. For example, imagine this phrase placed in the development section of a slow movement. Sometimes such a completely altered harmonization may have a special charm, as in a set of variations, where the simple symmetrically harmonized theme would later appear in an entirely different harmonic version.

Beethoven makes use of this device in the variations of his A major

quartet, Op. 18, No. 5. He answers the simple theme later with a harmonization which replaces the harmonic roundness of the theme by something entirely new. The theme uses the progressions of I V, V I, I V, a modulation to the dominant (V). The variation modulates from D major, to A major, B minor, F sharp minor. A setting like this second one would usually occur in the middle of a composition. At the beginning it would create an unsettled, restless effect and would obliterate any impression of an exposition. In order to observe this, imagine that the theme and the variation in the Beethoven movement exchange places with each other so that the variation stands as the theme at the beginning of the piece. The absurdity of such a transposition would be clear immediately (see p. 44).

the treatment of cadences in four-bar groups

A few examples suffice to make clear that for a songlike, simple, and well-rounded melody, only a symmetrical harmonization is proper, with cadences in nearly related keys, making use preferably of the half-close and the authentic cadence in the principal key. In this parallelism, every rising progression is balanced by a correspondingly descending progression. If the fourth measure has the cadence I V, the eighth measure will naturally have V I. If the fourth measure modulates to the dominant, the eighth measure will return to the tonic.

Some of the simplest and most common cadences are the following:

In C Major	*In A Minor*
(1) Half-close on G; Full close C.	(1) Half-close on E; Full close A.
(2) Modulation to G; Full close C.	(2) Modulation to C major; Full close A.
(3) Full close C; Modulation to G.	(3) Modulation to E minor; Full close A.
(4) Modulation to A minor; Full close C.	

Naturally all the refinements of cadence known from the study of harmony may be freely used in the harmonization of well-rounded melodies: alterations, substitute tones or chords, deceptive cadences, suspensions, and so on. In all these cases only harmonic embellishments are employed by which the basic functions of the simple chords are not at all changed. To illustrate the various possibilities of cadence the following little piece has been especially devised. The first cadences are quite simple. Towards the end they grow more and more involved:

The cadences numbered one to six are as follows: Half-close on G; modulation to the dominant G; variant of the half-close at three; the progression C to B in the bass is changed to C sharp to B flat; half-close I V at four; modulation to E flat major; full close in C major after a series of rather complicated deceptive modulations through the use of passing chords. The themes of Mendelssohn's variations, Op. 54, Op. 82, and Op. 83, abound in similar interesting modulatory turns and cadences.

The distinction between strong and weak measures is not always easy. In certain cases one can hardly determine whether a certain measure is strong or weak. In doubtful cases several successive measures together must be examined, as it is easier to make the proper distinctions in a larger complex.

Although a composition begins normally with a weak measure, a strong measure sometimes occurs first. In such a melody the strong beats are shifted, and the eight-bar phrase usually gets a feminine ending, a close on an unaccented beat of the measure. Such constructions starting with the strong measure can best be understood by calling the strong measure the "second" measure. Thus the phrase starts with the second measure. The preceding first measure has been omitted. The identical phrase in two different versions may illustrate how the accents are distributed in such cases:

Version *a* illustrates the normal eight-measure phrase with the strong beats at the even measures; *b* shows the same phrase with the first measure omitted. The paradoxical beginning with the "second" measure will thus be comprehended in its true meaning. The measure which is lacking at the start is added at the end. This explains the extension of the E flat at the end, the feminine ending, while at *a* the sharply marked masculine ending enters. The first note of example *b* is not the start but the close of a motif whose beginning has been omitted. The following rhythmical interpretation, though frequently found, is nevertheless wrong because the coherence of the motifs from measure to measure is thereby broken up.

It would also be wrong to interpret the beginning of Schumann's "Warum" (Op. 12) in the following manner:

In this case the strong measures are not the second and fourth, but the third and fifth measures. This apparent contradiction to the rule is explained by Schumann's incorrect notation. The melody ought to have been written in 4/4 time, two 2/4 measures contracted into a single 4/4 measure. This correction makes it evident that the heavy "second" measure coincides with the third measure in Schumann's notation. The correct notation would be:

Certain two-bar and four-bar groups do not end with the accented beat of the measure, but rather with a so-called feminine close. In a feminine close the cadence does not end on the strong beat, but is carried over to a weak unaccented beat:

b, c, d show feminine endings; *d* is particularly noteworthy, because here it is manifest how a feminine ending may extend into the next weak measure, without losing its character as an unaccented close. If such a feminine ending is melodically extended, motifs of a peculiar type occur, for which Riemann has coined the term, *Anschlussmotive,* or appendage motifs. These motifs have the power of turning a weak measure into a strong one or vice versa. The following example illustrates this phenomenon:

The same melody in two versions: *a* with masculine endings; *b* with feminine endings and appendage motifs. Because the strong accented measures of *a,* the second, fourth, sixth, and eighth, are melodically extended, they lose their emphasis, and example *b* shows a new type of motif with the strong beat at the beginning.

A good example of this type with its appendage motifs and strong beat at the beginning is found in the finale of Beethoven's C major sonata, Op. 2, No. 3:

If one changes the appendage motifs into masculine endings, the strong beats also are shifted and occur one measure later. The theme then would appear somewhat as shown at the top of page 49.

the linking together of successive phrases

As soon as one goes beyond the eight-bar phrase, the problem of how to connect successive phrases becomes important. The simplest proceeding, of course, would be to complete the first phrase, before starting the next one, i.e., direct smooth coördination of two phrases. Frequently, however, an overlapping of the phrases occurs: the last measure of the first section is at the same time the first measure of the second section:

First measure

Eighth measure

This example also illustrates how sometimes the strong measure may coincide with the weak measure. The eighth measure as such would be strong, but since it is also the first measure of the next section, it loses its strong accent and is changed into a weak measure. In the direct coördination of two phrases it often happens that a pause occurs between the end of the first phrase and the beginning of the next one. This break is usually filled in by a prolonged upbeat (a *Generalauftakt* in Riemann's terminology), usually containing a more or less rapid scale- or passage-figure, as we see in the first movement of Haydn's quartet Op. 54, No. 2:

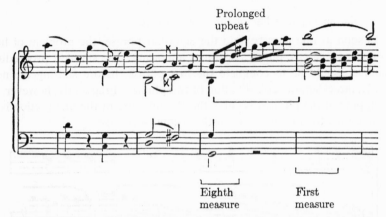

Sometimes a prolonged upbeat will be extended to cover several measures. Particularly instructive examples of this type occur in the first movement of Beethoven's sonata Op. 31, No. 3. A two-bar passage of this type is found in the transition from the first to the second eight-measure phrase (measures eight and nine):

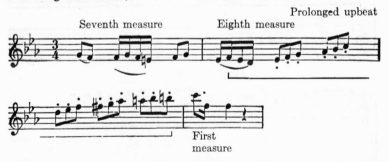

In measures 53–57, at the repetition of the second theme, the upbeat is prolonged to four measures:

This insertion of four measures could have been replaced by an upbeat of only one measure in length:

By this contraction, however, the sweep of the melodic line would be impaired. It is expressly in order to obtain this elegant curve that one employs these prolonged upbeat passages. The corresponding measures in the reprise section of this sonata extend this four-measure passage even further to six measures. Compare also the introduction of the second theme in D major in Chopin's B minor sonata, first movement.

Insight into the nature of such passages teaches us that in actual performance they should not be played in strict time with sharp accents on the first beat, nor with differentiation of strong and weak measures, but rather rolled off as a prolonged upbeat in a single onward surge. It would even be logical to write them without bar lines in order to make manifest to the eye at first glance their nature as merely filling out, transitional, ornamental features, like arabesques. Just as the light upbeat does not like to be weighed down by chords or harmonization (with rare exceptions, as in old part songs of the sixteenth century and Bach chorales) so, too, passages replacing the upbeat require no harmonization, and are better written without any chord accompaniment. The preceding final chord is prolonged by them and dies away within them.

the song forms and their application to the dance and march

The student who has comprehended the elements of musical construction, who has learned to build eight- and sixteen-bar groups, to vary them by extension or contraction, to connect the single phrases, is now prepared to proceed to the study of larger forms. Our somewhat theoretical introduction may now be followed by the practical application of these theoretical principles and by the study of entire pieces. First we will consider the simpler types of dance, march, and song form, later, the more complicated forms, such as the prelude, fugue, canon, passacaglia, the suite and sonata, in all their varieties. Finally we will examine the most important of the vocal forms.

the dance

There is an important distinction between the real dances, intended for dancing, and the idealized dance forms. The latter, while retaining the general outlines of the dance, add refinements of structure, of harmony, and of musical treatment which would be disturbing and inappropriate in actual dancing, and by its excessive pretentiousness would divert attention from the dance itself. First of all, a piece of dance music must clearly mark the rhythm of the dance. Besides this, it should have a characteristic and pleasing melody. Dances are written partly in duple, partly in triple time. The most popular ballroom dances of nineteenth-century music are the polka, galop, waltz, polonaise, mazurka, contradance, quadrille.

THE POLKA

The polka is a Bohemian dance which originated in the nineteenth century. It must not be confused with either the polonaise or the polacca. The polka is written in 2/4 time and in a rather lively tempo; the polka rhythm is 2/4:

The purest polkas are to be found in the works of Bohemian composers, in the ballet music of Smetana's operas and, not infrequently, in Dvořak's compositions. Johann Strauss, Ziehrer, and others have written polkas strictly for dancing. The polka occurs frequently too in Swedish folk music. Like the march and mazurka, the polka has a short introduction preceding the dance proper, a trio in the middle, and a coda at the close, after the repetition of the polka.

THE GALOP

Similar to the polka, but much faster is the galop, which is a leaping dance, with a characteristic rhythm in dotted notes, somewhat as follows:

The galop is built throughout like the polka. In both dances there is an introduction of a few measures. The dance proper is written in three-part song form, containing either 3 × 8 or 3 × 16 measures. Extensions or contractions of the eight-measure phrase are rarely used here. The trio,[1] too, is built in two- or three-part song form, usually in a tonality different from the main section, preferably in the subdominant. Dances in the minor keys

[1] In the study of musical form, the trio means a middle section, a contrast to the principal section in its more reposeful, broader character. Because this middle part was originally written for three voices, in the old French ballet suites, it received the name trio; in later compositions, however, strict three-part writing is by no means a characteristic feature of the trio.

are rare, except in the music of Slavic countries. The coda is an appendix which does not belong to the dance proper. Eight or sixteen measures generally suffice for the coda.

THE WALTZ

This most popular of nineteenth century dances is one of the youngest of them all. Waltz literature first arose around 1800, particularly in Vienna. The masters of the classic waltz are Joseph Lanner, Johann Strauss, father, and Johann Strauss, son, whose worthiest successor was Emil Waldteufel. The waltz, written in 3/4 time, usually if it is a fully developed work begins with an introduction, often in a slow tempo, more or less in the style of a fantasy. Next follows the *Eingang* (entry), a short phrase of a few, generally four, measures marking the waltz rhythm sharply and introducing the waltz tempo before the dance proper begins. Generally five waltzes, though sometimes less, are written in sequence, contrasting with one another in melodic character. Each waltz is built on a regular pattern usually of 2×16 measures, with clearly defined cadences and rather simple modulation.

Occasionally, the waltz is written in three-part instead of two-part song form, with the third part repeated at the end. Often, in two-part waltzes, two entirely different sixteen-bar periods succeed one another without any thematic connection. Several of the five waltzes are generally written in different tonalities. The whole work is concluded by a finale, which links together the various waltz melodies in the manner of a potpourri, occasionally elaborating one of them still further and winding up with a brilliant climax at the end. The artistic value of a waltz lies in its wealth of light, agreeable, varied, and graceful melody. Generally only the accompanying dance rhythm is allotted to the bass and middle parts, whereas the composer's art is displayed in the melody of the uppermost voice. Exceptionally, the roles are reversed, the melody is placed in the bass, and the upper voices indicate the dance rhythm.

The new "Paris" waltz is written in a somewhat shorter form: 2×16 measures : || : transition to the trio || : 2×16 measures : || the waltz da capo, followed by the finale and coda.

In the nineteenth century the waltz was transformed into concert music, just as earlier the old dances had been adapted to the concert suite. Thus, Chopin's famous waltzes and Brahms' "Liebeslieder" are meant as salon or concert pieces, not as dance music. Even symphonic music does not disdain a waltz occasionally, as is shown in Berlioz' "Symphonie Fantastique," in Tchaikovsky's Fourth and Fifth symphonies, in Liszt's "Mephisto" waltzes. In such cases the composer, free from the restrictions imposed by the actual dance, can apply much more elaboration of harmony, modulation, and polyphony to his concert waltz. The characteristic feature of the waltz rhythm accompaniment consists in the sounding of the bass note alone, on the first beat, followed by the full chord on the second and third beats:

Chopin. Op. 64, No. 3

THE MAZURKA

The mazurka, the Polish national dance, is written in 3/4 time. Frequently shifted accents constitute the rhythmical peculiarity of this dance. It gets its main accent on the third, sometimes the second beat, instead of on the first beat. These sharp accents make the mazurka energetic, forceful, and fiery, entirely foreign to the soft charm of the waltz. The accents correspond to the violent motions of the dance, to the leaping, the stamping of feet, the clapping of hands.[2]

Through Chopin's masterly piano music, the mazurka was introduced into art music, along with the Kujawiak and Oberek. The Kujawiak is a peasant dance. It is slower and quieter, more monotonous and melancholy than the mazurka. At its end, the Kujawiak generally passes over into the very fast Oberek, often in 3/8 time. The mazurka, like many other dance types, often has a short introduction preceding the dance proper and a trio in another tonality as intermezzo, followed by the repetition of the mazurka plus a coda. The typical mazurka rhythm is illustrated by Chopin's Op. 68, No. 1:

[2] Felix Starczewski published a very illuminating study on the mazurka in the *Sammelbände* (1902) of the International Society of Music. The Chopin mazurkas are treated in detail in my *Frédéric Chopin* (Berlin, 1905), and *Analyse der Chopin'schen Klavierwerke,* 2 vols. (Berlin, 1920–21).

THE POLONAISE

The polonaise is a stately march dance in 3/4 time, generally of a gallant, pompous, and festive character. Its distinctive features are the rhythm of its accompaniment:

and its typical conclusion:

The origin of the polonaise is generally traced back to a banquet given by Henry of Valois who later became Henry III of France, at the Polish court in Cracow in 1574. Recently, Spanish origin has been claimed for it.[3] Polonaises are found occasionally in the suites of the eighteenth century, also in Bach's French suites, but these do not reveal much of the characteristic rhythmical pattern. In the so-called "polonaises" of the song collections of the eighteenth century, the rhythm at least is hinted, as in the following song from Sperontes'[4] "Singende Muse an der Pleisse":

Un-ter euch, ihr lieb-reich stil-len Schatten, sucht mein Herz die

Ein-sam-keit zum Gat-ten und ge-neust der an-ge-nehmsten Ruh.

Even much earlier in the songs of Heinrich Albert in the seventeenth century, pieces are found "in the Polish manner."[5]

---

[3] See Tobias Norlind, "Zur Geschichte der polnischen Tänze" in *Sammelbände* (1911), p. 502, of the International Society of Music.

[4] See Max Friedländer's *Das deutsche lied im 18. Jahrhundert*, I, 2, 219.

[5] See new edition of Albert's "Arias" in *Denkmäler deutscher Tonkunst*, XII, XIII.

The literature of the polonaise as an actual dance is restricted mainly to a few Polish composers, like Oginski, Kurpinski, Moniuszko. The polonaise entered the realm of art music through Chopin, whose example inspired Liszt and other musicians, such as Tchaikovsky, Mussorgsky, Moszkowski, Xaver Scharwenka, and others.

In its construction the polonaise resembles the march; it uses a sort of trio or intermezzo, contrasting with the main theme, and it shows a preference for a large three-part form. Chopin's much more complicated polonaises are not intended as dance music proper, but as concert pieces in polonaise style. Thus, for example, the E flat minor polonaise is in rondo form,[6] with two subsidiary sections. Op. 40, No. 2 is built on the same plan. The outstanding example of this form is the great A flat polonaise, Op. 53. The chief theme of the F sharp minor polonaise will illustrate the characteristic polonaise rhythm:

THE MINUET

The minuet is a French dance which became an art form in the seventeenth century. Its name is sometimes derived from the short, dainty steps (*menus pas*) of the dance. The characteristic features of the minuet are a certain amiable charm, a certain artful grace of the salon. It is written in 3/4 time; its tempo rather slow, its melody pleasing. The French suites of the seventeenth and eighteenth centuries abound in charming minuets. Indeed, this dance, more than any other, expresses the rococo spirit to per-

[6] See p. 110.

fection. The minuet is virtually the only one of all the old dances which has survived in modern music. As the second or third movement, it has become an indispensable feature of the sonatas, quartets, and symphonies of Haydn and Mozart. It is precisely here that the most remarkable masterpieces are to be found, since both Haydn and Mozart displayed the entire refinement of their art of rhythm most brilliantly in their minuets. Nowhere, in fact, can one better learn what is meant by refined, distinctive, and ingenious rhythm. Beethoven took over the minuet, but frequently replaced it with the scherzo.[7] Although the scherzo was favored during the nineteenth century, the minuet likewise kept its modest place in the sonata form. As the best known model of its type, the minuet from Mozart's *Don Giovanni* is sketched out here:

The minuet, as part of the sonata, is generally written in a three-part form of the type *a b a* with da capo. The first part, *a,* is the minuet proper, *b* is the trio; the last *a* is the repetition of the minuet, often with an added coda. Each of the three parts has its own subdivisions in the style of the three-part song form. As an example of a minuet with all the refinements of the species, let us consider the minuet from Mozart's G minor symphony.

First part: fourteen measures, a contraction of the sixteen-measure period, caused by the two three-bar phrases at the beginning.[8] The first phrase, the antecedent, closes in the tonic. The second, the consequent, modulates from G minor to D minor, the dominant:

[7] See below, p. 62.

[8] This three-bar phrase might be restored to the normal four-bar construction somewhat as follows:

Middle section: continuation of the three-part main motif with an additional new countermotif. The structure is $3 + 3 + 7 = 13$ measures. One measure is lacking at the end. Modulation from B flat through G minor, E flat major, and C minor returns back to G minor:

Third part: very free recapitulation of the first part. At the reprise of the minuet, the masters often take considerable liberties with this form. Thus, instead of mere repetition a more or less complicated variation may occur, in this particular case, a canonic imitation of the chief motif. The nine-measure phrase is an extension of the eight-bar phrase by one measure.

This interpolation will become clearly manifest by special attention to the bass (at *a*):

Coda: simple repetition of the main theme, 2 × 3 measures:

Trio, G major, 3/4 time: First part (3 × 2) = 6 + 8 + 4 measures. At the beginning, a contraction [9] of two measures at *a* and an extension of four measures at the end, increases the sixteen-bar phrase to eighteen measures. At the close, the dominant D major is reached by modulation:

[9] In normal construction, the beginning, in four-bar sections, would correspond to the four-bar ending as follows:

Second part: eight measures of regular construction, 2 × 4 measures. Modulation from D major back again to G major:

Third part: the reprise of part one (3 × 2 = 6) + (5 × 2 = 10) = 16 measures. This is therefore a sixteen-measure section, irregularly built by the division into 6 + 10 instead of 8 + 8 measures. The last section has two measures more than expected, compensating for the two measures lacking in the first section. This time the second section has an extension of only two measures, whereas at the corresponding place of the first section an extension of four measures was interpolated:

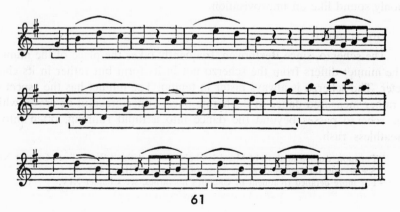

short instrumental pieces

The small or large three-part song form, with or without a trio, as used in the minuet, is preferred in instrumental music for short pieces, such as the song without words,[10] the nocturne, impromptu, and romance, which do not however, make use of this form exclusively. Their titles have reference to the character rather than the form of the music.

THE NOCTURNE

The term nocturne (Italian, *notturno*) translated literally means night piece or night music and is used in the eighteenth century as the equivalent of serenade,[11] cassation, or divertimento. Music for wind instruments, filled with the dreamy, soft sound of the horn, was popular in those sentimental "Werther" days, especially for nightly serenades or nocturnes. In the nineteenth century the nocturne became a species of piano music, brought to perfection mainly by John Field and Frédéric Chopin. Franz Liszt introduced his edition of the Field nocturnes with a remarkable literary appreciation of Field's nocturnes as lyric little masterpieces.

Chopin's nocturnes are generally written in three-part song form in slow tempo, with a more rapid middle section, a tempo scheme quite frequent in music: andante, allegro, andante.[12] Robert Schumann's "Nachtstücke" sometimes approach this form, and sometimes make use of a still more involved song form similar to the rondo. Schumann was particularly fond of this complex song form.

The reversed order—allegro, andante, allegro—is used by Chopin in his impromptus, as well as by Schubert in his impromptus. Schubert's "Moments musicaux" have a similar construction although they are shorter. The term impromptu (derived from the Latin words *in promptu,* in readiness) means almost the same thing as improvisation. The piece should commonly sound like an improvisation.

THE SCHERZO

The scherzo, since Beethoven, frequently takes the place of the minuet. The minuet differs from the scherzo not in its form but rather in its character. The scherzo is always faster in tempo. The minuet has the aspect of a rather measured dance in deliberate pace, either graceful or grave, while the scherzo passes beyond the dance into a rapid running, often into a breathless rush.

10 For more explicit analysis of Mendelssohn's "Songs without Words," see Chapter XIV.
11 See section on Serenade, at the close of Chapter VIII, p. 173.
12 For more detailed treatment of Chopin's nocturnes, see Chapter XIV.

As its name suggests, jest and humor are its chief attributes. Beethoven, particularly, expressed its presto style with most brilliant effect. He always preserved the humorous character of the form. Even in his less frequent scherzi in minor, which are sometimes charged with a strange, demoniacal, and restless motion, a humorous tone occasionally breaks through, as in the jolly, rollicking trio in the scherzo of the Fifth Symphony. Hurried, sprightly rhythms, sudden sharp accents, shiftings of the accent by syncopation, clever use of staccato, great leaps in the melodic line, violent dynamic contrasts are the main characteristics of the Beethoven scherzo. Nearly all the later composers down to Brahms, Bruckner, and Mahler have retained in their scherzi the features of the Beethoven scherzo.

Mendelssohn introduced a new note into the scherzo. He is the master of the fantastic, the diaphanous, airy scherzo, nimble-footed and delicate, like a fairy's dance, a carnival of elves. For Chopin, the scherzo was a piano piece of larger dimensions, in rapid tempo. His four *Scherzi,* among his best works, abandoned the Beethoven-like humor, but stressed the fantastic, the demoniacal, the savage and nocturnal traits to a degree hitherto unknown in piano music. The rapid tempo of the scherzo permits a much larger extension of the form as compared with the minuet. This greater extension need not actually mean an extension in time, however. Beethoven, in some of his larger works, extended the scherzo to nearly twice its usual length by expanding the basic form *a b a* into a larger pattern *a b a b a,* thus bringing in the trio twice, and the main section of the scherzo three times. Later composers occasionally go even a step further by employing two different trios instead of the repeated trio. Schumann, in particular, is fond of this form of scherzo. In his symphonies and chamber music many an example may be found. The Schumann "Novelettes" for piano, and also the "Nachtstücke" are written in this free song form, closely related to the rondo. The structural formula for pieces of this type would be *a b a c a,* with two different intermediate sections, or *a b a c a d a,* with three intermezzi.

THE ETUDE

The etude is a short, instrumental piece devoted to the practice of some particular technical formula. Its purpose is to offer the player a certain technical problem in its various aspects and in a musically coherent form. Generally some type of song form underlies the etude. A single motif, just as in a variation or in a song accompaniment, is usually carried out through the entire etude. Since the study gains coherence by being limited to a single motif, the etude can, on the other hand, permit itself a much greater freedom of harmony, modulation, and structure than would be feasible in a straightforward song.

Many etudes confine themselves to the stressing of technical problems (such as those of Czerny, Bertini, and frequently, Clementi). But the great masters of piano composition have always striven to combine musical value with technical purpose in the etude. In this respect, the etudes of Cramer, Moscheles, and especially those of Chopin and Liszt are eminent models. The greatest master of the etude is Chopin, who knew how to set forth ingenious, novel, highly interesting technical problems in such a way that they became poetry in sound. Three etudes by Cramer, Moscheles, and Chopin may be briefly examined here.

Cramer, No. 39. Bülow edition

The technical motif is a scale figure for the left hand, with a briefly struck octave at the beginning of each measure. The pianistic difficulty of this piece lies in this brief octave, from which the etude mainly derives its practical value for the suppleness of the left hand. In the right hand there is a light, chordal accompaniment interrupted by rests. The musical value of the etude lies in the even flow, the lovely contour of the bass figure, and in the counter melody to which the right hand chords contribute their share; it lies also in the climax of the second part, in the elegant descent towards the end, and in the balance and polish of the form. The piece has seventy-two measures, so divided that each of the two parts is precisely equal in length, namely, thirty-six measures.

Moscheles. Op. 70, No. 15

The technical motif is a light staccato touch, alternating with legato, and resulting in the desired *leggierezza*. In this three-part form, the first section, of forty-seven measures, is a development of the motif quoted. The second, the middle section, aims at contrast. Now the motif is played by the left hand, forte, while the right hand plays heavy, full chords. The climax is attained in the middle, fortissimo, the motif now being played by both hands. Following this an abrupt change occurs, with the return to the original setting of the first section, again leggiero and piano, and then a surprising modulation from E flat back to A flat major. The middle section starts at measure 49 and ends at measure 108. The third part, measures 109–141, returns to the version of the first part without being an exact repetition. It has the character of an enlarged coda which replaces the reprise. Here is an interesting illustration of the above-mentioned free and ingenious treatment of the formal scheme. The musical refinement of the piece is manifest in the climax of the middle section, in the sudden contrast (the E flat section) in the second part, in the interesting harmonic return to the A flat tonic and in the broadly extended coda.

Chopin. Op. 10, No. 9
Allegro molto agitato.

The technical motif is widespread accompaniment figure in the left hand, an onrushing and receding wave of sound, which, together with the rhythmical rubato, produces the "agitato" of the piece. Its form is two-part. The first section contains thirty-six, the second, thirty-four measures. The two parts run completely parallel to each other. In the first part the relative major A flat and the dominant C predominate; in the second part the tonic key of F minor is central, in accordance with the general procedure of the song form. The musical values of the piece are manifest in the passionate melody, rising over the surging bass, in the powerful climax at the end of each section, in the magnificent expression of the agitato character, in the abrupt change from passionate outcry to timid anxiety, from forte to piano.

the march

The march is closely related to the dance. Since a march is a piece of music suitable for marching, that is, for forward motion in regular steps, the rhythm of the march must be adapted to this purpose. It must be in duple time, corresponding to the regular alternation between the right and left foot. All marches are therefore written in 4/4 time, with few exceptions.[13] Sometimes they are written alla breve, and, as quick marches, in 6/8 time.

Generally the form of the march is simple, developing from the eight- or sixteen-bar form. It is quite important to mark the accents strongly. Most military marches are written in the three-part form *a b a,* as used in minuets and scherzi: first the march proper, then the trio as contrasting melodic middle section, often in the key of the subdominant, and finally the repetition of the march. When the march is taken over into opera and concert music, not infrequently it is symphonically treated, planned on a larger scale and more extensively developed than an actual march. The march proper is represented by a great many military marches, among which are found pieces of outstanding musical value, such as the German marches of Hohenfriedberger, Dessauer, Torgauer, "Pariser Einzugmarsch," Sousa's American marches, and others. Masterly marches of solemn, religious character are found in the works of Gluck in *Alceste* and of Mozart in *The Magic Flute.*

Models of the pompous, festive march are: Mendelssohn's "Wedding March" from the *Midsummer Night's Dream* music, the "Coronation March" from Meyerbeer's *Le Prophete,* the "Entrance of the Guests into the Wartburg" from Wagner's *Tannhäuser,* Wagner's "Kaiser Marsch" and "Huldigungsmarsch."

The most famous funeral marches are by Handel, in *Saul,* Beethoven, from the sonata, Op. 26 and the second movement of the "Eroica" symphony and Chopin, in his Piano Sonata in B-flat minor. To this group may be added the funeral music from Wagner's *Götterdämmerung,* which, however, is quite different in construction.

At least one of these pieces can be closely examined here, namely the "Marcia funebre" from Beethoven's "Eroica." The piece shows a mixture of various elements of form. It begins in regular march form with trio, but at the reprise of the march theme, an elaborate development is inserted, somewhat similar to the middle section of the sonata form, or to a subsidiary section in a rondo. Towards the close, a second episode of this same type is interpolated.

(1) Main theme in C minor: 2/4 time, 8 + 8 measures. New theme in E flat major (touching the keys of C minor and F minor in passing); 20 + 20 measures (with allusion to the main theme twice). Concluding motif in C minor; 12 measures.

---

[13] Schumann, for example, in his *Carneval* writes the march of *Davidsbündler* against the Philistines in 3/4 time.

(2) Trio in C major, three-part form. First theme, C major; 12 measures. New theme, F major; 10 measures. Repetition of the first C major theme, and transition to F minor; 15 measures.

(3) Reprise of the Funeral March theme in C minor, with a transition to F minor; 9 measures. Development of a fugato section for forty measures, whose motif is derived by inversion of the E flat motif of the first section:

Two new contrapuntal counter motifs

To this is added the preparation of the reprise; 19 measures.

(4) The reprise of part (1) in a more complicated version, somewhat shortened by the reduction of the E flat section to half its original length; 8 + 20 + 10 measures.

(5) New episode in D flat major, 4 + 10 measures, with a new motif leading back to C minor to a resumption of a motif from the second part of (1); return to the main theme; 16 measures. The main theme again at the end; 8 measures. The most famous feature of the Coda is the concluding section where the melody is broken up by short, sobbing pauses.

CHAPTER *IV*

the contrapuntal forms

the invention

What Johann Sebastian Bach called an invention is a short two- or three-part piece in contrapuntal style, not bound to any particular form, written sometimes in free polyphony, sometimes in strict canonic or fugal style. The most ingenious results follow from the manipulation of the subject and countersubject. In Bach's inventions, playful lightness and elegance of motion are combined with the strictest logical structure. More detailed discussion of the invention technique will be found in the second part of this book.

the prelude

The prelude,[1] especially in its older, contrapuntal form, may be called the precursor of the etude. The preludes of Bach's *Well-Tempered Clavier*

[1] For the sake of brevity the prelude is placed here under the title of contrapuntal forms, though many preludes are written in homophonic style. With reference to the preludes and fugues of the *Well-Tempered Clavier,* attention may be called to Busoni's edition, rich in profound insight and in illuminating comments on formal problems as well. Riemann's analysis will also prove of value. Landshoff's scholarly edition of Bach's autograph, now a treasure of the Yale University library, is a most valuable contribution to recent Bach literature.

and those from his organ works are certainly to be regarded as the most eminent models of their species. In their plan they have something in common with the Chopin etudes, though their style, their manner of expression, are different. The two- or three-part song form is used also in the Bach preludes, and here, too, a single motif dominates the entire piece. One of the simplest and, at the same time most beautiful, examples is the first prelude in C major in the *Well-Tempered Clavier,* a lightly undulating motion of chords dissolved into arpeggios and always retaining the rhythmical motif:

The second prelude in C minor is similar in method, though very different in character. Here again the character of an improvised prelude is manifest. A rushing torrent of sound, an onward impelling motion characterize the piece. It represents admirably that type of the tempestuous, florid, and playful prelude which, as a virtuoso piece par excellence, is the direct consequence of the technique of the instrument, shaping in an artistic manner the elementary peculiarities of piano technique. This prelude pattern is closely related to the toccata.[2] The preludes, Nos. 5 (D major), 6 (D minor), 15 (G major), 21 (B flat major), all from the first book of the *Well-Tempered Clavier,* belong to this type, as well as No. 6 (D minor) from the second book.

A third type is represented by preludes like Nos. 11 (F major), 14 (F sharp minor), 17 (A flat major), 20 (A minor) from the first part of the *Well-Tempered Clavier.* This type of prelude is contrapuntally-treated prelude limited to a certain number of parts, strictly developed, evolved from the subject and countersubject with application of double counterpoint. It can hardly be distinguished from pieces which Bach in other works calls two- or three-part inventions. The only difference lies in the fact that the invention is in itself complete, whereas the prelude generally serves as an introduction to an immediately following second piece, generally a fugue. Bach's organ preludes belong mostly to this third type, but are usually planned on a larger scale.[3]

Chopin's Preludes (Op. 28), the most beautiful modern examples of the species, are short, independent pieces which may be regarded mostly as etudes in miniature. They, too, are built entirely on a single motif. Pianistic

[2] On the toccata, see p. 84.
[3] The second part of this book, Chapter XV, contains more detailed investigation of the preludes of the *Well-Tempered Clavier.*

figuration and virtuosity play an even greater role than with Bach. Others, again, are sustained and slow, reminiscent of the first section of a nocturne. Mendelssohn's Preludes (Op. 35) stand midway between Bach's and Chopin's. In their contrapuntal texture, their broad development, they approach the Bach organ preludes. On the other hand, however, they make effective use of brilliant modern pianistic technique. The organ preludes of César Franck, like those of Max Reger, dating from more recent years, are derived from Bach; Rachmaninov's preludes for piano continue the style inaugurated by Chopin.

Until about 1725 the dance suites often contained a first movement called the prelude. This prelude not infrequently was a work planned on a larger scale, and because of the richness of its thematic material, was different from the usual prelude types. Often it contained two or three separate themes. It really was a sonata movement in the sense of the older sonata type. Perfect instances of this type are found in the first movement of Bach's English suites. Such a prelude differs from the other movements of the suite in not being related to the dance forms. It is a freely constructed, contrapuntally complicated piece of music. The terms sinfonia, concerto, or sonata are often used instead of prelude. The older composers were somewhat careless in designating their works; consequently, a great confusion existed in reference to such forms as the sinfonia, concerto, sonata, and prelude. Only late in the eighteenth century were these various species cleanly separated from each other. The term "preluding" is applied to a free improvisation, often without reference to a formal type. Organists still practice this kind of improvisation, which was formerly fashionable with pianists, but is now rarely heard.

THE CHORAL PRELUDE

A very special type of prelude is the choral prelude, which has dominated organ literature for centuries. Its greatest master was Bach. Yet it was also known two generations before him, as well as among many composers of the nineteenth and twentieth centuries, who have attained remarkable results with this form. One may easily become acquainted with the older choral prelude through an extensive collection edited by Karl Straube in the Peters edition. The choral prelude has no definite form. There is considerable variety in its construction. Yet several types in common use stand out.

(1) The choral melody in one part as cantus firmus is written throughout in notes of long duration (whole or half notes). The other parts are written as counterpoints in shorter notes, linked to each other by imitations. The motifs of the counterpoints are usually derived from the chorale itself in diminution. To this species belong the following pieces in Straube's col-

lection: No. 2 by an unknown composer, "Ach, Gott im Himmel, sieh darein," the cantus firmus in the bass; No. 4, by Johann Michael Bach, the cantus firmus in the discant; No. 31, "Von Himmel Hoch" by Pachelbel, the cantus firmus in the bass—this time as an exception, the contrapuntal parts are freely written on new motifs; No. 32, "Gott sei gelobt" by Heinrich Scheidemann, the cantus firmus in the bass.

(2) The second type is like the first, only broader and more involved. The preludes, interludes, and postludes are more extended. Often each stanza receives a different treatment in conformity with the expression of the words. An approach to the variation form is here evident, of which No. 37, Franz Tunder's "Jesus Christus, unser Heiland," is a good example.

(3) The choral melody in one voice is more or less dissolved into fioritura while the other voices, partially free and partially thematic, weave their counterpoint around it. Examples are No. 16, "Auf meinem Lieben Gott" by J. N. Hanff, also Nos. 17, 19, and 20 by the same composer; No. 21, "Herzlich tut mich verlangen," by Johann Peter Kellner.

(4) The chorale is not retained in a single voice, but distributed among the various parts in fugato style. No. 6 is an example: "Was mein Gott will" by Wilhelm Friedemann Bach.

(5) A fairly free fantasia, in which the choral melody, broken up into fragments, is woven through the other parts. The first part of No. 11, "Vom Himmel kam der Engel Schar" is an example of this type.

(6) The choral melody is used simply as a theme, followed by a number of more or less complicated, figurated variations. An excellent example of this so-called "partita" is offered by Johann Gottfried Walter's "Jesu, meine Freude" (No. 40). A similar type of choral prelude works out the choral melody verse by verse, the number of variations dependent on the number of verses.

(7) Ingenious canonic treatment, especially in Bach's music. Often the choral melody is elaborated canonically, with free voices added. Sometimes, however, the opposite is preferred, and the choral melody enters as counterpoint to the canon, which is founded on entirely different motifs. Compare Bach's "Von Himmel Hoch," "In dulci jubilo" (a double canon), and "Ach Gott, und Herr."

(8) A chorale fugue is a strictly worked out fugue, in the course of which the chorale intoned as counter melody is the culmination of the entire piece, generally towards the end. Compare Bach's "Jesu meine Freude."

The choral preludes of J. S. Bach are a world in themselves. Every young composer is strongly advised to study them thoroughly, and whoever wishes to devote himself to a more intensive study of their rich variety of formal treatment, their wealth of characteristic expression, will find valuable guidance in the famous books on Bach by Philipp Spitta and Schweitzer, and also in Pater Isidor Mayrhofer's *Bachstudien*.[4] The choral prelude, with its contrapuntal style, leads to the strict contrapuntal forms of which the fugue and canon are the most important.

the fugue

Of all the musical forms the fugue has the greatest logic in its construction. It manifests the art of building up a complex piece from a single motif of a few notes. The fugue as a contrapuntal form is always limited to a fixed number of voices. Its principle consists in transferring one theme to all the participating parts. In a three-part fugue, for instance, a single voice begins with the theme. As soon as it is completed, a second voice takes up the theme a fifth higher, while the first voice continues with a counterpoint to the theme. The third voice enters with the theme again in the tonic key, while the other voices continue their counterpoints. When all three voices have stated the theme, the exposition is brought to a close. Two other sets of entries usually follow, in which the theme is occasionally heard in some tonality other than the tonic or dominant. The last entries often contain as an additional feature the so-called stretta [5] or contraction, which consists of a canonic imitation in which one voice enters with the theme before the other has completed it. The plan of a regularly constructed three-part fugue is sketched in the following diagram:

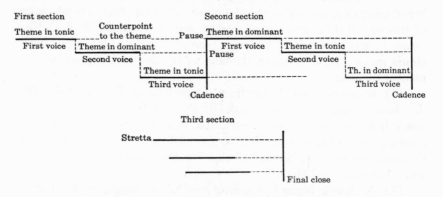

In practice, this plan is adhered to only in its general outline. In particular cases many variants occur in fugal structure. Sometimes the theme enters more frequently, sometimes less frequently. Occasionally, keys other than the tonic and dominant appear. Sometimes the stretta is entirely lacking, or

[4] All three books published by Breitkopf & Härtel, Leipzig.
[5] Canonic imitation is treated further on in this chapter.

it may enter as early as the second set of entries instead of in the third only, as would be normal. Any number of these variants is to be found in Bach's *Well-Tempered Clavier,* which is indeed the incomparable school of fugal composition. For more detailed instruction on the structure and character of the theme, of the counter subject, the answer, and cadences, and so on, the reader must be referred to the text books specializing in fugue composition.[6] In general outline of musical form, only the essential features can be treated.

FUGUE THEMES

Not every melody is fit to be the subject of a fugue. Songlike tunes demanding chordal accompaniment are particularly unsuitable fugal treatment because of their symmetrical construction. The theme may appear a dozen or more times in the course of a fugue and must therefore be so built that it can stand frequent repetition. Thus a theme less symmetrically constructed is better fit for such a purpose than a songlike tune which, on account of its eight or sixteen measures, would be much too long. The fugue theme must be extremely plastic, short rather than long, in order that one may quickly recognize it even in a rather dense polyphonic texture, and so that one may introduce it frequently without undue extension of the piece. The fugue theme or subject is also called *dux* or leader (*proposta*). The continuation of the theme by the second voice is called "answer" or *comes,* companion (*riposta*).

The counterpoint (counter subject, contrast) should be a good counter melody to the answer and at the same time, a satisfactory continuation of the dux. It should make the theme stand out rhythmically, should have definite individuality, an independent line, and really serve as a counter melody, not a mere accompaniment in homophonic style. Free episodes or intermezzi are frequently inserted between the main sections. In these episodes the theme itself is not heard, but motifs from it are workd out thematically. With the help of these short episodes, modulation progresses from one key to another and weightier cadences are formed at the end of each of the main sections. In the stretta, slight thematic alterations are permissible, provided the theme is not disfigured by them and provided the stretta cannot otherwise be written satisfactorily. Even at the very first answer of the theme it often becomes necessary to alter it slightly in order to preserve tonal

[6] From the extensive literature on the fugue, the following authors (besides those already mentioned) deserve special attention: Cherubini, Iwan Knorr, Michael Haller, Bellermann, Henri Gédalge (very thorough), E. Prout. The *Well-Tempered Clavier* is treated in Riemann's analysis and in Busoni's edition with detailed, formal, stylistic, and aesthetic commentaries. The mathematical aspect has of late been stressed by Wilhelm Werker's analysis. Dr. F. Staden's edition, with explicit analytic remarks, is very useful (Steingräber edition, Leipzig).

unity. Thus the skip of a fifth is often answered by a fourth, as in the A flat fugue of the *Well-Tempered Clavier:*

In the F major fugue, Bach answers the fifth degree of the scale with the fourth:

This so-called "tonal" answer, in which the fifth is answered by the octave instead of the ninth, stands in contradistinction to the so-called "real" answer, the intervals of which correspond exactly to the intervals of the subject.

INVERSION, AUGMENTATION, AND DIMINUTION OF THE THEME

In the course of longer, more involved fugues, the theme is sometimes inverted for the sake of variety, that is, each upward interval of the theme is answered by a corresponding downward interval, or vice versa:

Bach, *Well-Tempered Clavier,* vol. I, no. 6:

Theme   Inversion

Sometimes the theme is introduced in augmentation or diminution. Occasionally the theme appears simultaneously in the original form (*recte*), in inversion (*inverse*), in augmentation (*per augmentationem*), or in diminution (*per diminutionem*), which results in ingenious intricacies. A classic example is found in the D sharp minor fugue in the *Well-Tempered Clavier:*

74

Several other types of inversion are described in the chapter "Contrapuntal Forms" in the second part of this book.

A few more examples from the *Well-Tempered Clavier* will illustrate what has been said above on the structure of the theme and its continuation as countersubject or counterpoint:

The theme is one and one-half measures long. The counterpoint is a natural continuation of the theme itself. Mark the rest at the beginning of the theme, which makes its entrance more striking and gives the counterpoint opportunity to be conspicuous. The theme, though well rounded, is really more of a "phrase" than a theme of songlike character.

The theme is three measures long. It begins with a rest and consists of equal quarter notes. For this reason the counterpoint must introduce an entirely new motif. If the counterpoint simply continued the theme, it would not serve as an effective contrast.

In many figures (as in the above-mentioned F minor fugue), the counter melody is written in double counterpoint. The advantage here lies in the fact that one can then retain the counter melody throughout the entire piece, inasmuch as the inversion at the octave will permit new combinations of the parts, especially when free voices are added.

THE DOUBLE FUGUE

The use of double counterpoint is indispensable to the double fugue in which two themes are developed. One type of double fugue is closely related to the fugue with retained countersubject. Both themes should be rhythmically independent of each other. One theme usually enters in advance of the other in order to facilitate the perception of the two different themes. An example of this type of fugue is the Kyrie Eleison from Mozart's *Requiem:*

le - -

As indicated, the piece begins with both themes in close succession. They appear together throughout the entire piece. Handel was particularly fond of double fugues of this type.

In the second type of double fugue, the initial theme is at first given regular treatment alone. Then follows a fugal development of the second theme alone. In the third section the simultaneous entrance of both themes, freely developed in various combinations, leads to the climax. Examples of this species are found in Bach's Art of the Fugue.[7] The fugue begins with the exposition of the first theme:

The second section introduces an entirely new theme, likewise developed alone:

Finally, the two themes are combined. Only one of the many combinations is shown here:

[7] Busoni's "Fantasia contrappuntistica" applies an abundance of contrapuntal combinations to an extremely ingenious restoration of the final quadruple fugue left unfinished by Bach.

THE TRIPLE AND CHORALE FUGUES

There are also triple fugues, with three themes worked out in various combinations. Structurally, the triple fugue hardly differs from the double fugue. The best known example, an unequaled masterpiece, is the C sharp minor fugue from Book I of the *Well-Tempered Clavier,* in which the following three themes are treated singly and in combinations:

Bach's E flat major triple fugue for organ is constructed on a still more colossal scale.

Not infrequently, especially in Bach, one finds the chorale fugue. Its special feature consists in a chorale, given forth either in sections or appearing in its entirety as the crowning climax of the close. A splendid example is found in Mendelssohn's piano fugue in E minor, Op. 35, No. 1, also at the close of Max Reger's "One-Hundredth Psalm."

One finds at times the artificial inverted fugue. Here the theme gets its own inversion as answer. Bach has incorporated such pieces into the "Art of the Fugue" (Nos. 5, 6, 7, 14).

A fugato is a short piece of music written in fugal style without being submitted to the strict laws of fugal form. A fugato can never represent a special formal type. It is rather a sort of improvisation, a free fantasia, written in fugal style.

THE CANON

One speaks of a canon when theme and counterpoint are identical, when the theme becomes its own counterpoint, entering a little later in the manner of an imitation. The canon is the strictest and most artificial of all musical forms because from beginning to end all voices participating in the canon play or sing exactly the same melodic phrases successively, one voice, like a shadow, following the other. The difficulty of the canon increases with the number of voices. A well written three- or four-part canon is a master test of skill and construction. Canonic imitation must be interrupted at some point or other in order to terminate the piece. Many canons become infinite, moving as it were in a circle, the end of the theme returning to its beginning. Canonic imitation may enter at any interval. There are canons in unison and at the second, third, fourth, fifth, sixth, seventh, octave, ninth, tenth, and so on. Frequently, one or more free voices are added to the canon. A short example from Bach's "Goldberg" variations may illustrate the nature of canonic technique:

Here is a two-part canon at the sixth for the two upper voices, with an added free part as bass. Canonic imitation enters at the distance of half a measure. One must be very cautious in the use of chromatic tones in the theme proper, as every chromatic tone engenders a new chromatic tone in the imitating voice, provided the canon is carried through strictly. In most cases, as is evident from the above examples, one will be forced to take slight liberties. Thus, the notes B, A of the first two measures are answered by G, F sharp. In other words, a major second is here answered by a minor second. If one insisted on strictest canonic imitation, the first four measures would look as follows:

The natural flow and unity of tonality would thus be lost, especially in a longer continued canon. Bach justly contents himself here with simply writing a canon at the sixth, not at the major or the minor sixth. Bach's "Goldberg" variations contain a whole collection of masterly canons at different intervals. Some are quite artificial, as Variation 12, "Canone alla quarta in moto contrario," which imitates the leading voice throughout the exact inversion; similarly, Variation 15, "in moto contrario." The beginning of this piece may illustrate this mode of treatment. The two higher voices are in canon, the bass free:

80

Strictly constructed canons for three or more parts are rare in modern music, which usually is content with a two-part canon to which one or more free parts are added. Three- and four-part canons are found in Friedrich Kiel's Op. 1, a collection of excellent canons in various styles for piano, and also in Alexander Klengel's ingenious opus, "Canons and Fugues in All the Major and Minor Keys." The four-part canon, "Mir ist so wunderbar," from the first act of Beethoven's *Fidelio* is a masterpiece. It belongs, however, rather to the class of "rounds" to be discussed later.

Another type of the four-part canon is the double canon representing the canonic continuation of a double theme by another pair of voices. The finest examples of this type of canon are to be found in the music of the old Flemish and Italian masters of the fifteenth and sixteenth centuries, the period of the greatest technical perfection in canon writing. Included in this category are not only four-part double canons, but also canons for six or even more parts. The start of the chanson "Basies moy, ma doulce amie" by Josquin de Pres will illustrate this technical method. Three separate two-part canons are fitted together:

The simplest and most popular form of canon is the round. It is a canon in unison, generally written for voices of the same range. The theme is song-like, with its single sections so invented that every single section will fit the preceding one as counterpoint. Haydn has written charming pieces of this sort, such as the three-part canon, "Ein einzig böses Weib":

with various transpositions of the three voices. Sections I, II, III are so constructed that they serve as mutual counterpoints. Practically every eight-measure phrase, if carefully written for three or more voices, is fit for a round, provided that each pair of voices is written in irreproachably pure harmony. Cherubini, Mendelssohn, and Brahms have written excellent pieces in this style. Mendelssohn's "Wie lieblicher Klang" from his Op. 49 is a double canon in this simplified style.[8]

the basso ostinato, chaconne, and passacaglia

A basso ostinato is a constantly recurrent bass figure, over which the upper voices move in continuous melody. The basso ostinato is rarely expanded into a whole piece. Generally, it is used only in episodes. If the bass figure is expanded to two or more measures, the resulting structure is called chaconne or passacaglia. Strict distinctions between basso ostinato, chaconne or passacaglia however, cannot be maintained. In general, the ostinato bass consists of a short motif of one measure or less, whereas the chaconne or passacaglia is constructed on a phrase of several measures in length, or even on a fully developed bass melody. The recurring feature in all these constructions is melodic variation above a constantly repeated bass theme or motif. These forms were especially popular in the older instrumental music of the seventeenth and eighteenth centuries. Their origin may be traced back to the contrapuntal technique of the old Flemish masters of polyphonic music. They were used extensively in masses and motets.

The passacaglia (known also as *passecaille* in French, or *passacaglio* in Italian) is, like the chaconne (*ciacona*), an old dance form. It has not yet been determined whether the constantly recurrent bass figure is an inherent feature of the dance, or whether it is to be regarded as a later musical refinement. Also, the difference between the passacaglia and chaconne—if there

[8] More detailed treatment of canonic technique may be found in a number of textbooks on counterpoint by Padre Martini, Paolucci, Marpurg, Dehn, Ziehn, Jadasson, Bussler, and Riemann. H. Leichtentritt's *Geschichte der Motette* treats canonic problems (p. 32, Ockenheim's thirty-six part canon; p. 49, Pierre de la Rue; pp. 69, 90, 180, 194, 398). Some remarks on the use of the canon in works of contemporary masters, especially in Schönberg, are found below, in Chapter XV.

really is any difference at all—has not yet been definitely determined. Sometimes the explanation is given that in the chaconne the theme always remains in the bass, whereas in the passacaglia it may sometimes pass into an upper voice. But this view is not sufficiently corroborated by musical literature.

One of the most eminent examples of basso ostinato technique occurs in the Crucifixus of Bach's *B minor Mass* with its chromatically descending figure in the bass:

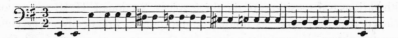

In more recent literature, a basso ostinato is used in Chopin's "Berceuse." Here the rocking of the cradle is happily suggested by the indefatigably repeated bass figure. The most famous models of the chaconne and passacaglia come from Bach, namely, the Violin Chaconne (D minor) and the great Organ Passacaglia in C minor.[9] Superb passacaglias are also found in the works of the old organ masters, Buxtehude and Pachelbel.[10] Excellent recent works of this type are the passacaglias for two pianos by Hugo Kaun and Max Reger, also Karg-Elert's E flat minor passacaglia for organ.

The basso ostinato is found in short episodes in the first movement of Beethoven's Ninth symphony towards the end of the coda (in the character of a funeral march over the chromatic bass figure):

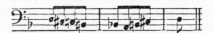

in the middle section of Chopin's A flat polonaise, in Wagner's *Walküre* prelude, in the first movement of Liszt's "Dante" symphony, in the finale of Brahm's orchestral variations, Op. 56. Brahms used the form of a chaconne with extraordinary effects in the final movement of his Fourth symphony.[11]

the toccata

In the instrumental music of the seventeenth and eighteenth centuries the toccata (derived from *toccare, toucher,* to touch or strike the keys) meant a type of fantasia, based on two different elements: Powerful broad chord columns and brilliant, rapid passage work. Toccatas of this type occur in the organ works of Frescobaldi, Scheidt, Froberger, Buxtehude,

[9] See analysis in Chapter XV.

[10] Buxtehude's three admirable organ chaconnes have been discussed in detail most ably by Spitta in his *Johann Sebastian Bach* (German edition), I, 277–282.

[11] Analysis in Chapter XV.

and Pachelbel. Bach once again furnishes the most brilliant models in his organ toccatas. Best known, perhaps through Tausig's piano arrangement is the D minor toccata. The toccata often takes the place of a fantasia or prelude. Generally it is followed by a fugue. In modern literature another type of toccata occurs, a vivid, virtuoso piece for piano with rapid passage work in the manner of a *perpetuum mobile*. Robert Schumann's toccata, Op. 7 and Rheinberger's toccata belong in this category. The characteristic beginning of a toccata may be illustrated by an example from Johann Kasper Kerll, a pupil of Frescobaldi: [12]

---

[12] More detailed discussion of the old forms of toccata, ricercar, canzone, capriccio, symmetrical inversion, the various inversion forms, mixed forms in contrapuntal writing, will be found in Chapter XV.

the suite

The suite is the most important of the larger forms of older instrumental music. It dominated the whole of piano music from about 1650–1750, just as later the sonata became preëminent in the time of the great Viennese masters.

A series or sequence of dance pieces is called a suite. The number of single pieces in the suite varied from three or four up to twelve and even more. Yet nearly all suites have a common framework. The older suites generally contain four pieces, the pavane, gaillarde, allemande, and courante. From about 1620 onward, the suite normally consisted of allemande, courante, sarabande, and gigue. To these, many other dances could be added at will, like the minuet, and rigaudon, passepied, loure, gavotte, musette, rondo, branle, passacaglia, and so on. The Italian name of the suite is partita, and sometimes the term partie is found.

Generally, the same tonality prevails in all the pieces of the suite. But there is a change of rhythms and of character in the contrast between two successive pieces, either through more rapid or slower tempo, or by duple and triple time. The suite had its origin in the lute music of the sixteenth and seventeenth centuries. About 1650 it became the chief form of piano music and in fifty to seventy-five years it rose to its greatest eminence in the

works of J. S. Bach. The greatest suite composers were Johann Jacob Froberger, François Couperin, Rameau, J. S. Bach, and G. F. Handel.[1]

The suite of the seventeenth century also shows a constructive idea
characteristic of its epoch. One movement is formed from the preceding one
by a variation of the theme. Thus the courante is often evolved from the
allemande by metrical transformation. In some Handel suites (the one in
E minor, for instance) all movements, including even the gigue, are built of
the same thematic material. Bach gave up this manner of construction. One
is reminded of it only occasionally in his suites when he uses a sarabande
with "doubles" or variations.

THE PAVANE AND GAILLARDE

The pavane, also called padovana or paduana, is a stately, fairly slow
dance in duple time, distinguished by its solemn, dignified, almost pathetic
character. The beginning of a pavane from J. Rosenmüller's "Studenten-
musik" of 1654 will give a fair idea of this dance:

As contrast to the pavane, a quick dance in triple time follows, the gaillarde, or gagliardo. The pavane and gaillarde correspond to the old and
well-known "round dance" in duple time, to which a lively after-dance, a
jumping dance, the gaillarde itself, was linked. Originally, this jumping
dance in 3/4 time was called a *proportio*, in Italian, a *saltarello* again meaning jumping dance, or romanesca.

[1] Details on the history of the suite will be found in Max Seiffert's *Geschichte der
Klaviermusik;* in Spitta's *Bach,* I, 693–709; in Oscar Bie's *Das Klavier und seine Meister,*
in W. Niemann's *Das Klavierbuch.* A more detailed account is easily accessible in Dr. Apel's
Harvard Dictionary of Music, under "Suite."

The first part of a gaillarde by the Spanish lutanist, Alonzo de Muddara, published in 1546, will show the character of this dance:

THE SALTARELLO AND TARANTELLA

The saltarello has survived down to the present time. Mendelssohn has written a saltarello as the finale of his A major "Italian" symphony, a rapid whirling piece in 6/8 time somewhat like a tarantella, that wild Neopolitan dance whose name is derived from the tarantula spider. It was the common belief of the Italians that the dangerous bite of this insect would engender a dance madness, and that only through wild dancing could one avert its evil consequences.

THE ALLEMANDE

The later suite, from about 1620 onwards, usually begins with an allemande, which replaced the pavane. The allemande, like the pavane, is written in duple time, but is less solemn and dignified in its style and only moderately fast. Like all the dances of the suite, the allemande, a "German dance," gradually lost its dancelike character, becoming concert music in the style of a dance or so-called idealized music. The Bach suites are, for instance, as far removed from real dances as the Chopin waltzes are from the dance waltzes of Lanner or Johann Strauss. The start with an upbeat is characteristic of the allemande. A few measures from an allemande by Froberger will be sufficient to illustrate its character:

THE COURANTE

The courante, a running dance, corresponds to the older gaillarde. It is a lively dance in 3/4 time with an upbeat and a predilection for the dotted rhythms on the second beat of the measure. The later Bach courantes no longer show the older rhythmic patterns of the dance. Their characteristic feature is the constant running motion in eighth or sixteenth notes, with an upbeat of three eighth notes. Bach often writes his courantes in 3/2 time, adding rhythmic spice by expointing the double connotation of 3/2 through subdivision into triple or duple time ($=6/4$). Not infrequently one hand plays in 3/2 time simultaneously with the other hand in 6/4 time. This rhythmical combination is manifest in the second double of the second courante in Bach's English suite, No. 1:

THE SARABANDE

The sarabande, a slow movement of the suite, is noble in character, often sorrowful in expression, broad in its melodic line. Its distinctive rhythmical feature is the strong accent on the second beat of the measure. The rhythmical patterns $\frac{3}{4}$ ♩ ♩. ♪ or $\frac{3}{2}$ 𝅗𝅥 𝅗𝅥. ♩ occur frequently in the sarabande. A famous example is the well known aria from Handel's opera, *Rinaldo*, "Lascia ch'io pianga." The following illustration is from Bach's English suite No. 4:

THE GIGUE

The gigue, the finale of the suite, is a very lively dance in 6/8, 9/8, or 12/8 time. An incessant flow of motion is its characteristic feature. Bach makes his gigues more complex by working out the theme in contrary motion in the second part of the piece. The beginning of the gigue from the Fourth French suite will illustrate this procedure:

The gigue often lends itself to fugal development.

THE GAVOTTE, MUSETTE, PASSEPIED, RIGAUDON, AND OTHER DANCES IN THE SUITE

Besides these four main dances, the suite may contain a good many others, the already enumerated intermezzi. For the minuet, see pages 57–62.

The gavotte is a graceful dance in 2/2, 2/4, or 4/4 time, with an upbeat of one-quarter or two-quarter notes. It is made up of two-measure phrases. In the suite two gavottes often follow one another, the second a kind of trio to the first. One first plays gavotte No. 1, then gavotte No. 2, and finally No. 1 da capo. The second gavotte is often treated "à la musette" in the style of a bagpipe piece with constantly repeated or long-sustained bass note, the bourdon or drone bass. Good examples may be found in Bach's Third and Sixth English suites.

Genuine dance gavottes, together with many other dance types, are found in the ballets and ballet operas of Lully and his school, in Rameau, and in the masters of the French comic opera of the eighteenth century, Philidor, Monsigny, Grétry. Rameau and Grétry particularly abound in the most exquisite dance music. We quote the beginning of a gavotte from Grétry's "Colinette à la cour:"

Lully's gavotte from "Roland" illustrates another type:

For the musette, a few measures from Bach's Third English suite serve as an illustration. At the same time they show the trio in its original meaning as a contrasting intermezzo for three voices:

The passepied, of Breton origin, is a round dance of nimble, lively character in 3/4 or 3/8 time. One of the loveliest examples is found in Bach's Fifth English suite:

The bourrée, from Auvergne, is a rather quick dance in 4/4 time with an upbeat. The rhythmic pattern is with the second and third beats often tied by syncopation:

The agile rigaudon, the Provençal national dance, resembles the bourrée in character. It is written in 2/2 time with a quarter-note upbeat, for which a peculiar dance step was customary. Charming rigaudon melodies are found in Rameau's "Pièces de clavecin" of 1724:

Loure (the name of an instrument of the bagpipe type formerly used in Normandy) is also the name of a dance. The loure is written in triple time, rather slow in movement. Its dominating rhythm is

92

Bach. French Suite

The air or aria,[2] an instrumental piece without special dance character and without a definite formal structure is usually written in broad, lyric, vocal style. Bach's "Air for the G String" from one of his orchestral suites is a famous masterpiece.

The rondo is one of the main forms in the studies of the French masters. Its constructive idea consists in the frequent return of the principal theme, introduced in an interesting manner. In the chapter on the rondo as part of the sonata more detailed treatment will be given to this form, which is so important in the classical sonata.

The branle, a dance in duple time of moderate speed, with a refrain after every stanza when employed as a dance song, is found only in the older suite of the sixteenth and seventeenth centuries. Henry Expert has recently published many charming branles.

As a pendant to the allemande many suites contain a polonaise or an anglaise. The polonaise, as found in Bach's Sixth French suite, has practically nothing in common with the dance now known by the same name. The anglaise (Bach's Third French suite) is better known as the contredanse, a counter dance in distinction to the round dances, the couples dancing towards each other instead of behind each other. The dance was introduced into France from England and was later imported into Germany as the française.

THE OVERTURE AND PRELUDE

Suites laid out on a larger scale often have a broadly conceived overture or a prelude preceding the allemande. Bach has brilliant examples in his English suites. Here a series of dance pieces is introduced by a piece of purely concertizing music without dance character. This prelude often re-

[2] For the aria in vocal music, see Chapter IX.

93

sembles a sonata of the older type. Especially in orchestral suites it makes use of the so-called "French ouverture" of the Lully type: adagio, allegro, adagio. Models of orchestral suites of this type are found in Bach and in the publications *Denkmäler deutscher Tonkunst,* in suites by Johann Fischer, in the "Journal du Printemps" and in Muffat's *Florilegium, Denkmäler der Tonkunst in Oesterreich.*

Owing to the rapid development of the new sonata form and the ever increasing popularity of the Viennese classics, the suite went out of fashion in the nineteenth century. Still, it was not altogether forgotten. A few masters had a predilection for it, as Franz Lachner in his important orchestral suites, Otto Grimm, with suites in canonic form, Joachim Raff (piano suites), Tchaikovsky, Dvořak, Moszkovski (orchestral suites).

In many of these modern suites, new dances like the waltz, polka, and polonaise replaced the older forms. On the whole, the suite in the nineteenth century no longer had as fixed and definite a form as in the eighteenth. Any series of loosely connected pieces of entirely different types (with the exception of the sonata form) could now be linked together in a suite.

modern suites

Thus Tchaikovsky's orchestral suite contains an elegy, a valse melancholique, a scherzo, and a theme and variations. Dvořak's Suite for Orchestra, Op. 39, is made up of a prelude, polka, minuet, romance, and furiant. This type of suite is closely related to the serenade. In Tchaikovsky's serenade, Op. 48, is found the following combination: Pezzo in forma di sonatina, Valse, Elegy, Allegro con spirito. In France, the suite has recently been revived from a different approach. D'Indy, Debussy, and others have composed suites in the old dance forms, utilizing at the same time the modern technical devices in harmony and orchestration. In modern times the form of the suite is employed in order to make accessible to the concert hall theatrical music originally written for drama or opera. The inartistic potpourri, with its bits of melody strung together is not considered here at all. What is meant is a combination of complete pieces, either in their original form or in a special arrangement for concert use. Examples of this type are found in Bizet's important "L'Arlesienne" suites, in Grieg's "Peer Gynt" suite, in Busoni's "Turandot" suite. In all these suites, pieces from the music for the dramas of Daudet, Ibsen, Gozzi are simply put together. Busoni proceeded differently in his "Brautwahl" suite, in which he arranged and remodeled music from his opera, adapting it for concert use by extensions, cuts, new transitions, altered endings. So conceived, the suite might receive a new impulse for further growth and might reach new and fascinating achievements, serving the double purpose of making suitable pieces of dramatic music available for the concert hall and at the same time showing them in a new light by transformation.

theme and variations

Simple songs, marches, and dances are popular in character, whereas the theme and variations belong more to the domain of art music. Variations, as bravura music, allow the player's virtuosity to shine forth brilliantly, or may, through their abundance of thematic transformations, emerge as complicated structures demanding greater powers of appreciation on the part of the listener. There are thus two main types of variation to be distinguished:

(1) The ornamental variation, which aims at brilliance and virtuosity.
(2) The characteristic variation, based on the art of thematic transformation.

Both styles are legitimate, both have been cultivated by great masters.

The ornamental variation retains the harmonic basis of the theme, dissolving the melodic line into figurations, passage work and arabesques, encircling the theme in fanciful ornamental play. The characteristic variation transforms the theme into something entirely new, gives it a totally different character, and strays away from the theme, without, however, losing contact with it. If one may call the ornamental variation concentric, the characteristic variation may be termed eccentric. Many works in variation form mingle the two styles.

the theme

In every style of variation the theme should be clear, concise, easy to grasp, in order to make its impression quickly and be easily recognized by the ear, even when it appears in disguise. Almost always the smaller song form is chosen, since its symmetry, brevity, and its cadences make it especially appropriate for the end in view. Significant, simple, and clear harmonization of the theme is of the greatest value.

DEVELOPMENT OF THE ART OF VARIATION

The art of varying a theme represents one of the most important problems of composition. Independent of all changes of taste, of all the phases of development in musical form, the variation has played a great role uninterruptedly from the very beginning of musical art down to the present. A comprehensive discussion of the art of variation would demand an extensive and special book. Here only the briefest indications regarding the nature of the variation can be made. We must at least mention the variation-like, ornamental coloratura of Gregorian chant and the technique of variation in the polyphonic vocal music of the Dutch and Italian masters of the fifteenth and sixteenth centuries. Variation became even more important for instrumental music. The English harpsichord or virginal players had a special fondness for variation. Their manner of ornamental variation, found as early as 1625 in the *Fitzwilliam Virginal Book,* became quite generally a model for variation in piano music. Even earlier, in the music of the lutenists, variation was popular. Spanish lute music [1] published by Morphy shows fully developed *differencias,* that is, variations, as early as 1536.

The older type of variation is almost entirely ornamental in character. It dissolves the melody of the theme into notes of shorter value, playfully encircling it with runs, trills, arpeggios, utilizing transposition into the various octave registers of the keyboard. The harmony of the theme is usually retained in the variations. Examples of this type of ornamental variation may be frequently seen in the music of the French suite composers, in the so-called "doubles," and also in the Bach suites. This sort of variation lasted well into the nineteenth century. Haydn's F minor variations belong to this type, as do the majority of Mozart's and Clementi's variations, and in certain respects also Beethoven's C minor variations. This type of variation, unless treated with exceptional taste and discrimination, will easily degenerate into a shallow play of sounds, into brilliant virtuoso pyrotechnics without musical substance. Actually this type led to a class

[1] See Morphy, *Les Lutistes espagnoles du XVI siècle* (Leipzig: Breitkopf & Härtel, 1902).

of fashionable salon variations in the nineteenth century (Herz, Hünten, Kalkbrenner) representing a low-water mark in composition, hardly any longer in touch with genuine art.

A second type of variation, the contrapuntal variation, had already been extensively practiced in the organ music of the seventeenth century. In the chorale preludes the chorale melody, the cantus firmus, in correspondence with the text of the various stanzas, is treated differently several times in succession, the character of the music being changed to fit the poetic contents of the various stanzas. Variations based on imitation, canon, fugue, and fugato also belong to the contrapuntal type. Brilliant examples of this sort are found in Bach's "Goldberg" variations, already mentioned [2] elsewhere. The forms of the basso ostinato, the English "ground bass" (meaning the same as the ostinato or the Italian *follia*), the chaconne and passacaglia belong here. Bach's "Art of the Fugue" is another example of variation form.

The characteristic variation is found less frequently in older music. It became predominant, however, in the nineteenth century after Beethoven had shown its possibilities. One of the oldest and most amusing examples is the Aria with Variations by the Viennese court cembalist, Alessandro Poglietti (who died in 1683), in which, as a birthday gift to the empress, he made the nations of the Austrian Empire pass in review. One hears the Bohemian bagpipe, the Dutch flageolet, the Polish "Sablschertz," the Bavarian Schalmei, the Hungarian violins, the honor dance of the Hanackj, and many other curious titles, such as the "Old Women's Funeral," the French "Baiselemen" (kiss the hands), the "Soft Lyre," the clown's "Rope Dance," and so on.[3]

Though the theme is clearly heard in all the variations, nevertheless the contrivances of the characteristic variation are abundantly utilized: theme in the bass, with a new, figurated upper part in constant motion; rhythmic alterations of the theme, 3/4 time changed into 12/8, 3/2, or 6/4; contrasts between the different variations through the use of legato and staccato, forte or piano, high or low registers; thin three-part writing and vigorous, full chords; strict obligato part writing and pianistically free treatment. Beethoven brought this type of variation to its highest perfection: his F major variations, Op. 34, are a modern counterpart to Poglietti's work. Each variation is a sharply outlined character piece, very different from its neighbor:

> Variation 1: 3/4 time, D major, a richly ornamented, playful piece in Mozartean vein.

[2] See Chapter IV.

[3] Published in *Denkmäler der Tonkunst in Oesterreich*, vol. XIII, 2; also separately by Bruno Hinze-Reinhold (Breitkopf & Härtel, Leipzig).

Variation 2: 6/8 time, B flat major, with sharply dotted rhythms and horn effects.

Variation 3: 4/4 time, G major, gently flowing.

Variation 4: 3/4 time, E flat, a grave minuet.

Variation 5: 2/4 time, C minor, in the style of a funeral march.

Variation 6: 6/8 time, F major, in graceful motion.

Then follows a long coda joined to the last variation and leading back to the theme which is once more freely developed in a brilliant, ornamental variation as finale. An unusual feature of this work is the constant change of tonality in the variations. Generally Beethoven, like all masters of the variation form, retains the same key throughout the work, at most changing from major into minor, or vice versa. Among the modern composers, Max Reger is also fond of changing tonalities in his variations.

the final variation

The number of variations is always left to the composer's choice. Sometimes he ends the work quite simply at the close of a variation. But in most cases the end is reached in a special coda which finally returns to the theme. Sometimes the coda is confined to but a few measures, as in the case of Schubert's B flat piano variations, where at the end of the fifth variation, two connecting descending measures introduce a shortened reprise of the theme, now effectively placed in the lower range of the instrument. Often, especially in Mozart's variations, the coda is written in the style of a brilliant cadenza. Beethoven, however, prefers a thematic, symphonic treatment of the coda. The F major variations show a fusion of brilliant thematic development and cadenza in the coda.

A favorite coda device is a broadly expanded fugue, whose subject may be derived from the main theme of the variations. Such a "Finale alla fuga" is found in Beethoven's so-called "Eroica" variations, Op. 35. Here the fugue is followed by another broad nonfugal repetition of the original theme. Other works end directly with the fugue, as Brahms' Op. 24, Reger's Variations on a Theme by Bach (Op. 80), and Beethoven's Op. 81. Beethoven's Op. 35 has the rare feature of a special introduction before the theme proper. Generally, one begins immediately with the theme. Chopin also, in his Op. 12, starts with a broad introduction leading into the theme.

Beethoven's variation technique

The possibilities of the characteristic variation are manifest on the loftiest scale in Beethoven's Op. 120, "33 Veränderungen über einen Walzer von Diabelli," the greatest masterpiece of the entire species. In a multicolored procession of the most diverse types, the single variations pass in array, the skill of the Beethoven Op. 34 now intensified into gigantic proportions. The power of imagination dominating this work is astounding. From the jolly "Biedermeier" theme Beethoven extracts the most arresting profusion of fantastic visions, now reminiscent of a droll masquerade, now of powerful and sinister apparitions. The hand of the master is already evident in the theme by the manner in which he makes the rather commonplace Diabelli melody interesting, distributing the music between the right and left hand, applying sudden accents and refined harmonizations. The blazing march rhythm, the heavy armored march step of the first variation, is followed by the light, floating, and airy second variation, the graceful and serene third, the ingenious texture of the fourth, a roguish hide-and-seek in the fifth. In the next variations he creates sturdy, valiant activity; a tender longing and meditation ("dolce e teneramente") in the eighth variation; rough, boorish humor and a roundelay of aerial spirits in the scherzo, No. 10; and so on, with infinite variety. No. 13 deserves special attention for its witty, aphoristic brevity. The piece has more rests than notes, presenting a sharply marked dialogue with the barest possible touches of melody; No. 14, is grave, filled with mystic awe; the deeply moving and profound Andante, No. 20; the imaginative, humorous allusion to Mozart's *Don Giovanni* in No. 22; the Largo No. 31, with its soulful melody, the delicate ornament of its transparent fioritura; the masterly, broad fugue, No. 32; the enchantingly beautiful minuet, full of Elysian bliss, with which the entire opus comes to its close.[4]

Beethoven's technical process deviates considerably from the usual variation style. The theme never returns in either its original form or in any easily recognizable version all through these thirty-three variations. A new motif is invented for each variation and this motif is worked out on the essential harmonies of the theme, not closely, chord for chord, but in such a way that the cadences and the striking modulations also reappear in the variations. The strict development of the motif throughout each piece is an essential requisite of the variation technique for every type of variation. Nevertheless, the master is not constrained to retain the given system of harmonies and cadences. Some variations, for example, the fifth and fourteenth, modulate at the end of the first section to E minor instead of G major. Also, at the beginning of the second part, some variations take liberties with the harmony. In most cases the motifs of the single variations show some manifest relation to the theme. Beethoven chooses some characteristic point in the theme, continuing with it consistently throughout the variation and evolving thereby his variation from a seed formed within the theme itself. A comparison of the first four measures of the theme with

---

[4] In his concert programs, Hans von Bülow gave each variation of this Op. 120 a title with additional characterizing designations, an aid of considerable value to the student of this work.

variation motifs will make this clear. The beginning of the theme shows a number of characteristics:

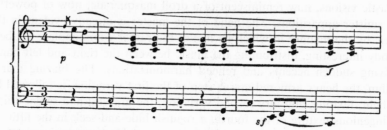

The appoggiatura figure:

is used by Beethoven in Variation 9:

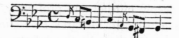

in Variation 11:

in Variation 27:

in Variation 31:

Related to the appoggiatura is the trill, on which Beethoven bases several passages, like Variation 6:

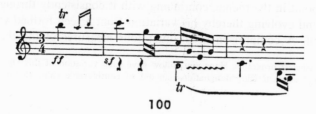

Variation 12 (slow trill):

Variation 21:

Trill together with the chord repetition in the bass which in the theme appears in the top voice.

On this repetition of chords

are based moreover:

Variation 2:

Variation 10:

Variation 25:

Variation 32, the fugue theme:

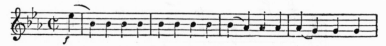

Variation 33:

From the first five notes of the theme

Beethoven obtains the motif for Variation 1, calling particular attention to the last note of the upbeat and to the leap of a fourth in the second measure:

Notice the chord repetition in the right hand and the bass descending in oblique motion. Compare Variation 10, where the same elements are differently treated: here unyielding, relentless rhythms; there a light and airy play of sound:

The descending leap of a fourth becomes important in Variation 5:

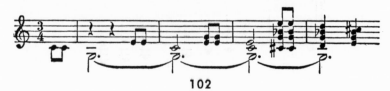

Variation 15:

Variation 17:

Variation 20:

Variation 22:

Variation 24, fughetta:

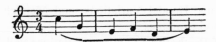

These examples are sufficient to show what an abundance of different motifs a master is able to extract from a comparatively insignificant theme.

different types of variation

Variations may be of many types. One may retain the melody, like a cantus firmus, or alter it in tempo or in note values; invent new accompanying harmonies, new rhythms for the accompanying voices or new counter melodies. The harmony of the theme may be essentially preserved and an entirely new melodic structure erected upon it. The theme may be ornamented in an infinite number of ways. It may be dissolved into shorter note values, into runs, passage work, and trills. Finally, the variation may be an entirely free construction, showing hardly any relation to the theme, either by melodic resemblance or similarity of harmony. It is enough for the theme to hover over the variation, as it were, hidden or imagined. To many variations of this type one might add the theme as counterpoint. Such an observation could be made of Mendelssohn's "Variations sérieuses." Lastly, we might remember the methods analyzed in Beethoven's Op. 120, where new structures are shaped from little fragments of the theme.

Rigid rules for the treatment of variations in their continuity cannot generally be laid down. The charm of the variation lies precisely in the fact that it gives the imagination endless opportunities without losing itself in limitless space, that the theme is a fixed point shining through the variations and offering to both listener and composer alike a secure foothold. Notwithstanding, some especially popular systems can be illustrated by numerous examples from musical literature. One may therefore consider these systems as well tested by actual experience without accepting them as binding laws. The classical masters, for example, are fond of gradually increasing the speed of motion in the first variations until a climax is reached. If the theme is dominated by quarter notes, the first variation will be written in eighth notes, the second in sixteenth, the third in thirty-second notes. Then follows an abrupt turn in the opposite direction, a very slow variation with the theme perhaps in its original form, but differently harmonized. Afterwards the tempo again will gradually become more animated. An example of this type is shown in the variations from Beethoven's A major quartet, Op. 18, No. 5.

Larger works in variation form demand special care in construction. The climaxes must be well prepared and must enter at the right places. One often writes the variations in pairs, so that frequently two successive variations are closely related to each other. Beethoven's thirty-three variations in C minor, Brahms' Handel Variations, and Mendelssohn's "Variations sérieuses" offer good examples.

An analysis of Beethoven's C minor variations will illustrate these observations. Here Beethoven follows the usual plan of elaborating a certain motif in every variation on the basis of the harmonic structure of the theme. The thirty-three variations are clearly arranged in four main sections:

    (a) Variations 1–11 inclusive.
    (b) Variations 13–22 inclusive.
    (c) Variations 24–29 inclusive.
    (d) Variations 31–33 inclusive.

Between these four sections the slow and sustained variations 12, 23, and 30 are interpolated as restful intermezzi.

The last group (d), consisting of but three variations, is built up through interpolations, connecting sections, and the coda-like final extension in such a way that in its dimensions it corresponds approximately with the other three groups. All four groups are therefore of practically equal length. Each of them comes to its own climax.

(a) Variation 1, 2, 3, all on the same sixteenth-note motif, 1 in the right hand, 2 in the left, 3 in both hands.

Variations 4, 5, 6, 7, 8 form a new group. Variation 4 on a triplet motif, staccato and piano. Variation 5 with the melody in octaves. Variations 7 and 8, again in octaves, both on the same motif.

Variation 9, piano espressivo, in contrast to the immediately following group.

Variations 10 and 11, in thirty-second notes on the same motif. Here the climax of (a) is reached. This is followed by

Variation 12, in the character of an intermezzo, which reverts to the original form of the theme, piano, slow, but brighter in color by virtue of the major harmonies.

(b) Variations 13 and 14 on the same motif in sixteenth notes.

Variations 15 and 16 on the same triplet motif.

Variation 17 corresponds to Variation 9, as a contrast to the immediately following climax.

Variations 18, 19, 20, 21, and 22 bring the second climax. They are all forte. The most powerful of all is No. 18, with its lightning-like precipitate scale passages in thirty-second notes. Variations 20 and 21 are likewise coupled together. Variation 22, a powerful outburst of sound in double octaves at the end of the group, corresponding to Variation 18 at the beginning. Next follows an

Intermezzo, Variation 23, pianissimo.

(c) Variations 24 and 25, both still piano and light staccato so that the three piano variations form a counterbalance to the preceding forte series.

Variations 26 and 27, forte again on the same staccato motif in sixteenth notes.

Variation 28, piano and legato, corresponding to variations 9 and 17, as a contrasting transition to the third climax which is reached in

Variation 29. Now the third

Intermezzo follows, Variation 30, pianissimo, with sustained, slow chords.

(d) Variations 31 and 32 again are paired by the use of the same motif in thirty-second notes. Gradual rise to the highest summit in Variation 33. The Coda, starting with a long diminuendo, like a vast wave of subsiding sound, followed by a pianissimo variation, before a new crescendo ushering in the powerful emotional close.

The plan of the finale of Beethoven's "Eroica" symphony is also an authoritative model, with its formal working-out of the beginning, middle, and closing sections. Brahms' Händel variations, Op. 24, and Mendelssohn's "Variations sérieuses" can also serve as models of effective, thoughtful construction.

variations on two themes

Many variants of the variation form [5] may be found combined with other forms, especially in Beethoven's works. In the slow movement of the C minor Symphony, two themes are varied:

Theme (a):

Theme (b):

The two themes are in this case related to each other, the second being a continuation of the first. The structure is:

(a) Measures 1–21.

(b) Measures 22–49 (with development and return to the first theme).

(a) Variation 1, measures 50–72.

(b) Variation 1, measures 73–98.

(a) Variation 2, measures 99–124. (Only the first part of the theme is varied—three times with different instrumentation. This is the central point of the entire movement.)

Thematic interlude, measures 125–148.

(b) Curtailed and repeated with return, measures 148–167.

(a) Used as thematic interlude in A flat minor, measures 167–185.

(a) Variation 3, measures 185–204.

Further continuation of (a), with reminiscence of (a), measures 204–228.

Coda, measures 228–246.

Here is a combination of free rondo form with variation form.

[5] For examples from Bach and from modern literature, see Chapter XVI.

The slow movement of the Ninth symphony also consists of variations on two themes, which, however, are entirely different, both in character and in rhythm and tonality. The structure is:

Two measures of introduction.

Theme (a):

Theme (b):

(a) Variation 1, measures 43–64.
(b) Variation 1, measures 65–82. Here the variation consists only of a new, richer orchestration.

Thematic contrapuntal interlude on theme (a), measures 83–98, equivalent to Variation 2 of (a).

(a) Variation 3, measures 99–120.

Coda, measures 121–158, with a free development of (a).

Altogether there are three variations on theme (a), interrupted twice by theme (b), followed by a long, thematic coda. The relationship to rondo form is evident.

The third famous example of modified variation form is found in the finale of Beethoven's "Eroica" symphony:

Intrata, free, brilliant introduction, measures 1–11.

Theme (a), at first very primitive, actually no more than the bass of the theme, measures 12–43.

(1) Variation theme in the middle parts, counterpoint in eighth notes, measures 44–59.

(2) Variation theme in the upper voice, counterpoint in triplets, measures 60–75.

(3) Variation. A new melody above the bass theme, theme (b), counterpoint in sixteenth notes, measures 76–107.

Interlude (episode) with transition from E flat major to C minor, measures 107–116.

(4) Variation. Rather free, in the style of a fugato. C minor, A flat major, transition to B minor, measures 117–174.

(5) Variation. Theme (b) in the upper voice; in the repetition, rapid counterpoint in sixteenth notes, later triplets. Modulations to B minor, D major, G minor, measures 175–210.

(6) Variation. Theme (a) in the bass, an entirely new counter melody in the upper voice. Hungarian in character with dotted rhythms; extension in the second part, measures 211–255.

(7) Variation. Takes the place of a development section. Themes (a) and (b) worked out in complicated contrapuntal manner, even in inversion. C major, C minor, leading to E flat major; the climax of the whole movement, measures 256–348.

(8) Variation. E flat major. Theme (b) developed broadly as an andante. Measures 349–380.

(9) Variation. Continuation and intensification of the preceding variations. Theme (b) in the bass, counterpoint in sixteenth-note triplets in the upper voices; transition to A flat major, measures 381–403.

(10) Variation. A flat major, rich modulation to G minor. Theme (b) hidden in the upper voice, with free continuation, measures 404–419.

(11) Variation. Organ point on G, theme (b) in G minor, faintly apparent in the upper voices, measures 420–430.

Coda, introduced by the intrata from the beginning of the movement, measures 429–471.

We see here a freer type of variation form with introduction, combined with the development section of a sonata.

As models for the study of variation technique, the following selection of eminent works from older and modern periods is recommended:

Fitzwilliam Virginal Book (about 1625).

Allessandro Poglietti, Aria with Variations.

Pachelbel, in harpsichord and organ works.

Rameau, in clavecin music.

J. S. Bach. Aria with Thirty Variations—the so-called "Goldberg" variations.[6] Passacaglia for Organ.[7] "Art of the Fugue." Chaconne for violin.

Joseph Haydn's variations in the "Emperor" or "Kaiser" quartet. F minor variations for piano.

Mozart variations from the D major quartet, from many sonatas, and the independent series of variations.

Beethoven, variations from the A major quartet, Op. 18, No. 5; from the E flat major quartet, Op. 74; from the C sharp minor quartet, Op. 131; "Dankgesang eines Genesenen an die Gottheit," from Op.

[6] See the analysis of the "Goldberg" variations in Busoni's edition, published by Breitkopf & Härtel.

[7] See the analysis in Chapter XV.

132; from the violin sonata, Op. 12, No. 1; the "Kreutzer" Sonata; the piano sonatas, Op. 14, 57, 109, 111. Variations Op. 35, 120 for piano. Finale of the "Eroica" symphony. Adagio of the Ninth symphony.

Schubert, variations from the A minor and D minor quartets; B flat major piano variations.

Chopin, variations on a Theme from Mozart's *Don Giovanni,* Op. 2; B flat major variations, Op. 12.

Schumann, "Abegg" variations, Op. 1; Impromptus, Op. 5; Etudes Symphoniques. Variations for two pianos, Op. 46.

Mendelssohn "Variations sérieuses"; variations in E flat major.

Liszt, variations on a Basso Ostinato of Bach.

Saint-Saëns, variations for Two Pianos on a Theme of Beethoven.

Brahms, Händel variations, Op. 24; from the string sextet, Op. 18; from the clarinet quintet; variations on a theme of Haydn for orchestra, Op. 56; Finale of the E minor symphony.

César Franck, "Variations symphoniques" for piano and orchestra.

Grieg, G minor ballad.

Xaver Scharwenka, Theme and Variations, Op. 48.

Richard Strauss, *Don Quixote.*

Max Reger, Variations on a Theme by Bach, Op. 80. Variations on a Theme by Beethoven for two pianos, Op. 81; Variations on a Theme by Hiller for orchestra, Op. 100.

Paul Dukas, Variations on a Theme by Rameau for piano.

Edward Elgar, "Enigma" variations for orchestra.

F. Busoni, choral variations from the second violin sonata.

Arnold Schönberg, Variations for orchestra.

CHAPTER **VII**

the rondo

The characteristic feature of the rondo form is the frequent return of the theme. Like a ring, the rondo describes a complete circle which ends by returning to its starting point. Although the sonata form is also based on the return of the theme, the rondo differs from the sonata form in that the main theme of the rondo returns at least three times. Moreover, the episodes coming between the reappearances of the theme are not so weighty and independent in the rondo, not so much opposed to the principal theme, as are the second and third themes and the development section in the sonata. The character of the rondo, furthermore, differs considerably from that of the sonata in regard to general sonority, melodic contour, and expression. The rondo in allegro tempo is amiable, cheerful, smoothly flowing, graceful, delicate in expression, and playful. The complex profusion of moods, the anticipation of threatening conflict, the seriousness and weightiness of ideas, the dramatic accents with their sudden contrasts, are features characteristic of the sonata form and foreign to the rondo.[1]

[1] This analysis of the rondo seems all the more necessary because of late the character of the rondo has been fundamentally misunderstood. Too strong a mixture of rondo and sonata elements does injury to both forms. Not every piece called a rondo is a real rondo. The following pages will give more detailed information on this matter.

There is no particular rule for the construction of a rondo. The theme may return three or four times, even more frequently, generally in the original key. Only in more extended rondos the theme may, at a later stage of the piece, sometimes enter in a different key for the sake of contrast. The various repetitions of the theme are separated by episodes, or intermezzi, sometimes consisting merely of passage work of transitional character. In other cases these episodes may be melodious expansions which, like a secondary theme, serve as a continuation and extension of the main theme or stand in slight contrast to it. Often the main theme in the rondo is concluded by a clearly marked cadence. In that case, it does not glide over imperceptibly into the episode as in the sonata where the first and second themes not infrequently merge into each other. The secondary theme in the rondo prefers to enter in a new key, not through modulation, but with a sudden bound.

The essential characteristic of the rondo is the transition at the end of each episode back to the main theme. The composer's most difficult task consists in making these transitions to the principal key at each return of the main theme and differentiating them by ingenious variations. The aesthetic fascination of the rondo form lies in the fact that only through these interesting and frequently varied transitions is the constant return of the theme justified. Unlike the theme, the episodes are not separate, closed sections. They glide back into the principal theme skillfully, gently, and gradually.

the rondo theme

In the rondo, as in all forms, thematic material and treatment are controlled by the nature of the form. One may also reverse the statement: a particular type of thematic material and development requires a particular form. Thus one may rightly speak of a "rondo theme," a melody especially suitable for a rondo and therefore less appropriate for either sonata, song form, or variation. Since the rondo theme returns often, it must be appropriate to such repetitions. It should be neither too weighty nor too light. A weighty theme may be suitable for a sonata, but is less fit for a rondo because through repetition it loses both force and significance. Dignity and grandeur do not go hand in hand with loquacity. A very light theme, however, serviceable enough in a song, is inappropriate for the rondo. Through constant repetition such a theme becomes flat and insipid. A clever witticism should not be used too often. The pathos of solemn utterance is likewise foreign to this form, as is the sober simplicity of ordinary speech. One may more aptly compare the rondo to the polished conversation of a highly cultured social circle. The gay chatter, the witty remarks, ingenious turns, the constant flow of words without hesitation, the tactful avoidance of unbecoming themes, in short, the art of social conversation transferred to music characterizes the rondo as an artistic form. It is perhaps not a mere coincidence that the fairest flower of the rondo appears simultaneously with the brilliant and refined salon of the *beau monde* in the eighteenth and the early nineteenth centuries.

rondo and variation themes

Still another form demands frequent repetition of the main idea: the theme and variations. Yet the rondo theme and the theme for variations differ considerably. The latter is intended for variations following each other without transitions or interludes. In the rondo, however, the ornamental changes should not be as far-reaching as in a variation. Moreover in the rondo, it is precisely the return to the theme which is the salient feature of the form. Thus a theme for variations will have the effect of a title, brief, pointed, simple; whereas the rondo theme may unfold more broadly. The one is firm, rigid; the other, flowing and elastic. Both may be in song form. The character of the music makes the difference. Two Beethoven themes, each typical of its own class, will illustrate these points:

Op. 26. *Andante con variazoni.*

Op. 27. *Rondo. Allegretto.*

One might make a rondo theme out of the variation theme by recasting the rigid rhythms into more flowing contours, by giving the sharper edges a softer curve, as for instance:

The Beethoven rondo theme could be transformed into a theme for variations by simplification and reduction to its melodic essentials somewhat as follows:

development of the rondo theme

There are various ways of developing the main theme of a rondo. Some rondos state the main idea briefly, ending with a full cadence and proceeding immediately to the episode. An excellent example of this type is the finale of Beethoven's Op. 10, No. 3, where the main theme is only eight measures long.

This simple type is not found very often. A longer exposition of the main theme occurs more frequently. In the adagio of Beethoven's Sonata "Pathétique," Op. 13, the main theme (2 × 8 measures) is treated in a two-part song form.

The normal rondo exposition makes use of the three-part song form, a-b-a, thus making the main theme in itself a little rondo, with the episode b between the twice-recurring a. The largo, as well as the finale of Beethoven's Op. 2, No. 2, also Op. 7, Op. 22, and so on, illustrate this rather frequent type.

There are rondos whose main sections do not end in the tonic, but modulate to the dominant, gliding into the episode gradually. This procedure, much less frequently encountered in the rondo than in the sonata style, is often seen in mixed forms—half sonata, half rondo—as, for instance, in the finale of Beethoven's Op. 2, No. 3.

The episodes may be thematically more or less independent. They some-times contain entirely new material, and at other times are derived from the main theme, continuing it in thematic development.

There are some very ingenious rondos, planned on a larger scale, which have but one theme from which all the material of the work is derived. The finale of Beethoven's Op. 54 is a genuine *perpetuum mobile* built in this way on the motif:

Here, to be sure, Beethoven found it necessary to modulate more exten-sively into distant keys than is ordinarily the case in his rondos, expressly in order to obtain interesting effects in the full extent of the piece from the insignificant motif. The main theme appears in various tonalities, F, C, A, G major and C minor, and the transitions touch F minor, A flat, D flat major, and so on.

Splendid examples, masterpieces of this type, are to be found in Haydn's symphonies; for instance, in the finale of the E flat Symphony (Peters Edition, No. 1). The theme, with its countersubject in the bass, is:

The artistic value of such a work rests in the fact that, deliberately fore-going all contrasts, it expresses a single and fundamental mood in various gradations. The ease, the cheerfulness, or, if you prefer, the naïveté, of the rondo form lies in just this leisurely expansion of many details, this display of but a single emotion. The great value of a form which allows this kind of artistry is manifest. Sonata form, in this respect, is secondary to the rondo. In the fugue only is such conciseness possible. As a counterpart, one should compare Haydn's Rondo with the Fugue in D major from the *Well-Tempered Clavier* of Bach, second volume:

in order to see how very differently the fugue and the rondo work out two almost identical, or at least very similar, themes, and in order to realize that one form may never become a substitute for the other, despite the close resemblance of the theme and the similarity of the artistic problem. In fugal development a merry theme of this kind takes on a certain gravity which heightens the humorous character of the music and adds its characteristic coloring. In its turn, the rondo has a lightness, a nimbleness, a sly humor inaccessible to the fugue, but it cannot, on the other hand, attain the good-natured bonhomie of the fugue. The contrast between the corpulent burger and the street urchin might be said to be parallel to the difference between the fugue and the rondo.

Other rondos do not go so far as to dispose of all thematic contrasts, but retain sufficient thematic material for the episodes so that the main theme is always thrown into sharp relief. Beethoven, in the finale of his Op. 7, works out the first long episode with thematic strictness. The episode elaborates the following motifs derived from the eighth and ninth measures of the theme. Also, the chord repetitions of the accompaniment are taken from the main theme.

episodes with new material

Sometimes the episodes consist of entirely new thematic material. In this case, also, distinctions can be made. Many rondos mark the episodes very strongly as insertions of little pieces complete in themselves, while others treat them as something secondary or transient by making them more flowing, less weighty in content. The second type of treatment is more in accordance with rondo form. The strongly marked episode, carrying sonata features over into the rondo, is antagonistic to the idea of the form. A better effect is made by a contrasting episode in the manner of a trio, or a "minore" section in a major piece. Rondos in the Clementi sonatas are frequently treated in this manner. In minor pieces, just the reverse is often found, a contrasting "maggiore" episode, as in the second episode of the attractive rondo in Mozart's piano sonata, No. 16, in A minor. This rondo is also noteworthy on account of the first episode with its new melody shaped from motifs of the main theme and closely related to it.

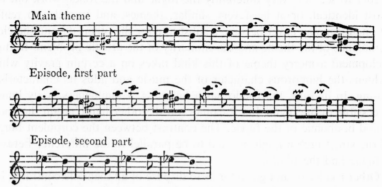

The division of the episode into several parts should not be overlooked in this example. Similar construction is often found when the episode introduces a new theme. In the rondo of Beethoven's Op. 90 the first section closes quite normally in E major at measure 32. The last figure of the preceding close is taken up immediately by the episode:

leading over as a connecting link from C sharp minor to the dominant of B major (up to measure 41) to the entrance of the second section:

This shows a close relationship to the main theme, both in melody and accompaniment. The new melody finally enters in B major (measure 59),

but, with fine feeling for the peculiarity of the rondo style, it is not developed to any degree, leading back instead to the main theme after ten measures. The composer makes very ingenious use here of the new episode melody as a surprising introduction to the reprise.

Several of the most important types of the rondo may be briefly illustrated by a few masterpieces of the form. The simplest type of rondo form is *a-b-a-c-a.*

The adagio cantabile from Beethoven's Sonata "Pathétique," Op. 13, shows a perfectly pure model of the simple rondo. The rondo is not very commonly found in a slow movement, but is most often applied to the finale. In the above-mentioned Beethoven piece, however, the main theme, *a,* is $2 \times 8 = 16$ measures in length:

After a full close in A flat major at measure sixteen, the first episode, *b,* enters abruptly in F minor without modulation. A modulation to E flat major follows, then another to A flat, bringing in the principal theme, *a,* after twelve measures. For the first repeat of the theme eight measures are sufficient. Then the second episode, *c,* enters in A flat minor, leading in a novel manner through very interesting modulations back to A flat major and reaching the main theme after fourteen measures. Then follows a coda of eight measures. The Largo of Beethoven's Op. 2, No. 2 is similarly constructed. Here, however, the main section is somewhat expanded at the reprise and a thematic development is inserted in the transition. An analysis of the piece follows:

(*a*) Main theme, three-part song form, measures 1–19, D major.

(*b*) First episode, measures 19–32, B minor, modulating to D major.

(*a*) The first reprise, measures 32–50.

(*c*) Second episode, measures 50–68, D major, D minor, B flat major, D major; thematic development in the second section.

(*a*) Second reprise with coda, measures 68–80.

Another structure frequently found is *a-b-a* | *c* | *a-b-a.*

The whole piece is in three-part form. The first section consists of the main theme, *a,* the first episode, *b,* the repetition of *a.* The second section is filled out by a broadly developed second episode, *c.* The third part is approximately the same as the first. This type of rondo, approaching the sonata form, is modified by a new episode, *c,* in the middle, in place of the development section of the sonata. Many of Beethoven's final rondos are of this type: Op. 2, No. 2; Op. 7; Op. 22; the G major rondo, Op. 51, No. 2.

The rondo theme is often ornamented in various ways at the repetitions. An interesting, thematically developed coda, too, is suitable to the form. Sometimes the material of the middle section, *c,* is found adaptable for the coda, as, for example, in Beethoven's Op. 7: *a-b-a-c-a-b₁-a.*

Sometimes a rondo with three themes occurs. The most remarkable example is perhaps the finale from Beethoven's "Waldstein" Sonata, Op. 53 in C major. Each episode expands into a development section of a new, individual theme. An actual middle section is lacking. The construction of the piece is:

(*a*) Main section, three-part song form, three different versions of the same theme, rising to a climax, measures 1–62.

(*b*) First episode, in several sections, similar to Op. 90 already mentioned: first a C major transition, then the new theme itself in A minor, finally the return to the rondo theme, measures 62–114.

(*a*) First repeat of the main section, normally built, measures 114–174.

(*c*) Second episode, beginning immediately with the new C minor theme, is again in several sections; at first we find a development of the new theme (to 118), then the preparation for the reprise by thematic elaboration of the main theme in sections, measures 119–137, 137–149, 149–212; throughout this passage the note repetition at the start of the principal theme is ingeniously elaborated.

(*a*) Second repetition of the main section, somewhat shortened, but otherwise regular, measures 212–243.

(*b₁*) Third episode brings in no new thematic material, but takes up the first motif of the first episode, expanding it more than before, measures 243–302.

(*a*) Third repetition of the main theme, this time considerably modified by a more rapid tempo and different continuation. Starting here the piece assumes the character of a broad thematic coda, elaborating the motifs in various groups. Measures 302–325, 325–339 (F major, C major to A flat major), 339–383 (A flat, D flat, back to C major), 383–413 (main theme in a new version), 413–441, coda with strong emphasis on the main theme.

Care must be taken that the episodes, notwithstanding their extension and importance, should never lose their character as transitional episodes.

The great variety of the rondo form is by no means exhausted with the few main types here indicated. A knowledge of their structure will, however, suffice for an appreciation of other rondo types.

mixed forms

Formerly, the rondo forms were classified much more elaborately. One spoke of a rondo of the first, second, third, fourth, and fifth type, according to the number of themes. This old distinction is, however, no longer accepted, since many of the so-called rondos of the first to fifth class are in many instances not rondos at all, either in character or structure, but are mixed forms, belonging partly to the song form, partly to the sonata form. These mixed types are indeed also legitimate and are found in many great works. To call these forms rondos is, however, detrimental to the rondo form, because they obscure one's insight into the characteristics of the real rondo. We have already mentioned mixed forms in several chapters. Here we might consider a few of the most important cases which are often confounded with the rondo. The abbreviated sonata form, *a-b-c* | *a-b-c*, without development section, belongs to this class. It is generally used in slow, less frequently in allegro movements. The finale of Mozart's C minor sonata is constructed somewhat in this manner. A regular sonata exposition with its three themes is here brought back three times in succession with only small changes. In this particular case, one may be doubtful whether the piece is written in rondo or in sonata form. The decision would finally be in favor of the sonata on account of the greater independence of the episodes. The formal scheme would be: *a-b-c* | *a-b-c* | *a-b-c*.

rondo-like constructions

Closely related to the rondo is the somewhat loose construction so favored by Schumann in his piano music: in Op. 21, "The Novelettes," for instance, and the "Faschingsschwank aus Wien," Op. 26. A main section alternates with a whole series of constantly changing new episodes. But as each of these is in itself rounded and finished, the charm is lost which was obtained in the classical rondo by the constantly varied reprise. In Schumann one piece stands next to the other without making manifest the inner mutual relation of the individual pieces. Thus the form loses its convincing coherence and creates an impression of looseness, even somewhat of inartistic treatment. In Schumann's case, certainly, the precious musical contents serve as a counterbalance and make it easier for the listener to pardon any formal deficiency. The first movement of the "Faschingsschwank" makes use of the formal scheme *a-b-a-c-a-d-a-e-a-f-g-a* and a coda which derives its material from *a* and *c*.

This plan of construction has considerable resemblance to the rondos of the preclassical epoch in the suites of a Couperin and Rameau. This type of rondo was most popular in French clavecin music of the seventeenth and eighteenth centuries. Though very similar to Schumann's manner, the French suites surpass Schumann in artistic finish, as their episodes are less extended, thus maintaining their character as intermediate connecting links and giving precedence to the principal theme.

the rondo in classical music and in the nineteenth century

The classical era of the rondo is the period from about 1775 to 1825. It is in the music of Haydn, Mozart, Beethoven, Clementi, Field, Hummel, and Weber that the refinements of the rondo form can best be studied. Later in the nineteenth century the rondo went out of fashion. Mendelssohn may still boast of a piece in best rondo style, the brilliant "Rondo Capriccio," and Brahms has occasionally, though not frequently, written some pieces in true rondo character. Elsewhere, however, one rarely finds pieces of that vivacious lightness, that carefree mirth, that graceful and elegant motion, so characteristic of the classical rondo. Richard Strauss's brilliant *Till Eulenspiegel* pretends, on its title-page, to be written "in rondeau-form," adding, however, to this statement the revealing confession "after the old-fashioned roguish manner." Thus the listener is warned to accept the rondo as one of Till's "merry pranks."

After the neglect of the rondo in the romantic and neoromantic music, a surprising revival of the rondo form took place in the neoclassical music of the Stravinsky and Hindemith schools, this time, however, amply seasoned with the discordant spice of the grotesque, burlesque, and parodistic traits favored by ultramodern music.

CHAPTER VIII

the sonata

A sonata at the present time designates a composition in several movements, of which at least one, generally the first movement, is written in the so-called sonata form. Generally two outer movements of larger dimensions, the first and the last movement, include one or two shorter intermediate movements. These intermediate pieces tend to employ song or dance material. If there is only one middle movement, it receives the character of a slow movement. In the event of two middle movements a minuet or scherzo is added.

The usual typical sonata thus consists of:

(1) Allegro
(2) Andante or Adagio
(3) Minuet or Scherzo
(4) Allegro, either in sonata, in rondo, or in variation form.

The slow movement and the scherzo sometimes change places, so that the scherzo or minuet forms the second movement.

Sometimes, especially in more extended works, the first or the last movement, or both of them, have a special slow introduction. (See Beethoven, Sonata "Pathétique," Op. 13; and the Second, Fourth, and Seventh symphonies.)

Since the sonata form is the chief form of modern instrumental music, it dominates the whole of chamber and symphonic music. Not only the piano, violin, violincello sonatas belong to this species, but also the trios, quartets, quintets, sextets, septets, octets of all kinds, the concertos, symphonies, and most of the overtures.[1]

historical development

The importance of the sonata form for modern music is clear enough, but the earlier history of the sonata, in the seventeenth and eighteenth centuries, is intricate and complex. The term sonata is first found in the seventeenth century, when instrumental music had just begun to separate itself from vocal music. Originally "sonata" (derived from the Italian word, *suonare,* to play) meant a piece for playing, in distinction to "cantata," a piece for singing. For some time the term sonata did not imply a definite type of form. Sonatas were at first written mainly for the violin, and in the course of time a certain formal type was evolved, predominating until late into the eighteenth century. This type is shown in its highest perfection in the sonatas of Bach, Handel, Tartini, who followed older Italian models and employed a type attributable to masters such as Corelli and Vivaldi.[2]

This older Italian sonata form differs considerably from the later sonata as we find it in the works of the Viennese classical masters. Between the two main types, the older Italian and the more modern Viennese sonata, various transitional types are manifest in the middle of the eighteenth century, in the works of the Mannheim composers, Stamitz, Richter, Philippe Emanuel Bach, and many others. The piano sonata had its inception with Johann Kuhnau, the predecessor of Bach as cantor of Saint Thomas' church in Leipzig. Kuhnau was the first one to transfer the Italian violin sonata to clavier music. The clavier sonatas of Domenico Scarlatti form a separate and distinct species, written mostly in one movement, in song form, and in homophonic style. Scarlatti's sonatas too represent a transition type between the older and the Viennese sonata. In Italy a distinction was made in older times between the *sonata da chiesa* (church sonata), written in fugal style, and the *sonata da camera* (chamber sonata), which was really a suite mixed with sonata elements, not derived from the dance.

A most essential difference is found between the older sonata of the Bach-Handel epoch and the later Viennese sonata. The older sonata generally has only two movements, often with a slow introduction prefixed to each movement. The plan is:

(1) Adagio, Allegro

(2) Adagio, Allegro

[1] On the overture see pp. 167f.
[2] See Part Two, Chapter XVII.

The various movements are generally written in the same key. There is, however, often a change of time, 3/4 interchanging with 4/4. The older sonata does not employ a second theme proper, as is so conspicuous in the Viennese sonata; and the idea of thematic development of the motifs, in the modern sense, is still foreign to it.[3]

The sonata form, as practiced later by Haydn, Mozart, and Beethoven, is constructed on the following plan:

First Part. Exposition of the themes: First or principal theme in the tonic. Transition to the dominant. Second theme, in the dominant. Third or closing theme in the dominant.

Second Part. Development or working-out section: Free fantasy on motifs from the first part, chosen at will. Much more elaborate modulation, final return to the main key, the tonic, and to the principal theme.

Third Part. Reprise: Repetition of the entire first part, this time, however, the second and third themes are not written in the dominant key, but in the tonic. The little appendage at the very close of the movement is called a coda (in Italian, a tail). In case the coda is considerably expanded, as often happens in Beethoven's larger works, it is considered a special fourth part.

Fourth Part: Often corresponding to the second part, as a second development section. In this case the parallelism between the first and third parts and the second and fourth parts is apparent.

This ground plan is of course valid only in its general features. In their details the various sonatas often differ considerably, consequently an understanding of the sonata form necessitates a closer study of its various constituents.

exposition of the themes

The exposition of the theme is the function of the first part. As the sonata is a large and complex form, it is important for the sake of clearness and conciseness to state the thematic material as clearly as possible at the beginning of the piece. In accordance with this maxim, the best masters of the sonata keep the exposition section rather free from complications. The most brilliant example of an efficient exposition is given by Beethoven in the first movement of the C minor symphony, where the entire thematic material is clearly stated with the utmost brevity and impressiveness.

As the sonata has to deal with three (or at least two) main themes, it is essential to understand clearly the mutual relation of these themes. It is of course useful to make a certain contrast between these themes; the melodic

[3] On details in the older sonata type, see Part Two, Chapter XVII.

contours will thus be more differentiated, and occasion provided for more pointed antithesis, for interesting transitions. The manner, for instance, in which Chopin builds the first movement of his piano concertos is not to be recommended, for there is too great a similarity of the first and the second themes, putting the whole piece in danger of lengthiness and monotony. It would be equally inadvisable, however, to introduce into the exposition complications which anticipate the later development section which comes in the middle of the movement. In general, it is useful to differentiate the character of the three chief groups. Beethoven's usual practice is to give to his principal theme sharp and plastic contours, to underline the rhythmical features; whereas he likes to write his second theme in softer, flexible lines, in a lyric, ariose style. For the third theme in the closing group a rhythmically pointed, significant, but brief idea is best, because such a theme is suggestive of a conclusion. The closing theme should appear as the logical consequence of the preceding themes rather than as a variant or an amplification of the second theme.

the principal theme

Not every musical idea is appropriate for the principal theme of a sonata. The principal theme should be so invented that it lends itself to thematic development. For this purpose, a phrase with sharply pointed motifs is best adapted; characteristic contour is always of great advantage for the main theme. The nature of the principal theme may be illustrated here by examples from Beethoven's works:

a) Beethoven, Op. 2, No. 1

b) Op. 10, No. 1

h) Quartet. Op. 51, No. 2

i) Quartet. Op. 95

All these themes, with their sharp contours, are of the same type, characterized by angular zigzag lines and wide leaps. Many of them contain something of dramatic tension, as examples (b), (c), (d), (f), (h), (i). Sharply pointed dialogue phrases express violent contrasts between forte and piano, excited exclamation and soothing reply, separated by expressive pauses. Such themes are well adapted for development because they can be broken up into small strongly differentiated segments, possessing plastic outline and impressiveness by virtue of their rhythmical precision.

Numerous themes of quite different character occur, however, themes of melodic flow, of simpler, more unified emotional expression. They are rather epic in character. A number of themes of this more reposeful type are collected here:

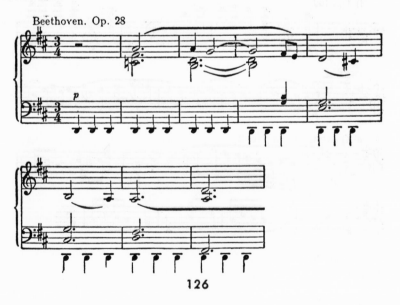

Beethoven. Op. 28

This class of principal themes, often idyllic in character, is frequently found in Brahms' music:

There is a class of principal themes, based on regular sequence or on progression of the tones of the triad, which has already become somewhat antiquated in our present taste. They are typical of many weaker works of the classical masters. One finds them quite frequently even in the nineteenth century, in the Mendelssohn and Schumann epoch. Illustrations follow:

Also the principal theme of the Sonata "Appassionata" would have to be included in this class, were it not that Beethoven knew how to impart so striking an expression to the F minor arpeggio through rhythm and timbre.

The exposition of the principal theme can be accomplished in various ways. In general, the problem is to strengthen the tonal element and to fix the tonality at the start. In most cases there is little reason here for deviating very much from the straight line of harmonic coherence; the aim is to let the transition to the second theme display its full force in the modulation to the new key. Sometimes the first theme is expanded in the manner of an eight- or sixteen-bar song theme, ending with a half or full close, to which is joined the transition section, utilizing either the motifs of the first theme or introducing a new motif. In other cases, however, the principal theme receives no real close at all, but merges almost imperceptibly into the transition episode, modulating to the dominant, or (in minor) to the relative major key, until finally the second theme is reached. It also happens sometimes that the first section has not only one principal theme, but a whole chain of themes. All three types may be illustrated by examples from classical literature:

(1) The first theme ends with a full or half close.
Beethoven, Op. 10, No. 1. Main theme extended to thirty-one measures, with full close in the tonic. The subdivisions are: $8 + 8 + 5$ measures (antecedent, consequent phrase, coda) + 10 measures, taking up the principal motif.
Beethoven, Op. 10, No. 3. Similarly constructed: $4 + 6 + 6$ measures.
Beethoven, Op. 22. First group $3 + 4 + 4$ measures. Half-close.
Beethoven, Op. 28. First group $[1 + 6 + 3] + [1 + 6 + 3] + 8 + 11$ measures. Full close.
Beethoven, Op. 90. First group $16 + 8$ measures.
(2) Principal theme without real close, merging with transition.
Beethoven, Op. 2, No. 1.
(3) Principal theme (first group) as a chain of themes.[4]
Beethoven, Op. 2, No. 3.

transition episode

The transition episode is often built on motifs from the principal theme, and in this case it somewhat anticipates the development section proper in the middle of the movement. In general, one will have to take care not to elaborate the transition episode too much; the impression of a transition should always be retained. The transition should certainly be interesting, through its ingenious and fine manner of treatment; on the other hand, how-

[4] See page 133.

ever, it should not give the impression of something fixed, or broad and solid—rather it should pass in a flowing manner over to the following broader level of sound, the second theme.

In this way are built the transition episodes in the following works:

Beethoven, Op. 2, No. 1.

Beethoven, Op. 13: the first group closes in the sixteenth measure with a full cadence, followed by an appendage of four measures, again half-close, and modulation on a motif from the principal theme, passing over to the second theme.

Beethoven, Op. 14, No. 2: a two-part first theme, antecedent phrase eight measures with full close. The consequent phrase glides imperceptibly into the transition episode, which is in fact nothing but a continuation of the consequent phrase.

Beethoven, Op. 31, No. 1: first theme with transition comprises three parts. First part until measure 30 with full close in G major. Second part, measures 30–46, elaborates a figure from the first theme with full cadence in G major. Third part, return to the first theme, with brief modulation to B major, measures 46–66, where the second theme is reached.

Beethoven, Op. 31, No. 3: quite similar to Op. 31, No. 1.

Beethoven, Op. 53: the repetition of the main motif (starting in measure 14) leads into the transition, which takes its motif from the principal theme.

Beethoven, Op. 57: repetition of the main motif (starting in measure 17) leads into the transition, which this time is built on a new motif.

Other sonata movements bring the first theme group to a full close and introduce the second theme with a new motif. In this case transition by passage work is quite usual. Of this type are:

Beethoven, Op. 2, No. 2 (transition starts in measure 32).

Beethoven, Op. 10, No. 1 (transition starts in measure 32, this time based on a new melodious motif).

Beethoven, Op. 10, No. 2 (similar to Op. 10, No. 1).

Beethoven, Op. 79 (transition starts in measure 12 with running passages).

Beethoven, Op. 110 (transition starts in measure 12 with running passages).

the second theme

The second theme is generally written in the dominant key, therefore a modulation from the tonic to the dominant is required. The classical masters prefer a roundabout way for this modulation, passing to the dominant of the dominant (V of V), the second higher dominant. In order to go from

C major to G major, the chords of A major, D major, and G major would thus have to be touched. The advantage of this manner of modulation lies in the fact that the modulation, passing beyond its real aim, must go backwards again, thus prolonging its journey, gaining the aspect of a larger line, and giving to the second theme the impression of greater repose. For the introduction of broad, calm melodies, this more diffusive preparation is often useful. Examples of this "superdominant" are found in:

Beethoven's Op. 2, No. 2 (A major. B major, F sharp major, B major, E minor).

Beethoven's Op. 10, No. 3, starting at measure 42, before introduction of the E major triad, leading to A major.

Beethoven's Op. 28 (similar to Op. 10, No. 3).

For pieces in minor keys, the normal procedure is to write the second theme in the relative major key. The classical masters very seldom introduce the second theme in another key besides the dominant or the relative major. Beethoven sometimes employs the mediant or third above, as, for example, with the most brilliant effect in the "Waldstein" sonata, Op. 53 (first theme in C major, second theme in E major).

In introducing the second theme, modern composers take more liberties with modulation. These liberties, however, should not obscure the fact that the dominant and the relative major are the normal and most natural keys for the second theme, and that the choice of other keys will be effective for well-planned, special effects only after thorough consideration.

The construction of the second theme can be just as varied as in the case of the first theme. Here also the theme may be melodically rounded off in eight or sixteen measures; it may be repeated with certain variations or amplified by an appendage. The treatment of the first theme, as it is explained above, may therefore be applied also to the second theme.

Sometimes, especially in modern works, the second theme is contrasted with the first theme not only in its character and tonality, but also in its different time. In his Third symphony, Brahms opposes to the 6/4 time of the first theme a 9/4 time in the second theme.

the closing group

Just as the second theme is introduced by a full cadence in the dominant, so too a cadence is required before the entrance of the closing group or third theme. The first main section of the sonata, the exposition of the themes, will thus show two well defined cadences in the dominant key. The closing group is, in general, brief and concise, without greater elaboration which would deprive it of its character as a close. A significant feature of this third theme group is its straightforward, direct, plain manner, without much irrelevant digression. Thus one achieves the effect of a final clause. In a very extended movement, the closing group may be composed of two different ideas in the manner of an antecedent and consequent phrase within the period. Such a doubled closing group is found in Beethoven, Op. 7:

The organ-point (long-held note) on the tonic is very serviceable for the closing group, since it produces an impression of broad expansiveness, of calm breathing. A similar plan is followed in Beethoven's Op. 10, No. 3; the Eighth symphony; and the Ninth symphony.

On account of its rather plain construction, the closing group often repeats the same closed melody, be it in different octaves, in different dynamic degrees (now piano, now forte), in different tone coloring (changing the orchestral instrumentation). As regards these repetitions, attention may be called to Beethoven's Op. 2, No. 1; Op. 2, No. 2; Op. 10, Nos. 1, 2, and 3; Op. 13, and so on. The close tends to be strongly marked through dynamic effects, whether it be a climax, a crescendo up to fortissimo, or a diminuendo down to pianissimo. In this way distinct and orderly subdivision is attained; the form gains in plasticity, the piece is more easily comprehended by the listener. The older sonatas generally repeat the entire exposition, and consequently some transition becomes necessary for joining the close of the exposition section to the beginning of the movement. In many sonatas close and beginning are simply opposed to each other without any special connecting link, as in Beethoven's Op. 2, Nos. 1, 2, 3; Op. 7; Op. 10, Nos. 1 and 2. Here the dominant at the close simply leaps to the tonic at the beginning. In such cases the impressiveness of the effect is based on contrast, on opposition or quick succession.

In other cases a gradual transition is preferable. A special appendage is then subjoined to the closing group, anticipating the motif of the first theme so that the principal theme appears as the logical continuation of the final group. Beethoven gives an interesting illustration of this procedure in Op. 10, No. 3. The motif:

is directly related to the first theme. The modulation from A major to D major is accomplished by introducing the minor seventh G, instead of the preceding G sharp.

Similarly, Beethoven makes a distinct allusion to the first theme at the close of the exposition in Op. 31, No. 3; in Op. 14, No. 1; in Op. 22. In Op. 106 the rhythm of the principal theme is distinctly marked at the close.

Occasionally composers go even a step beyond hinting at the first theme. In such cases the entire closing group is based on the principal theme. Beethoven's Second symphony illustrates this case. Compare the third theme in the closing group:

with the principal theme:

groups of themes

In more broadly laid out works, the first movement is sometimes complicated by large aggregations of themes. The first, second, and third theme sections are no longer composed of single themes, but of groups of themes. Beethoven's rather ample C major sonata, Op. 2, No. 3, shows this type of construction. Its formal analysis follows here:

Principal theme with full close in the tonic, measures 1–12

Transition episode with new, passage-like motif; modulation to the dominant with full close, measures 13–21

Annex with plagal cadence on G (IV–I), measures 21–26

First secondary theme, G minor, modulating to A minor, measures 26–39

Transition from A minor back to G major on a new motif, measures
39–47
Second secondary theme in G major, modulating at the close to C major,
measures 47–61
Restatement of the first transition episode from the principal theme
section. Modulation from C to G, with thematically new appendage,
measures 61–77
Closing group, first phrase, measures 77–85
Closing group, second phrase, measures 85–90

Beethoven's Op. 7, first movement is similarly constructed:
Principal theme group: first introductory phrase, measures 1–4
Second phrase, theme proper, measures 5–17
Appendage, measures 17–25
Transition episode: first phrase formed from the first motif of the prin-
cipal theme and a new motif in the manner of a dialogue; modula-
tion to the dominant, half-close on F, measures 25–39
Second phrase, measures 39–59
Second theme, with repetition and continuation; modulation touching
F, C, back to B flat major, measures 59–93
Transition to closing group, with new motif, measures 93–111
Closing group, first phrase, measures 111–126
Second phrase, measures 126–135

A similar plan of construction is followed in Beethoven's sonatas,
Op. 10, No. 3; Op. 53, the "Waldstein" sonata; Op. 47, the "Kreutzer"
sonata; Op. 106; the three quartets, Op. 59; the Second, Third, Fourth,
Sixth, Seventh, Eighth, and Ninth symphonies.

the development section

The central portion of the sonata form, the so-called development section, has to deal with the thematic elaboration and working out of the
themes or motifs of the exposition section. In the exposition, the various
themes were presented; the development section has to bring about interesting complications of this thematic material and finally to unravel the
knot by a return to the principal key and a repetition of the entire first part.
As this return is the final aim—the climax of the entire development section—the rule seems logical that the principal key of the piece should not be
strongly marked during the development section; otherwise its return in
the third part would miss the point by anticipating the aim.

Free modulation is the section's characteristic feature. Although the exposition was limited mainly to the tonic and dominant (or relative) keys,
the development section has no such limitations. All keys are at its dis-

posal, with the exception of the tonic. Towards its close, the development section will aim at the dominant, in order to arrive at the tonic again at the beginning of the third part of the piece.

This freedom of modulation does not, however, mean lawlessness or arbitrariness. In the development section, as in other parts, consistency and logical modulation are of prime importance. In its use of the thematic material, the development section has much freedom. Its motifs may be taken from all three themes of the exposition or it may show a predilection for one or two of the themes. It is not tied to the original order of the themes, but may jump from the first to the third theme, and may join together originally separated parts of the exposition. It may combine new, freely invented themes with the original thematic motifs. The art of combination and contrapuntal skill enjoys free play in the development section.

Only by way of exception can the introduction of an entirely new theme thematically unrelated to the original motifs be justified in the development section. The manner in which a new theme in the development section can be brought into interesting relationship with the motifs of the exposition is frequently observable in the works of Schumann, who was fond of this method. Examples are found in his piano sonata in G minor, in the B flat major symphony, in the D minor trio.

The extension of the development section is not determined by any fixed rules. But in general it is advisable to make exposition and development section about equal in length. One cannot very well oppose a lengthy development to a brief exposition. The consequence would be a lack of proportion, somewhat similar to a house with a very little basement and a mammoth upper story. Also the reverse holds true: extensive exposition with brief development is not advisable. The development then loses its point, it appears insignificant. Of course, all these prescriptions have only general validity. Sometimes the exposition preponderates, sometimes the development. But one ought to take care that the two sections retain a just proportion.

In order to demonstrate clearly the possibilities of thematic development, one of the most astounding models may here be analyzed in detail, the development section of Beethoven's "Eroica" symphony.

The central part of the first movement, comprising 246 + 4 measures, is constructed on a vast scale. It is divided into a number of larger sections, which, down to their smallest fragments, are worked out organically on the thematic material. The plan of construction is as follows:

(I)   Measures 1–15 (to these must be added four measures preceding the double bar)

(II)   Measures 15–27

(III) Measures 27–69

(IV)   Measures 69–85
(V)   Measures 85–133
(VI)   Measures 133–149
(VII)   Measures 149–171
(VIII)   Measures 171–187
(IX)   Measures 187–246.

(I) Measures 1–15, joined to the closing motif of the exposition, developing this motif derived from the principal theme:

in pianissimo, in dim contours, modulating from the dominant B flat to G, the dominant of C minor. These fifteen measures, together with the four measures preceding the double bar, represent the introduction of the development proper, connecting the exposition and the development. In the works of the masters one often finds application of the formula: extract from the close of the exposition a short transition phrase, which in modulating into another key leads to the beginning of the development proper. The fifteen-measure phrase represents an eight-measure phrase extended through interpolation.[5]

(II) Measures 15–27; this episode works out the motif

[5] For the sake of convenient reading, the measures are numbered starting after the double bar, though the development section actually starts four measures before the double bar. The numbers above the notes have reference in all the following examples to the continuous counting of the measures throughout the section, whereas the numbers and brackets below the notes indicate the real, heavy measures, the extensions and elisions of the single phrases.

derived from the transition to the second theme (starting in measure 45 of the exposition). To this is newly added a counter motif in double counterpoint:

These two motifs in various inversions fill out the entire section. A secondary motif in eighth notes serves for the harmonic accompaniment:

which likewise has its origin in measure 45 of the exposition. The construction of this episode is rather simple. Its 3×4 measures are subdivided into three equally long phrases, representing an extended cadence on the chords V_7, I 6/4, V_7:

(III) Measures 27–68; thus far all has been by way of preparation. Now the first goal is reached. The principal theme enters in C minor:

moves on slowly, in rising sequences, from C minor to C sharp and D minor. The first four measures of the principal theme had so far been employed as motif; from here on only the first two measures of this theme are retained (measures 35 and following), the phrases expanding in majestic breadth in fortissimo.

The figure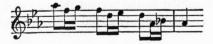

serves as counterpoint. It may be traced back to the second theme in the exposition (measure 65). In his development sections Beethoven often likes to combine motifs taken from widely separated places in the exposition:

After a development of sixteen measures the continuation is interrupted by an interpolation of four measures in piano. The coherence with the foregoing is maintained by retaining the contrapuntal motif in eight and sixteenth notes in the middle part. The motif of the upper voice appears like a diminution of the principal theme. This becomes manifest especially in the second measure at *

With a quick crescendo this little interlude leads to a repetition of the preceding twelve measures, fortissimo, in G minor:

The same little four-bar interlude in its second half is now used for the further development, leading to a half-close on the dominant of A flat major:

(IV) Measures 69–85; here follows a new elaboration of the two motifs, already used in (II). In 4×4 measures the modulation turns toward F minor:

(V) Measures 85–133; a great climax is being prepared. It is introduced by a fugato on two motifs already much employed:

After eight measures, the motifs are fused together. The tones flow on with a colossal power like a mountain torrent in a narrow bed of rocks. The softly wailing phrase, which but a few moments ago, in sections (II) and (IV), preceding the fugato, had sounded so plaintive and delicate, now recalls the thundering roar of a cataract. This impression is caused by the sforzati, the sharply jagged, octave leaps of the motif, and by the syncopation, squeezing into the 3/4 measures what the ear interprets as 2/4 time. Moreover, the continuous tension also has its effect, working at full power until the climax is reached, which sounds finally like a desperate outcry. Immediately afterwards the raging tumult is calmed, and a moment of rest enters.

This episode, together with the preceding section (IV), shows a brilliant model of thematic development, by virtue of the three different versions of the same motif, which thereby undergoes a complete change of expression. At first the motif appears in piano and legato, descending diatonically or in little leaps. In the fugato, sforzati enter and leaps of sixths, finally of octaves, in fortissimo:

At the place where the syncopation starts, a motif from the exposition (measure 28) is introduced with splendid effect, producing the climax by the same above-mentioned "wedge" in 2/4 time:

The modulation turns from D minor to A minor and E minor. An interesting constructive feature is offered by the constant extensions of two-bar phrases so that a two-bar phrase is attached to almost every four-bar phrase: $4 + 6 + 6 + 6 + 6 + 2 + 2 + 2 + 2 + 4 = 40$ measures.

133.

(VI) Measures 133–149; the first summit has been surmounted. After the recent passionate outbursts, a moment of relaxation enters. An entirely new theme in E minor makes its appearance. This is an exceptional case; usually new themes are avoided in the development section. Beethoven, however, finds a justification for his new theme by bringing it into relation with the principal theme, as will be evident in sections (VII) and (VIII). The construction is simple: 2 × 8 measures, 8 measures in E minor, transition to A minor, 8 measures A minor, transition to C major:

(VII) Measures 149–171; after the close of the new theme, the principal theme appears as an answer, in a new thematic elaboration. The motif for the continuation is derived from the third measure of the principal theme:

To this is attached a newly formed phrase:

With these motifs the thematic material of this episode is exhausted. The construction is 4 + 4 + 4 + 2 + 2 + 4 + 2 = 22 measures. The extension of six measures is brought about by the repetition of an appendage at the close of both eight-bar phrases. Four measures are attached to the first eight-bar phrase and two measures to the second eight-bar phrase (at the placed marked *). The progressions touch C major, C minor, E flat major, E flat minor:

(VIII) Measures 171–187; this episode corresponds to (VI); the former E minor, however, is now replaced by E flat minor, and the modulation now touches G flat major in the middle and then quickly turns to the chief dominant, B flat. Here also the formal construction is quite normal, 2 × 8 measures:

(IX) Measures 187–247; the quiet intermezzo of (VIII) prepared the great final climax now entering in section (IX). The entire modulation revolves around the dominant B flat, as preparation for the return to E flat at the end of the development section. The construction is simple in its basic features, but complicated in its details. As on a staircase, the bass mounts in four-bar sequences, through 7 × 4 measures, until it reaches the summit. On this bass, progressing irresistibly in huge giant strides, the principal motif is built up in the top voices in canonic imitation. What follows after this grandiose structure, the crown of the entire movement, is nothing but a slow falling off, the dying reverberations of an echo. Fragments of the episode linger hesitatingly, the melodic contours grow dimmer and dimmer, until finally nothing is left suggestive of a plastic motif: at this moment, however, the principal theme enters in the bass with decisive impulse and shoves everything into the right track—the beginning of the reprise follows directly:

144

187.

146

The modulation in the nine sections progresses as follows: B flat major—C minor—G minor—A flat major—F minor—C minor—G minor —D minor—A minor—E minor—A minor—C major—C minor—E flat major—E flat minor—G flat major—B flat major—E flat major. The close concatenation of the various keys is worthy of notice. The progression moves forward to four flats (A flat, F minor), then backwards step by step, from four to three, two, one flat (C minor—G minor—D minor), to the neutral key of A minor (no flat), still further to E minor, where, approximately in the middle of the development section, a reposeful episode enters. Of all the tonalities which appear here, E minor is farthest distant from E flat major. Further on, the neutral key, C major, is the starting point for a return to the flat keys, and in effective concatenation the movement reaches the dominant B flat of the main tonality.

The development section is built up in three climaxes. From the dim pianissimo in section (I), the motifs proceed in playful progression from piano, section (II), in rapid crescendo, reaching fortissimo in (III) (D minor and G minor). Again the sprightly, playful motion starts in piano and in the following fugato (V), the powerful climax is prepared and attained. Next follows impressive contrast: a moment of rest (VI); soon, however, a new ascent begins (VII), once again interrupted (VIII), finally, however, continued with irresistible power to the highest peak (IX). Also certain parallels of construction are remarkable. Section (II) corresponds to (IV), (VI) corresponds to (VIII). These parallels are of special importance in so broad a structure, which otherwise might easily fall apart into single, incoherent phrases.[6]

the reprise

Essentially, the third part of the sonata form contains a repetition of the entire first part, the exposition. Instead of the dominant, however, the second and third themes now appear in the tonic key. Consequently, there is no modulation to the dominant in the reprise, and therefore the transition from the first to the second theme must be different from what it had been in the exposition. Besides this inevitable change, still other smaller variants must be introduced in order to avoid the impression of a merely mechanical, dull repetition. One may even call it a law of artistic construction that a repetition should never be made verbatim or quite exact, but must be made with little variations in its details. The most important and most frequent change is in the principal theme itself as it emerges from the development section of which it is the crowning consequence. A soft principal theme may under certain circumstances be changed in the reprise into a brilliant fortissimo phrase, as for instance, when the development is worked out to a great crescendo, and the beginning of the reprise appears as a brilliant climax. Beethoven's Seventh, Eighth, and Ninth symphonies; Schumann's C major symphony and piano quartet, Op. 47; and Brahms' C minor symphony demonstrate this mode of composition.

THE VEILED REPRISE

Sometimes it is of good effect, however, to do just the contrary and to veil the entrance of the reprise by a deceptive cadence, or by new, refined harmonization of the principal theme. In Brahms' trio in B major, Op. 8, this case is well illustrated. The principal theme is introduced at the reprise in G sharp minor and only in its further continuation does it modulate back to B major.

In the first movement of his G minor symphony, Mozart anticipates the beginning of the reprise by letting it enter while the close of the development is still continuing on the long sustained dominant G. This is one of the most enchanting examples illustrating this manner of transition on the dominant organ-point:

[6] In his excellent study on the "Eroica" development (in the *Beethoven Jahrbuch*, 1925), Professor A. Lorenz comes to the conclusion that the entire development is built in the large bar-form (see page 19f.): *Stollen, Stollen, Abgesang*, if one considers section (I) as introductory, and combines the other eight sections into four larger parts: section (II) and (III), 54 measures, first part (*Stollen*), thesis; section (IV) and (V), 64 measures, second part (*Stollen*), antithesis; sections (VI), (VII), (VIII), 54 measures, third part, and section (IX), 60 measures, fourth part (*Abgesang*), synthesis.

Reprise.

THE REPRISE IN A FOREIGN KEY

The great masters have shown much ingenuity in the treatment of the
reprise. One of the refinements of construction may consist in introducing
the reprise not through the regular full cadence from the dominant, but
through some surprise of modulation. Beethoven in his Second symphony
finishes the development section in the first movement with a broad cadence
in F sharp minor, and then passes quickly in a single measure to the reprise
in the main key of D major.

Haydn, in his C major quartet, Op. 33, No. 3, similarly turns the close of the development section to E minor, and even retains E minor in the start of the reprise before modulating quickly back into the main key of C major:

The reprise enters surprisingly with a delightful effect of freshness in Haydn's "Emperor" quartet in C major. The key of E major is firmly established in a lengthy cadence towards the close of the development section. This vigorous E major, however, loses its force and brightness by passing hesitatingly into E minor in the softest pianissimo. Suddenly the reprise, entering in forte with the C major theme, sweeps away all timid hesitation.

the sonata

Reprise.

THE TONIC IN THE BEGINNING OF THE REPRISE

Brahms, in his G major string quintet, Op. 111, proceeds differently with great effectiveness. He places the modulation back into the main key not in the close of the development section, but in the beginning of the reprise. The development ends with a widely extended, firmly established E flat major, and the reprise enters not after the expected G major cadence, but in the cadence itself.

151

The harmonic extract of the passage in question is:

The reprise commences with the chord of the sixth and fourth of the tonic instead of the fundamental position of this triad. In a piano reduction the transition looks as follows:

In Philipp Scharwenka's string quartet in D minor, Op. 117, the reprise enters very elegantly and surprisingly, after a long F major passage, by interpreting the chord B flat, D, F, G (subdominant of F major) as sub-dominant of D minor. Here also the return to the principal key takes place not before but within the reprise:

153

THE DECEPTIVE REPRISE

On the analogy of the deceptive cadence, a composer may sometimes employ a deceptive or mock reprise. The development section is brought to an apparently normal close with a full close; the principal theme then enters, not, however, in the main key, but in a very different tonality; harmonic artifices then lead the ear back surprisingly to the tonic, and suddenly, almost imperceptibly, the reprise has reached the main key and is now continued normally. This case is finely illustrated in Beethoven's F major sonata, Op. 10, No. 2. The rather extended development of the first movement is closed with a cadence in D major, the principal theme now follows in D major through twelve measures, making the listener believe that the reprise has already started. Quite surprisingly, however, a transition is made to F major, and only now, with the fifth measure of the theme, does the reprise proper begin.

The various methods of beginning the reprise briefly indicated here have validity not only for the third part of the sonata form. Wherever the problem arises of making a new section enter effectively and in an interesting manner, similar methods may be employed. Such cases may occur at the introduction of the second theme in the sonata; at the repetitions of the principal theme in the rondo; in the finale of a set of variations, provided the theme is brought back again; in the song form, and so on.

Sometimes the entire structure of the reprise is considerably changed. Beethoven, in his D minor sonata, Op. 31, repeats in the reprise the slow introduction from the beginning of the movement. He even amplifies it, but omits the principal theme entirely with its long exposition and passes over immediately to the second theme. The reason is found in the development section, which had already busied itself considerably with the main theme. By being repeated once more in the reprise, this theme would have lost its impressiveness. Similarly Chopin, in his B flat minor sonata, Op. 35, omits the principal theme entirely in the reprise, and starts the reprise with the second theme because the development section had treated the principal theme almost exclusively and had already exhausted its interest.

differences between reprise and exposition

In the transition from the first to the second theme with its change of modulation (tonic instead of dominant), will generally be found the main difference between the reprise and the exposition. The masters have taken advantage of most of the possibilities for attractive effects at this point of the sonata structure. Looking over the Beethoven symphonies, one will find in almost every one some ingenious, novel idea. In the First symphony the long sequence, effectively introducing the second theme, is newly inserted here. The "Eroica" symphony exhibits a much broader development in respect to harmony and constructive design, thereby effecting a climax which contrasts with the corresponding phrase of the exposition. The Fourth symphony builds up this transition in the reprise splendidly, with a broad sequence of powerful sound, mounting upwards forcefully (see the half-notes in the first violin) and a little later descending again with firm step, merging into the second theme. The Seventh symphony introduces at this point an entirely new, broad development of the main motif. In the Eighth symphony the reprise amplifies the entire first theme group and varies it by frequently placing the melody into the bass. The Ninth symphony presents that famous passage with the long roll of the kettledrum, starting fortissimo and vanishing into the piano of the second theme. Also in the three famous Mozart symphonies (G minor, E flat, C major) the transition passage in the reprise shows further extraordinary refinement.

the coda

The coda is a shorter or longer appendix at the end of a sonata movement or any other form. Not all sonatas, however, make use of a coda. Beethoven's Opp. 22 and 49, for instance, close without any coda.

Many sonatas are ended with just a few measures appended to intensify the final cadence. In such cases one can hardly speak of a real coda because of the lack of an independent finial structure. Examples to illustrate this typical ending are found in Beethoven's Op. 2, Nos. 1 and 2; Op. 10, Nos. 1 and 2.

There are two species of coda. The shorter coda usually resumes the principal theme once more at the close, treating it with more or less elaboration. The large coda is a separate part of the sonata form, its fourth part, somewhat corresponding to the second part. It contains a new development section and may in many cases, as regards wealth of elaboration, vie with the first development. A few examples may illustrate the two kinds of coda:

Beethoven's Op. 2, No. 3, contains, quite exceptionally for a sonata, a brilliant concerto cadenza, beginning with the deceptive cadence (G to A flat major) and leading back to the principal theme; to this is added a motif from the development (syncopated octaves in the bass) and finally the closing passage from the exposition (octaves in both hands).

Op. 7 has an elaborate coda, starting again with a deceptive cadence developing the first motif briefly, then turning to the second theme, recapitulating the last phrase of the closing section, and finally returning once more to the principal motif. The harmony hovers near the tonic throughout.

Op. 10, No. 3, deals in the coda with the principal motif only, but compensates for this lack of variety by an interesting harmonic treatment and a well built climax (D to G major, G minor, E flat major to D major).

Op. 13 brings into the coda a reminiscence of the slow introduction, and to this joins once again the principal theme of the allegro.

Op. 14, Nos. 1 and 2, and Op. 28 have only a short coda, utilizing the principal theme without harmonic complications.

Op. 31, No. 3, mixes motifs from the first theme and the transition episodes, which results in a plastic short coda. Op. 110 treats the coda similarly.

Opp. 54 and 57 have broad codas in the style of a development section; in correspondence with the extension of the coda, the modulation deviates further away from the tonic. A similar construction of the large coda is found in Opp. 81 and 106.

One of the most brilliant examples of a broadly constructed coda is found in the first movement of Beethoven's "Eroica" symphony. It is strictly thematic in character, representing a second development section, and showing definite relationship to the first development.

The coda can be divided into six sections:
  (I)   Measures 1–16
  (II)   Measures 17–30
  (III) Measures 31–52
  (IV)   Measures 53–80
  (V)   Measures 81–121
  (VI)   Measures 122–140.

(I) Descending sequences built on the principal motif, on E flat for six measures, on D flat for four, on C for six measures.

(II) Modulation from C major to F minor: $2 + 4 + 2 + 2 + 4$ measures. The principal motif is combined with a counterpoint, whose first part is derived from the first development section:

and whose second part (figure in eighth notes) is newly added.

(III) F minor passing through E flat minor to the dominant B flat.

8 + 14 measures. The new theme of the first development is taken up here again, thus strengthening its appearance of legitimacy.

(IV) The four-bar motif

already heard at the close of the first development as its crowning climax, is reintroduced here. This time, however, the complicated canonic construction to which it previously served as substructure is lacking. A flowing melodious top voice is now added. 7 + 4 measures. Use of the low B flat in the manner of a pedal point, followed by the E flat major cadence.

(V) Combination of the principal theme with the counterpoint, from (II), of the coda. Various inversions of these two themes, followed by an appendage of ten measures, representing an amplified E flat major cadence, embellished by passing notes.

(VI) Return to the second theme of the exposition followed by cadence in E flat major.

In the development section, as has been shown, the introduction of a new theme is justifiable only under special circumstances. In the coda a new theme will be appropriate even more rarely; examples of this are therefore very scarce. Beethoven closes the first movement of his Op. 111 with a melodically new motif, which, however, is connected with what precedes it by the accompaniment figure of the left hand, which had been an importart feature throughout the piece. Schumann introduces an entirely new melody in the coda of the first movement in his B flat major symphony. This little theme has its justification only in its extraordinary delicacy and beauty. Berlioz also introduces an entirely new idea at the end of the first movement of his "Symphonie fantastique," excusing its presence with the "religious consolations" of which he speaks in his program.

the same thematic material in one movement

Sometimes all the themes of a sonata movement are derived from the same thematic material. Beethoven gives us a number of striking examples. In Op. 2, No. 1, the second theme is formed by the inversion of the first theme:

The difference in character between the first and the second theme is here made manifest by the staccato in the first case, the legato in the second version, and by the replacing of the sixteenth triplets at the close with quieter eighth notes. Similarly, Beethoven proceeds in his Sonata "Appassionata," Op. 57:

Here one should compare the rhythmically more plastic and forceful first theme with the softer, curved outlines of the second theme. Especially instructive and interesting is Beethoven's sonata, Op. 81, "Les Adieux." Here all the themes of the first movement are derived from the principal motif of the slow introduction, with its three descending notes:

Le - be - wohl!

The main theme of the allegro is:

Le - be - wohl

The transition to the second theme makes use of the same motif in *motu recto* and *motu contrario,* in the original motion and in contrary motion at the same time:

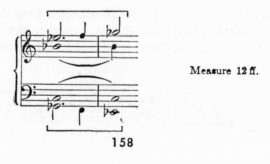

Measure 12 ff.

158

The second theme is based on the same motif:

Also the final group is dominated by it in diminution and in augmentation:

Also the entire development section, the reprise and the extended coda are dominated by this motif of three notes. Here is seen one of the most brilliant examples of thematic development.

the slow introduction in the sonata

The slow introduction is sometimes brought into relation with the following allegro. The simpler case is seen in pieces such as Haydn's E flat major symphony, Schubert's C major symphony, Schumann's F sharp minor sonata, Op. 11: here the theme of the slow introduction is effectively worked out later in the development section and at the close of the movement.

Sometimes the introduction contains the thematic material of the following sonata movement either completely or in part. Thus Wagner evolves his entire *Faust* overture from the slow introduction, similarly Brahms the first movement of his C minor symphony.

the intermediate movements of the sonata

If the sonata has only three movements, it will generally have a slow piece as its middle movement, either an andante, adagio, larghetto, largo, or so on. The form of the slow movement may be:

159

(1) Simple songlike, as often in Mozart's piano sonatas (see the F major sonata, for instance); in Beethoven's sonatina, Op. 79.

(2) In the manner of a rondo, as in Beethoven, Op. 13.

(3) In the sonata form, as in Beethoven, Op. 22.

(4) In an abbreviated sonata form without development section, as in Beethoven, Op. 10, Nos. 1 and 3.

(5) With theme and variations, as in Haydn, "Emperor" quartet; Beethoven quartet, Op. 18, No. 5; Schubert, D minor quartet.

Also mixtures of various forms occur. It has been pointed out that the quick scherzo has a contrasting slower trio. In the adagio often the reverse occurs. A slow first part alternates with a fast second part. Brahms is especially fond of these mixtures. In his F major string quintet, Op. 88, the second movement combines an adagio with a scherzo. The plan of construction is:

Grave, 3/4, C sharp minor, measures 1–31

Allegretto vivace, 6/8, A major, measures 32–78

Grave, 3/4, C sharp minor, measures 79–115

Presto, A major, measures 116–162

Grave, 3/4, A major, measures 163–208.

Here is seen a rondo form with two vivid intermezzi, after the pattern: *a-b-a-c-a.*

In this particular case *b* and *c* are thematically alike, but rhythmically different.

Similarly Brahms mixes an adagio with a scherzo in his Second symphony in D major.

If the sonata has four movements, a minuet or scherzo is generally added (see Chapter III).

the finale

The last movement of a sonata-like composition is not nearly so fixed in its form as the first movement. For the finale a variety of forms may be used. Most frequently employed are the rondo, theme and variation, sonata form, and fugue. Sometimes, however, as in Tchaikovsky's "Pathétique" symphony an adagio takes the place of the finale, occasionally also a minuet, especially in the earlier Haydn-Mozart epoch.

Even if the sonata form is used in the finale, it nevertheless differs in character from the first movement. The complicated texture of the first movement is less favorable for the finale, for this last movement usually requires plain, straightforward form, less interrupted by digressions. The demand for largeness of form can well be reconciled with subtle workmanship in the details. Even a graceful rondo may have breadth of proportions, as can be seen in Beethoven's Op. 7, in Mozart's symphony in E flat, in Haydn's quartets and symphonies. These masters possess a subtle skill in distinguishing the finale character from the middle movements, especially in regard to thematic invention and treatment. The attempt to reverse the order of the minuet and the finale rondo in Beethoven's sonata, Op. 10, No. 3, will show how senseless such an arrangement would be. The interchanging of the two outer movements in the same form, as in Beethoven's A major symphony, would likewise be a fatal mistake.

deviations from the normal structure of the sonata

Deviations occur quite frequently. Sometimes the number of movements is increased or diminished, or one movement may be replaced by a piece in less usual form. Extended sonatas place a slow introduction before the first movement, as in Schumann's F sharp minor sonata, Op. 11. Here the introduction is even more closely related to the first movement, through its reappearance in the middle of the development section as climax of the entire movement. Other examples are found in Beethoven's "Kreutzer" sonata and "Les Adieux," Op. 81; Schumann's violin sonata in D minor, and in many overtures and symphonies.

SONATAS IN TWO MOVEMENTS

The earlier masters of the sonata, Haydn, Mozart, Clementi, Beethoven, often are content with only two movements. The second movement in such cases frequently combines the character of an andante with that of a finale, being conceived as a rather broadly extended andantino or allegretto; sometimes the minuet is thus made to serve as finale. In Haydn's G minor piano sonata (Peters Edition, No. 4) the first of the two movements combines the allegro and andante character, representing a slow movement in the form of a first sonata movement, but also approaching the allegro type by the bustle of its motion, the multitude of notes. The second movement, an allegretto, serves the double purposes of minuet and finale.

Similarly in Haydn's G major piano sonata (Peters Edition, No. 10) the first movement, *allegretto innocente,* combines an andante movement. Also Beethoven's F major sonata, Op. 54, is similarly constructed: *In tempo d'un menuetto* and *finale.* Beethoven's two little sonatas, Op. 49 (G minor and G major) have two movements only, but since they are actually sonatinas, they are normally built as such. Even in the monumental "Waldstein" sonata, Op. 53, Beethoven is content with two movements only, though certainly of vast proportions; the short adagio in the middle is only an intermezzo, an introduction to the rondo, into which it leads without any stop. Beethoven therefore calls it an *Introduzione.*

Especially in the last sonatas Beethoven shows a special predilection for two movements. The E minor sonata, Op. 90, consists only of allegro and rondo. Op. 109 ushers in the first movement by a long and elaborate introduction which might be considered a movement in itself, were it not so inseparably tied to the following prestissimo in strict sonata form. A theme with variations serves as finale. Quite similarly constructed is Op. 111, the very last sonata. Variations are much favored in the finale, as will be seen by an inspection of the literature. A few examples only may suffice here: Mozart, D major sonata; Haydn, violin sonata No. 6 (Peters Edition); Beethoven, piano sonatas Opp. 109, 111; violin sonata, Op. 30, No. 1; string quartet, Op. 74; "Eroica" symphony; Brahms clarinet quintet; Fourth symphony.

Sometimes a sonata starts with a set of variations, as Beethoven's Op. 26. For an irregular plan of construction Beethoven applies terms like: *Sonata quasi una fantasia,* in Op. 27, Nos. 1 and 2; Op. 31, No. 2. In these latter three cases, the irregularity is seen in the first movement, which in Op. 27, No. 1 and Op. 31, No. 2, shows fantasy type, by the mixture of adagio and allegro. The so-called "Moonlight" sonata, Op. 27, No. 2, commences with an adagio. Occasionally the fugue is used as a finale, as in Beethoven's Opp. 106 and 110, in Brahms' F major string quintet, Op. 88, in Max Reger's string quartet, Op. 131. The fugue as first movement is found in Beethoven's C sharp minor quartet, Op. 131; the minuet as first movement in Beethoven's Op. 54.

FIVE OR MORE MOVEMENTS IN THE SONATA

Sonatas are written not only in two, three, or four movements, but sometimes also in five, six, or more movements. Beethoven has been the first to make use of this amplified form in his last quartets. His Op. 130 has six movements: besides the first movement and the finale, there are two slow movements and two scherzo-like pieces. Op. 131 has seven movements. More recent examples are found in Schumann's E flat major symphony in five movements, and Brahms' F minor sonata, Op. 5, which is also in five movements.

The impression of unity of all the movements in a sonata is of great importance. It does not suffice that every single movement in itself be well invented and well constructed; the different movements must also match in emotional expressiveness, contents, and style. A heroic, pathetic first movement is badly coupled with a dainty and graceful rococo minuet; a jolly, jovial, unpretentious allegro moderato does not fit together with a bacchanalian, tumultuous, winged scherzo; a plain, short songlike andante can hardly support a gigantic polyphonic structure as finale. The unity of mood and style must not degenerate into monotony, so perilous to the listener's interest. Variety within unity is the problem. Its solution is a matter of aesthetics, of style rather than of formal construction; consequently one can only hint at the problem. Formal construction is appealed to only where the various movements are closely related to each other in their motifs. The following paragraph treats of these cases.

ONE MOVEMENT MERGING INTO ANOTHER

Generally the several movements of a sonata are separated from each other by brief pauses. In earlier times, however, attempts were made at letting the various movements follow each other without any pauses. The form of the fantasy, often related to the sonata, lies behind these attempts. Attention may be called here to Mozart's C minor fantasy and to Schubert's C major fantasy. Beethoven in some of his sonatas *quasi una fantasia,* makes use of this welding together of the successive movements. In Op. 27, No. 1, the first two movements are merged into one without pause; the third movement, the adagio, passes immediately over to the finale. Similarly in Op. 27, No. 2, the first two movements are joined together. Mendelssohn goes one step further in his "Scotch" symphony, in which all the movements succeed each other without interruption. Also in his G minor piano concerto and in the violin concerto, Mendelssohn makes artistically interesting transitions from one movement into the next one. Liszt, in his concertos and sonatas, welds the four movements together into a single, large movement.

ONE THEME FOR ALL MOVEMENTS

In the first movement of his sonata, Op. 81, Beethoven based all the themes, the entire development section, on a single motif. Thus he set an example later composers adopted and varied. The idea was to base all the movements of a sonata on the same theme. In his C major fantasy, Op. 15, Schubert utilizes the principal theme for all four movements by various processes of variation and transformation. This model became quite important for the later treatment of the sonata form, by Liszt, César Franck, and more recent composers. In his "Symphonie Fantastique" Hector Berlioz interweaves his principal motif, the so-called *idée fixe* into all the movements. He does not, however, limit himself to the *idée fixe* as thematic material, but he invents new and characteristic themes for each movement and to these he opposes the *idée fixe* as countermelody, counterpoint. Franz Liszt went still further by deriving the entire thematic material for all the movements of a sonata-like composition from a single theme, through melodic, rhythmical, and harmonic transformation. Brilliant examples can be found in his piano concertos in E flat and A major, in the B minor sonata, the "Dante" and "Faust" symphonies, and in many of his symphonic poems.

In modern times the French School founded by César Franck has appropriated this Lisztian sonata type. In the second part of this book César Franck's violin sonata in A major and Debussy's G minor string quartet will be analyzed in detail with respect to these thematic transformations.

The idea of gaining various themes in larger compositions by transformation of an original motif appears new if one is acquainted only with the music of the eighteenth and nineteenth centuries. In truth, however, this idea represents one of the oldest methods of instrumental music. Towards 1600, and even earlier, when the first organ toccatas, fantasias, ricercar, and canzone were evolved in Venice and Rome, it was quite customary to transform the principal theme rhythmically in every new section. In the modern editions of the music of Claudio Merulo, Frescobaldi, Sweelinck, Froberger, Kerll, and many others, an abundance of instances illustrate this procedure. The following example shows the principal motif with its various transformations in Froberger's Twelfth Capriccio:

Later one became tired of the monotony arising from the continued application of this method. It fell into oblivion, and upon its rediscovery in the nineteenth century, claimed novelty for itself.

THE LEADING MOTIF

It is now relevant to discuss the "leading motif" to which Wagner has assigned so important a part in the construction of his scores. In order to characterize a certain person, a certain sentiment or situation, a motif is either repeated exactly, or varied, somewhat similarly to the Froberger example above. The use of the leading motif does not, of course, imply a certain fixed form. The advantage of the leading motif consists exactly in the fact that it may enter at any place and may be associated with any musical idea. A work based on leading motifs may best be compared with the development section of a sonata. The use of leading motifs permits an even greater freedom because in such a piece no heed need be taken in respect to the extension of the music or a following reprise. The first entry of the leading motif can certainly be compared with the exposition of a sonata theme. In the sonata, however, the exposition of a theme always presupposes a certain formal frame; it must consider the demands of melodic character, tonality, rhythm, time, whereas all these demands are of no importance for the leading motif, which derives its justification not from the formal construction, but from the scenic requirements, the characteristic emotional expression.

UNIFORM ROUNDING OFF OF WORKS IN SEVERAL MOVEMENTS

Various attempts have been made to round off a large work and to bring the several movements into an especially close mutual relationship. In all the movements of his great C minor symphony, Beethoven gives a more or less important part to the fundamental motif of the first movement:

At the beginning of the finale of the Ninth symphony Beethoven, in a fantasy-like introduction, makes the main themes of the preceding three movements pass in review again, thus awakening the impression of meditation, of recollection of the past.

A similar poetic idea is expressed by Hector Berlioz at the start of the finale in his "Harold" symphony. Here the main themes of all the preceding movements suggest how Harold quickly recalls to memory his impressions of the day. In this way formal elements are used for expressing a poetic idea. Schumann applies a similar method for purely formal reasons in his piano quintet. At the end of the finale, the principal theme of the first movement is woven in as a counterpoint, thus effecting a direct relation between the close and the start of the entire work. At the close of his clarinet quintet, Brahms resumes the principal motif of the very beginning of the first movement, thus restoring the original mood and rounding off the entire composition. Following such models, modern composers have frequently applied similar methods. In song cycles, too, some composers have attained very impressive effect by recalling former themes. With the touching postlude at the close of Schumann's *Frauenliebe und Leben,* the first song of the cycle is resumed, creating an impression as of a dream of long vanished bliss. Schumann rounds off his cycle, *Dichterliebe,* in like manner.

Glancing over this great variety of modifications, one perceives clearly why the sonata form was able to rise victoriously above all earlier forms. Not only does it offer a vast field to the imagination, but it is also extremely flexible, is equally adaptable for large and small pieces, for simple and complicated music. It can ally itself with many other forms such as dances, marches, fantasies, fugues, variations, songlike music, rondos, canons, and so on. The phenomenal rise of instrumental music during the time of the Viennese classical masters would have been impossible without the sonata form.

the sonatina

The sonatina is a sonata *en minature*. It is not only shorter than the sonata, but also simpler in structure, plainer in its contents. A special treatment of the sonatina form is superfluous to a student who knows the character and the construction of the sonata. Only a few characteristic features of the older sonatina may be pointed out here.

The thematic invention is lighter than in the sonata; pathos and grandeur are foreign to the sonatina. One may consider it an easily grasped introduction to chamber music for beginners and children.

The development section is limited to a few measures; sometimes it is altogether lacking. The coda also is confined to a minimum of extension. Hardly ever does the sonatina have more than three movements. The second theme is frequently not introduced by a modulation to the dominant, as in the sonata, but by a half-close. One of the best known examples, the first movement of Beethoven's sonatina, Op. 49, No. 1, may illustrate this feature:

Half-close in G major

Second theme in D major

The classical masters of the sonatina are Clementi, Dussek, and Kuhlau. Their sonatinas abound in formal refinements which, however, are duly appreciated only exceptionally, because the sonatina is considered music for children, and only beginners pay any attention to it. Mozart occasionally has something in the sonatina type. Beethoven has written three sonatinas, Op. 49, Nos. 1 and 2, and Op. 79; the latter sonatina has that uncommonly pretty andante which Hans von Bülow has fittingly called "the first song without words," the prototype of the genre later cultivated so successfully by Mendelssohn.

In modern times a revival of the sonatina has taken place. Its intimate character attracted composers again, while its instructive, didactic aims have become less emphatic. Ferruccio Busoni has created a new type in his four sonatinas. They represent indeed "little," but by no means "easy sonatas." The first sonatina belongs to the "cyclic type" of César Franck. The entire thematic material is exhausted by these two plain motifs:

The sonatina consists of a single movement in four sections, as in Liszt's concertos and B minor sonata. An ingenious constructive idea has been evolved here by Busoni. The single movement takes the place of the typical first movement sonata form with its various sections, but at the same time it also corresponds to three different sonata movements. The analysis follows:

(1) Principal theme, at the same time representing the first movement (allegro moderato).

(2) Second theme, stands also for the second movement (andante).

(3) Development section, represents also the finale (allegro).

(4) Reprise of part one and appendix, corresponding to a coda (allegro).

Max Reger has also written works of similar type, piano sonatinas and the charming little trios of Op. 77. Ravel's "Sonatine" and the remarkable sonatinas by Erwin Lendvai may also be mentioned in this connection.

the overture

An overture means an opening, introductory piece. It is found for the first time in the seventeenth-century opera as a short introduction, called sinfonia or sonata, without a well defined formal type. When in the course of time the instrumental forms became more and more differentiated, they were taken over into opera as well and in the second half of the seventeenth century, two main types of overture were generally accepted, the French, Lully, overture and the Italian, Scarlatti, overture or sinfonia. Both types have a three-part construction. In the French type two slow sections include a quick middle piece, whereas the Italian type has two allegro movements with a slow intermezzo:

French Overture: adagio, allegro, adagio.

Italian Overture or Sinfonia: allegro, adagio, allegro.

Very often the Lully overture has actually only two parts, without a concluding adagio, which in other cases has the effect of a coda rather than of a real piece.

In the eighteenth century the French overture became a chief form of instrumental music, not only as an introduction into opera, but also in concert music. Also the suite often contains an "ouverture" as first movement, frequently identical with the prelude.[7] An extensive literature of orchestral suites with overtures bears witness to the popularity of the French form.

The Italian sinfonia became important for instrumental music, especially in the second half of the eighteenth century, when the form of the new sonata was evolved from it, through the efforts of the Mannheim masters and the Viennese predecessors of Haydn, of Phillip Emanuel Bach, Pergolesi, Gluck, and others. Thus the overture gradually accepted the form of the first sonata movement. In this form the overture has entirely replaced the older Italian type, in opera and oratorio as overture proper, as well as in instrumental music, as concert overture. As a relic of the old French type, some overtures have a slow introduction. Generally the overture omits the repetition of the first part, customary in the sonata form. Lighter operas dispense with the symphonic type of overture and are content with a kind of potpourri overture, stringing together with more or less artistic treatment the principal tunes of the opera. In French and German comic opera (Auber, Hérold, Adam, Boieldieu, Bizet, Meyerbeer, Lortzing), in Italian opera (Rossini, Bellini, Donizetti, Verdi) many examples of this type may be found. A higher artistic rank must be accorded to those overtures building up a symphonic structure from themes of the opera. The overtures of Cherubini, Weber, and Schumann's "Manfred" and "Genoveva" overtures would belong to this class.

Wagner's preludes

Wagner goes a step further in his *Vorspiele* (preludes), not binding himself to a certain formal type, but making his prelude a freely constructed symphonic piece on motifs of the opera. In his later works, starting with *Lohengrin,* he replaces the overture by the prelude, in order to indicate that its form is quite free. The Rheingold prelude is built on a single motif, the E flat major arpeggio

[7] See page 68 on the prelude. The history of the French overture has been cleared up by Henri Prunière: "Notes sur l'origines de l'ouverture française," in *Sammelband* 12 of the International Society of Music.

building an undulation of variegated sound in manifold rhythms. The chord of E flat is retained through no less than 136 measures without the slightest harmonic change. One can speak of form and construction only insofar as a planned rhythmical order and climax is made manifest. From the long-held tonic and dominant at the start (E flat and B flat), the above-quoted motif evolves after sixteen measures. The next section, beginning with measure 49, is dominated by the more fluent 6/8 rhythm, every measure of 2 × 3 eighths always filled with motion. The sixteenth notes entering in measure 81 are retained to the close of the prelude, which may be called an introduction and theme with variations. The analysis would be as follows:

Introduction, measures 1–16.

Theme, measures 17–49.

First variation, measures 49–80.

Second variation, measures 81–97.

Third variation, measures 98–113.

Fourth variation, measures 114–129.

Coda, measures 129–136.

The theme is not stated clearly at the start, but unfolds gradually to the ears of the listener, and therefore, as a total complex of forty-eight measures, it appears larger than each of the four variations extracted from it, with thirty-two, sixteen, sixteen, and sixteen measures. The crescendo of sound in these variations is produced less by dynamic means than by the ever-growing animation of rhythm, half, quarter, and sixteenth notes successively dominating the various periods, together with an ever-growing fullness of orchestral sound and the gradual trend upwards from the lowest bass region to the higher octaves. The desperate problem to sustain an E flat major chord through 136 measures without any change of harmony has been solved here with superior art through the formal construction as well as through coloristic orchestral and rhythmical means. The title of this prelude is "In the Depths of the Rhine." It is indeed a landscape painted with the resources of music, depicting in tone the quiet flowing of the deep waters.

All Wagnerian preludes are to be interpreted as expressions of a certain mood, as *Stimmungsbilder,* or descriptions of nature, tone-painting. The master creates his form anew for every piece in conformance with his particular problem. Though the older types of form are no longer used here, yet the art of formal treatment is not inferior to that of the most complex symphonic structures. A great master of form may create new formal types, for he knows everywhere how to obtain his effects with the elements of musical construction. In the *Lohengrin* prelude, for instance, a most effective use is made of showing the theme each time in a different light: at first in aerial heights, resplendent in radiant light; afterwards a little lower and fuller in sound; and finally with full force in the medium range, as if firmly resting on the ground. The entire piece symbolizes the gradual descent of the Grail.

The admirable *Tristan and Isolde* prelude demands a special analytical study, which will be given in the second part of this book.[8]

the symphony

From about the middle of the eighteenth century the symphony meant an orchestral work in sonata form, with several movements. The symphony naturally tends to larger proportions. Most symphonies have four movements; symphonies with three or only two movements are rarely found, and also the numerous varieties of formal treatment pointed out in the sonata are found much less frequently in the symphonies.

HISTORY OF THE FORMS

Terms like sonata, concerto, cantata, and also sinfonia were very vague in meaning in the sixteenth and seventeenth centuries. Heinrich Schütz calls one of his chief works "Symphoniae Sacrae." In it are contained vocal compositions for many parts and solo songs with instrumental accompaniment. Symphonia has here no reference to a definite form. Also Giovanni Gabrieli, in his "Sacrae Symphoniae," uses the term in a similar sense. A generation later, when the new independent instrumental style had gained considerable ground, the name "sinfonia" was preferably applied to instrumental pieces, as a synonym for "sonata." Until late in the eighteenth century, sinfonia meant an instrumental introduction, or an instrumental intermezzo in opera, oratorio, or cantata.

"Sinfonia" was especially applied to the so-called Italian overture, whereas the Lully overture always retained its title "overture." As this French overture became very popular in the orchestral suites, the next step was also to call such suites in several movements overtures. The confusion of titles was so great that even Haydn symphonies were called overtures in England. Only after the new sonata form had asserted its predominance, later in the eighteenth century, more precision was demanded in the titles, and from that time on a sonata for orchestra was commonly called a symphony.

Since the days of Haydn, symphony and sonata have been identical in form; therefore we need to add nothing new to what has been already discussed in the section on the sonata.

the concerto

A sonata for a solo instrument with orchestral accompaniment is generally called a concerto, though the term does not seem to be quite correct

[8] See Chapter XVIII.

in certain cases.[9] The solo part in a concerto has an outspoken virtuoso character. The brilliant treatment of the solo part, however, was not inherent in the idea of the concerto form from the very beginning. Originally the concerto meant a contest between the solo part and the orchestra, a dialogue, an opposition of the two factors. In modern times, however, the orchestra has constantly gained in fullness, power, brilliant sound and coloring, and the solo was likewise obliged to increase its power so that it would not become inferior to the opponent.

The modifications of the sonata form are very slight here; they mainly concern the first movement. Usually the first part, the exposition of the themes, is so managed that a tutti of the orchestra plays the entire first section up to the customary double bar (sign of repetition); the repetition, however, is varied by giving the exposition to the solo instrument. The development section is generally introduced by a second tutti. Towards the end of the movement usually a cadenza is inserted; that is, in the ordinary cadence IV, I 6/4, V, I, between I 6/4 and V an insertion is made which is called a cadenza. It represents a free fantasy for the solo instrument without accompaniment of the orchestra, based on themes and motifs of the exposition. The cadenza is richly ornamented with runs, passages, trills, and a manifold display of virtuosity; in regard to contrapuntal elaboration and in modulation, it is not restricted. Finally, the dominant is reached, and on V the orchestra enters again, bringing the piece to a rapid close in conjunction with the soloist. Between approximately 1725 and 1825 it was customary to improvise the cadenzas at the performance. Later, when the art of improvisation was less and less practiced, it was preferred to work out the cadenza in advance and write it down. Some composers have written their own cadenzas, as Mendelssohn in his violin concerto; others, such as Beethoven in his violin concerto have left it to the player to provide a fitting cadenza.

HISTORY OF THE CONCERTO FORM

The history of the concerto form is rather complicated. In the seventeenth century, when instrumental music began to evolve its own forms, the concerto was a collective term for solo pieces of various kinds, just as sonata, sinfonia, cantata were also such collective names. At first, the concerto was used for ecclesiastic vocal pieces accompanied by the organ or by other instruments. "Concerti ecclesiastici" of this type were already written before 1600 by Andrea and Giovanni Gabrieli.[10] The term concerto here means, as has been already mentioned, a contest, opposition of two tonal groups,

[9] On the difference between concerto and sonata see below, pp. 172ff.

[10] Details on the history of the concerto are found in Arnold Schering's *Geschichte des Instrumentalkonzerts* (Leipzig, 1905).

the dialogue between voices and instruments. These "concerti ecclesiastici" are the ancestors of the church cantata, and even Bach often calls his cantatas "concerti." After a period of experimentation, the instrumental concerto assumed more definite shape and was practiced under two main classifications: (1) The chamber concerto, *concerto da camera;* and (2) the church concerto, *concerto da chiesa.* These in general are equivalent with *sonata da camera* and *sonata da chiesa.* In the seventeenth century there arose an especially important species, the concerto grosso.

THE CONCERTO GROSSO

This is a composition for a small group of solo instruments (called concertino, the small concert) and the entire mass of the orchestra (the real concerto grosso, large concert). The dialogue of these two groups produce attractive problems of sound in this form. Corelli, Torelli, Vivaldi, Handel are the great classical masters of the concerto grosso. Also J. S. Bach has left us in his "Brandenburg Concerti" [11] some of the greatest masterpieces in this form.

THE SOLO CONCERTO

The concerto grosso was the immediate predecessor of the solo concerto, as it is now practiced.

In the new concerto three types must be distinguished:

(1) Concerti in which the solo instrument predominates and the orchestra has mainly an accompanying part. Concerti for violin by Viotti, Kreutzer, Rode; for piano by Hummel, Field, Chopin belong to this type.

(2) Concerti in which the solo and the orchestra are well balanced factors of about equal importance, as in Mozart, Beethoven, Schumann, Mendelssohn.

(3) Concerti, in which the orchestra predominates, really symphonies with a piano obligato, as in Brahms' piano concerti.

MODIFICATIONS OF THE CONCERTO FORM

In modern times, the attempt has been made to modify the sonata form for the concerto, or replace it entirely with some other form. One of the earliest attempts in this direction was made by Spohr in his "Gesangsszene," his eighth violin concerto: he starts with a broad introduction after which recitativo and aria follow with an allegro as finale. Max Bruch chose a similar plan of construction for his violin concerto in G minor. Liszt's manner of thematic elaboration has already been discussed. His concerti do not consist of four separate movements, but of one large movement in four sections.

[11] For a detailed study on the Brandenburg concertos, see Chapter XIX.

In detail of treatment, the great masters show many subtle differences between the concerto and the symphonic form, and these differences prove that they did not consider the concerto a solo sonata with orchestral accompaniment.[12] The introductory orchestral music resembles an extended ritornello before the aria. It has more the character of an introduction than of a typical symphonic exposition. This impression is strengthened by the predominance of the tonic key in the various themes, whereas in the sonata the second and third themes are usually written in the dominant key. Mozart, who has treated the concerto form more ingeniously and with greater variety than any other composer, sometimes makes the solo enter with a theme quite new and different from that of the introduction. Beethoven in his G major concerto does not permit the orchestra to come to a full close in the introductory tutti; quite unexpectedly the solo piano sneaks in on the chord of the dominant seventh and searches its way through the orchestra before reaching the principal theme.

the serenade

The Italian word *serenata* means evening music. At the time when nocturnal serenades were popular, in the eighteenth century, a special type was fashioned for them. A distinction must be made, however, between the vocal serenata and the instrumental serenade.

VOCAL SERENATA

Serenata designated a type of music for some festive occasion, a kind of dramatic cantata, often equivalent to a series of operatic scenes, though theatrical performance was not always demanded. Numerous serenatas of this kind are left to us; the Italian opera composers of the eighteenth century and their German contemporaries: Keiser, Hasse, Graun, Telemann cultivated this field.

INSTRUMENTAL SERENADE

The instrumental serenade was music usually written for performance in open air, and therefore it had a predilection for the wind instruments. Haydn and Mozart have written many serenades of this kind, often calling them divertimenti or divertissements (a suitelike combination of various pieces, especially dances) or cassations. As the sonata form was then being evolved, the serenade adapted itself to the sonata. At present one may call a serenade a symphony of somewhat lighter, more popular type. The movements of a serenade are shorter, but more numerous than the symphony movements. Two andantes, two minuets are quite customary in a serenade. In more recent times Beethoven's serenade for string trio and Brahms' two sere-

12 See Donald Francis Tovey, *The Classical Concerto, Its Nature and Purpose.*

nades, Opp. 11 and 16, in reality two little symphonies, claim principal attention. Formerly popular were serenades by Robert Volkmann for string orchestra, partly with cello solo, and by Robert Fuchs.

the fantasy

A fantasy is a piece freely constructed without a definite formal scheme. Since fantasies are therefore extremely varied, hardly anything definite can be said about the fantasy as a musical form. It may utilize elements of any formal type. In the older instrumental music of the sixteenth and seventeenth centuries for lute, harpsichord, and organ, pieces entitled fantasia hardly differed much from customary forms, such as ricercar, praeambulum, sonata, save in some liberty of fugal answer and contrapuntal treatment. Later, when the fugue had become a fully developed form, fantasia meant something opposed to the strict fugue, in a rather free, improvisatory style. In this sense fantasia is often nearly equivalent to the toccata and prelude, which in their freer types come quite close to the fantasy style.

FANTASY OF THE CLASSICS

The most grandiose examples are Bach's "Chromatic" fantasy and the organ fantasy and fugue in G minor (transcribed for the piano by Liszt). Just as fantasy is opposed here to fugue, so later we find it associated with the sonata after this form had become dominant. Mozart's fantasy and sonata in C minor offers a classical example. The Bach fantasies contain a colorful mixture of contrapuntal, toccata-like, and fugal elements; Mozart derives the elements of his fantasy from the sonata. Here the thematic invention, rhythm, and harmony are decidedly sonata-like. Although the Mozart fantasy contains thematic material enough for three sonata movements, it does not, however, really develop any theme in sonata-like manner. Mozart's fantasy style consists in quickly jumping from one theme to another, in a rapid change of emotional expression, in a free treatment of harmony and modulation. Beethoven, following Mozart's example, frequently introduced fantasy elements into his sonatas. Sometimes he indicates it by titles as "Sonata quasi una fantasia." Op. 27, Nos. 1 and 2, show the fantasy element in the unusual construction of the first movement, whereas the other movements are quite normally constructed. Often, however, in the last sonatas and quartets, fantasy episodes occur without special title or designation.

FANTASY OF THE ROMANTICS

Among the fantasies of more recent time, the following have acquired especial fame: Schubert's C major fantasy, Schumann's Op. 17, and Chopin's Op. 47. Schubert offers us a sonata interspersed with fantasy-like elements, manifest in the transition from the first to the second movement, in the beautiful interconnection of both pieces. Also Schumann's fantasy is, like a sonata, built up cyclically in three movements. Here the fantasy elements are found in the slow G minor episode (*legendenartig,* in the middle of the first movement), and in the slow last movement. Chopin's fantasy resembles a first sonata movement with an introduction. The fantasy features consist here in the freedom of modulation and in the little adagio episode in the middle. All these fantasies, in spite of a certain laxity of construction, still show a real consciousness of form. The popular "fantasies" of modern salon music are a medley of loosely-joined tunes, opera potpourris, paraphrases of songs or opera airs in a showy, brilliant manner. Among this class only the Liszt paraphrases and fantasias have an artistic value by virtue of their most effective and clever pianistic treatment.

symphonic tone poem

Richard Wagner believed that Beethoven with his sonatas, quartets, and symphonies had exhausted the possibilities of the sonata form and that instrumental music had to seek new ways in order to create something of artistic moment. Wagner's view was later refuted, as is proved by the instrumental music of a Schumann, Brahms, Dvořak, Tchaikovsky, César Franck, Mahler, Reger, Debussy, Sibelius, and others. Yet Wagner's opinion has contributed considerably to the creation of a new type of instrumental music, intent on translating a poetic idea into terms of music without, however, binding itself to a fixed, formal scheme.

Modern program music,[13] whose most eminent representatives are Hector Berlioz, Franz Liszt, Richard Strauss, today no longer concerns itself with symphonies or sonatas per se, but with a certain title, a more or less detailed program, illustrating the poetic idea to be expressed musically. A treatise on form has little to do with these "symphonic poems," because they do not represent a definite type of form. This does not mean that a symphonic poem must needs be formless: it creates its form anew in every single case in the light of the problem at hand. Whatever may be the construction of a piece, one should never confound freedom of form with illogical development. Even the most poetic symphonic poem should in itself have logical coherence, quite apart from the program, so as to be musically intelligible. The leading motifs are of great importance; in themselves they ought to be sharply characteristic, and besides, they should be serviceable in satisfying the demands of the program through constantly fresh transformations.

[13] See F. Niecks, *Program Music in the Last Four Centuries* (London, 1907). Alfred Heuss published an exhaustive thematic analysis of Liszt's "Ce qu'on entend sur la montagne," in the *Zeitschrift* (October 1911) of the International Society for Music.

analysis of Liszt's "Les Préludes"

Liszt's "Les Préludes" may be briefly analyzed here. The construction of the piece follows the program. Lamartine had inspired Liszt to this composition through his poem "Les Préludes," where he develops the idea that the whole of human life is nothing but a series of preludes to the final song of death. The poet paints some of these prelude scenes, and the composer, following the poetry, translates these images into music. The titles of the program indicate the emotional content of the various sections:

(I) "Love, the luminous dawn."

(II) "The first delights of happiness interrupted by the raging of the storm."

(III) "What deeply wounded soul after such agitations does not gladly seek to lull its memories in the lovely quiet of rural life?"

(IV) "A man does not stand the restful quietude for long . . . when the trumpet signal arouses him, he rushes into the fray."

In correspondence with this program the music is constructed as follows (the letters *a* to *i* have reference to the motifs):

(I) Andante (*a*), 4/4, C major with transitions to various keys, crescendo until andante maestoso, (*b*), 12/8, C major, fortissimo, agitated. (*c*), 9/8, C major to E major, F minor, E major, tender. (*d*), second theme, E major, soft.

(II) Allegro ma non troppo (*c*), stormy climax, F minor, much modulation to the summit (*f*) in A minor, A flat major.

(III) Interruption by a longer, idyllic episode. Motif (*c*), and a new motif (*g*), later combined with (*d*), climax at the close.

(IV) Allegro marziale, (*h*) and (*i*) in continuous climax, until the triumphant close is reached, resuming (*b*).

Here we see a four-part construction, contracted into one large movement with some liberties, but with the object of achieving variety and contrast. Part (I) is introduction and exposition; (II) leads to the summit in powerful climax; (III) introduces contrast by a soft, idyllic episode; (IV) leads to a brilliant, majestic close in true finale style. The well planned modulation, the order of tonalities (not bound any more to the tonic dominant scheme of the sonata) have their part in the effectiveness of the piece.

The entire thematic material is limited to the two themes (*a*) and (*d*). From these themes the other motifs are evolved by remodeling, variation, and various combinations to satisfy the changing demands of the broadly expanded piece. The transformation of the motifs will be easily perceived in the illustrations on the next page. From motif (*a*) all the following motifs are derived.

A brief comparison will show that the expressive power of the various motifs is much differentiated in spite of their family likeness. The second theme (*d*) is less subject to variation. Its chief change consists in the contrapuntal combination with motif (*g*):

CHAPTER *IX*

the vocal forms

One can speak of real vocal forms in a limited sense only. Vocal music, so far as it is at all of artistic value, is more dependent on the text than on any definite constructive scheme such as is found in the dance and march, in the rondo of the sonata form, and so on. This definition, however, does not exclude a similarity to or even identity with instrumental forms, whenever the text favors such similarity of plan.

Gregorian chant

The vocal forms may perhaps best be studied under the headings: church music and secular music. Church music has its subdivisions into one-part and polyphonic music. In the medieval ecclesiastic music, especially in Gregorian chant, one-part or unison music is exclusively used. The arrangement and collection of the Gregorian chants is generally attributed, not without some contradiction to Pope Gregory the Great (who died in 604), whose intention was to provide the church with appropriate liturgical music for the entire year. Leaving aside a few scanty remnants of antique music, Gregorian chant is the oldest music which we possess, and without doubt the oldest European music still alive at the present time. Gregorian chant is extremely important for the study of Catholic church music, not only on account of its great musical value, its expressive melody, but also because almost the whole of polyphonic church music is based upon it.

CANTUS FIRMUS

Countless motets, hymns, masses, magnificats are built on the Gregorian cantus firmus, that is, a fixed, unalterable chant.

PSALMODY, ANTIPHON, ACCENTUS

Psalmody, the traditional psalm chanting, was taken over into the early Christian divine service from the Jewish temple liturgy. Graeco-Christian liturgy practiced psalmody in the form of an antiphon, a chanting in dialogue between two unison choirs, a men's and a boys' choir. The Milanese bishop Ambrosius introduced the antiphonic psalmody into the occidental church. Nowadays psalmody does not mean real melodious singing, but rather a quick recitation on one tone or a few tones, with rising and falling of the voice at the important signs of punctuation. Accentus is another name for this style of chanting. A fragment from a Gregorian Pater Noster may serve as example:

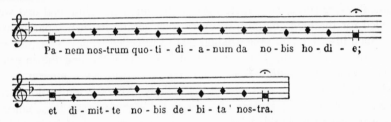

Bar rhythm does not exist in psalmody; the proper accent of the words also dominates the singing. The starting tone of every section is a little protracted, and the final tone is held out still longer. Psalmodic accentus is employed not only for the chanting of entire psalms, but also in a number of other species of liturgical music in which only single psalm verses are sung, or other texts, not taken from the Book of Psalms. Such pieces are *graduale* or graduals, sung by the deacon on the "steps" (*gradus*) of the ambo, the little pulpit, and *tractus* or tract, a wailing chant sung in one "tract," without antiphony, with responses and interruptions by the congregation or a second choir.

The responsorial style or concentus, often sung with rich coloratura by soloists, is musically more developed than the accentus. The so-called Ambrosian hymns came quite close to our modern conception of melodic construction:

em - que   qui   re - gis,   et   tem - po - rum   das

tem - po - ra,   ut   al - le - ves   fas - ti - di - um.

(This hymn is written here in 4/4 time, following Hugo Riemann's version; other scholars, like Gevaert, read these hymns in 3/4 time, since the question of the rhythm of Gregorian chant is not settled.) The hymns are written to original Latin verses, new poetry, whereas most of the other liturgical chants, such as the psalms and antiphons, are taken from the Bible.

TROPES, SEQUENCES

Among the medieval ecclesiastic solo chants the tropes and sequences are especially important. The Gregorian chants with their rich melismatic ornaments were sometimes treated in syllabic manner: additional text was provided for the long coloraturas, every tone getting its own separate syllable. Such insertions into the original text were called tropes. Thus, for instance, the Kyrie of the Mass was amplified in text through the inserted words: *cunctipotens genitor Deus omni creator eleison, Kyrie eleison,* without, however, adding more tones to the melody. Also the long coloraturas at the close of the Alleluia were often provided with new text; these coloraturas were called jubilatio, jubilus, or, when new words had been added, sequence. Later the sequence became an important species of composition. Its classical master was Notker Balbulus, who lived around 900 A.D. as a monk of the famous Convent Saint Gall in Switzerland. The most famous of the sequences ascribed to him is "Media in vita in morte sumus," which in Luther's time was transformed into the Protestant chorale: "Mitten wir im Leben sind." At least a part of the extended original melody may illustrate the sequence style:

Me - di - a in vi - ta__   in   mor - te ___   su - - - - - mus,

quem quae - ri - mus___   ad - iu - to - rem___   ni - si__

te__   Do - mi - ne___   qui pro pec - ca - tis   no - stris____   usw.

HYMNS, SEQUENCES, PROSA

The essential difference between hymns and sequences (which, of course, differ from what are called sequences in modern music) may be seen in the similarity of the hymns to modern song, with the same melody recurring in the various stanzas (called in German *Strophenlied*), whereas the sequences are more like a composition with continuous, not recurrent melody (called in German *durchkomponierter Gesang*). Generally the sequence retains the same tune for two successive stanzas, after which a new melody is introduced, and so on. For sequence one often finds the term *prosa,* which has nothing to do with our word prose, but is simply an abbreviation for *pro sequentia.*

From the sequences are derived the lais, similar in style to the sequences, with numerous stanzas and melodies. They form a transition from ecclesiastic to secular music.

POLYPHONY, ORGANUM

Starting with the tenth century, music was gradually placed on an entirely new basis by the discovery of polyphony. A chain of new vocal forms marks the various phases in the development of polyphony. The oldest documents of chanting in several parts are found in the so-called organa, concerning which the monk Hucbald of Saint Amand has left us a Latin treatise. Hucbald's organum consists mainly in doubling a melody in the upper fourth or lower fifth. Sometimes the two-part organum is amplified into a four-part organum, by doubling both parts in the octave. The parallel fifths and octaves, which in later practice were strictly forbidden, are a conspicuous feature of organum style:

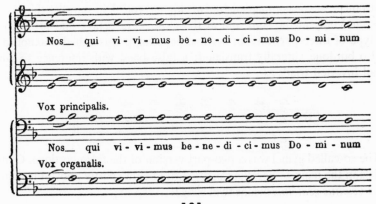

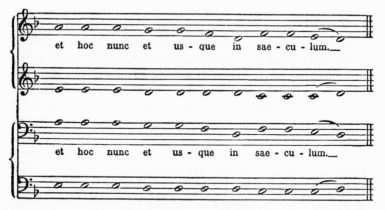

The third part, the vox principalis, has the Gregorian cantus firmus. To this is added in the lower fourth the vox organalis, in parallel fourths, except towards the close when the third and prime are heard. The two upper parts simply double the lower voices in the octave.

This is not the proper place for discussing the varieties of the organum. Mention may be made here only of that form of organum based on a primitive organ-point: the cantus firmus moves up and down above a long held or often repeated bass note.

discant, fauxbourdon, gymel

From the organum was derived the discant. The characteristic feature of the organum lies in the parallel motion of the parts. Discant, however, is based on the idea of contrary motion. Thirds and sixths, formerly occurring only exceptionally, were after 1200 used freely in artistic music. The parallel thirds and sixths, the contrary motion, established the basis of music as practiced even now. Various species of discant are found in England, where polyphony was already at home at a rather early period. A cantus firmus, for instance, was accompanied by two higher voices in parallel thirds and sixths, and only at the start and at the close were octave and fifth heard. This type of three-part discant became popular; it was called fauxbourdon or falso bordone (literally translated: a false bass, with reference to what we call inverted triads):

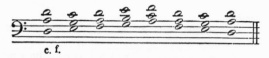

c. f.

The so-called gymel was a two-part version of the falso bordone. Gymel consists in the main of parallel thirds, partly below, partly above the cantus firmus (*cantus gemellus* means twin song).

The fauxbourdon became a generally accepted form of Catholic church music. In later times it was no longer limited to the plain series of chords of the sixth, but any simple harmonization of the cantus firmus, note against note, occasionally adorned with suspensions, was called fauxbourdon. More detailed information on medieval music may be found in Gustave Reese's book, *Music in the Middle Ages* (1940).

Discant was developed mainly in France. Here is the initial impulse of counterpoint, based on the idea of individual part writing, each voice being more or less different in melodic ductus from the others.

rondellus, old french motet

Some other important forms in the early times of discant are the rondellus and the old French motet. The rondellus or *rota* (wheel) corresponds to our canon. The most famous early sample is the six-part English rondellus "Summer is icumen." This pretty round has been frequently reprinted. In the rondellus the idea of imitation enters as a new constructive element.

The old French motet is not to be confounded with what was called a motet after the fifteenth century. The old French motet of the thirteenth and fourteenth centuries is a polyphonic piece, with as many different texts as it has different parts. All three parts have not only different texts, but they also differ considerably in rhythms and melody. The total sound effect is still crude, wanting in what we call euphonious harmony, but sometimes of a peculiar primitive strength.

the motet

Since the fifteenth century one calls a shorter polyphonic vocal piece, written on words from the Bible, or on a devotional text, generally without accompaniment, sometimes accompanied by the organ or other instruments, a motet. The motet is the main form of ecclesiastical vocal music. It reached its climax in the fifteenth to seventeenth centuries, and in the eighteenth century Bach in his motets attained a new summit. In the classical epoch every section of the text introduced a new motif and led it through the parts in contrapuntal writing. Polyphonic style reaches a culmination in the motet. The masters of the various Flemish, German, English, Italian, Spanish, French schools, have created immortal masterpieces in motet style, Josquin de Près, Orlando di Lasso, and Palestrina being the leading masters. Strictly speaking, the Bach motets are not motets at all but rather cantatas, since they contain several movements and reveal in their entire structure and thematic treatment a style considerably different from the motet proper.[1]

[1] On details in the long development of this form see H. Leichtentritt, *Geschichte der Motette* (Leipzig, 1908).

In order to illustrate the typical motet a part of a motet by Vittoria is here reprinted. The single phrases of the text—*Domine non sum dignus—ut intres sub tectum meum—sed tantum dic verbo—et sanabitur anima mea*—are treated separately, each one with a new motif, either in fugal imitation or in free polyphony, or, as at the close, in entirely homophonic style. One section follows the preceding one without any special transition. Whoever has some familiarity with the nature of musical architecture, will, of course, not be surprised at finding much technical refinement in the entries of the new sections. Note, for instance, in this four-part motet, how at the entrance of new motifs (measures 7 and 16) one or two parts are held over from the preceding section in order to cover the "seams" better. Plain entry of all parts together occurs in 3/2 time towards the close:

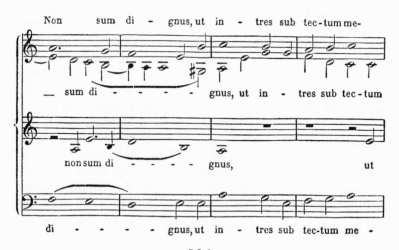

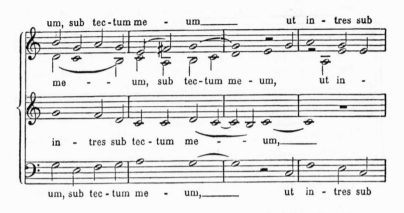

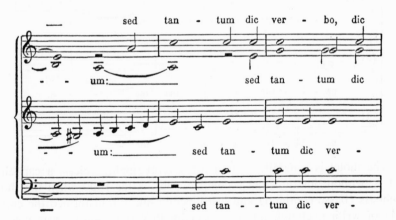

The motet is generally written for several singing voices, a cappella, that is, without instrumental accompaniment. After 1600 when the thoroughbass (basso continuo) and instrumental music transformed the entire style of writing, church music, especially Protestant music, was considerably transformed.

the cantata

The cantata became the most important form in the eighteenth century. A cantata originally meant quite generally any piece fit for singing, in distinction to the sonata, a piece for playing. In the seventeenth century, when many new elements deriving from the opera penetrated into church music, the cantata was gradually evolved as a new form. Cantata now meant a piece in several movements for singing voices and instrumental accompaniment. Its essential characteristics are the predominance of ariose melody, the aria, and the recitative. There are solo cantatas for a solo voice, ensemble cantatas for several solo voices, and choral cantatas in which the chorus is leading. One can best learn what there is to be known about the cantata through the study of J. S. Bach, who, in his enormous output of cantatas has led this species of musical art to its summit.[2]

On the cantata form nothing special is to be said here. Its various constituents, such as choral fugue, chorale, aria or duet, recitative, and chorale variations have already been treated elsewhere in this book.[3]

the mass

The Mass, the principal part of the Catholic liturgy, acquired a definite form during the time of a cappella polyphonic music. The Mass consists of two different types of music: (1) The so-called *ordinarium missae,* the chants with constant, invariable text in Latin, the "ordinary" chants, and (2) the *proprium missae,* pieces with changing text, according to the varying demands of the liturgy on weekdays, Sundays, holidays, the chants "proper" for every occasion. Motets, gradualia, offertories, hymns, and anthems, comprised the repertory of the *proprium.*

We are here concerned mainly with the *ordinarium missae.* The Mass, written on a fixed, unchangeable Latin text, has the following movements:

(1) *Kyrie eleison.*
(2) *Gloria in excelsis.*
(3) *Credo in unum Deum.*
(4) *Sanctus Dominus Deus Sabaoth.*
(5) *Agnus Dei.*

Frequently, however, these five principal pieces are subdivided. Thus the Kyrie is often written in three separate movements: "Kyrie eleison—Christe eleison—Kyrie eleison." The Gloria generally is intoned solo by the cele-

---

[2] An excellent introduction into the marvelous art of the Bach cantatas, demanding a profound special study, is found in P. Spitta's great Bach biography; on the refinements of formal treatment, see Spitta, vol. II, pages 287f., 552, 580. See also Schweitzer's book on Bach, H. Kretzschmar's *Führer durch den Konzertsaal,* and Terry, Bach Cantata texts.

[3] See pp. 78ff.

brating priest, and at the words, "et in terra pax" the chorus enters. The beginning of the Credo is often treated similarly. In the Gloria the words "Qui tollis peccata mundi," and in the Credo the "Crucifixus" are often treated as separate pieces. In the Sanctus often the "Benedictus" is written as a special piece, sometimes also the "Pleni sunt coeli" and "Hosanna." The Agnus Dei is sometimes sung two or even three times in succession, in varying musical versions.

The style of the a cappella Mass is identical with motet style. Most Masses are written on a cantus firmus taken from the Gregorian chant, sometimes from a motet or even a folk song, often with complicated thematic elaboration. Palestrina writes one of his most brilliant and extended Masses on the hexachord, the six-tone scale C, D, E, F, G, A. All movements of this Mass are based on the same scale motif, rising or descending, in shorter or longer notes. The master is inexhaustible in the invention of interesting counterpoints. The entire Mass may be regarded as a long series of contrapuntal variations on the hexachord motif. In the new complete edition of the works of the Flemish master Jacob Obrecht [4] the Mass "Je ne demande" is especially outstanding. Its theme is a song by Busnois, "Je ne demande." This song furnishes Obrecht with the motifs for his Mass; for every movement of the Mass a new little section of Busnois' melody is used. In the "Pleni sunt coeli" a song motif is treated as basso ostinato, twelve times in succession, with constantly changing upper voices. In the Benedictus, Obrecht takes over the entire bass part of Busnois note for note, adding three new higher parts.[5]

THE REQUIEM

A special type of the Mass is the requiem, the Mass for the dead, with a text considerably different from the ordinary Mass text. Here Gloria and Credo are omitted, only the Kyrie, Sanctus, Benedictus, and Agnus Dei remain. For the missing parts new texts are added, such as "Requiem aeternam"—"Dies irae"—"Domine Jesu Christe"—"Lux aeterna."

MASSES WITH ORCHESTRA

In later times, since the eighteenth century, the orchestra and the closed forms of fugue and aria have been more and more incorporated into the Mass. At the present time one no longer speaks of a definite form of Mass and Requiem, or of Passion music and oratorio. In all such cases a whole series, a chain of pieces, are linked together; the composer is free to employ any form so long as he observes certain liturgical rules. Closer information

---

[4] Published by Breitkopf & Härtel.

[5] A detailed technical analysis of this Obrecht Mass by H. Leichtentritt is found in the *Kirchenmusikalisches Jahrbuch* (1911).

can be obtained in the Catholic liturgical handbooks such as Haberl's *Magister Choralis* (Ratisbone).

The Mass is a musical work of art in a limited sense only. The older a cappella Masses, especially, are not concert music, but rather liturgical music. In order to produce their full effect, they need the liturgical frame, the pomp and solemnity, the ceremonial of the Catholic service. One therefore obtains an inadequate impression of this music upon hearing the several pieces of an old Mass in uninterrupted succession at the concert hall. The liturgical Mass separates the individual pieces by long interruptions, interpolations of many kinds, ceremonies of the priest, motets, graduale, and so on. Modern Masses, however, are best fitted for the concert hall. Gigantic works like Bach's *B minor Mass,* Beethoven's *Missa Solemnis* are autonomous to such an extent that they do not fit into the liturgy and can be used in the divine service only exceptionally. Other Masses such as Beethoven's *C major Mass,* Masses by Haydn, Mozart, Schubert, and Bruckner have found a place in the liturgical repertory.

THE CHORAL MASS

Finally we must consider the oldest and simplest type of Mass, the so-called choral Mass, or Gregorian Mass. Here polyphony and instrumental accompaniment have no part at all, the Mass is sung in unison, on the basis of Gregorian chants.[6] For the Mass particularly the Gregorian chant offers an abundance of beautiful and expressive melodies, namely the concentus, whereas the more declamatory accentus is more appropriate to the original form of choral Passion music.

choral passion music

Historical references to the musical treatment of the Passion of Christ go back as far as the thirteenth century. The Passion text, according to one of the Gospels, was sung in declamatory tone with distribution of the parts. Whenever the crowd of the people, the *turba,* has something to say, the soloists or "soliloquents" form a little chorus, in which the clerics also participate. This primitive form of Passion music has survived in some parts of the world until recently. Even the Sistine Chapel in Rome makes use of a similar type of Passion music, in a mixture of lecture tone, accentus in the solo parts, and of plain falso bordone in the choral sections, with music composed by L. da Vittoria.

The next higher step in artistic development, following the venerable choral Mass, was the motet Passion.

---

[6] Details on everything connected with the Mass are found in Peter Wagner's monumental *Geschichte der Messe* (Breitkopf & Härtel: Leipzig, 1913).

THE MOTET PASSION

This form treated the entire text in polyphonic style, in motet manner. Valuable models of this species are available in the works of Dutch and German masters of the sixteenth century, composers such as Obrecht, Cyprian de Rore, Jacobus Gallus, Johann Walter, Orlando di Lasso, and many others. The seventeenth century, with its predilection for recitative, aria, thoroughbass, instrumental accompaniment, created the new type of oratorio Passion.

ORATORIO PASSION

The first great master of this form is Heinrich Schütz. In their formal construction, Bach's Saint Matthew's and Saint John's Passions are not much different from a Handel oratorio, except in the use of the Protestant chorale, which is much more important for Bach than for Handel. The musical structure is the same for Bach and Handel: vast fugal choruses, recitatives, arias, ensemble pieces in aria form, instrumental music in overtures and intermezzi. The same style, in smaller proportions, dominates the cantata.

oratorio

The oratorio was originally a sacred opera. Soon after the inception of Florentine opera, the first sacred, allegorical music drama was performed theatrically in Rome, Emilio di Cavalieri's "Rappresentazione di corpo e di anima." The term oratorio is derived from the prayer hall (*oratorio*) in which the first performances of works of this type took place. For some time spiritual and secular opera flourished side by side. Only later was the oratorio proper evolved, which finds its first classical master in the Roman composer, Giacomo Carissimi. In this new species, following remarkable predecessors in the older spiritual dialogues, theatrical performance was abolished.

The action of the drama was told in recitative by the *testo* or *historicus,* the storyteller (comparable to the Evangelist in Bach's Passion music). Thus the older spiritual music drama was gradually changed into a musical epic, retaining, however, the forms of opera. A special oratorio form does not exist. One may, however, speak of an oratorio style, characterized by epic breadth and repose. In oratorio the chorus is much more ambitious than in opera because the oratorio chorus need not be sung by heart. Moreover, in oratorio the center of gravity lies in the mighty choral pieces, so apt for powerful display of sound and grandiose climax. Compared with these the solo arias give the impression of lyric resting places.

Handel, the greatest master of the oratorio, fashions it into something intermediate between secular and ecclesiastical music.[7]

early forms of secular vocal music

Secular vocal music comprises solo songs with accompaniment, part songs without accompaniment (a cappella), and works in larger dimensions with rich instrumental accompaniment, like the cantata and opera.

TROUBADOURS AND MINNESÄNGER

The solo song of artistic type makes its first appearance in the songs of the troubadours and minnesänger of the twelfth to the fourteenth century. To this first flowering of secular music we owe a treasure of fresh, well formed, expressive melodies, mainly from France and Germany. In their structure these songs hardly differ much from what we recognize as songs. They were generally accompanied by some stringed or harplike instrument. As these accompaniments, however, were not written down, but only improvised, they must be replaced by new accompaniments.[8] The Spring Song of Neidhart Von Reuenthal may serve as a sample:

1. Mei hat wun-nik-lich entspros-sen Berg und tal darzuo die gruene
2. liegt das veld mit touw be-go-ßen, al-ler cre-a-tur ist niemer

1. Hei - de, da man brach der Vi - ol un - ge-zalt. Dez
2. lei - de, schon ge-zie - ret steht der grue - ne   Walt.

1. Man sieht gein der Sun-ne Glesten niu-we bluet uf-dringen,
2. o-ben in des wal-des e-sten hoert man voglin   sin-gen, ein

---

[7] See A. Schering's *Geschichte des Oratoriums* (Breitkopf & Härtel: Leipzig, 1911), the standard work on oratorio. Handel's oratorios are treated in detail in H. Leichtentritt's *Händel* (Berlin, 1924), a special chapter being devoted to Handel's treatment of chorus and of the choral forms.

[8] See: Von der Hagen, *Die Minnesänger*; Ambros, *Musikgeschichte*, vol. II; R. Von Lilieneron and W. Stade: *Lieder und Sprüche aus der letzten Zeit des Minnesangs*; Riemann, *Handbuch der Musikgeschichte*, vol. 1, 2. Songs of Oswald Von Wolkenstein in *Denkmäler der Tonkunst in Österreich*, Vol. IX, 1; Pierre Aubry, *Trouvères et Troubadours* (Paris, Alcan); Jean Beck, *La Musique des Troubadours* (Paris, 1910).

THE OLD GERMAN FOLK SONG

The chivalric troubadours' song was followed in the thirteenth and fourteenth century by a unique rise of folk song, especially in Germany, productive of a musical treasure of precious melodies, which have retained their value for German music of all later epochs. On these popular tunes were based all the thousands of German part songs. Our knowledge of the old German folk song is derived from great song collections such as the Lochheimer Liederbuch [9] (fourteenth century), the song manuscripts of Jena, Munich, Berlin, Vienna, Colmar, and so on, and from the famous Ott and Forster song books (both printed at Nuremberg in the sixteenth century). An extensive collection of old German folk songs, arranged as part-songs is easily accessible in the *Volksliederbuch für Männerchor* and especially in the *Volksliederbuch für gemischten Chor* (both published in the Peters Edition, Leipzig, by order of Emperor William II).

THE PROTESTANT CHORALE

To folk song also belongs the Protestant chorale, a religious folk song; its musically characteristic trait is the continuously equal rhythm. German chorale tunes as well as the essentially similar English hymns are so universally known that examples seem superfluous here.

THE PART SONG

The part song is of great importance, especially in the older literature of the sixteenth and seventeenth centuries. Dutch, French, and German masters have cultivated it, and especially the German part songs of great masters like Heinrich Isaak, Heinrich Finck, Ludwig Senfl, Hans Leo Hassler, Hermann Schein, and many others belong to the very best achievements in the entire history of German song. There is an essential difference between this older and the modern style of song. The older masters were satisfied with merely arranging a well known popular tune for several voices, whereas the ambition of modern composers is centred in the invention of a new, original melody. Old part song is, therefore, always based on a cantus firmus, a folk song melody divided into several sections, ornamented with more or less coloratura and generally given to the tenor. The other parts are freely invented, opposed to the melody as counterpoints. In technical treatment, part song is almost identical with the motet. In both cases fugato, canonic, or plain imitation are extensively used, and in both cases also, a new motif is worked out for every new section of the text. There is, however, no lack of plain homophonic part song. The be-

[9] A facsimile edition of the Lochheimer Liederbuch was brought out in 1925 in Germany.

ginning of a famous song by Heinrich Isaak may illustrate the style of the older contrapuntal part song:

CANZONETTA, VILLANELLA, FROTTOLA

This older, Dutch style of writing was abolished in the later sixteenth century. Towards 1600 a new song style, derived from the Italian canzonetti and villanelle became popular. The songs are popular tunes in fresh, vivid rhythms, plainly written in homophonic manner without much contrapuntal complication. Another essential feature is the placing of the melody in the soprano, whereas formerly the tenor had invariably sung it. Dancelike rhythms are found frequently; indeed, many of these songs are real dance tunes (*ballata*). Also the frottola belongs to the same species: a flippant little love song, a humorous, joking or scurrilous tune, it intentionally avoids artistic treatment and coquettishly applies an amateurish, rough, naturalistic style of writing.

From these various Italian elements a new and original style was shaped by the great German master Hans Leo Hassler, who holds an especially high rank in the history of German song.[10] Hassler's part songs are of various types, sometimes in plain homophonic writing, of canzonetta or dancelike character, sometimes in more complicated madrigal writing. The principal melody, however, is always given to the soprano.

A few measures from a Hassler song may illustrate this style:

---

[10] A complete edition of Hassler's works is published in the *Denkmäler deutscher Tonkunst*. See also H. Leichtentritt's edition of old German part songs (Breitkopf & Härtel) containing thirty-six songs by Isaac, Finck, Senfl, Hassler, and so on.

Notice the dance rhythms, the chordal writing, the dance refrain "fa la la," fashionable in that time and found in thousands of songs, the echo dialogue of the two upper voices in the second section, typical Italian traits throughout. This type of part song was very successfully continued by Johann Hermann Schein.

QUODLIBET, POTPOURRI

A special type of part song is found in the jocose, often burlesque quodlibet, potpourri. It consists of a medley of various melodies in no way related to each other. The quodlibet resembles our modern potpourri. It far surpasses this vulgar species, however, by a superior artistic technique. In the quodlibet the point is not only to introduce the tunes successively, as is seen in the potpourri, but to let them also be heard simultaneously. The different voices sing different words and different tunes. The quodlibet, of course, is meant for listeners well acquainted with the parodied melodies; the joke misses its point, if the listener does not readily catch the meaning. For this reason many of the very ingenious old quodlibets merely impress us as clever curiosities.[11] A little quodlibet by Matthes Greiter from the Schmelzel Songbook may illustrate this style:

[11] See Elsa Bienenfeld, "Das Schmelzel'sche Liederbuch" (in *Sammelband*, 1904/5, of the International Society of Music) on one of the most important quodlibet collections of the sixteenth century.

the madrigal

In secular music, between 1550 and 1650, the Italian madrigal [12] held the foremost rank. By madrigal is meant a piece composed for several voices in rather pretentious artistic style, set to artistic poetry. Compared with the part song, the French chanson, the villanella, and frottola, the madrigal represents the noblest artistic type in text and music, intentionally excluding all allusion to the popular element. In the madrigal there is no cantus firmus any more, for all parts are freely invented by the composer. Its polyphonic technique resembles that of the motet style.

In the madrigal the refinement of Italian music reached its acme, as regards exquisite sound effects, tone painting, harmony, and declamation. One may well call the madrigal the most precious flower of older secular vocal music. The greatest masters of the madrigal are Luca Marenzio, Gesualdo, the Prince of Venosa, Claudio Monteverdi. A complete edition of Marenzio's madrigals (by Alfred Einstein) was begun a few years ago. Also a number of Gesualdo's madrigals are available in Peters' edition and elsewhere. Monteverdi's madrigals have been published in Malipiero's complete edition; a selection of Monteverdi madrigals has come out in two volumes (Peters' edition), edited by H. Leichtentritt and Arnold Mendelssohn. A detailed study on Monteverdi's madrigals by H. Leichtentritt appeared in the *Sammelband* 1910 of the International Society for Music. A part of a famous Marenzio madrigal is here reprinted. It may be observed how the music is influenced by the text. In the beginning the undulating figures of the two upper voices above the long tenor notes paints the rocking of the little birds on the twigs. Further on one should observe the tone painting in the bass at *onde* ("wave"), at *garrir* ("soft rustling"), at *taccion*

---

[12] This polyphonic Italian madrigal must not be confused with the still older solo madrigal, mentioned later in this chapter.

gl'augelli ("the birds are silent"), at *alto risponde* ("loud answer"), like a strong echo from voice to voice. Such little picturesque illustrations are characteristic of the madrigal. The text in approximate English translation means: "Lovely birds in the green foliage try out enchanting sounds. The wind is hushed, and moves the leaves and waves with soft rustling as it strikes them. When the birds are silent, the air echoes loudly."

The idyllic sound of the piece, its local flavor, are distinctly madrigalian in type, as can be seen on the pages immediately following.

The Italian madrigal found favor around 1600 especially in England, where great masters like Byrd and Morley, Gibbons, Weelkes, Wilbye, and others created a great number of English madrigals, now recognized as one of the most valuable achievements of English music. Dean Horace Fellowes has written a classical book on the English madrigal and has published hundreds of masterly English madrigals.

Towards the end of the seventeenth century the madrigal style had become so deeply rooted in Italy that it also extended its domain into ecclesiastical and dramatic music. It seems unnecessary to discuss here in what manner madrigal elements penetrated into the motet, Mass, cantata, oratorio, and Passion music, because this question deals with problems of style rather than of form.

The madrigal comedy, however, which was the immediate predecessor of opera, must be mentioned here at least briefly. Whole dramas composed of polyphonic madrigals were sung with parts distributed among the various characters. A dramatic character was not represented here by a solo voice, as in opera, but by an ensemble of three, four, or more voices. Nevertheless, the composers succeeded in making the dialogue impressive even in a many-voiced madrigal, thanks to their eminent skill in polyphonic writing. High and low voices were utilized for purposes of dialogue most effectively.

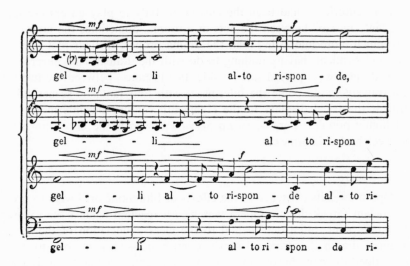

The most famous one of these madrigal comedies is Orazio Vecchi's "Amfiparnaso" (1597),[13] but there are known a number of other interesting works of this species by Alessandro Striggio, Giovanni Croce, Adriano Banchieri, and others. Also the dramatic Italian intermezzi or intermedia have been of importance in the history of the Italian theatre.

[13] Details on madrigal comedy and intermezzi are found in H. Leichtentritt's revised edition of Ambros' *Geschichte der Musik,* IV (1909), 264. Vecchi's "Amfiparnaso" in H. Leichtentritt's arrangement was heard in a number of American cities, excellently performed by the Marguerite Dessoff choirs.

For centuries it had been the custom in Italy to play an entre-acte, a little "intermezzo" between the acts of a drama. Sometimes the intermezzi were much more interesting than the drama proper. In their plot they are quite independent, having nothing to do with the drama. Thus several different dramas were played side by side. For instance, between the five acts of a tragedy would come the intermezzi with four fantastic scenes full of brilliant theatrical display. In the eighteenth century the intermezzo was still highly popular. Pergolesi's *La Serva Padrona* is the best known and most celebrated intermezzo.

opera

Opera owes its existence to the efforts of Florentine art lovers to revive the ancient Greek drama. Opera was also a reaction against the excesses of counterpoint, often detrimental to the clear enunciation of the words. In music drama the principal aim was an expressive recitative, to which were added the new thoroughbass accompaniment, invented towards 1600, and a few instruments.

Beginning with recitative, the dramatic style gradually took over a good many other forms: choral pieces in madrigal type; preludes and orchestral intermezzi in the style of the instrumental canzone, ricercar; solo songs, starting with arioso and gradually evolving the closed form of the aria; duets and other ensemble pieces in contrapuntal manner, in chamber duet style; dances of suitelike type. In every century opera changes its face. The forms just mentioned are typical for the later seventeenth century, the operas of the Venetian School, of Cavalli, Cesti, Lully, Steffani, and others.

In the eighteenth century opera declined more and under the influence of the Neapolitan School, also in regard to variety of forms. Virtuoso singing was by far the main factor so that the entire opera consisted chiefly of dozens of arias, connected by indifferent secco recitative. The second half of the eighteenth century meant a new rise for opera, through the reform of Gluck, who repressed virtuoso solo singing in favor of true dramatic expression. Also a new rise of Neapolitan opera took place, due to masters like Jomelli, Traetta, Hasse, Piccini, and finally Mozart, who brought Neapolitan opera to its greatest perfection.

FORMS OF THE MOZART OPERA

A Mozart opera is a marvel of form, as regards variety, wealth, elegance of structure, and the distinction and force of the melodic line. It suffices to cast a quick glance over the pages of any Mozart opera in order to get an idea of this abundance of formal art. *Le Nozze di Figaro* contains an overture in sonata form, many recitatives and arias, cavatinas, canzone, a number of complicated duets and terzets, one sextet, choral pieces, marches, dances and two great finales. The cavatina is a simplified aria, more songlike in melody, shorter, plainer, in two-part form, with less repetition of words and less coloratura. The canzone is a similar type. Mozart's dramatic ensembles differ from the chamber duets and terzets through less use of an imitative contrapuntal style. Mozart works out each single part and makes it dramatically expressive of the acting character. The terzetto No. 7 from the first act of *Figaro* differentiates sharply and accurately the three persons Susanna, Basilio, and Count Almaviva, every one singing in conformance with his character and emotional mood. Mozart's finales, the closing sections of each act, are great masterpieces. The finale had been slowly evolved: at the end of an act something impressive was desired, and thus the close of the act was transformed into a kind of symphonic fantasy. The division into single, separate pieces is abandoned in the finale in favor of a constant single flow. Most diverse elements are welded together, aria-like pieces with recitative, symphonic orchestral interludes, choruses, dance music, ensembles. Usually the act closes with a splendid climax and a brilliant tutti of all the soloists, the chorus, and the orchestra.

SECCO RECITATIVE, ACCOMPAGNATO, ARIOSO

A most important innovation of dramatic music consisted in the introduction of declamatory singing, the recitative, which later was taken over into church music, cantata, Passion music, sometimes even into instrumental music. The recitative can only be comprehended through the text, not through its purely musical contents. It has no musical structure like the song, but is determined solely by the words in its extension, in the rise and fall of the voice. In recitative one quickly glides over the unimportant words in order to underline and to mark the essential words, either by lingering, holding the principal tone longer, or by harmonic or rhythmical means in the accompaniment. There are two kinds of recitative: secco recitative and accompanied recitative, or accompagnato. The secco recitative is a quick declamatory singing, accompanied either by a few sustained or staccato chords. It serves in opera to glide quickly over stretches of narration and dialogue offering scant opportunity for musical treatment, or to call attention to a dramatically important moment when it is essential to understand the words distinctly. Occasionally, where weightier music is needed, this nimble recitative is concentrated into a more expressive declamation, allowing the accompanying orchestra greater free play in depicting the situation. In such a case one speaks of an accompagnato. If the vocal part stresses even greater expressive melodiousness, the arioso results, more or less approaching the aria.

Short examples of the first two kinds of recitative follow here; first a secco recitative from Mozart's *Magic Flute,* finale of Act I:

Notice the skillful manner in which the chords of the accompaniment fill out the pauses between the single sections of the text.

The accompagnato was applied for the first time in admirable manner by Monteverdi. Ever since then all great opera composers have made use of this means of expression peculiar to the music drama.

Several fine examples may be found in Mozart's *Don Giovanni.* One of them is reprinted here in part:

THE WAGNER STYLE OF RECITATIVE

In Wagner's operas, too, accompagnato plays an important part. There is, however, a significant difference, inasmuch as Wagner does not oppose the recitative to the aria, as its introduction, but makes it a part of a most pretentious symphonic architecture, of an organic construction manifest everywhere in the totality of the structure as well as in the details. This subtle organism gives the Wagner style its unique position in operatic music.

207

In recent years the various books of analysis by Alfred Lorenz (*Das Geheimnis der Form bei Richard Wagner,* and so on), rich in new insight, have made us acquainted with the fascinating constructive side of Wagner's art.

As an example of the arioso a beautiful passage from a Bach Cantata has already been presented at the close of Chapter I.

RECITATIVE IN INSTRUMENTAL MUSIC

Occasionally the principle of recitative has been applied to instrumental music as well. Beethoven, for instance, inserts recitative several times in the first movement of the D minor sonata, Op. 31. An outstanding example is the famous recitative of the basses before the finale in Beethoven's Ninth symphony. Spohr's violin concerto "In Form einer Gesangszene" (in the form of a vocal scene) is an outstanding example, as also the third movement in César Franck's A major violin sonata.

the aria

The aria, which is of especial importance in older opera, is a somewhat extended vocal piece, generally accompanied by the orchestra (also the cembalo), in a closed, larger form, in distinction to the song, which is shorter, more simply constructed and less pretentious in content. There is no fixed form for the aria. Often the large two- or three-part song form is used; sometimes the aria approaches the rondo, even the sonata form.

DA CAPO ARIA

Especially in older Italian music the so-called da capo aria is a favorite form, in three-part structure according to the pattern *a-b-a*. As is true of all the vocal forms, the aria depends for its structure largely on the text, which accounts for whatever liberties of form or even striking irregularities there may occur. In the eighteenth century, when the da capo aria flourished, it was customary in opera and oratorio to vary the reprise of *a,* the da capo, and to ornament it with trills, passages, suspensions, cadenzas. These variants, generally not written down at all, but left to the skill and taste of the performer, are an essential stylistic requirement for the right effect of this type of aria. The art of singing, as well as of ornamental improvisation, have in our times declined to such an extent that the old aria is hardly ever heard in its genuine style. Chrysander is to be credited with the revival of this almost lost art of proper aria treatment in his editions of various Handel works.

various species of opera

After this consideration of the various formal constituents of opera, the art form of opera in its totality demands attention. Opera has various types.

Opera seria, serious opera, often called grand opera, is a tragedy set to music throughout.

Opera buffa or opera comique, comic opera, generally employs spoken dialogue in place of the elaborate recitatives and ariosi of opera seria. The *Singspiel* (musical comedy) is more popular, has spoken dialogue and songlike soli instead of the arias predominant in opera. The Singspiel came into being in the eighteenth century; in Germany especially the Hiller Singspiele were favorite pieces of the public. The popular Lortzing operas are a cross between Singspiel and comic opera. Of late the Viennese operettas have been immensely popular in many countries. Operetta is to opera as farce is to drama; it is not scrupulous in the choice of its means and is not afraid of vulgarities. Only in its very best representatives, such as Offenbach, Johann Strauss, Sullivan, Lecocq, Audran, and a few others can operetta be called a really artistic genre.

elements of Wagner's music drama

The Mozartean finale together with the complex modern art of musical declamation, recitative, may be called the elements of the new Wagnerian music drama. To this Wagner adds the *Leitmotive* (leading motifs), which give thematic unity to the entire drama and prepare the work for the application of Beethoven's grand symphonic style; Wagner also, in his later works, gives up the single numbers of closed forms, typical for earlier opera.

vocal chamber and solo music

It remains to cast a glance at the vocal chamber and solo music. Mention has already been made of the troubadours and minnesingers. In the fourteenth century an artistically pretentious style of accompanied solo song was already cultivated in Italy, especially in Florence. The characteristic forms of this *ars nova* (new art in contrast to the older French *ars antiqua*) were the *caccia* (catch, chase), a canonic form for two solo voices with instruments, the *ballata* (dance song, ballad), and the solo madrigal (very different from the later, already mentioned polyphonic madrigal). In recent years a considerable number of ars nova pieces have been published singly or in collections. Nevertheless, the interpretation of the instrumental part in its relation to the vocal part is a problem not yet settled beyond a doubt. In Riemann's *Handbook of the History of Music* (vol. I, 2, p. 305), and "Musikgeschichte in Beispielen," in Arnold Schering's *Beispielsammlung zur Musikgeschichte,* and various essays in Johannes Wolf's fundamental studies on ars nova, the material can be found, and the opposing methods of interpretation can be studied.

VOCAL MUSIC WITH THOROUGHBASS

Monody had a revival in opera toward 1600. A new style had been evolved: solo vocal music with the accompaniment of thoroughbass or basso continuo. Giulio Caccini's collection of vocal chamber music pieces, the *nuove musiche* of 1601, is the first important publication in the new style. There exists a very extended Italian music literature in this branch of the art. The solo canzonetta with continuo and the dance song constitute a species of their own in the seventeenth century, quite apart from the pieces in declamatory style or recitative. For Germany the *Arien* of Heinrich Albert from Koenigsberg was an epoch-making publication.[14] Under the collective title *Arias* are found vocal pieces of various kinds with thoroughbass, inclusive of a number of real songs. The new type was cultivated in a still purer and more original style, especially by Adam Krieger, whose *Arias* are *Strophenlieder* (same tune for all stanzas) with continuo. The characteristic feature of the Krieger songs are the interludes between the single stanzas. In these so-called ritornelli, a five-part instrumental body plays a real little concerto.[15] The Krieger songs are students' songs, written for the Leipzig students. While drinking their mugs of beers and cups of wine at their convivial gatherings (*Kneipe*) the students accompanied their libations with singing. The instruments hung up at the backs of the chairs were taken down after every stanza for the playing of the ritornelli. This fresh, spirited, artistic song music of Krieger with instrumental ritornelli represents the finest achievement in this style.

SOLO CANTATAS

The solo cantatas, consisting of recitative, aria or duet, with basso continuo, to which occasionally obligato instruments were added, are vocally still more pretentious, a virtuoso music for the great masters of Italian bel canto. An immense number of such cantatas was accumulated around 1700. The chief masters of this type are Carissimi, Alessandro Scarlatti, Handel, Bach, besides almost all composers of note in Italy and France.

CHAMBER DUETS

Steffani's chamber duets with thoroughbass, a very noble form of art, had its classical master in Agostino Steffani, whose duets have been published in a valuable selection by Alfred Einstein in the series *Denkmäler der Tonkunst in Bayern*. Here are found finely chiseled polyphonic part leading, exquisite refinements of vocal treatment, carefully elaborated form. Many

---

[14] Now easily accessible in the *Denkmäler deutscher Tonkunst* (vols. 12, 13).

[15] See *Denkmäler deutscher Tonkunst*, vol. 19. Some samples of Krieger songs also in H. Leichtentritt's *Deutsche Hausmusik aus 4 Jahrhunderten* (Berlin, 1905).

of these duets approach the cantata type in the musical delineation of a dramatic scene. A little sample of Steffani's art follows here:

SONG WITH PIANO ACCOMPANIMENT

In more recent times the song with piano accompaniment occupies by far the foremost rank among the other vocal forms. What instrumental music calls two- or three-part song form, is, of course, derived from the real vocal song. What has been said on the song forms earlier in this book applies also to the vocal song. Since the song, however, has to deal not only with the structure of the melody, but also with the relation of the text to the music, these relations demand some consideration.

A distinction is made between what in German is called a *Strophenlied* and a *durchkomponiertes Lied*. The *Strophenlied* (strophic song) repeats the same melody for all stanzas of a poem, the *durchkomponiertes Lied* (song composed throughout) does not bind itself to the same melody for all stanzas, but invents a new melody for every stanza, according to the contents of the text.

The same melody repeated throughout all stanzas is the characteristic feature of the folk song. Also popular songs and plain art songs make uses of the Strophenlied principle. A modification of the Strophenlied sometimes occurs. The melody may remain unchanged throughout the various stanzas, yet the character of the various stanzas is marked by changes of harmony, of the accompaniment formula at important places of the text. Robert Franz is given to the treatment of the Strophenlied in this sense. The melody of his Op. 4, No. 9, may illustrate the above-mentioned modifications. The first two stanzas are only slightly different from each other; in the third stanza it is worth observing how warmth, cordiality, beautiful culmination of sentiment are brought into the Strophenlied by means of the broader melodic curve at the close:

213

A comparison of the single stanzas in Franz' famous song, "Die Haide ist braun" shows how climaxes increasingly gain in interest through change of harmonization. Brahms also is a great master of this type of Strophenlied; many of his admirable folk song arrangements prove his masterful treatment in this respect. Brahms and some other composers make a distinction between Lieder and Gesänger. Lied (song) applies to every melody close to the Strophenlied type, while Gesänge means freely constructed vocal pieces of the type of *durchkomponiertes Lied*.

ACCOMPANIMENT OF THE *Durchkomponiertes Lied*

In the *durchkomponiertes Lied* the accompaniment acquires still greater importance. It is here not merely the harmonic support of the vocal part, but at the same time it lends color and expression. In Schubert's songs the introductory prelude often paints the scene, the locality in which the action takes place, with a few significant strokes. Examples can be seen in almost every Schubert song. In No. 13 of the *Winterreise* cycle, "Die Post," one hears the post horn in the introduction; further on, the accompaniment suggests the throbbing of the excited heart. In No. 16, "Letzte Hoffnung" ("Last Hope"), the prelude depicts the gentle falling of the withered leaves from the tree. In No. 17, "Das Dorf," the prelude refers to the clanking of iron chains, to the barking dogs mentioned in the poem. No. 5, "Der Lindenbaum," is introduced by the tone painting of the softly rustling foliage. It is a principle of the modern art of song to derive the motif of accompaniment from the text as significantly and plastically as possible. The talent of the song composer is shown, so far as the accompaniment is concerned, in the manner in which he knows how to gain from the text a fitting motif of accompaniment and to develop this motif properly. All the means of expressive melody, of impressive declamation, and finely nuanced colorful harmony are evident in the creation of one of the most admirable manifestations of artistic spirit, the modern German art song, as it is represented by the combined productions of Schubert, Beethoven, Schumann, Franz, Mendelssohn, Cornelius, Jensen, Brahms, Wolf, Strauss, and others. A treatise on form cannot have much to say on this most subjective of all species of art; it must be satisfied with pointing out briefly some of the most important stylistic problems.

THE BALLAD

A special class of art song is represented by the ballad, a poem not of purely lyric, but rather narrative, descriptive character. Because of the peculiar and rarely found admixture of temperamental qualities demanded by it, the ballad has always been a domain reserved to a few specialists. The music demands great distinctness, plastic design of the motifs, broad and large outlines, and at the same time much care for detail, marked artistic character without too much individual sentiment, and a rather objective attitude. The narrative tone should always predominate, as the ballad does not represent the poet's and composer's own individual experience and sentiment. Carl Loewe is the master of the ballad par excellence; of his forerunners Zumsteeg deserves most attention. Occasionally the other great masters of song have also tried their hand in ballad, like Schubert (*Erlkönig*), Schumann (*Belsazar*), Brahms (*Verrat*), Hugo Wolf (*Der Feuerreiter, Die Geister am Mummelsee*).

THE INSTRUMENTAL BALLAD

Instrumental ballads, derived from the vocal ballad, also occur in the literature—pieces of a fantastic rhapsodical character. The term ballad refers here more to the content and character of the music than to the form. Chopin was the first great master of this genre, with his four grandiose ballads for piano. Influenced by him, Liszt and Brahms have also written remarkable piano ballads.

PART TWO

CHAPTER **X**

aesthetic ideas as the basis
of musical styles and forms

Even a superficial acquaintance with the history of music
reveals the fact that musical forms have a close and inseparable relation to
musical styles. Evolution of forms coincides with the evolution of styles.
Every new style carries with it a new form or set of forms adapted to the
aesthetic ideas underlying each change of style. It will be useful for us to
study these mutual relations in a rapid, brief, fundamental survey of the
field.

The first part of this book aimed at presenting the basic facts of musical
forms, as abstracted from the works of the great masters. The following
second part supplements this elementary presentation by a more detailed
and penetrating study of what one may call the metaphysics of musical
construction. It deals with problems of style and psychology, of logic and
coherence, and aims to discover and formulate at least a few of the laws
governing musical structure. In view of the close connection of forms and
styles, it seems desirable to point out briefly, by way of introduction, the
origin of musical styles, and to explain the ever-changing ideas of style
and structure by reducing them to their roots. Aesthetic ideas are the soil

from which the various forms of our art grow and expand themselves, until they have exhausted their vitality and are superseded by other new aesthetic ideas.

Music is not able to use the outward aspects of nature, the visible, material world, directly as the starting point of its creative impulses. In this respect the other arts, painting, sculpture, poetry, and drama differ considerably from music, as they spring from the model of the outward world which they depict, describe, or interpret. Lacking this immediate model, music must derive its problems not from concrete reality, but from the world of the spirit, from ideas, sentiments, and emotions. It is the aim of this essay to point out at least a few of these fundamental ideas from which were derived what we call the various styles in the history of music. Some of these basic ideas are mathematical in their nature, others are architectural, philosophical, psychological, poetic, or dramatic. In spite of their different origins, all these ideas, as they are applied to art, become aesthetic ideas.

All music is dominated by the idea of "up" and "down," high and low, or rising and falling, though strictly speaking, there is actually no up and down at all in the world of sound. What we call higher or lower sounds are in reality only different frequencies of vibrations, air waves not discernible in space at all, but only in time. Yet the attributes of space are universally applied to an art existing in time only, for practical reasons, symbolically, and for the sake of an easily explainable theory of music. When in ancient Greek music the twenty-four letters of the alphabet were made to serve likewise as the names for the twenty-four tones of the Greek system of vocal music, the idea of up and down was not yet connected with this nomenclature. But even in that early stage it was found necessary to take refuge in the idea of high and low when the twenty-four tones were subdivided into groups of four tones each. For these tetrachords the names of *hypaton* (low), *meson* (middle), *hyperbolaion* (high) were invented as practical means of distinction.

A still greater importance was attached to these terms of space when the eight-tone groups, the octaves, were introduced into the theory of music, and when to them the name of *scala* was given. Here is added to the rather vague, indefinite concept of high and low the idea of a strictly regulated progress from one tone to its neighbor. Within this *scala* (staircase) on which the tones promenade up and down according to a certain norm, distinctions are also made. In a certain scale each tone may be equally distant from its next neighbor, in another scale this equality of distance or interval is replaced by two or even three kinds of intervals. Thus the "chromatic" scale is composed only of half tones, twelve within an octave; the "diatonic," so-called major scale introduces two different kinds of intervals, half tones and whole tones, following each other in a certain norm: either two whole tones plus one half tone or three whole tones plus one half tone. In what we call a "minor scale" an interval of one and one half tones is added to the whole and half tones.

A great variety of scales based on whole and half tones is manifest in the literature of music; indeed, the study of scale formation has become a favorite topic of modern musical research. The importance of scales for the art of music is easily understood as soon as one has comprehended the fact that scales are an essential aesthetic factor. On the structure of the various scales the character, impressive value, and the style of the melody largely depends. The scale indeed is comparable to the alphabet in language; it is a reduced alphabet.

The severe, ecclesiastic, sublime expression of a Gregorian chant is conditioned by its diatonic church modes, a rejuvenation of the ancient Greek modes. Major and minor scales have determined the melodic invention of more recent music of a song and dance type in the seventeenth, eighteenth, and nineteenth centuries. The emotional ecstasy of romantic melody is a consequence of the chromatic scale mixed with major and minor. The chromatic half tone, used more profusely, is a realistic echo of wailing, sighs, of question, melancholy, soliloquy, anxiety, and agitation, as well as sensuous delight. The works of Chopin, Schumann, Liszt, and Wagner offer abundant examples of this. The pentatonic scale with its jumps, its five tones, instead of the seven of the major scale, is largely responsible for the strange charm, the far-away mood of the music of the distant East, China, Siam, India, and Java, as well as the northern tinge of ancient Scotch, Irish, Finnish, and Russian melodies.

From Oriental music Debussy has taken over his six-tone scale, with six whole tones to the octave, which in this case is no longer the eighth tone of the scale, but the seventh tone. The absence of half tones in this scale and the upsetting of the octave balance give these hexatonic melodies their exotic tinge. Arabic and other Asiatic music also makes use of quarter and three-quarter tones, which in the European system and notation have no place at all. They cannot be reproduced on any of the European instruments, but only by phonographic records, nor can they be indicated by our system of notation.

The possibilities of scale formation are far from exhausted. The great musician Ferruccio Busoni has found out by experimental trial that in the tempered tuning of our modern piano more than one hundred and ten different scales are possible between the tone C and its higher or lower octave. Most of these scales do not even possess a name and have hardly ever been exploited in actual melodies. Nicolas Slonimsky has been very inventive in tracking down novel scale formations in a highly stimulating volume of scale studies. This means that many new types of melody are still possible.

Another idea of vital importance for music is the conception of motion. With motion the idea of rhythm is inseparably linked. The involuntary bodily functions of the heart beat, pulse, breathing, and circulation of the blood stream are one source for rhythm, even as employed in music. Another source is derived from the voluntary activities of the animal body: walking, marching, dancing, jumping, creeping, limping, crouching, and running, and so on. Music is very apt in translating into its own terms these numerous types of motion so that they may be recognized. Though motion is perceptible both in space and in time, yet motion in music generally occurs only in time. Motion in space cannot be perceived by the ear, but only by the eye. Only when music is linked with drama, in an opera scene or ballet, is motion in time and in space combined.

Motion is indeed an important attribute of style, different styles being dominated and characterized by certain well defined types of motion and rhythm. Thus the ecclesiastic Ambrosian hymn of medieval times, the model for the later German Protestant chorals and the English hymn tune, has a solemn rhythm, due to its broad, slowly moving tones, its absence of sharp, cutting accents. These hymn melodies are adapted to the measured steps in a solemn religious procession. With stronger accents on the downbeats and a little faster motion, this procession rhythm is changed to a march rhythm, of which music has quite a variety, from the funeral march to the festive, military, and quick-step march. With the march one generally couples the dance. In both march and dance music, the ideas of repetition and symmetry are added to motion. A certain rhythmic pattern characterizes every type of dance, and this characteristic pattern is repeated as often as required, sometimes repeated in the literal sense, more frequently, however, repeated not on the identical notes, but in what is called transpositions, either higher or lower, or repeated with slight variants.

We can touch briefly only a few of the inexhaustible manifestations of motion in music. The most up-to-date variant of that idea has been the introduction of the machine-like "motoric" motion, with speed and force combined. The master craftsman of this new motoric music is Stravinsky. He applied it most convincingly in his ballet *Petrouchka,* with its world of mechanical dolls assuming human passions. In this exceptional case the soulless but brilliant motoric music was legitimate. It has later been abused for burlesque, grotesque, and satirical effects. It represents a modernized variant of the older, more amiable, humorous, and gay "moto perpetuo," of which we find outstanding samples in a few Haydn quartet finales, in the finale of Weber's C major piano sonata, in Paganini's brilliant moto perpetuo, in Schumann's Toccata and in Rimsky-Korsakoff's "Flight of the Bumble-Bee."

The principle of repetition is one of many rudimentary, constructive ideas latent in the musical mind and applied by instinct even in early stages of human civilization. Such primitive ideas, however, become aesthetic factors only when applied, not instinctively, but with consciousness and knowledge of facts. Repetition in music, very much like repetition in architecture, is a means of obtaining the effects of continuity, coherence, order, and symmetry. It is, therefore, evidently a primary factor of importance for artistic work. Of all constructive ideas, repetition is the simplest and most elementary one, because the easiest thing for the mind to do with any idea just uttered is to repeat it. Thus any characteristic pattern of motion, a motif in the musical terminology, may be repeated exactly, once, twice, or many times.

This is what primitive people in remote parts of the globe have done and are still doing in their music as a first step towards a more involved art. But also in highly developed art music this kind of constant repetition of a motif is still practiced. Russian music delights in these so-called "ostinato" phrases, now, however, changed from a primitive, monotonous device into a much more ingenious procedure, as a "basso ostinato," a constantly repeated phrase in the bass, accompanied by ever-changing counter melodies, "counterpoints" in the higher parts. The Crucifixus in Bach's *B minor Mass* shows the aesthetic possibilities of basso ostinato in the most exalted manner. In a lyric, idyllic mood Chopin's "Berceuse" is a masterpiece of basso ostinato. Other much admired examples occur at the close of the first movement of Beethoven's Ninth symphony and at the very beginning of Wagner's *Die Walküre*.

When a short ostinato phrase of one or two measures is expanded into a coherent theme of eight or more measures, and when this bass theme is constantly repeated, with ever new counterpoints in the upper parts, the form of the passacaglia or chaconne is obtained. Some of the greatest and most ingenious music in existence is molded into this form. Bach in his organ passacaglia and his chaconne for violin solo, and Brahms in the finale of his Fourth symphony represent the artistic culmination inherent in this structural plan.

Another ingenious and advanced variant of the repetition principle is the canon, one of the oldest and most important forms of musical structure. In the canon the same tune is exactly repeated by several voices. The different voices participating do not, however, sing the same tune simultaneously, nor does one of them wait until its predecessor has finished the tune, but the repetition of the tune is started by the second voice somewhere midway, just a little after the first voice has started the tune, but before it has finished it. A simple diagram may illustrate the different types of repetition (see page 224).

223

First voice   —————————   } simultaneous repetition
Second voice —————————   } of the same tune.

       —————————
               ————————— } successive repetition

       ————————— } canonic repetition
             —————————

This overlapping of melodic lines raises a number of new problems of a harmonic, contrapuntal, rhythmical nature with which the masters of the art had to grapple for at least three centuries, roughly from 1300 to 1600. Only one of these novel problems can be treated briefly here.

In canon the principle of strict imitation of one voice or instrument by another had been developed. Flemish masters devised besides canon a method of free imitation, relaxing the rigid constraint of canon and thus opening a road to new possibilities. No longer a whole tune, but only a short phrase of one or two measures is stated by one voice and reiterated exactly or approximately by several other voices in succession. The result is not a canon, but a dialogue based on identical thematic matter, thus ensuring logical coherence. The fugue also is based on the principle of free imitation, as well as the form of the motet. Every sonata, quartet, and symphony makes constant use of this principle. In its most concentrated type it is found in the fugue, which may be compared to an animated conversation of three or four people on a certain theme. The conversation is not dominated by one leading speaker. All participants discuss the main theme in dialogue, none of them being superior or inferior in the contents of his part, and all of them are intent on speaking logically, always remaining close to the theme, not allowing themselves to be far diverted from it. How to produce the effect of logical coherence in music is indeed one of the most amazing discoveries. Imagine the material of sound—nothing but air waves—and associate with this fleeting, unsubstantial motion of the air the idea of logical coherence. It seems absurd at first sight, and for thousands of years the problem was never even approached, just on account of this apparent absurdity. Yet the invention of counterpoint, the conception of constructive music, of architecture and form, pointed out the right direction for the solution of this tremendous and difficult problem.

The principle of symmetry was taken over into music from the metres, verses, and rhymes of poetry. The metrical schemes of Greek and Latin poetry have dominated music for centuries, especially in the form of song. With symmetry must be coupled its opposite, asymmetry. The asymmetric principle is derived from the prose recitation in a language, with its irregular accents and subdivisions. This musical recitative in its oldest form is a descendant both of Greek drama and the Hebrew psalmody. It became the main pattern of the declamatory Gregorian chant of the medieval Christian church, as the so-called accentus, whereas the Ambrosian hymns preserved the metrical symmetry of ancient poetry, in the style of concentus.

In the later development of the art of music, in the polyphonic, contrapuntal styles, still later in the instrumental sonata and symphonic styles, the ideas of symmetry and asymmetry were mixed in an endless variety of combinations. The aim of this mixture was to impart to the music both the stability of symmetry and the interesting animation of asymmetry. Too much symmetry becomes tiresome; an excess of asymmetry endangers the coherence, tends towards a vague formlessness. But in mixing asymmetric phrases at well chosen points into a symmetrical melodic line, new and interesting effects were gained. The details of this mixture, never yet adequately formulated and described, would fill a sizable chapter in a book on the constructive laws of music, the evolution of musical forms. The simplest samples of such a mixture may be found in plain, songlike melodies, where the prevalent four-bar phrase is occasionally replaced by a three-bar phrase or a five-bar phrase, resulting in its diminution or enlargement.

A great elaboration of this method occurs in the "free rhythms" of Flemish polyphonic music in the sixteenth century, where the different voices in a motet or part song often sing in different time simultaneously, thus mixing 4/4 with 3/4 or 6/8 time in a manner upsetting the common measure. This mingling of irregular, unexpected accents and different time results in a fascinating interplay of accents, an effect which is lost to modern music with its regular bar lines. It is comparable to the play of the small waves on the surface of a river or to the motion of clouds in the sky, always producing changing, unpredictable patterns.

A discovery of immense artistic value and incalculable consequences was made during the Gothic era in France and later during the sixteenth century in Italy when the dimensions of space were for the first time utilized in music. In medieval times music had been in one dimension only one-part music, without accompaniment. Gregorian chant, purely linear, melodic, without any addition of chords or harmony, is indeed the ideal realization of the first one of the three dimensions of space: length, width or breadth, and depth.

These three dimensions in musical terms would be:

(1) Linear extension or melodic line = length or height.

(2) Harmonic or contrapuntal filling out, accompaniment = breadth.

(3) Dynamic and color effect = depth.

Melody and rhythm are the only attributes of the linear element of length, horizontal extension, as we find it in Gregorian chant and the troubadours' songs of the thirteenth century. The combination of Gregorian chant and troubadours' song in the French motet of 1200, a startling novelty in spite of its harmonic crudeness, added the element of breadth to the dimension of length for the first time. Vertical extension or breadth is provided by the opposition of one or two countermelodies to the Gregorian theme in the tenor. If Gregorian chant is comparable to the groundplan of a one-room bungalow, as an architect sketches it on a sheet of paper, the French motet of ars antiqua may be likened to the façade of a structure of three widely different stories, one placed on top of the other. This combination of two dimensions of space was so fundamentally novel and striking in effect that it must be considered one of the great basic discoveries of lasting value to all later music.

The Gothic idea of a complex musical structure distinguishes European from antique and oriental music, and in its enormous consequences it is certainly the most fruitful idea ever applied to the art of music. In its most primitive aspect, the combination of length and width is perceived when one plays with both hands on the keyboard of a piano or an organ: the right hand represents the horizontal element of linear extension, length; the accompanying left hand adds the element of breadth. Quite appropriately, even the visual aspect of the two staves in piano music suggests length and breadth. For three centuries music was content with these two dimensions, exploited in the most refined and ingenious manner by the Flemish masters in their linear, contrapuntal art, which one may liken to a "white and black" design.

A principle peculiar to music and hardly applicable in any other art is that of inversion. It is used in three meanings in music. Reading a melody backward, from its close to its start, in so-called retrograde, or cancer, crab motion, is a device frequently applied in contrapuntal music. Bach's fugues and canons are full of such inversions, but also in recent music it is not rare, and the leader of radically modern music, Arnold Schönberg, makes the "crab" inversion one of the pillars of his sensational "twelve-tone system." This kind of inversion is comparable to reading a sentence in a book backward. But whereas in a language this inversion generally makes no sense, it may make good sense in music, under certain conditions, by evolving from a melody an entirely new and different melody, without changing a single note, but merely by retracing the melody's path from the positive, plus direction, geometrically speaking, to the opposite, negative, minus direction. In architecture and in the ornamental arts this kind of inversion is also used, but in a much more restricted sense, as when a certain geometrical or ornamental pattern is turned about on its axis from right to left, as a pendant to the original pattern—the ordinary mirror inversion. Here the effect of symmetry in opposite directions is intended: ⌒ ⌒ since the pattern re-

226

mains essentially the same, whereas in music a crab inversion changes the effect and expression of the original melody fundamentally.

Besides this inversion from right to left, the inversion from high to low, top to bottom, is also a frequent device in music. The so-called double and triple, invertible counterpoints depend on this idea. This kind of inversion is not applicable in a tune without accompaniment. It presupposes two voices that may be exchanged, a soprano becoming a bass, and vice versa, like turning a sleeve inside out. If three voices are written according to the rules of triple counterpoint, the same three parts can be exchanged with each other in six different combinations, every time with a different effect, according to the formula

a-b-c, b-a-c, c-a-b

a-c-b, b-c-a, c-b-a.

Four parts written in quadruple counterpoint: a-b-c-d, admit of twenty-four exchangeable combinations. The five-part triple fugue in C sharp minor in the first part of Bach's *Well-Tempered Clavier* shows in the most eminent degree the artistic possibilities of three themes in ever-changing inversions and combinations.

The third species of inversion answers every step or leap upward in the theme by a corresponding leap downward in the inversion, and vice versa. The piece thus inverted becomes an entirely new piece, with altogether different harmonies. What Bach achieves with inversions of all three kinds in the "Art of Fugue" and in the "Musikalisches Opfer" is unique in its kind and has no parallel anywhere in the world, neither in nature nor in any other art. Some of these mirror fugues, canonic fugues in inversion and augmentation and diminution of the theme, are technical virtuoso feats never surpassed in the ease and elegance with which Bach treats them. To find a description of some of these pieces one would have to imagine a whole house turned upside down, with the roof below and the basement on top, yet not falling apart, but preserving its coherence and orderly arrangement, its logic of structure. The reflection of a house in a pond would be a significant parallel. But while this reflection is only an illusion of the eye, the musical inversion has concrete reality.

From the spectacular progress of Renaissance painting in Italy, music profited immensely in the sixteenth century by adopting the principle of color, and adding to the dimensions of length or height and width also depth and background, perspective, so to speak. Plastic effect, a projection of contours in space, light and shade, color impressions, dynamic and agogic effects, forte, piano, sforzato accents, crescendo and diminuendo, ritardando, accelerando, are new attainments invented by the masters of the Italian madrigal. The incitement for these innovations came from the picturesque Italian poetry, the canzone and sonnetti of Petrarch, Tasso, and their schools, that served as texts for the madrigal writers. This was the age of tone painting. Composers exercised their imagination and inventive power to suggest to the listener the pictures evoked by the poetry. The new colorful chromatic harmony, introduced by Luca Marenzio, Claudio Monteverdi, Gesualdo Principe di Venose, the three greatest madrigalists, was of great assistance in these coloristic efforts, but also the cut of the melodic line, rhythm, dynamic accents, and polyphonic structure were powerful means for tone painting.

In an aesthetic sense, the problem of "expression" has become a central problem. Art acquires value in proportion to what it expresses. Expression is the opposite of impression. To express something one first has to be impressed, and in order to impress somebody else one has to express something. Impression is made possible by the senses of seeing, hearing, and feeling. Thus in a general way we get realistic, objective impressions from the physical, outer world, the experiences of daily life. The problem of art is to translate these sensual impressions into expressions fit to impress others.

The elaborate history of musical expression has not yet been written. Yet the titles of the chapters in such a book may be briefly sketched out here. The importance of emotional expression was stressed in Greek antiquity by Plato when he defined the expressive character of the various modes and scales, the sensuous, dissolute, Asiatic Phrygian mode, as opposed to the more constrained, manly, native Dorian mode. Perhaps the oldest detailed description of the expressive power of music is given by Saint Augustine in his commentary on the Twenty-Second Psalm. In enthusiastic and inspired words he describes the effect of the jubilant strains in the brilliant coloraturas traditional for this psalm in the Jewish temple service: "One who is jubilant does not utter words but sounds of joy without words." This "jubilus" was taken over into Gregorian chant, together with its opposite, the wailing "tractus," expressive of sorrow by coloraturas of different character. In both cases we are concerned with coloraturas, that is, with more or less extended chains of tones sung on the vowel of one syllable. The precise expression of the words in their meaning was something of less importance to medieval music. The declamatory psalmody sufficed for centuries. Only around 1500 Flemish music began to tackle the problem of the words. In the meantime the newly discovered Gothic art of counterpoint, polyphony, was concerned with expressing the entirely new ideas of construction in terms of space dimensions, as explained above. The words of the text were cherished in a new sense when the humanistic tendencies of the Renaissance, the more profound study of Greek and Latin literature, made the masters of music conscious of the rhetoric and expressive power of the words in antique poetry. Josquin de Près is

228

credited with the idea of the so-called *wortgezeugte,* word-engendered motifs, thematic phrases that take their rhythm, accent, tempo, and mood from the dominating words of a motet, translating these rhetorical features into musical terms faithfully, and thus multiplying their expressive value by the recurrence of the same motifs in the dialogue of the voices.

All the new styles in art, with their different demands on the plastic means of expression, are reflected in music. The Romanesque ideal dominates Gregorian chant, the Gothic mind builds up its elaborate polyphonic structures, the Renaissance mentality adds the rhetorical element and a little later, in the Italian madrigal, the concepts of tone painting, of color, light, and shade in the quality of sound, plus the illustrative effects. The Baroque taste adds pomp and grandeur, in polychoral structures, of which we find the most striking examples in Heinrich Schütz' concerti ecclesiastici, in Handel's oratorios and Bach's Passion music. Only a few of the numerous attributes of Baroque style in music can be hinted at in this rapid review. They have been described at greater length in a chapter of the author's book, *Music, History and Ideas.*[1] The new Baroque interest in sumptuous, resplendent colors, in clair-obscur, the fascinating effects of light and shade, was transferred to music in the amazing, chromatic harmony of Monteverdi around 1600, which found its parallel only in the romantic music of Chopin, Liszt, and Wagner. The severity of the Gregorian modes, the orderly structure of the major and minor tonalities, are suggestive of the art of linear drawing with its clear outlines, whereas the new Baroque chromaticism, by deliberately obscuring the purity of the linear design, suggests the element of color. In a sense, Monteverdi and Rembrandt rendered similar services to their respective arts.

When, in the middle of the eighteenth century, rationalism began to invade the European mentality, we see the reflex of this new philosophy in music in a new analysis of expression, in the doctrine of thematic invention manifest in the symphonies of the Mannheim School and of Philipp Emanuel Bach, the direct predecessors of Haydn and Mozart. Here the various "affetti" are mixed as in a bottle, the ingredients of a melody rapidly changing its emotional expression within a very few measures.

In a similar manner one might continue to point out the influence of dominating aesthetic ideas in Gluck, Beethoven, the great romanticists of the nineteenth century, in Wagner, Brahms, Debussy, and Stravinsky. But to do this would require a special book. Enough, however, has been said here to show to what an extent the growth and change of the art of music depends on aesthetic ideas born in the sphere of the intellect and transferred in a hardly explainable creative process to the sphere of the imagination, the real soil of art.

[1] Cambridge, Massachusetts: Harvard University Press, 1938.

logic and coherence
in music

The question of logical coherence, so important for the aesthetic value of a piece of music, is inseparable from the problem of formal structure. What is meant by sensible continuation of a musical idea—how does a musical idea logically (not mechanically or fortuitously) engender a second, new idea? To investigate such problems, one must first gain clear insight into the role of logic in music.

Scientific, mathematical logic reaches certain conclusions from given premises with strict certainty; it proves that a certain fact must necessarily be as it is under the given conditions. In this keen and cool intellectuality the work of art has no place. To be sure, the musical work of art is also in need of intellectual activity, of orderly arrangement, of weighing and judging. The aesthetic sense, however, is satisfied with the impression as if the connection of two ideas, the continuation of a phrase, should be just as it actually is. The aesthetic world of imagination is opposed to the material world of reality; absolute certainty is demanded by reality, whereas aesthetics needs only the logic of imagination. This explains the fact that the same themes may be connected with each other in different ways, and yet every one of these different connections may appear convincing and natural. The reprise in a Beethoven sonata sometimes shows a transition from the first to the second theme different from what it had been in the exposition. Both transitions may appear equally natural and logical; their difference adds one more charm to the work of art without detracting from its logical coherence. One might possibly say that owing to its position after the development section, the transition episode in the reprise is subject to conditions different from the exposition, with its first, direct presentation of the themes. It would therefore be a logical error to let the two transitions change places with each other. In the rondo the aesthetic charm lies in the varied introduction of the same theme: different roads to the same goal. Here, too, the order of the transitions is not a matter of indifference: the third transition would probably be unsatisfactory if it took the place of the first one.

The sensible continuation of a musical phrase is based upon the coherence of the single tones. The technical methods of composition in regard to coherence may be classified under two headings:

(1) Physiological coherence.

(2) Psychological coherence (treated in detail a few pages further on).

physiological coherence

Coherence effected through retention of motifs is of a physiological nature because it is based on the natural capacity of the organ of hearing, the ear. There is a tendency to persevere in a given direction, towards repetition and similarity of successive phrases. The most primitive method consists in the exact repetition, note for note, of a melodic phrase. In the practice of composition this method is of little use. From an aesthetic point of view it can be justified only by skillful harmonic and contrapuntal elaboration, which may contribute much towards making even prolonged melodic repetition more interesting. Here follow some examples of melodic structure, solely by means of repetition of the same tone:

Mozart, *Don Giovanni,* the utterances of the Commendatore's marble monument in the finale of Act II.

Schubert, *Der Tod und das Mädchen* (*Death and the Maiden*), second part.

Schubert, "Die liebe Farbe" ("The Lovely Color"), continued reiteration of the note F sharp in the accompaniment, with changing chords and melodic line in motion.

Cornelius, "Ein Ton" ("A Tone"), a single, long-continued tone in the melody, with shifting harmonies.

Reger, "Aeolsharfe" ("Aeolian Harp"), a constantly held third in the accompaniment, with the melody in motion.

In all these cases, more or less, a sort of inverted organ point is found, which, to be sure, only obtains significance and aesthetic charm through the changing harmonies of the accompaniment.

Exact repetitions of an entire motif are called *ostinato* (obstinate) voices. Their usefulness is generally determined by the interesting structure of the contrapuntal countermotifs, Basso ostinato, chaconne, passacaglia are based on this principle. As examples one might study:

Bach, Crucifixus of the *B Minor Mass*.

Beethoven, first movement of the Ninth symphony, coda.

Chopin, Berceuse.

Liszt, "Dante" symphony, first movement.

Wagner, Prelude to *Walküre*.

Brahms, Finale of the Haydn Variations, Op. 56.

Debussy, scherzo of the string quartet in G minor.

Next to the primitive tone repetition, the following step in melodic structure is the repetition of a phrase on different degrees of the scale, called sequence. The third step consists in the continuation of an already established rhythm, the characteristic means of constructing a melody by retaining the rhythmic motif.[1] Then come those melodies which are composed of two or three different motifs, and finally, freely constructed melodies with changing rhythms.

Here is the proper place for a more thorough discussion of the conception of the motif. A distinction is made between a motif and a closed melody, or theme, the motifs being considered the component parts of the melody. The question, how far can a motif be extended, how many tones or measures may it contain as a maximum, can best be answered by a comparison with the power of the eye in perceiving various objects in their totality, without counting and reasoning. Thus one can take in at a glance five black dots on a white sheet as a totality of five, not, however, thirty dots. In music similarly, a group of five notes will normally be perceived without further calculation by the ear as a coherent group, a unit or motif, but not, however, a group of thirty tones. The exact limits of a motif cannot be found because these limits vary with the velocity of the sounding groups; in a quick motif one may employ many more tones without endangering its distinctness than would be feasible in a slow motif. Thus, for instance, the passage:

---

[1] Cf. Chapter I.

may well be considered a single motif, whereas the same tones in the Adagio:

are no longer comprehensible as a single unit, but as a compound of smaller groups, the motifs (marked by square braces) producing a larger melodic line.

To listen to this phrase takes such a long time that at its close the beginning is only dimly recollected; the entire phrase cannot therefore be perceived as a series of tones grouped around a single center of gravity; in other words, a phrase of this nature is no longer a single motif, but a compound of motifs.

The basic material of composition consists of motifs. One might call these the cells of the musical body; every expressive value in music ultimately goes back to the primitive motifs: reason enough for the student to observe constantly the nature of the motifs, to analyze their structure, and to investigate how the melodic succession of tones and the rhythms of the motif influence the expression. The closer study of these problems would require a special exhaustive research into the fundamentals of musical expression. This difficult task has, however, not yet been satisfactorily accomplished, and no book is thus far available which adequately treats these problems.

The most useful and most frequent, the really normal means of melodic construction consists in retaining the rhythm of the chosen motif for a longer or shorter time. How long it is proper to retain the same rhythmical motif depends on the manner of its development, on its harmonic, melodic, coloristic interest. Here, as everywhere in musical composition, the aesthetic laws of unity and variety, of stability and contrast are the deciding factors. Stability without variety, mere repetition, if continued for any length of time, is aesthetically objectionable because the ear finds it uninteresting and dull. The opposite also holds true: variety without constancy is unwarranted. A somewhat extended piece of music which almost constantly changes its rhythms, figures of accompaniment, harmonies and color from bar to bar has a jerky, confused effect, and as it shows no manifest order of treatment, it finally becomes fatiguing and repulsive.

Nevertheless, contrast, if properly applied, may be a means of promoting coherence. Two phrases may belong together not only by virtue of their rhythmic and melodic similarity, but in their differences they may even complement each other like light and shadow, day and night. Very

233

impressive melodies can be found compounded of contrary motifs, as, for instance, the dramatically intense, pathetic, declamatory themes of some Bach fantasies, some Beethoven sonatas and quartets.

Beyond the confines of monodic and of homophonic music, new means of coherence are found in polyphony, in the use of imitation, of canon and fugue. A motif or theme carried through the various voice parts of a piece binds these parts together into a higher, spiritual unit. The powerful logic of polyphonic writing is thus explained. A Bach fugue is comparable to a conversation between four clever persons discussing a theme on which everyone has something essential to say. Therefrom results a most profound and convincing coherence. The devices of augmentation and diminution, of inversion, may all be helpful in attaining coherence and in consolidating the logical impression of a piece of music.

Repetitions not only of single notes, single motifs or themes, but of longer sections and even entire movements are of constructive importance; they occur frequently, wherever symmetry on a larger scale is favored, in the dance and march forms as well as in the song form and the sonata.

psychological coherence

The theme once stated and continued, a second problem of importance for musical structure presents itself; how can a new melodic idea be logically evolved from the first idea?

Here we have to deal with the art of transition from one emotional mood to another. Psychological connection, the second type of coherence above mentioned, becomes effective here. What matters now is not so much the continuation of an idea, but the connection of two different ideas. Aesthetic effects and logical connections are derived not from the similarities, but from the differences. There are three possibilities of transition: it may enter suddenly, by a leap, or glide gradually from the former rhythm into the new rhythm; finally, the various rhythms may be bridged over by running-passage interludes. The most primitive case is transition by leap: two different states of emotion are crudely placed next to each other, exciting the ear by means of violent contrast. This method loses its impressiveness by too frequent use. The second method consists in reconciling the contrasts by gradually gliding over from one state of emotion to another. The older musicians including Bach generally content themselves with a juxtaposition, a coördination of closely related emotional moods within the framework of the same piece, or with a sharp contrast.

The transition to the second theme in Beethoven's sonata, Op. 53, may be quoted here as an example of that manner of bridging over to the second theme by employing figures derived from the arpeggio or scale which obliterate the original rhythm:

234

The arpeggio figure in sixteenth notes descends lower and lower, losing its power, and from its downward curved line the upward moving scale figure, somewhat lessened in power, reverses the motion, now in eighth notes; in slower motion, this scale figure passes step by step into the still broader rhythm of the second theme. This kind of transition obtains its effectiveness more from the balance of the upward and downward swing of the lines and also from the equilibrium of its dynamic values than from relationship of the motifs in the various themes.

The great achievement of modern music, especially manifest in Beethoven, is the art of transition, which reveals to music much greater possibilities of emotional expression by teaching how even the most antagonistic sentiments may be welded together logically into a new spiritual unity. This concerns the reprise after the intermediate trio, in the large song form, the transition to the second theme in the sonata, and still more the development section where the triumph of this method is attained. The technical means of transition is chiefly the gradual approach and finally the merging together of the different rhythms and the two melodies to be connected. The return to the main theme of the presto from the entirely different trio, in Beethoven's string quartet, Op. 130, may illustrate this case (see page 236).

Measures 1 and 20 are the starting point and the end of this development. The 6/4 time and the scale figure from measure 3 are at first continued by repetition and imitation. In measures 7 to 10 the scale figure appears in triple augmentation, in measure 12 in the original metre, but inverted, turned upside down at the end in measure 13. This measure already uses the new time 4/4, alla breve. By this metrical change and through the succession of the notes F, F, G flat, the return of the theme in measure 20 is prepared. Measures 14 to 19 vacillate between 4/4 and 6/4 time, and finally bring about a state of equilibrium, the chromatic scale gliding down, in diminution, in eighth notes, at first starting the downward swing from high E flat, then in a still wider curve from high G flat down into the E flat minor theme, now reached with convincing logic.[2]

Beethoven's art of development has created new possibilities of coherence. There is a considerable difference between the older and the modern style of development between Bach's and Beethoven's system. Bach makes use of the elaboration of motifs (*motivische Arbeit*), taking from his economically stated themes (which moreover are closely related to each other in the same piece), the motifs for interludes, developments, transitions and reprise. This accounts for the continuity of rhythms in Bach's music,

---

[2] On Bruckner's remarkable art of transition, E. Kurth's monumental book on Bruckner contains an abundance of instructive material. See also Chapter XXI, below.

and the corresponding similar steadiness of harmony and of modulation.

Beethoven obtains his effects through thematic elaboration (*thematische Arbeit*). His development section takes its motifs not only from the principal theme—which, in comparison with Bach, is generally much freer and more differentiated in its rhythms—but also from the second or third themes, both very different from the principal theme. Consequently, Beethoven's development section has not the rhythmical steadiness and continuity of Bach's elaboration, but makes up for this lack by a wealth of changing rhythmical constructions, an abundance of new combinations derived from a variety of motifs, of thematic material. Corresponding to this is the unlimited range of modulation. These two different methods may be called rhythmically concentric and eccentric, repeating a terminology once before applied to the variation form.

A still more intensive inner coherence of logical, even of psychological nature is manifest in larger cyclical works by the manner in which the various movements are coördinated through inner relationship, in spite of strong exterior differences, as in the prelude and fugue, or in the four movements of a sonata. Beethoven knew how to relieve this type of coherence most admirably. Richard Wagner in his "programmatic analysis" of the "Eroica" symphony interprets the inner connections of the various movements;[3] in his essay, "Beethoven," he gives a similar analysis of the C sharp minor quartet.[4] Also the reader may be reminded of what is said in this book on the cyclical sonata form, as practiced by Beethoven, Liszt, César Franck, Debussy, and Bruckner.[5]

logical consequence

A third question may be raised: does a given theme demand only one certain melodic idea as its logically convincing consequence? The answer to this question can only be in the negative. Experience as well as reasoning teaches us that any musical idea might be continued differently and may be brought to a different close from that of the chosen single instance. What matters is that this single case should appear convincing; another continuation might have been more, less, or equally convincing.

The reason for this peculiarity of musical structure lies in the fact that a composition is the product of two different factors: the creative force of the motif, and the individuality of the composer. Understanding the nature of any single motif is a prime condition for its natural and logical development. But the composer must develop its portions, its color, and its direc-

[3] Wagner, *Gesammelte Schriften*, V, 169.
[4] *Ibid.*, IX, 96.
[5] See Chapter XVII.

tion. A seed can produce only a plant of its own kind, but this plant may grow soundly or poorly, according to the influences of soil, sunlight, water. It is the composer's duty to provide good soil, sunlight, and water, and to care for their proper efficiency. From a cherry stone no apple tree will grow, and a wailing adagio motif cannot engender a merry, playful rondo. The first problem is to recognize the nature, the possibilities of the motifs, and to develop them accordingly. From this aptitude of the composer there follows the second ability of finding the proper sort of motif for every purpose. Fundamental mistakes of composition arise generally from a wrong estimation of the musical idea. The choice of suitable motifs, however, is merely the raw material of the composition. The personality of the composer must add the ennobling, beautifying cultivation of the motifs. One speaks of cultivation or culture in the domain of spiritual activities as well as in agriculture. Without culture no higher art is possible, but at best only a healthy but crude naturalism.

The same theme may be developed simply or in a complex manner, briefly or extensively, and yet in each way it may appear convincing and impressive, provided the composer knows how to execute properly the adopted plan. It is the composer's task to bring about coherence by fitting transitions from one emotional mood into the other. Even the strangest, most unexpected combination of different themes may in a particular case be justified. Berlioz, in the finale of his Fantastic symphony, couples together the sublime Dies Irae with a vulgar dance tune, solving the problem of making this combination credible, of changing aesthetic hideousness into aesthetic charm. To evolve unexpected, surprising, novel consequences from a theme is a characteristic trait of romantic art. Classical art, too, occasionally in search of more remote effects, sometimes transgresses into the domain of romanticism. Bach and Mozart have their romantic traits when they aim at colorful effects, at picturesque contours, at the connection of distant emotional moods.

The logic of a structure is sometimes perceived and justified only by what follows it. If, for instance, two entirely different themes are developed fugally in succession, one cannot in the moment of listening perceive a coherence of both fugues. Such a coherence, however, might be brought about in the further continuation of the piece by a double fugue, in which the two different themes are combined and enter into a higher unity. If the development section of a complicated sonata movement were played without the exposition, the logic of its structure would not be intelligible because the understanding of the coherence presupposes an acquaintance with the themes of the exposition. The order of the single parts of a complex whole is decidedly important; it would be senseless in a composition to let the first

238

and third part change places. It has, to my knowledge, not yet been attempted to reverse the entire principle of construction, but in a special case, according to a special plan, it might not appear absurd to try this reversal.

In the case of the double fugue the earlier part of the composition is made intelligible by the later part. Could one not, after this analogy, start a symphony with a complicated development section and later extract from it the simple basic themes and motifs? Or in other words, could one not place the exposition at the end of the movement? This would mean application of an analytic method, whereas all principles of construction thus far mentioned aim at a synthetic structure.

The principle of anticlimax would here attain importance. So far anticlimax has been applied only occasionally, in exceptional cases, and rather timidly, not yet a legitimate principle of construction. Something similar, in the much simpler form of variation, has been tried by Vincent d'Indy in his "Istar." [6] Only the practice of great composers could prove whether the principle of anticlimax is aesthetically fertile, and whether new possibilities of composition might be based on it.

A few rare places in the works of the masters may, however, be pointed out, showing the germ of this idea and illustrating the peculiar effects to be derived from the dissolution, the breaking up of the theme into its elements. Beethoven sometimes aims at similar effects in his development sections, as in the piano sonata, Op. 28, in the development section of the first movement. Here the firmly shaped four-bar phrase is split at first into a two-bar phrase by omission of the first half. This is followed by another splitting up into one-bar motifs; this fragment, already cut up four times, is still more diminished, until the plastic design of the original motif has entirely lost its shape, and finally there remains only a long single chord, an elementary sound without any clear structure at all.

Another main example is found in the first movement of Beethoven's Fourth symphony; here the development idea consists mainly in breaking up the theme into smallest fragments. A famous example also occurs in Beethoven's Fifth symphony: the transition from the scherzo to the finale, that strangely exciting and stirring pianissimo, with the softly beating kettle drum extending through nearly fifty measures. Also the E minor sonata, Op. 90, contains two interesting examples, measures 17 to 25 and 41 to 53, in the development section of the first movement. In the Diabelli Variations, Op. 120, Variation 13, would have to be singled out, that witty *aperçu* consisting merely of torn shreds of motifs and pauses. The C sharp minor quartet, Op. 131, brings in its fourth movement (Variation 5) a complete dissolution of the theme into its harmonic elements (see page 240).

[6] See Chapter XVI.

Brahms ends his cycle of variations, Op. 9, with a similar effect. Variation 16 hovers about like a pale, inanimate shadow of the theme, with strangely touching effect.

Very important for musical construction is the proper handling of the small contrasts (like high and low, light and dark, strong and weak) which help to give a long rhythmical phrase those many new little stimulants constantly demanded by the ear. These small contrasts within a homogeneous melodic line must be well distinguished from the large contrasts, aiming at variety of the successive ideas. In one case the purpose is to make unity or steadiness more impressive, more agreeable; in the other case variety is expressly sought.

Musical logic is derived from a compromise between unity, continuity,

or steadiness and variety or contrast. To balance properly these two opposing factors, to assimilate them to each other, is a problem to be solved
anew in every particular case. General rules can hardly be stated beyond
broad outlines. To demonstrate this balance of opposing factors in many
individual cases is the main object of the analysis of masterpieces in this
book.

In summarizing, one might say the following about musical logic: there
is a logic of variety, sufficient reason for any change; a logic of harmonic
succession, tonal relations in a narrower or wider sense, and the opposite,
atonality; a logic of melodic structure, the relation of high to low, of long
to short tones; a logic of tone coloring, timbre. All these various aspects,
however, are not active in isolation, but solely in coördination. Without logic
there is no style. One might define style also as the ratio of unity to variety.
Accordingly, the characteristic feature of classical style would be variety
in unity, whereas modern style aims rather at unity in variety.

In other words, the classical masters attach prime importance to unity
or continuity, the modern composers more to variety. No genuine work of
art, however, whatever style it may have, should favor one of these two
elements to the complete exclusion of the other.

the accompaniment in its formal and stylistic significance

The accompaniment has its structural function, the purpose of which may vary considerably. Sometimes it is sufficient as a mere background, from which the contours of the solo can stand out effectively; in other cases a considerable part of the rhythmic activity is allotted to the accompaniment, as in dance and march music.

The accompaniment may also strengthen and intensify emotional expression by characteristic rhythms and tone painting, as can be observed in many modern songs. And finally, it may serve as a framework holding firmly together the fragments of a rhapsodic, declamatory piece which otherwise would fall apart; or it may bind several quite different successive melodies together by means of its common rhythm. It may alternate in dialogue with the solo, it may interrupt the solo at fitting places, or be opposed to it more or less independently; it may employ polyphonic art to a greater or lesser degree. In other words, the accompaniment may be subordinated to the solo, coördinated with it, or superior to it. The intention may be to present to the ear only one essential melodic line at all times, either in the solo alone, or distributed between solo and accompaniment, so that during the pauses of the solo the melodic line is transferred to the accompaniment. In other cases, two or three melodic lines may be presented to the ear simultaneously: the accompaniment opposes a new melody to the solo so that both melodies are heard simultaneously or alternating in dialogue. All these typical cases will now be explained in greater detail and illustrated by examples.

accompaniment as background

Often a single held note suffices for background; a sustained chord; or single chords struck successively, tied in legato, or interrupted by rests. This type of accompaniment is extensively used in the secco recitative of opera, oratorio, cantata, and also instrumental music in passages of a recitative-like character. The stylistically plain form of accompaniment adapts itself well to the declamatory tone of the solo, and strengthens the realistic effect of recitation, lifting it into a higher plane by the sound of the singing voice. Though the most primitive of all forms of accompaniment, yet this type is one of the most natural, useful, and durable forms since, because of its primitive nature, it is not subject to fashion and therefore not in danger of becoming antiquated or old-fashioned. On the other hand, it hardly permits finer differentiation, is altogether lacking in refinement, and is only rarely serviceable for more precise expression.

The second order of background treatment consists in the network of chords as employed in an ordinary thorough bass: a more or less densely filled-in background (according to the frequency and velocity of the change of chords), without aiming at extraordinary coloristic effects. This is the normal procedure in older musical practice and has its origin in the motion of the bass, in the basso continuo (thorough bass), whose restless movement to and fro and steady rhythm gives its stamp not only to the entire accompaniment, but also influences the style of melody. Every type of melody has a close relation to the type of bass leading, as can be easily observed in the recitative, the aria with thorough bass, in Haydn's melodic types, in the chorale, song, folk song, the dances and marches, in Beethoven's symphonic type of melody, in Wagner's declamatory singing with symphonic orchestra.

formulas for homophonic accompaniment

A simplified bass leading, in comparison to the constantly moving thorough bass, with preference for longer held bass tones, a more sparing change of chords, characterizes the new melodic type of Haydn. Since homophonic writing is the norm in this melodic type, a more vivid rhythmical motion cannot be produced by the scanty bass notes, but only by applying various formulas of tone-repetition, of broken chords and scales. Here the various kinds of tremolo, called "batteries" in French, make their appearance (there is no adequate English translation for "batteries"), either in all parts simultaneously; or alternately high and low; or one hand after the other; or syncopated in various rhythms, in dotted rhythms, in legato or staccato, in full or thin sound.

A special study is required for the many variants of the arpeggio, for stringed instruments, harp, and especially the piano, whose normal manner of motion lies precisely in the arpeggio. The possibilities of the older arpeggio can be studied in the piano works of Bach, Mozart, Clementi, Beethoven, Schubert; the more modern, much more refined and differentiated applications of arpeggio are manifest in the works of Chopin, Schumann, Henselt, Liszt, Brahms, Debussy, Busoni. The accompanying scale figures occur in numerous variants, in the bass, the middle or the upper parts, most frequently intermingled with the arpeggio as passing or changing notes.

All these formulas of accompaniment can best be studied in that class of songs with piano which content themselves with supporting the vocal melody plainly by simple figuration, in greater or lesser motion, without especially aiming at tone-painting or refined characteristic effects. A figurated accompaniment of this type strives to support the melody, to buoy it up so that it may lightly float on a moving substratum like a boat on a lake. To obtain such effects requires a fine ear and cultivated taste, and the figuration must be rationally elaborated according to the requirements of every single case. Otherwise, the melody will be dragged down by a clumsy accompaniment, as if one had tied heavy stones to the bottom of the boat. How the lifting and soaring of the melody, the support of the voice, the plastic contour of the solo against the background may be achieved through these means is evident in many songs of Schubert and his predecessors, Zelter, Reichardt, Zumsteg, in many songs of Mendelssohn, Robert Franz, and Brahms.

Accompaniment formulas of these types depend of course on certain well defined melodic types, or vice versa; a singable, popular, symmetrically built, smoothly flowing, pleasingly rounded melody is characteristic for this type of accompaniment. Similar observations may be made in violin or violoncello solos of a song or aria-like character, accompanied by the piano or orchestra. Piano and string literature abounds with such pieces: moments musicaux, impromptus, nocturnes, romances, songs without words, and so on, which in their character depend on a certain definite type of melody as well as of accompaniment. This extended class of pieces of course easily degenerates into something formalistic, into triviality and platitude, into mechanical repetition of hackneyed melodic turns. This explains the artistic inferiority of many pieces of this type. The blame, however, must be attributed to the dull abuse of the technical pattern more than to the pattern itself, from which numerous valuable pieces of this simpler style have been evolved.

The figurated accompaniment is especially serviceable for songlike, symmetrically built melodies. Almost never is such an accompaniment appropriate for declamatory, fantasy-like, recitative music. But also the reverse is true—a songlike tune generally should not be accompanied in the style of recitative or arioso. The reason for this is the apparent contradiction between the nature of the melody and its accompaniment. The problem is rather to find for each type of melody the appropriate manner of accompaniment. Here questions of good taste, of artistic tact and decency are touched upon, questions for which attentive observation and intelligence may to a certain degree find an adequate answer. Also the sharply marked march and dance rhythms have their own code of proper treatment. Imagine for instance a solemn recitative accompanied by polka rhythms, or a march tune accompanied by long held chords, or briefly struck chords interrupted by rests, and the absurdity of such combinations will be immediately evident. Sometimes in exceptional cases they may prove serviceable for grotesque, bizarre effects. Nothing in fact, no matter how strange, could be imagined which might not prove to be the very effect suitable for some out of the way and remote purpose. We have here, however, to deal principally with the normal cases.

Here follow examples illustrating many typical cases. For convenience' sake all these examples have been taken from volume two of the Schubert songs in the Peters' edition.

(1) Broad, long held chords, slowly changing: see Schubert, "Meeres Stille"; Hugo Wolf, "Du bist Orplid, mein Land." The effect is solemn, broad, sublime, the leading of the melodic line in conformity with this character.

(2) In "Wanderer's Nachtlied," plain chord accompaniment on a simple, rhythmical motif is seen. Without great trouble it would have been possible to continue the motif of the first measure throughout the entire song, as can be seen in dozens of other Schubert songs. In this case, however, Schubert makes use of at least five rhythmical variants of the original accompaniment motif. The reason lies in the aria-like character of the melody, which approaches recitative. Schubert, with his delicate sense for the finest emotional shades, has perceived that the typical song accompaniment with its strictly symmetrical formulas would not do justice to the melodic type here chosen. The five variants of the accompaniment are shown on page 246.

How excellently these rhythmical variants adapt themselves to the changing expression of the words will best be observed if one accompanies the entire song according to the first formula. Other songs of the same type are: "Erster Verlust," "Die Liebe hat gelogen."

(3) Strictly continued, simple accompaniment motif

taken from the declamation of the text, retained through long stretches: "Die Sterne." The character of the melody corresponds to this formula, the whole song is a *Strophenlied,* with the same melody repeated in every stanza. As the piece is very long, monotony would be unavoidable had not Schubert counteracted it by refinement of modulation and finely nuanced harmonic color. In like manner: "Der König in Thule," "Du liebst mich nicht."

(4) Chorale-like, strictly measured pace of chords: "Der Kreuzzug," "Pax vobiscum," suitable to melodies of ecclesiastic mood.

(5) Motion of chords in the manner of the thorough bass: "Das Echo," "Das Weinen," smoothly led in quarter notes. The effect is somewhat quaint and old-fashioned, well in accordance with the plain text. Of similar technique, though altogether different in emotional expression: "An die Türen will ich schleichen," from the *Gesänge des Harfners* (Goethe). This *schleichen* (stealthily passing by) is suggestively expressed by the restless onward motion of the bass figure in quarter notes.

(6) Ostinato-like figure, with repeated chords in the upper parts: "An Sylvia," continued throughout the song, strictly as regards rhythm, freely as regards the melody. The effect is lute or guitar-like, a serenade with pizzicato bass:

The vocal melody above this accompaniment forms a duet with the bass. The four-bar ostinato phrase is extended to six bars in the first two sections of the text, and interrupted by an echo in the seventh measure, extended again in the third section to 2 × 4 measures by repetition of the text. Between the single stanzas, and at the close, the first four measures recur as a ritornello. Of similar technique "Der Einsame," "An die Musik," "Auf der Bruck."

(7) Fanfare-like, rhythmically incisive accompaniment motifs, continued from the start to the close without interruption, fit for songs of a military, warlike character such as "Normanns Gesang":

"Lied des gefangenen Jaegers":

(8) Pizzicato basses, with repeated chords after the beat, a commonplace, conventional type of accompaniment, suitable for pleasant melodies of serenade type: "Im Haine," with waltz rhythms:

In the ritornello a melodic design is added in the soprano above this accompaniment figure. There is a similar procedure in "Drang in die Ferne," with a new melody occasionally appearing in duet with the voice, moving in parallel thirds.

(9) Bass struck on the downbeat, figuration of the upper parts after the beat. "Dithyrambe":

A commonplace, threadbare formula, which needs an unusually attractive melody in order to have any artistic effect at all.

(10) Three- or four-part writing with one or two figurated parts. "Der Fischer":

The figuration sometimes passes over from the alto to the tenor and soprano.

(11) Held basses, singly or in octaves, with chords dissolved into one-part figuration above the bass. Found frequently in the first two *Gesänge des Harfners*. These two songs contain a considerable number of various formulas of figurated accompaniment. Similar effects in "Der Schiffer"—here the bass has figuration in eighth notes, the soprano in sixteenth notes.

(12) Tremolo of the upper parts, bass in contrasting rhythm. "Der Zwerg":

"Suleika":

(13) Tremolo in both hands, with figuration interspersed: "Kolmas Klage," "Gebet während der Schlacht," "Gruppe aus dem Tartarus." Serviceable in dramatically agitated pieces, in emotional episodes. Slow tremolo in low position for both hands is used with beautiful, sonorous effect in "Nacht und Traüme." Repeated chords (batteries) with solemn, sublime effect in "Die Allmacht."

(14) Three-part writing; calm bass, figurated middle part, melody in the soprano: "Thekla."

(15) Style of the accompagnato recitative and of aria, transferred to song: "An die Leyer."

(16) The arpeggio in many variants is found less frequently in Schubert than in the Mendelssohn and Brahms songs. The simplest, most typical example is perhaps Mendelssohn's "Auf Flügeln des Gesanges," accompanied throughout with the motif:

Sometimes a simple unpretentious accompaniment of the kind already described, not at all claiming any special significance, is inclined at times to step out of its subordinate role for a few measures. A little prelude, an interlude interrupting the single sections, a postlude (these little snatches of melody are called ritornelli, especially when they always come back to the same melodic phrase) afford the accompaniment opportunity to lead the melody for a little while. But also while the solo has a short rest, or holds a long note or trill, the accompaniment sometimes assumes greater importance and enters into a modest duet with the solo. In this manner, notwithstanding the predominant part of the solo, a more vivid dialogue between solo and accompaniment is made possible, and the entire composition gains in attractiveness.

249

scena and aria

In dramatic music the accompaniment has to solve new problems. Older opera had a predilection for combining "scena and aria"—meaning by *scena* something intermediate between recitative and arioso, with frequently intermixed tone-painting, suggested by the text, and calling an aria a melodically closed, rounded off piece. Examples from Weber's "Freischütz" are No. 8, scena and aria of Agathe. The "scene" begins with accompanied recitative approaching an arioso in 4/4 time: "Wie nahte mir der Schlummer," next follows the aria-like melody "Leise, leise fromme Weise," in 2/4 time, interrupted after eighteen measures by a recitative in 4/4 time. Shortly afterwards the second stanza of the melody is heard: "Zu dir wende ich die Hände," in 2/4 time. There follows an andante, 4/4: "Alles pflegt schon längst der Ruh," with delightful landscape tone-painting, thereafter again recitative, agitato, recitative, and after this amply varied preparation full of tension, the aria finally enters, vivace con fuoco: "All meine Pulse schlagen," elaborated and introduced most effectively.

In the great aria of Max (No. 3) the order is almost reversed. A short introductory recitative is immediately followed by the aria: "Durch die Wälder, durch die Auen"; the "scene" proper with its dramatic tension, its sudden changes of motifs, time signatures, tempo, and tone-painting, is worked into the aria. Another admirable masterpiece of this type is the scene and aria of Florestan, at the beginning of the second act in Beethoven's *Fidelio.* Here the magnificent introduction of the orchestra is directly carried over into the first recitative.

change of the motifs of the accompaniment

In many pieces no single formula of accompaniment is used throughout the piece, but the formulas change in accordance with the progressions of the melodic line in its up and down motion in order to do justice to the expressive climaxes and to the dynamic fluctuations. Older operas contain many examples of this type of accompaniment. A well known aria from Verdi's *La Traviata,* Violetta's "Ah fors' è lui," from the close of the first act, may illustrate this type. A ritornello of three measures is followed by the first part of the aria, accompanied by a motif of the plainest kind. From measures 28 to 46, the second part of the aria is based on a new motif because the culmination of the emotional expression demanded a more agitated accompaniment. This part is brought to a close with the ritornello. Next follows a repetition of both parts with new text. This is followed by an intermezzo: "Follie! follie!" in the character of an accompagnato recitative, with freely changing accompaniment motifs, and hereupon the third part of the aria enters, on a new motif in 6/8 time, again interrupted by the melody of Alfredo's serenade (3/8 with new accompaniment). A short

recitative follows and then the rhythm of the third part is taken up again. It is instructive to observe how every change of the accompaniment formula can be accounted for by some musical or scenic reason. The entire piece, though making use of commonplace, almost trivial formulas, nevertheless does not miss its mark since these formulas attempt to do no more than they are able to: namely to give an unpretentious, simple support to the vocal melody, and yet adapt themselves in the plainest manner to the changes of emotional expression. There is no trace of individual, independent expression in the accompaniment. At most, in well chosen passages the accompaniment is illuminated a bit more brightly, by doubling the vocal melody in unison or in the octave, quickly resuming, however, its subordinate role once again. But without these modest turns of the accompaniment, the solo would not be able to display impressively enough its manifold melodic inflections.

SOLVEIG'S SONG BY GRIEG

For all its simplicity, a piece like Grieg's well-known "Solveig's Song" shows much greater refinement. The accompaniment motifs are more numerous and change more quickly than in the Verdi aria. The aim here is to satisfy a demand for finer coloristic effect. One phrase is underlined more than another, has a deeper shadow, or more brilliant light, more luminous color. Higher and lower range, unison and chord, full and thin sound, long held chords, figuration, and occasional doubling of the vocal line are some of the means employed. Nevertheless, the accompaniment is decidedly subordinate to the solo and hardly ever makes an attempt at independent characteristic expression.

Following Schubert's example, the masters of modern song make frequent use of a type of accompaniment restricting itself to only one, or a few motifs for the entire piece, but making these motifs—in distinction to the above-mentioned typical "formulas"—intentionally characteristic, suggestively picturesque. Thus the accompaniment itself becomes more interesting. It is no more a mere harmonic filling out and support, a background in one color, but something like a landscape background, accentuating the emotional mood; it becomes the scene in which the lyric action of the work of art takes place. The music, nevertheless, is able to follow all the varying shades of emotion in the poem by utilizing the progressive modern harmonic art, adding manifold illumination and changing colors. A number of Schubert songs may be analyzed here with regard to such effects (volume one of the Peters edition).

SCHUBERT'S SONGS

"Liebesbotschaft" takes its accompaniment motif from the beginning of the text: "Rauschendes Bächlein, so silbern und hell, eilst zur Geliebten so munter und schnell." The "light rushing" of the little brook and its "joyful hurrying to the beloved" determine the shape of the motif.

"Der Atlas." The accompaniment motif paints the "unfortunate Atlas," who must carry the whole world of pains. The tremolo of the right hand, suggestive of a heavy load, and the pathetic, grief-laden gesture of the bass motif evoke the complete picture:

Notice particularly the low, dark bass octaves, the lamenting diminished fourth, B flat down to F sharp. The apparent change of motif in the middle at the words: "Du stolzes Herz" ("thou proud heart") is in reality only a variant of the original motif replacing the tremolo by a triplet figure after the beat and retaining in the low bass octaves the descending fourth, D sharp to A sharp; now no longer a diminished fourth, however, and thereby effecting a more direct expression for the "proud heart" and for the will to happiness. Also purely musical, formalistic reasons make such a change of motif desirable here. This entire central section in B major with its changed rhythms serves the purpose of making the return of the original mood doubly and triply effective. Above this accompaniment the vocal melody rises and falls, bringing to powerful impressiveness all shades of emotional expression. Truly inspired harmonic effects are reserved especially for the closing phrases in the first and third stanzas: here the magnificent modulation from G minor to B minor, there the striking and surprising use of the chord: B flat, D, F sharp, A flat, between two G minor chords; in both cases the impression is further strengthened by the powerful climax in the melodic line, with its outburst of bitter pain on the highest held notes:

"Die Forelle" ("The Trout") has an accompaniment motif which is, so to speak, a silhouette of the wriggling and writhing little fish.

"Auf dem Wasser zu singen" ("Singing on the River") paints in the accompaniment the "Schimmer der spiegelnden Wellen" ("shining, reflecting waves") and the gliding of the boat.

accompaniment in modern music

In all these songs the part of the accompaniment is considerably enhanced and complicated in comparison with the simple song. Yet even here the vocal part still dominates melodically. The accompaniment acquires even greater importance and independence in the songs of modern composers such as Hugo Wolf, Richard Strauss, and their followers. Here the main musical content of the piece is often confided to the accompaniment and the vocal part adds a sort of explanation, interpretation, or reënforcement of the instrumental symphony. In such cases the song takes over from the opera scene not only declamatory recitation, but also the symphonic texture and elaboration of the accompaniment.

SONGS BY WOLF

Here follow a few examples from Wolf's songs set to Mörike's poems.

No. 5, "Der Tambour" ("The Drum-Major"). The piano plays spirited march music. The voice adds declamation in the manner of a counterpoint, occasionally merely doubling the march melody. This conception of the accompaniment as a picturesquely designed character piece does not interfere with the ingenious use of illustrative tone-painting, like the drum-roll, significant for the entire piece, the humorous illustration of the "lange Wurst" ("long sausage"), the sentimental, delicate sound of the moonlight episode, and the falling asleep of the romantic drum-major. In general it may be remarked that tone-painting may be helpful to artistic effect, if applied discreetly, as a secondary ornament, without disturbing the organic structure and the logical coherence of the piece. It must be remembered, however, that an accumulation of tone-painting easily breaks the piece asunder into disconnected little episodes and thus becomes more harmful than useful for artistic impressiveness.

"Auf einer Wanderung." The accompaniment is a piece of symphonic development of a light and graceful motif in the pace of the "Wanderer." The piano suggests the landscape background, not so much, however, in the sense of the actually visible contour as in the coloring, in its reflection of sentiment. The vocal part is purely declamatory, interrupted by shorter or longer pauses.

The strange feature of pieces of this type is that their entire structure is determined by the text and based upon it, yet for the listener the entire piece does not produce the impression of music set to a given text. Rather the words as sung appear as an explanation, a justification, a convincing plea for all the peculiarities and changes of the symphonic structure. The closed melodic line always appears as the primary object. If this melodic line is given to the voice, as in the plain songs, the instrumental part appears as something secondary, subordinate, only intended for assisting and underlining the vocal line in the display of its beauty. If, however, the main musical line is given to the instrumental part, then the ear refers all musical activity to the instrumental part as leading factor, and comprehends the vocal part, if not as an "accompaniment" in the ordinary sense, then nevertheless as an explanation, a commentary of the music, as stated above.

This commentary is, however, an indispensable factor of the artistic impression. Though one might comprehend a song melody even without any accompaniment at all, a piece like Wolf's "Auf einer Wanderung" has no coherence whatever without any accompaniment, and without the vocal part it could not be properly understood. In spite of the close coherence from measure to measure, certain modulations occur, certain climaxes and irregular periodic constructions, sudden harmonic progressions, new rhythms which have not been sufficiently prepared in order to appear as logically convincing by themselves. They are, however, justified by the text and thus made intelligible. A distinction is therefore to be made between a piece of absolute symphonic music explaining itself by its progression from measure to measure, and between a piece of symphonic music in connection with a sung text, however similar both cases may appear at the first glance. In the song the text is the cause of the musical form, and the form therefore becomes fully intelligible only through the text. This thesis holds good also in the case of some instrumental works composed to a secret, undivulged text. A great part of Bach's chorale preludes for organ can be fully understood only when the text of the various chorale stanzas is also taken into consideration and compared with the music.

WAGNER'S SYMPHONIC ACCOMPANIMENT

In the above-mentioned lyric pieces of Schubert and Wolf, the accompaniment motif represents an extract of the concrete, visible, perceptible contents of the poem, arising directly from the poetry. Wagner has evolved a different type of symphonic development, originating not in lyric, but in dramatic aspects. The leading motifs are the Wagnerian formulas of accompaniment. These motifs are not adapted to the literal sense of the words in every single line of the text, but they are ready made, constant from beginning to the end, and are applied in all places accessible to them. They add a commentary to the text by pointing to hidden connections with what has already preceded, by reanimating the memory, by making clear a dimly rising sentiment of the soul, by effecting psychological connections. In their symphonic texture, often complex, they speak their own language, parallel to the vocal part, though sometimes contrary to it.

Here also one may sometimes be doubtful whether the symphonic orchestral part is meant to illustrate the words or whether the words interpret the sense of the musical contents. Both apparently irreconcilable cases may nevertheless happen simultaneously: in such places the vocal part and the orchestra are coördinated, each being musically complete and intelligible in itself. To be sure, the deeper dramatic meaning is first fully revealed by the mutual collaboration of both, in the totality of their ensemble.

To illustrate these observations, the famous monologue of Hans Sachs "Wahn, Wahn, überall Wahn" in the third act of Wagner's *Meistersinger* may be subjected to a detailed analysis.

The first glance at the entire composition shows the technical principle involved: just as in the development section of a sonata, the piece is cut up into a number of phrases, of which each is dominated by a different rhythmic motif. Within each phrase there is a natural, logical musical coherence, owing to the continuation of the same motif. The transition from one phrase to the next, and this succession itself, cannot be understood according to the principles of musical logic, but only with the help of the words in the vocal part. If the piece is played without the vocal part, it is, from a musical standpoint, cut up into phrases. Examining the text in its relation to the music does not, however, make it at all evident how this text is associated with just this music. The dotted motif:

has hardly in itself any reference to the "friedsam treuen Sitten" ("the peaceful, faithful customs") of "dear Nuremberg."

Imagine how a Verdi or a Meyerbeer would have composed this meditation. The result would have been an "accompagnato" recitative; the voice would have dominated, the orchestra would have contented itself with the customary recitative methods, single chords, rests, sustained chords; occasionally, where the text offered something tangible, either in sentiment or in picturesque expression, the composer would have taken advantage of the opportunity by fittingly displaying the orchestra for a little while.

The meaning and coherence of the Wagnerian music becomes manifest, however, only after one has grasped the various motifs in the significance which they have gained during the preceding acts. The recollection of something past, the act of reflection, is essential here. Something similar certainly also happens in the complicated development sections of a symphonic movement. In the latter case it suffices to remember and to recognize the motifs. Beyond that, however, Wagner demands that the listener should recollect not only the meaning of each motif, but also the complex within which it was heard for the first time. All this means a considerably increased reflective activity. It is facilitated on the other hand by the fact that the eye (through the scenic picture) and the ear, in collaboration, can retain impressions easier than the ear alone.

The monologue is divided into nine sections. A brief analysis of the first three sections will suffice to indicate Wagner's technical method.

(I) "Wahn, Wahn, überall Wahn!" (commencing in 4/4 time, measures 1–25).

(The motif recognized from the prelude to Act III, and its continuation):

(II) "S'ist halt der alte Wahn" (measures 26–38). Two measures of reminiscence from the *Meistersinger* theme:

(See measure 4 of the prelude to Act I.) Followed by:

(Recognized from the monologue: "Wie duftet doch der Flieder," in Act II.) In the last measure the trumpet enters with:

Trumpet

(III) "Wie friedsam treuer Sitten" (measures 38–63). A combination of the two motifs:

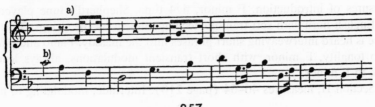

257

Motif (*a*) is always associated with "Nuremberg." Motif (*b*) is a variant of the "Meistersinger" motif, heard in the prelude to Act I.

The admirable treatment of the "Hirtenweise," ("shepherd's tune"), in Act III of *Tristan und Isolde* represents a somewhat different case. Here the Hirtenweise is heard at the beginning of the act in so marked and impressive a manner, in such a broad, melodious flow, that it remains firmly fixed in every musical ear. In the middle of the act (H. von Bülow's piano score, pages 208–219), it is taken up again in a magnificent symphonic treatment. This time the listener is hardly burdened with much reflective labor, because the text makes direct mention of it, and does not demand more or less precise recollection of former motifs. "Muss ich dich so verstehn, du alte Weise?" ("Must I thus understand you, old tune?") Tristan asks, and this question gives the most natural impetus to the wonderful piece of melancholy symphonic elaboration with the "Hirtenweise" as its kernel.

The text interprets all its changes of emotional mood, and at the same time the music reverberates to the words of the text and intensifies their meaning. Several times other motifs plunge significantly but unobtrusively into the melodious flow of the shepherd's tune, hardly interrupting its melodic continuity; sometimes later in the piece episodes based on earlier motifs alternate in dialogue with parts of the shepherd's tune, and in some places the relation is reversed: the shepherd's tune becomes a soft subordinate voice, a pale undertone in a melodic stream, whose flow in the main is caused by other motifs.

A special essay would be required to demonstrate the details of this method of accompaniment, as original and ingenious as it is impressive and touching. A few aphoristic indications must suffice here. All through the first part of the piece a broadly extended, coherent, in itself intelligible melodic line dominates. To the listener this broad melody is of primary consideration; what the voice recites into this melody and what other motifs add is of secondary importance for him, a mere ornamental feature that might, if necessary, even be omitted or overlooked without damage to the clearness of the melodic line. This explains the powerful emotional impression of this piece. Everything that might induce the listener to a reflective activity could be more or less relegated to the background, without much harm to the total effect. Here follows the analysis of the piece.

Section I (piano score by von Bülow, page 208, measures 9–45). Eight measures of introduction, F minor, 4/4 time. Shepherd's tune played by the English horn with soft tremolo accompaniment by the strings. Tristan's voice is heard interweaving short phrases into the melody. Piano and pianissimo tonality, F minor, with short transient modulations, always leading back to F minor.

Section II, measures 46–64 (page 210). Interlude, modulating to more distant keys; the tune abridged, distributed among bass-clarinet, oboe, clarinet, finally return to F minor.

Section III, measures 65–74 (page 211). Reëntrance of the English horn tune in F minor.

Section IV, measures 74–90 (page 211). Beginning of the elaborations and of a series of climaxes. Three entries of the commencement phrase of four bars, rising to a higher climax every time, starting on high F, G, and D flat, with aggressive, exciting, fiery violin figures, pushing on vehemently from one entry to the next. A significant motif from the second act is here combined with the shepherd's tune:

After the culmination, at the words "Vor Sehnsucht nicht zu sterben" a quick diminuendo to the next section.

Section V, measures 90–102 (page 212). Third entry of the English horn on the stage with the shepherd's tune, again in F minor. Basic dynamic color is piano.

Section VI, measures 102–118 (page 212). Combination of the shepherd's tune with the motif quoted in Section IV and a motif from Act I:

Section VII, measures 118–135 (page 213). Complicated interlude, former motifs in dense texture. The shepherd's tune introduces the section, but thereafter is no longer heard.

Section VIII, measures 135–164 (page 213). Growing agitation leading to a turbulent climax. Beginning and close of the section flanked by the shepherd's tune, the middle filled out by a wild tumult of tempestuous sound.

Section IX, measures 164–171 (page 214). Brief interlude, using former motifs.

Section X, measures 171–187 (page 214). The same motif from the shepherd's tune which introduced Section I, appearing now as a sort of basso ostinato, brings this grandiose fantasy on the shepherd's tune to its close. In the upper voices the shepherd's motif is coupled with the "Sehnsucht" motif (motif of longing) from the beginning of the prelude to Act I. The vocal part, in a frenzy of groaning and wailing, culminates in the desperate outcry:

Ich   selbst,   ich   hab   ihn   ge - braut!

Here the fantasy on the shepherd's tune is ended, but not Tristan's scene, which now takes on the character of a coda (measures 187–210, page 216), and shows an entirely new relationship between voice and orchestra. This coda, constructed on the closing measure of the phrase "Ich selbst, ich hab ihn gebraut," is developed with sweeping vehemence. With ever-growing force, orchestra and voice vie in snatching this phrase away from each other. Solo and accompaniment are here welded into a duet, a dialogue of most impetuous passion. With a final appearance of the shepherd's tune above the aforementioned motif (measure 210), the great monologue of Tristan is brought to a most impressive close. The same motif, by the way, dominates the following solo of Kurwenal as well as the orchestral accompaniment.

The analysis of the eleven sections of the monologue shows the clearness and roundness of the symphonic structure: introduction, theme, interlude, theme abbreviated, development section, return to the theme, new development, culmination, interlude, closing section corresponding to the introduction, and coda. These would be the formal terms applicable to the single parts of the structure, which in its totality resembles a rondo form.

accompaniment in the older concertizing style

The older music of the seventeenth and eighteenth centuries makes use of a peculiar kind of combination of solo and instrumental accompaniment by distributing the entire music among a number of "voices" or "parts" in the contrapuntal sense. The vocal solo is one of these parts, but enjoys no greater prominence than the rest, all being of equal importance. This so-called "concertizing" style finds its classic perfection in the works of Heinrich Schütz, Handel, and J. S. Bach, but worthy examples of this type are also contained in the music of smaller masters, like Hammerschmidt, Krieger, and Ahle. In order to illustrate this technique, a piece from Hammer-schmidt's "Musikalische Andachten" of 1642 follows:

BACH'S METHOD OF ACCOMPANIMENT IN THE CANTATAS

The favorite style of writing in the arias of the Bach cantatas and Passion music is the dialogue, the duet of the vocal solo and an "obligato" solo instrument, on a background formed by the other instruments with the thorough bass. Vocal solo and the instrumental obligato are here equivalent to each other and quite similar in content. Bach generally aims at a "picturesque" accompaniment. He translates some symbol or pictorial allusion of the text into a tone symbol, and bases the entire piece on such motifs, painting a concise essence of the dominating pictorial idea at each recurrence of the motif. In Albert Schweitzer's famous book on Bach, this pictorial technique is discussed in detail. It has a certain relationship to Schubert's method, described above. To this "picturesque" style of accompaniment, Schweitzer opposes the "poetic" method of Beethoven and Wagner. The contralto aria from Cantata No. 45: "Es ist dir gesagt, Mensch," may serve to illustrate this style of duet between a solo voice and a solo instrument, in this particular case, a flute. This dialogue is continued throughout the piece, with a thorough bass as substructure. The first few measures will suffice to indicate the method:

Wer Gott be-kennt aus wah-rem Her-zensgrund,

A few other examples, picked at random from hundreds, may illustrate the "picturesque" accompaniment. In the Cantata No. 64: "Sehet, welch eine Liebe," the recitative: "Geh Welt, behalte nur das deine, ich will und mag nichts von dir haben" ("Go world, keep your own, I will have nothing of you") is accompanied by a rapid rising scale in the bass:

This motif suggests a gesture of contempt, as if turning an unwelcome visitor out of doors: "Go hence," with the outstretched arm and pointed finger, as the tone-painting bass figure shows. Almost every pause in the recitative is filled with this gesture.

The first aria in Cantata No. 28: "Gottlob, nun geht das Jahr zu Ende" ("Thanks to God, the year is finished") is written in a brisk march rhythm, with trumpets and kettledrums clearly audible. The text explains Bach's intention: "Das neue rücket schon heran" ("the New Year is approaching"). This approach of the New Year is illustrated by Bach with the following motif, continued throughout the piece:

It is heard more than a hundred times, in many different combinations and with changing harmonies, until finally the hearer is fascinated by the picture of crowds of people marching in triumphant entrance.

In the Funeral Cantata, No. 198, Bach makes us hear a whole concerto of big and small bells in the recitative: "der Glocken lebendes Getön soll unsrer trüben Seele Schrecken durch ihr geschwungenes Erze wecken" ("The lively clangor of the brazen bells shall awaken the horror of our sad souls").

In the Christmas Oratorio the recitative No. 49, built on this motif:

must be interpreted as a tone-painting of awesome trembling, as the text explains: "Warum wollt ihr erschrecken, kann meines Jesu Gegenwart euch solche Furcht erwecken?" ("Why are you frightened, can the presence of my Jesus cause such fear?")

Once more the reader may be referred here to the valuable chapter in Schweitzer's book dealing in detail with the motifs, melodies, and accompaniments of the Saint Matthew's Passion music in their picturesque expressiveness.

accompaniment as connecting link or framework

A formula of accompaniment continued for some time often helps in tying together phrases with different melodic content, thus having the effect of a framework holding a number of objects together. This is illustrated by the first movement of Beethoven's F minor sonata, Op. 2, No. 1; almost the entire development section keeps its various motifs together in the successive phrases by the accompaniment motif in eighth notes, common to all the phrases. The scherzo of Beethoven's Ninth symphony keeps its various themes together by the rhythmical accompaniment formula

In the scherzo of the "Pastoral" symphony the rhythm

fulfills a similar task, as does the rhythm

in the first movement of the Seventh symphony, and the rhythm

in the allegretto of the same symphony.

accompaniment in dance music

The whole of dance music belongs more or less to this class. A Strauss waltz, for instance, consisting of introduction, five waltzes, and finale, has a wealth of different melodies, directly succeeding each other without any attempt at symphonic transitions, but kept together from beginning to end by the waltz rhythm of the accompaniment, common to all the sections. Similarly, the various themes of a Chopin polonaise are joined together by the common rhythm of accompaniment:

The barcaroles, cradle songs, spinning songs, and other pieces built on characteristic rhythms also find their proper classification here. In distinction to the modern dances, the characteristic feature of the older dances lies less in the rhythm of the accompaniment than in the rhythm of the melodies. They follow a certain rhythmical pattern, leaving, however, much more freedom to the accompaniment than the modern dances, and thus demand a reverse treatment. An inspection of the Sicilianos (with their melody in 6/8, 9/8, or 12/8 time on the rhythm

or of the pavanes, sarabandes, gavottes will show this characteristic difference between older and modern dance types.

evenly continued rhythms in ostinato-like pieces

Pieces based on ostinato rhythms, like basso ostinato, chaconne, passacaglia, long organ points, musettes, moto perpetuo, have evenly continued rhythms generally in the accompaniment, much more rarely in the melody. The older pieces of this type, as well as the Bach pieces, are usually written as variations on a rather constantly retained figure of accompaniment. The well known moto perpetuo from Weber's C major piano sonata, however,

265

frequently changes the rhythms of the accompaniment, but retains rather strictly the rhythm of the running figures in the melody. Would it not be possible to write a set of variations on a melody with a fixed uniform rhythm, and permitting the variations to retain this rhythm, but each time constructing a new melody on the recurrent rhythm? This proceeding, just the reversal of the passagalia idea, has as yet been scarcely attempted, let alone successfully coped with. Its formula would be: Equal rhythms in the melody, different accompaniments, different melodic progressions.

ostinato rhythms in Oriental and Russian music

The ostinato rhythms are a peculiarity of Oriental, also of East European, Slavic music. Russian music is full of them, sometimes in the melody, at other times in the accompaniment. The strictly applied ostinato shows a variety of graduations up to constructions of considerable freedom, avoiding the monotony of ostinato and yet retaining the peculiar charm of a constant rhythm heard for a considerable time. A characteristic and typical example is the scherzo from Borodine's Second string quartet in D major. The piece contains no less than exactly three hundred measures, which (with the exception of thirty-two measures of transition and cadence, distributed throughout the piece), content themselves with a single figure of accompaniment, productive of a certain ostinato effect, yet full of charming variations in harmony and melody. The upper, the middle part and the bass all participate in these variations, and occasionally the accompaniment figure takes over the leading melody for a few moments. The main variants of this figure follow here:

These four variants are not only used alternately, but also combined with each other in rhythmical polyphony, and interwoven into still more complicated patterns of accompaniment, like tapestry or wall paper designs. Thus, for instance, the principal melody of the viola at the beginning is accompanied by *a* and *d* combined in both violins. Further on, both violins play the formula *b* together; similarly the first violin and violoncello, in thirds; similarly first violin and viola, second violin and violoncello. Also *a* and *c* are combined in various groupings of the instruments, and likewise *b* and *c*. Sometimes a "hemiole" effect is brought about by the following rhythmical complication:

two measures in 3/4 time contracted into one measure of 3/2 time. In this connection, Debussy's string quartet may also be mentioned, with its fascinating scherzo, capriciously elaborating ostinato motifs.

accompaniment in rhythmical polyphony

Accompaniments based on rhythmical polyphony occur frequently in exotic music of all oriental nations, the Chinese, Japanese, Indians, Arabs, Turks, also the African negroes. From those countries they have been imported into European music, where they sometimes are employed for exotic, strange, and grotesque effects. The percussion instruments are naturally preferred for such purposes. Examples are found in the last two movements of Berlioz' "Symphonie Fantastique" and in the Lacrymosa of his Requiem. With still more fascinating effect, Busoni utilizes these complex rhythms of the accompaniment in his Turandot suite. The first movement is built on the ostinato kettledrum rhythm

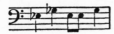

especially in the Turandot march (No. 4): timpani, triangle, tambourine, little drum, bass drum, cymbals, and tamtam are combined into an intricate rhythmical texture, filling out the middle part of the piece as an ostinato figure:

Similar effects also occur in the sixth movement: "Dance and Song," and in the eighth movement: "In modo di marcia funebre e finale alla Turca."

Finally, attention may be called to a famous place in Berlioz' "Roman Carneval" overture, that strikingly effective accompaniment in the introduction in which drums, triangle, timpani are joined in rhythmical polyphony to the woodwind and brass instruments. The percussion instruments have the rhythmical pattern shown on the next page.

This figure persists through eight measures. Also the last three measures of the introduction, before the allegro vivace, obtain their fascinating effect from the whirling, rattling, bell-like sound of the drums, triangle, kettledrums, to the accompaniment of the whistling, howling scale runs of the woodwind instruments:

The dynamic gradations should be particularly noted, the quick crescendi and diminuendi, sforzati, with their stimulating effect.

Javanese music

Polyrhythmic accompaniment finds a most remarkable application in the so-called *gamelan* of Javanese music. A great many different percussion instruments, wooden rods, metal, gongs, bells, plates, drums, cymbals, accompany the principal melody. The theme (based on the pentatonic scale), is at first played in unison or octaves by various instruments. A beat on the gong marks the close. Next follows a complicated elaboration. The melody is heard in the middle parts, accompanied by figurations of the higher instruments, the bass coming in occasionally with a few tones. Gongs, bells, and cymbals mark the close of the various sections. ". . . towards the middle section or on the first three quarters of the section, sounds are struck on the kenong (a kind of bell). Every one of these subdivisions is divided into still smaller phrases by the ketuk (also a bell), here however.

the beat is heard not at the end of the phrase, but in its middle." [1] In most cases these percussion instruments are tuned to a certain pitch. Here follows a short example of gamelan, taken over from an extended score by J. P. Land, who has been the first to call attention to this strange Asiatic music.

Xylophone	
Bronze chimes	
Metallophone	
Set of gongs I and II	
Set of gongs III	
Drums	

[1] See J. P. Land: "Über die Tonkunst der Javanen" in *Vierteljahrschrift für Musikwissenschaft*, V (1889), 193. See also: Bandara, "Das javanische Orchester" in the periodical *Die Musik* (February 1926).

CHAPTER XIII

the forms of unison music

European music is dependent on harmony to such an extent that unison music is allotted only a rather small though curious and interesting part, serving occasionally as a contrast to chordal accompaniment. Rarely only will one find unison, or one-part melody in the strict sense of the term, because even our plainest folk songs have a latent harmonic feeling.

We are not concerned here with unaccompanied music which becomes one-part music by the accidental lack of accompanying instruments, as, for instance, a tune that one hums on a leisurely promenade in the country. Opposed to such melodies, with their really implied harmony, are others which from the very beginning are truly *unisono* in character. All these truly one-part melodic structures have with few exceptions one trait in common: they are all derived from declamation, from the accent of word and speech. They are more of a declamatory nature than is the nature of song or dance. Hence their great rhythmical freedom, their aversion to symmetry, be it regular meter or periodic structure. In place of these supports of musical coherence, the chanted words, the declamatory melody had originally offered sufficient compensation. And even when the texts were later forgotten or neglected, these melodic types still retained the characteristic signature of their origin: in their unconventional irregularity they offer a welcome counterbalance to the excessive regularity of song and dance music.

unison in oriental music

Since oriental, exotic music is with rare exceptions almost exclusively one-part music, it receives its formal character from this peculiarity. Its lack of harmony allows the listener's attention to be less distracted from the melodic and rhythmical features than is the case in European music, with its weighty harmonic apparatus. Thus one finds in Arabic, Indian, Chinese, and Japanese music a subtlety of rhythm far surpassing anything ever attempted in occidental music. Complicated measures hard to grasp, frequent change of time, rhythmic vitality (with an overflow of activity), frequent use of quarter or third tones and other intervals unknown to us; these are the refinements through which oriental music makes up for its total absence of harmony. Reading the evolution of musical structure, from the most primitive to the most highly cultured peoples, one can follow simultaneously the history of the unison forms of music.

constructive principles common to all melodies

In this naturally very superficial comparison of melodic types of many different nations and epochs, it becomes manifest that certain constructive principles are common to all types and must even be the necessary basis of all melodic construction. Such principles are, for instance, repetition of motifs, correspondence, inversion, amplification, variation, culmination, contrast, symmetry, ornamentation by figuration, augmentation, diminution, and so on. This list enumerates rather exhaustively the tools of the melodist, but does not, however, come near touching the variety of structures. It is evident that primitive and exotic music applies these terms, familiar to our music as well, in a sense quite foreign to us, because our habit of harmonic associations prevents us from recognizing many other constructive possibilities. But if we perceive the logic and the aesthetic charm of such strange melodic and rhythmic unison constructions, our own music might be fructified by such knowledge.

music of the Wedda

The most primitive music known, even imaginable, is practiced by the aborigines of Ceylon, the Wedda. Their songs never pass beyond three tones; in the majority of cases, they are even content with two tones.[1] Seconds and a minor third comprise their entire tonal material. Gregorian

[1] See Max Wertheimer, "Die Musik der Wedda" in *Sammelband*, XI, p. 300, of the International Society of Music.

chant also has pieces containing only one to three tones, in the quick recitation of psalmody with cadence, a form which occurs also in the more recent operatic secco recitative. Here, however, the limitation of the rich tonal resources is intentional, whereas the Wedda possess no more than their three tones. It is of especial interest to observe that even in this most primitive state of music, the motif already shows its constructive power. This archetype of music consists, according to Wertheimer's observations, of "a little motif (equivalent to two quarter notes) heard twice in succession, followed by one or two quarter notes, reaching the lowest tone (preparation of the close), and the close, formed either by the second tone, or the lowest, or an upward progression from the first to the second tone." The cadence downward does not occur in this music. Here follows an example, showing a certain similarity with our periodic construction:

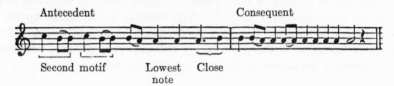

Similarly built, but not in period form is the following short phrase:

South Sea tribes and American Indians

The following example illustrates a melodic type frequent in the music of many primitive tribes, of the South Sea natives, the Indians, and so on. A high note at the start is held out with full force, or repeated plainly or in tremolo. From this loud tone the melody is evolved downwards in diminuendo. A remarkably beautiful example from the Australian west coast follows here: [2]

[2] Taken over from Karl Stumpf, *Die Anfänge der Musik* (Leipzig, 1911), p. 122. My disposition of the bar lines differs from Stumpf's version in order to make the periodic construction more evident.

272

Measures 4 and 5 are to be regarded as a somewhat simplified repetition in the lower octave of measures 1 and 2. The construction shows 2 × 3 measures, a sort of periodic effect in the third and sixth measure. These measures, if one may call them so, are of unequal length.

OSTINATO RHYTHMS IN THE MUSIC OF THE INDIANS

Almost all primitive people delight in ostinato rhythms. The following example (from Stumpf) shows how even the Patagonian Indians know how to interrupt the monotony of the strict ostinato by variation:

These Indians sometimes build something like a strophic tune. The melody returns with slight variations in every stanza, but amplified each time by insertions; sometimes these insertions show a certain arithmetical progression, 3/8 for instance being added every time beyond the extension of the preceding stanza.

SONGS OF THE INDIANS

The songs of the North American Indians show quite advanced thematic and constructive skill. Stumpf (pages 146–148 of his book), publishes a very long piece, in eight sections. The structure is as follows: Introduction: *a, b, c, b₁, d, b₂, c, b₃*. The first section *a* is heard only once, section *b* appears four times in interesting variations and amplifications; a combination of rondo and variation. As intermezzo in this rondo form, *c*, appears twice, *d* only once. The culminating points of the melody are sharply marked, every time after the close of *b*.

Here follows the harvest song of the Iroquois Indians:[3]

[3] From Julien Tiersot, "La Musique chez les peuples indigènes de l'Amerique du Nord," *Sammelband*, XI, of the International Society of Music, p. 159.

The entire piece consists merely of the triad G B D, arranged in interesting rhythms, with a kind of refrain, indicated by motif *a*. Sections II and III are nearly equal; one should observe the descending tendency throughout the piece. Section I had D as principal tone, II and III especially mark B, IV accentuates G. Simultaneously with the descent the groups become shorter: 9/4, 7/4, 7/4, 4/4.

EAST INDIAN MUSIC

The following East Indian melody [4] shows a curious mixture of repetition and variation by amplification. In order to show this feature clearly, the various sections (which are of unequal length, 4/4, 5/4, 7/4) are thus placed below each other so as to make the correspondences and amplifications immediately apparent. The five sections always commence with the same phrase, which, however, is differently continued every time. Thus these measures correspond with each other, as shown below:

1, 4, 8, 15;
2, 6, 10, 13;
3, 7, 11, 14;
5, 9, 12.

Part *a* has 3 measures, *b*, 4, *c*, 4½ measures (slightly prolonged), *d*, 3, *e*, 1 measure. Also the melodic line is lengthened towards the middle of the piece, decreasing towards the close. *b* is a variation of *a*, *c* a still more elaborate variant of *b*; next follows a picturesque decrescendo to the close. The single phrases of the melody in their mutual relations show the following interesting curve:

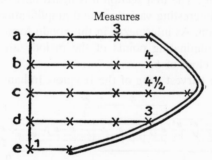

Our normal 8– or 16–bar period would represent a square or a rectangle. Here it becomes manifest that a firm construction may well be reconciled with fanciful asymmetry, a combination hardly known to European music, thanks to the tyranny exercised over it by measures and bar lines.

[4] From Abraham's and von Hornbostel's study on Indian music, in *Sammelband*, V, International Society of Music, p. 360. The bar divisions I have interpreted differently.

The following South Indian melody makes use of repetition and inversion.[5]
The repetitions of the motifs are indicated by square braces, the inversions
by zigzag lines. An effect of gliding, of soft melodiousness is the consequence.

The melody is based on two pentatonic scales, in the first half: C, E flat,
F, G, A flat; in the second half: E flat, F, G, B flat, C, or E, F, G, B, C.
The note D is entirely omitted; in the first part B flat is lacking (except for
its appearance as an auxiliary note before the double bar), in the second
part, A flat.

[5] From the collection of Albert Friedenthal.

TUNISIAN DANCE

The following Tunisian dance tune [6] has purposeful construction in spite of the complete asymmetry of its single sections. It represents a kind of free variation on a flexible theme, beginning each time with an ascending figure, rising to a climax, and then descending again. The ascent always starts on G: G, C, D, C, F sharp, G; or G, B flat, C sharp, E, or G, B flat, C sharp, E, F, D, C, G. The climax enters sometimes on the sixth, E, sometimes on the seventh, F sharp, or on the octave, G. The extension of the single sections differs considerably. The initial phrase, identical or similar every time, is followed by a different continuation in each section. The scale is: G, A. B, C, C sharp, D, E, F, F sharp, G—a mixed scale, partly diatonic, partly

[6] From E. von Hornbostel, "Phonographierte tunesische Melodien," in *Sammelband* VIII, International Society of Music, p. 14.

chromatic. The second part of this tune, not quoted here, does not adhere to the same plan of construction as the first one.

JEWISH SYNAGOGUE MELODY

The Jewish synagogue melody discussed below is similar in construction, though less complicated and less extended. Variation here consists in melodic amplification or contraction. The cadences of the single sections correspond very perceptibly to each other through the but slightly varied progression C, B flat, A, G.

The following Jewish synagogue melody,[7] without doubt very old and of oriental origin, as shown by its scale (on which, by the way, many synagogue chants are based: C, D flat, E, F, G, A flat, B flat, C), shows as its constructive principle the impressive "call" in the rising fourth or fifth, followed by descending tones. Every one of the four sections shows these features. The main climax enters in the third section, at the repetition of the confession: "Our father, our Lord, we have sinned before thee."

ARABIC MELODY

The following Arabic melody [8] is perhaps most easily explained as a stylized ascent and descent from tonic to dominant and the reverse, brought into a refined artistic form. Everyone of these five tones is playfully encompassed by the neighboring tones; the close C, G, G, C once more recapitulates in concise form the chief motivating idea. This piece is only the first number of a so-called *bashrav,* according to Idelsohn the largest form of oriental music, consisting of four to six pieces. In the present bashrav No. 3 has great similarity to No. 1, but commences with F instead of C, and rises from F to D, descending again to F and finally—in the manner of the plagal church modes—going down a fourth beyond the tonic F to C. All five sections have as a common motif (indicated below by a square

[7] See Joseph Singer, *Die Tonarten des traditionellen Synagogengesangs* (Vienna, 1886). A. Friedmann, *Der synagogale Gesang* (Berlin, 1908).

[8] See Idelsohn, "Die Maqamen der arabischen Musik," *Sammelband,* XV, of International Society of Music, p. 19.

brace), the progression of three successive tones, ascending or descending; thus a thematic elaboration of the same idea is evident throughout the melody.

The unison forms find a peculiar delight in rich, even extravagant, fantastically ornate ornamentation through figuration and coloratura. The desire to display highly developed virtuosity in unison music naturally leads to flowery ornamentation, since the lack of harmony and polyphony precludes almost every other possibility for virtuosity. All oriental music makes most abundant and passionate use of these ornaments, which are also well known to Gregorian chant.[9] A Tunisian piece (after Hornbostel) may serve to illustrate this peculiarity. It is based on the scale: G, A flat, B flat, C, D, E flat, F sharp, G. One must remember, however, that these intervals correspond only approximately to the actual sound, as the European system of notation has no means of imitating these oriental intervals correctly. The two sections *a* and *b* may be considered as theme and variation: *b* glides around the principal tones with arabesques, thus extending the basic melody considerably. Both parts have a common melodic nucleus, represented by the progression:

a scale descending from the octave A to the tonic. In the florid versions *a* and *b,* this diatonic scale is frequently deflected, pursuing its main direction in a roundabout manner. The essential tones supporting the melody are

<hr />

[9] Kurt Sachs has investigated this oriental ornamentalism in an interesting essay: "Kunstgeschichtliche Wege zur Musikwissenschaft," in *Archiv für Musikwissenschaft* (April 1919). He derives oriental music from the oriental industrial arts. A fine set of records: "Music of the Orient," compiled and explained by Prof. E. M. von Hornbostel, has been published by the Carl Lindström Company, Berlin. These twenty-four records deal with the music of Japan, China, Java, Bali, Siam, India, Persia, Egypt, Tunis.

marked *; they allow the florid passages to stand out as if set in parentheses. The effect is strangely wailing, pathetic, fantastic.

In melodic construction all oriental music makes use of a number of typical recurrent formulas, as in the Indian ragas, the Arabic maqams. Gregorian chant exhibits such formulas, too, characteristic of every one of the various church modes—formulas by which each one may be identified. It seems that every scale has the tendency to form such formulas; the richer the scale, the more varied its formulas. One might point out such formulas in the primitive two- and three-note system of the Wedda, in the Greek tetrachords, in the pentatonic scale of the Asiatic nations, of the Indians, Eskimos, the Scotch, in the hexachord of Guido of Arezzo, in the European seven-tone scale, in the six-tone whole-tone Asiatic scale, in the Arabic quarter-tone scale, in the chromatic scale, in the so-called gypsy scale with its accumulation of augmented seconds, and so on.

After more detailed acquaintance with all these scales, one probably would be able to state a constructive law, somewhat as follows: Every type of melody is dependent upon the scale on which it is based, and can be properly understood only through this scale. In Armenian church music, for example, melodies are frequently found with E in the lower octave and E flat in the higher octave. This type of melodic structure, foreign to European music, is explained by the Armenian tetrachord scale, consisting of three interlocked tetrachords of the same construction (whole tone, whole tone, half tone):

C D E F G A B flat C D E flat

The pentatonic melodic structure would also have to be discussed under this heading.

We have already pointed out several times that every type of melody (its dependence upon a given scale) also influences the manner of the bass-leading in the accompaniment. To investigate in detail the mutual relations between scale, melodic ductus, and bass-leading would certainly be a project well worth the effort.

Among modern composers, Béla Bartók has more than anybody else exploited unusual scales and the strange harmonic effects derived from them. The reader interested in this matter may be referred to an essay of the author,[10] containing an analysis of several Bartók pieces. In the "Allegro barbaro" for piano he uses a scale compounded of C major and F sharp minor-major plus the same scale a fifth higher, G major and C sharp minor-major. This strange scale, so far without a name, is as follows:

F sharp, G sharp, A or A sharp, B   C, D, E, F, G

and

C sharp, D sharp, E or E sharp, F sharp,   G, A, B, C, D

Here is seen a nine-, sometimes even a ten-tone scale, instead of the seven-tone scale; moreover the last two tones are chromatic lowerings of the first two, F sharp and G sharp at the beginning, F natural and G natural at the close; C sharp and D sharp at the beginning, C natural and D natural at the close. This fantastic scale, akin to the Armenian scale and to certain Arabic maqams, explains the simultaneous sounding of C major and C sharp minor-major at the start of the allegro barbaro, and many other features hardly otherwise explainable.

At the very start of Bartók's Second violin sonata, mixed tonality is used, derived from Hungarian peasant music; a combination of two descending scales: A, G sharp, F sharp, E, D, C, B flat, A and C sharp, B natural, A, G natural, F natural, E. This construction explains why the chromatically altered tones answer the corresponding natural, unaltered tones in Bartók's violin melody.

forms of Gregorian chant

The forms of Gregorian chant can be touched upon here only very briefly.[11] The main species are:

[10] Hugo Leichtentritt: "On the Art of Béla Bartók," in *Modern Music* (March–April, 1929).

[11] Detailed information is found in the extensive literature on Gregorian chant, as for instance P. Johner, *Neue Schule des gregorianischen Choralgesangs* (Ratisbone, 1906);

(1) Syllabic or recitative chants, to which the lection, oration, versicle, praefatio, psalmody, Te Deum belong.

(2) Plain melodic chants: antiphons, vesper hymns.

(3) Richly ornamented melodic chants: most of the mass chants: introitus, graduale, alleluia, tractus, sequences and tropes, offertorium, communio.

A chief means of expression in Gregorian chant is the responsorial singing of two choirs, used in psalmody, wherein the same recitative declamation is repeated, the verses being sung by the two choirs in alternation. This declamation on one tone is enlivened by little melodic turns at the halfclose and the final cadence. These turns, also called modulations (corresponding to the modulating of the voice in recitation), are more or less complex according to the style and the purpose of the single pieces. Thus there exists a "tone of question," a "fall or cadence in the fifth," a "tone of recitation," a "tone of lecture," of passion (distributed among three singers and the choir of the clerics, the so-called *turba*), the "solemn" and the "ferial tone of oration," and so on.

PSALMODY

Psalmody is composed of intonation, recitation on the dominant, the medium, and the final cadence. Every one of the eight church modes may occur in the psalmody. An example follows:

Coe - li   e - nar-rant glo - riam Do - i:

Intonation   Recitation Middle   Final cadence
cadence

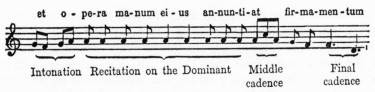

et   o - pe-ra ma-num ei - us   an-nun-ti-at   fir-ma-men-tum

Intonation Recitation on the Dominant   Middle   Final
cadence   cadence

RESPONSORIUM, OFFERTORIUM, COMMUNIO, INTROITUS

The psalmody as a so-called antiphonal chant must not be confounded with the responsorial chants—solo chants with responses from the choir,

---

P. Kienle, *Choralschule* (Freiburg i/B); "Choral und Kirchenlied," vol. I of P. Griesbacher's extensive work: *Kirchenmusikalische Stilistik und Formenlehre*. See also the numerous publications of the Benedictines of Solemnes. Gregorian chants in modern notation: Dr. F. X. Mathias, *Epitome ex editione Vaticana Gradualis Romani* (Ratisbone, 1909). See also Peter Wagner, *Einführung in die gregorianischen Melodien*, three volumes, Leipzig, the standard work on Gregorian chant. For more detailed literature see the article, "Gregorian Chant," in Apel's *Harvard Dictionary of Music*.

often in the manner of a refrain, alternately sung by the cantor and the congregation—for antiphony is the alternation of two choirs. The responsorial chants also include the graduale and the alleluia-jubilations, insertions between the various lectures from the psalms or the gospels. Offertorium, communio, introitus are accompanying music to the liturgical ceremonies, originally performed without words—rather decorative music. The offertorium was performed while the congregation brought sacrificial gifts to the altar, the communio during the holy sacrament, the introitus during the solemn procession of the pope and the clergy.

The praefatio in the solemn Mass signifies the expression of thanksgiving on the part of the congregation.

PERIODIC EFFECTS IN GREGORIAN CHANT

Gregorian chants sometimes make use of a kind of periodic effect, in a manner just the contrary of our practice. Whereas a periodic structure in modern music is characterized by the correspondence of the closing phrases, in Gregorian chant the correspondence is seen in the initial phrases. Here follows an example:[12]

Motif *a* terminates the phrase four times. These refrain sections of *a* enter, however, after irregular time intervals; here the four sections have an extension of 6/4, 5/4, 8/4, 11/4. The comparison of this Gregorian melody with the Indian theme from page 273 is quite interesting: both melodies depend for their impressiveness on the four repetitions of the end refrain, entering after unequally long verses.

THEMATIC ELABORATION IN GREGORIAN CHANT

Some of the more extensive Gregorian chants show a highly interesting thematic elaboration mixed with variation. Riemann proves that the thirty-two phrases of the Credo in the Easter Mass are without exception variations of three melodic motifs. Gregorian chant frequently employs a peculiar kind of melodic variation: almost all, or the greater part of its melodic sec-

[12] See *Zeitschrift* of the International Society of Music, VIII, 350.

tions are shown to be variations of the same tetrachord. Riemann [13] has proved this in detail by his analysis of the Gloria of the Missa in *festis simplicibus,* in which the greater part of the twenty-eight phrases are derived from the tetrachord E, F, G, A. The first six phrases are reprinted here in order to illustrate the technical method:

Glo-ri - á in ex-cel-sis De - o, Et in ter-ra pax ho - mi - ni - bus, Bo-nae vo - lun - ta - tis, Lau-da - mus te, Be - ne - di - ci - mus te, A - do - ra - mus

1 and 2 differ from each other mainly through different closes. 3 is an abbreviation of 1; similarly, 4 seems to be a more concentrated version of 3. 5 and 6 result from 3 and 1. Variation is achieved through the shortening and omission of tones: 3 to 6 leave out the initial tone, E. In our modern technique of composition, variation is usually effected by means of amplified ornamentation, whereas the shortening, compressing method of Gregorian chant has now become almost entirely forgotten.

ANALYSIS OF THE CREDO

As a most brilliant example of purposeful construction in the more extended Gregorian chants, the beginning of the Vatican version of the Credo is shown here (pages 284–285), according to the analysis of the Solesmes Benedictine Pater, Dom André Mocquereau.[14] The order of the single melodic phrases shows that the whole of this very extended Credo is composed of a few motifs only, always recurring either literally or in slight variants, in accordance with the text. Thus there is not a single melodic phrase in the entire piece which does not belong to one of these formulas. The interesting feature of the construction is that these formulas do not recur in a certain fixed order, like ostinato phrases or a set of variations, or *Strophenlieder,* but apparently without orderly rule. Yet they conform to a certain law, a structural plan derived from the psalmodic formula: intonation; recitation on the dominant; cadence; caesura with ascending transition to the second section of the melody, again followed by intonation, recita-

[13] See Riemann, *Folkloristische Tonalitaetsstudien,* I (Leipzig, 1916), 46.
[14] In volume X of the *Paléographie musicale.*

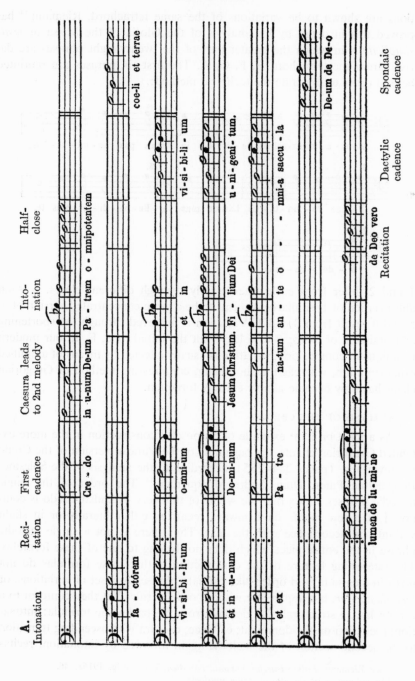

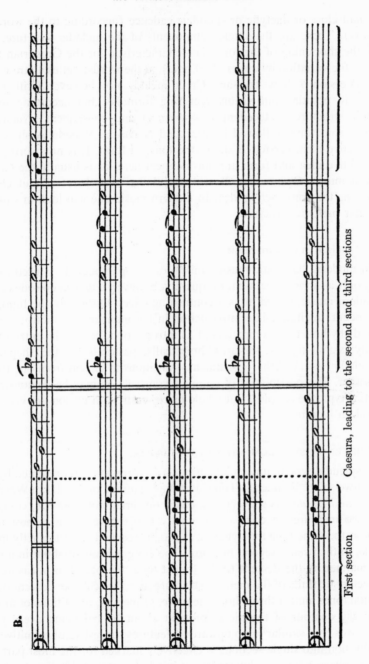

tion; half-close or dactylic or spondaic cadence (according to the words of the text). These are the single components of the melodic structure. Observe the shortening of the formula—characteristic for the Gregorian technique—the variation by omission of notes, at the words: "et ex Patre natum ante." Version B shows the same Credo melody, not, however, written with a view to pointing out visibly recurring formulas, but according to the melodic structure: antecedent (*Vordersatz*) and consequent (*Nachsatz*) phrases, sometimes followed by a second *Nachsatz*. Version A shows the constructive idea, version B shows the finished form. It is noteworthy that constructive idea and form are not identical here, as is usually the case in modern music. One may well understand the form here without clearly perceiving the constructive idea. In modern music one will look in vain for a similar melodic structure.

unison in modern music

In modern, harmonic music, unison or one-part melody is used extensively only as a rare exception. Frequently, however, a unison episode occurs in modern music, mixed in as a contrasting effect. Ordinarily the following cases occur: recitative-like introduction in the manner of a motto; sharply marked rhythms of accompaniment as introduction, before the entry of the melody; signal figures, fanfares, horn calls, pastorals for the shepherd's flute, chalumeau, or other instrument; transitions in unison from one theme to another. The possibilities of one-part construction may be demonstrated by a few typical examples. But whole pieces entirely in unison are very rare in modern literature.

"HIRTENWEISE" FROM TRISTAN UND ISOLDE

A splendid type of unison invention and expression is represented by the "Hirtenweise" ("Shepherd's Tune") at the beginning of Act III in Wagner's *Tristan und Isolde*. Its six sections, based on three motifs *a, b, c,* comprise forty-two measures, a compass of nearly two octaves. The highest tone, E flat, at the same time the dynamic climax, is reached almost exactly in the middle, in the twenty-second measure. The close is brought about in a masterly manner by the descent to the lowest tone, the bass F in measure 42. Characteristic traits of the melodic structure are: the scalelike descent of the essential tones almost throughout the piece, sequences, repetitions of motifs, the zigzag contour of the piece, brought about by balancing every jump downwards by a similar jump upwards—features suggestive of primitive art. The division into single sections is effectively marked for the most part just at those places where the longer values in whole notes and half notes enter.

A detailed analysis of the piece is given on page 287.

Section 1: 9 measures, 2 × 4 measures with one measure extension at the end. The motifs *a* and *b* serve as material for the construction. The melody is formed by a double series of descending tones (indicated by x above and below the notes).

Section 2: A repetition of *a*, 5 measures, the penultimate measure inserted as prolongation. The last measure is at the same time the beginning of the next section.

Section 3: Inversion of motif *a*, attached to it a new motif *c*, repeating the formula, G flat, G, A flat, G, in the manner of an ostinato voice.

Section 4: Motif *b*, in descending sequence, seven times.

287

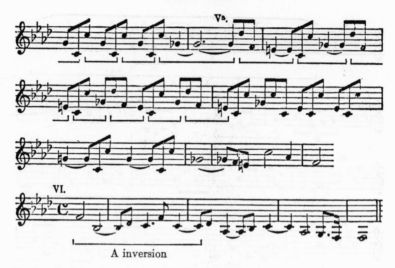

A inversion

Section 5: Motif *c* (a variant of *c*), six times in ostinato manner, followed by the next subsection.

Section 5a: A new variant of *c;* with the ostinato phrase G flat, F, E, parallel to, and almost an inversion of the second half of Section 3.

Section 6: Inversion of *a,* with added coda, descent to the close on the low F.

Although the piece is well built, brought to an effective climax, it is not, however, songlike in character, nor invented upon a latent harmony, but conceived as a pure melody of the unison type. For this reason the absence of a chordal accompaniment is not missed at all. For similar reasons the Gregorian chants likewise do not require an added harmonic accompaniment: they are, in their unison version, finished and self-sufficient works of art. Of course, chords may be added to such a unison melody. But the harmonic result will always be more complicated and pretentious than the natural, plain harmony of a real song tune. The age of Palestrina treated Gregorian chant contrapuntally, in complex polyphony. Wagner has also subjected the shepherd's tune to an elaborate, artistically ambitious orchestral treatment, at a later place in Act III, a passage which has already been analyzed in this book, on page 258ff.

THE VIRTUOSO PIECE IN UNISON STYLE

A special class is formed by those running, leaping tumbling virtuoso pieces in unison or in octaves, found for instance in Bach's solo sonatas and partitas for violin or violoncello. Such pieces, as also the beginning of Bach's great A minor prelude for organ, are not based on chords or fugal writing, but on quick, uniform passages. Johannes Brahms has transcribed one of these Bach solo pieces for the piano, in two versions for both hands. But it seems doubtful whether an even extremely skillful adaptation for several parts is really of any advantage to such a piece, whose main charm lies in the curve of the linear contour. One is somewhat hindered in the full enjoyment of these curves, if the attention is detracted by one or several new counterpoints in motion which likewise claim attention. The pieces of the moto perpetuo type generally retain the same rhythmical motif from beginning to end; there is no question at all of several contrasting themes; the whole piece is developed from the first motif, in manifold melodic circumflexions, frequently in sequences, in interchange of two and three measure groups, even and uneven groups, all these devices aiming at making the contour more capricious and more elegant. The presto finale from Bach's First solo sonata for violin may be examined here again. The grouping of the first measures is: $1 + 1 + 1 + 2 + 2 + 1\frac{1}{2} + 1 + 1 + \frac{1}{2} + 2 + 2 + 1 + 2$, and so on. In pieces of this type Bach generally prefers diatonic treatment, with modulation only to nearly related keys. He also prefers a two-part structure, though generally not according to the song form pattern *a-b*, or *a-b-a*, in the strict sense:

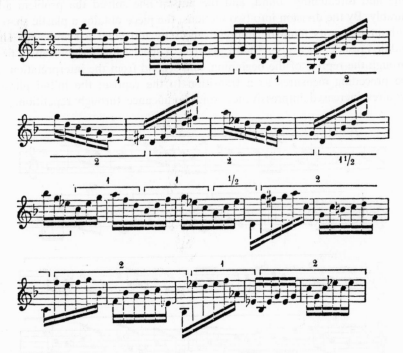

Some of these pieces offer instructive material for the technique of variation. They show how a theme with chordal accompaniment may be dis-

289

solved into a one-part melodic line. The "doubles" from Bach's Second sonata offer interesting material in this respect.

FINALE OF CHOPIN'S B FLAT MINOR SONATA

The strange finale of Chopin's B flat minor sonata [15] is quite similar in its constructive idea, though the use of chromatic sequences results in a very different coloring and emotional expression. The initial measures are grouped similarly as in the Bach example: $1 + 1 + \frac{1}{2} + \frac{1}{2} + \frac{1}{2} + \frac{1}{2} + 2 + 2 + \frac{1}{2} + \frac{1}{2}$, and so on. Of especial interest are the harmonic sequences, measures 9 to 12, owing to the minor ninths at the extreme points: B flat minor and A major, A flat major and G major, C flat minor and G flat major, C major and C flat major, B flat major and A major, in immediate succession. The piece has two main sections: (1) measures 1–39; (2) measures 39–77. The division is made exactly in the middle. The second section leads back to the beginning of the piece, but with a different continuation of the reprise. The constructive idea of the piece is two lines of different curvature starting parallel to each other. The intention of the piece was to produce a whispering, dark, mysterious, restless, running and threatening sound, and the unison line solved the problem admirably. By the division into two sections, the piece obtains a plastic shape, without losing its fantastic impressiveness by too great a symmetry. The middle episode, measures 30–40, receives a special inner significance, first through the reprise of the beginning, and second from the interpretation of the preceding measures as a transition to the reprise; the initial phrase acquires increased impressiveness and significance through repetition.

[15] A more detailed analysis of this fantastic piece is given in Hugo Leichtentritt's *Analyse der Chopin'schen Klavierkompositionen*, vol. II (Berlin, 1922).

UNISON IN INSTRUMENTAL RECITATIVE

Unison writing in recitative avoids moto perpetuo, constantly retained uniform rhythms, diatonic treatment, but rather prefers the contrary, that is, changing, free tempo, various rhythms, and chromatic melody.

In instrumental music recitative is a paraphrase of vocal recitative adapted to an instrument. Generally the unison line is interrupted by brief, interspersed chords at the cadences. Bach is fond of instrumental recitative; noteworthy examples are found in the "Chromatic" fantasy, at the beginning and further on. In the Adagio of Bach's organ transcription of Vivaldi's Third concerto, a broad "recitative" is introduced of the kind described as containing short inserted chords. This piece is of especial interest, because it points out the logic of the apparently illogical, free recitative. It is worth noting how finely the rising and descending lines are balanced. At the start a figure in eighth notes rises to the sixth, then lingers there for a while before diving down through two octaves. The second phrase starts again on a high note, descends more slowly, pauses on the tonic for some time, rises quickly in "terrace" form, sinks down again, ascends lightly, stops on a long held note, and afterwards rolls sweepingly downwards. This balancing of the melodic lines is full of grace, vivacity, and expression.

Beethoven also is fond of recitative. The most famous example is the recitative of the basses in the fourth movement of the Ninth symphony. Every phrase of the recitative is followed here not by the usual short chords of the secco recitative, but by a little symphonic intermezzo, representing each time a brief reminiscence of the themes of the preceding movements.

In Chopin's E minor concerto the middle section of the slow movement contains a recitative of fantastically curved melodic line, in unison or in octaves, interrupted by chords at the cadences. Also the F minor prelude with its storm-laden atmosphere employs a similar device, octaves interrupted by chords.

The dialogue of the piano solo with the orchestra answering in unison in the slow movement of Beethoven's G major concerto is also a very striking example. Here the effect of the unison is commanding, severe, inexorably tragic; filling out by chords would detract considerably from the simple grandeur, the impressive severity of its effect.

291

Gluck, who also treats unison in masterly style, often produces striking effects of a similar type. And later, Brahms, in the first movement of his
D minor concerto (at the beginning of the development section), introduces a dialogue of dramatic recitation between the piano in octaves and the
orchestra—just the reverse of Beethoven's G major concerto.

UNISON INTRODUCTIONS AND TRANSITIONS

Recitative-like, unison introductions and transitions occur sometimes,
as in the beginning of Chopin's C sharp minor etude, Op. 25, No. 7, or
before the reprise in Chopin's C sharp minor nocturne, Op. 27, No. 1.
Beethoven's sonata "quasi una fantasia," in D minor, Op. 31, No. 2, contains recitative-like episodes in the first movement. Those ornamental passages, trills, and runs issuing from a cadenza—already discussed under the
head of *Generalauftakt* (prolonged upbeat) [16]—are only apparently written
in one part. Generally in such places the chord on which the passage is based
continues to sound, sustained by the pedal, or at least it is supplemented
by the inner ear and by the imagination. Here we have to deal not with
real unison, but with a veiled, ornamented, dissolved harmony. Examples
are found frequently, as in the slow movement of Beethoven's Op. 31,
No. 1, with the ornamental return to the principal theme; in Chopin's B
minor sonata, first movement, in the transition to the second theme. In
Chopin's mazurka, Op. 56, No. 1, the unison has a different effect, replacing in very original manner a modulation from D major to B major, by
means of sequence-like figures:

QUICK UNISON OR OCTAVE PASSAGES

Sometimes quick, upward rushing unison or octave passages are used
with brilliant effect, in preparation for a triumphant outburst. A fine exam-

[16] See pp. 50ff.

ple is found in the brilliant, extremely effective unison of the violins in Weber's "Freischütz" overture. Wagner has well remembered this effect and has frequently employed similar unison passages in the introduction to the second C major theme of the *Meistersinger* prelude, measures 38–40, in this case with downward rushing passages. Also the last measures of the solo in the finale of Beethoven's E flat major piano concerto make a similar impression.

UNISON IN THE SENSE OF A TITLE

Unison is often used in order to state the theme impressively at the beginning of a larger composition, in the sense of a title or motto. Examples are frequent: Beethoven, in the beginning of the Fifth and Ninth symphonies, in the "Leonore" and "Coriolan" overtures, in the theme of the finale in the "Eroica" symphony; Schubert in the C major symphony; Wagner in his *Faust* overture, Brahms in his finale of the Second symphony.

The fugue themes which start in one part belong to this class.

SIGNAL FIGURES, FANFARES, HORN CALLS

Signal figures and fanfares are fond of employing unison because of their military origin. They have a martial effect through the associations they evoke, even when heard in the concert hall and theater. They must, however, in order to produce this effect, retain a certain realistic style and not be too polished in an artistic sense. Their character and their form are thus dependent on (1) one-voice leading or unison (reminiscent of the real trumpet signal, sounded by one trumpet only); (2) triad figuration in the melody, frequent leaps, dotted rhythms, repeated notes, all this a consequence of the technique of the horn and trumpet. Observe, for example, Beethoven, "Leonore" overture, and *Fidelio,* the trumpet signal. In Wagner, *Lohengrin,* Act III, close of the second scene:

Siegfried's horn call also belongs to this class, though the martial character is not expressed in its purest form, but combined with sentimental, idyllic, pastoral emotion (Act II, Scene 2). Its fifty-two measures are built in the three-part form, *a-b-a.* The first *a* is comprised of groups of 3 + 4 + 6 measures. The two-bar basic motif

is always extended by fermata, inserted measures, which are somewhat compensated for by the accelerando. Section *b* introduces an entirely new motif in minor, 4 × 10 measures. The second *a* resumes the principal C major motif, continuing it with a more urgent and triumphant expression, without fermata, in 16 + 10 measures; the last ten measures no longer maintain a strict unison, but are accompanied by the Fafner motif.

The horn calls form a class by themselves, different from the clear-cut, brilliant trumpet fanfares because of the darker, softer, more romantic sound of the horn. Hunting horn and post horn are the main source of associations. Modern literature contains a number of interesting examples of both kinds, either altogether in unison or with a very primitive accompaniment as background. Gustav Mahler, in the third movement of his Third symphony in D minor, evokes romantic, impressive associations by the quaintly old-fashioned, sentimental post horn solo. The very softly sustained chord of the string orchestra *con sordino* hardly weakens the unison impression. A similarly suggestive effect is obtained by the post horn solo in the orchestral prelude to Act III of Busoni's opera, *Die Brautwahl*. The beginning of the second movement of Mahler's Seventh symphony, the "Nachtmusik" (notturno) may be mentioned here. Sometimes a harmonic treatment of the fanfares and horn calls is also found, and it has its justification, just as does the polyphonic treatment of Gregorian chant. A closer examination of these cases, however, does not belong here. Nevertheless, a few examples of particular interest may be at least indicated: Berlioz, *Requiem,* the fanfare bands in the Dies Irae, the eight horns in Wagner's *Rheingold* prelude; the hunting horns at the beginning of Act II in *Tristan und Isolde*.

A few more examples of unison from famous works may be given here. Beethoven often applies unison for the expression of combined energy, of resolute activity, in the F minor quartet, Op. 95, first movement, measures 1, 2, 17–19, 37, 38, and frequently further on. The "Leonore" overture, No. 3, is especially instructive, showing a great many possibilities and admirable new effects of unison. At the very start a striking impression is made by the descent of a ninth from G down to low F sharp:

Here the unison not only has a picturesque, illustrative meaning: namely, the descent into the dungeon, but it also acquires something terrible, tragic, unrelenting in its expression, through the fortissimo entry, the quick diminuendo down to pianissimo. Moreover, it produces a striking harmonic effect by interpreting the low F sharp as belonging to the chord F sharp, A sharp, C sharp, so far distant from the main tonality, C major. The transition to the development section is achieved by a unison of the first violins, a brilliant specimen of unison effect and at the same time a striking means of contrast, bridging over a chasm, as it were, between two forte and fortissimo eruptions of the tutti:

Notice next the measures immediately preceding the trumpet signal. Here the unison has the effect of a furious onslaught:

The trumpet signal itself is only a thinly veiled unison and procures its realistic effect by virtue of this very unison (as has been pointed out above when signal figures and fanfares were discussed). The first great climax of the reprise likewise begins with a thinly veiled unison, preparing that famous, striking syncopated figure with its rhythmic displacement of the upper and lower parts. The result is a discord of harsh ninths, something like two big millstones grinding against each other:

The transition to the second theme in the reprise shows that "gliding" unison, already described when "transitions" were discussed:

Second theme

Finally mention must be made of that widely spanned unison beginning slowly in pianissimo and gathering power, like a gigantic, storm-lashed wave, until the jubilant, triumphant last tutti is reached:

In connection with the pauses and the acceleration of tempo, the unison here produces an incomparably powerful dynamic and emotional climax. Throughout the overture the frequent and powerful unisons give a popular, plainly human and elementary aspect to the piece.

Also the rarely played "Leonore" overture, No. 1, contains an abundance of interesting examples illustrating Beethoven's treatment of unisons.

unison in Berlioz

Of all the great composers, Hector Berlioz had the strongest feeling for the possibilities of the unaccompanied or almost unaccompanied melody. Almost all his scores contain striking examples. The first twenty-six measures of the "Lear" overture are almost entirely based on unison effect, and owe to it their impressive declamation and immediate appeal. Of similar effect is the pompous recitative of the brass instruments in the introduction to *Romeo and Juliet* (measures 78–145), with its sixty-seven measures only slightly interrupted by chords: one of the longest recitative passages in the entire literature. The few interspersed chords are written in the unpretentious and plain style of secco recitative. For Romeo's monologue (beginning of Part II), unison serves again as a striking means of expressing desolate loneliness. In the *Requiem,* the first twenty-four measures of the Dies Irae create the impression of simple sublimity, of timid expectation by means of their unison; still stronger is the expression of devout anxiety in the unison stammering that fills the first half of the "Quid sum miser," (No. 3). Through its unison treatment, the principal theme of the "Scène aux champs" in the Symphonie Fantastique achieves a vivid landscape impression, suggestive of the wide horizon in the plains. A firmly cut type of unison melody is found in *La Damnation de Faust,* in Faust's aria "Merci, doux crépuscule," at the beginning of Part III. Here the unison paints the "passionate curiosity," the slow steps with which Faust, trembling with inner excitement, passes through Margaret's room. In one place only do flutes and clarinets add to the unison a few measures faintly reminiscent of the principal theme. Every additional measure of accompaniment, every added chord would detract something from the convincing charms of these twenty-five measures, would make the piece lose the tender atmosphere of chastity and simplicity which it breathes.

Anton Bruckner is also a specialist in unison. His scores contain an abundance of novel unison effects of admirable impressiveness.

CHAPTER **XIV**

additional remarks on song form[1]

Mendelssohn's songs without words

As models in the formal treatment of the song form, the forty-two "Songs without Words" by Mendelssohn deserve a more serious study than is generally accorded them. Here Mendelssohn has varied the simple formal pattern *a-b-a* (without trio) no less than forty-two times, in ever new and ingenious variants, and in this difficult task he has evinced his great talent for form most brilliantly. Here the student may learn what an effective return means by observing how Mendelssohn manages to make the reprise (the return of part *a* at the close) most effective. The refined thematic structure of the coda also deserves close attention. The great variety of these little pieces may be illustrated by a number of examples chosen from them. Some of the simplest structures are:

No. 4. Introduction, 4 measures. *a,* 8 measures, *b,* 8 measures, *a,* 4 + 1 measures. Postlude, 4 measures. Prelude and postlude act as a framework around the piece. Remarkable features in the reprise are the climax and the

[1] An advanced continuation of Chapter III.

extension of one measure, introducing the coda as its logical consequence.

No. 9 is similar. Prelude, 4½ measures. *a*, 8 measures, *b*, 4 + 2 measures, *a*, 8 measures, postlude, 2 measures.

No. 6. Prelude, 6 measures, *a*, 4 + 6 measures, *b*, 8 + (8 + 1) measures, *a*, 6 measures. Postlude, 6 measures. Worthy of note is the fact that in part *b* the reprise starts nine measures later than expected. The consequence of this surprise is that reprise *a* and the coda are welded into one section, the reprise being just faintly indicated, not elaborated. Here, too, both prelude and postlude act as a framework.

No. 12. Prelude, 6 measures. *a*, 8 + 7, *b*, 8 + 6, *a*, 7, coda, 12 measures. In the prelude of this Venetian Barcarole the gondolier's call or cry (measures 3, 4, the ascending third, E sharp-G sharp) is important because it acquires thematic significance and is heard twice more during the piece as an effective culmination of the melodic line (measures 13, 14, 29, 30). Other noteworthy details are the shortened *Nachsatz* of *a*, 7 instead of 8 measures in the second half of the period, the effective introduction of the reprise, which at first is delayed for six measures and then in the cadence is made to enter earlier than expected (measures 37 and following).

No. 22. Prelude, one measure. *a*, 8, *b*, 8, *a*, 8, coda, 4 + 1 measures. In spite of the regular, symmetrical structure, it is one of the best balanced pieces of the collection. Remarkable features are the contrast of emotional mood in *b*, and the interesting transition to the reprise. The tonality seems to be tending towards A minor, but suddenly the dominant E is differently interpreted as the leading tone of F major, and thus the return to the chief tonality of the piece, F major, is effected very surprisingly. In the reprise attention should be given to the slight differences as compared with the first *a*. The coda logically returns to the agitated middle part, *b*, expressly on account of its strong contrast, which receives greater justification by being introduced twice; a quiet motif from *a* is, however, very effectively and soothingly opposed to the agitated *b*, and thus the contrasts are even more reconciled to each other.

No. 18. Introduction, one measure. Section *a* contains a double theme. a_1, 4 measures, a_2, 4, a_1, again 4, a_2, in the dominant, 4, *b*, 15, *a*, 7, coda, 12 measures. Section *a* has a double theme treated in dialogue between an upper and lower voice. In *b* the dialogue becomes more animated at the close, and an effective climax is reached with pauses in the bass; only at the reprise, the culmination of the entire piece, do the basses enter again. Here for the first time both voices in duet, in octaves. Since the coda must be rather extended after this powerful climax, the return to piano requires a considerable space. Thematic coda on motif a_2, and a beautiful diminuendo down to pianissimo.

No. 23. Prelude, 6 measures. *a*, 8 + 1, interlude, 4, *b*, 12 measures;

a, 10, interlude, 4, *b,* 12 measures; *a,* 16, coda postlude, 9 measures. This extended piece of more than eighty measures requires very little thematic material. Several returns of *a* and *b* make the piece approach the rondo form. The prelude is used here not only for the coda, but also for the interludes. The climax is brought about by crescendo, by extension of the melodic line, and by the pianistic treatment.

No. 34. Prelude, 2 measures. *a,* 8, *b,* 19, *a,* 12, *b,* 21, *a,* 15, coda (*a*), 17 measures. Its form is akin to the rondo; the graceful returns to *a* give the piece a special charm.

song form in Chopin's nocturnes

Chopin [2] treats the song form in so ingenious and novel a manner that a closer study of his works in respect to their constructive art would well reward the effort. The song form (in his waltzes, mazurkas, nocturnes, impromptus, scherzi, preludes, etudes) is his favorite form. The nocturnes differ from Mendelssohn's "Songs without Words" by their larger dimensions and by the important part given to the contrasting middle section, similar to a trio in the minuet or scherzo. This device affords opportunities of passing from one emotional mood to a quite different one, and Chopin knows how to utilize these opportunities with the greatest mastery. An analysis of his Nocturne No. 4, Op. 15, No. 1, follows:

(*a*) First part, andante cantabile, $8 + 8 + 5 + 3$ measures (note the charm of the unusual prolongation of $5 + 3$ measures, the close suddenly breaking off in the middle of the phrase in order to heighten the contrast of the agitated middle section even more.

(*b*) Second part, con fuoco, $12 + 12$ measures.

(*a*) Third part, tempo primo, $8 + 8 + 5 + 3$ measures. The transition from the second to the third part:

leads over most convincingly from the passionate outbursts of the "con fuoco" to the peaceful, bright tempo primo, not only by means of dimin-

[2] Chopin's art of formal construction is explicitly treated in my *Analyse der Chopin-schen Klavierwerke.*

uendo, rallentando, calando, but also by the prolonged extension of the last note of the motif, at *a, b, a:* at first a quarter, next two quarters followed by one quarter and three eighth notes, with rallentando, and finally the logically convincing long first note of the tempo primo.

In Op. 9, No. 3, attention should be given to the considerably shortened reprise, fully balanced, however, by the enticingly elegant coda.

In Op. 27, No. 1, a highly effective, dramatically agitated transition to the reprise.

Op. 27, No. 2, shows the mixed rondo and song form already pointed out in Mendelssohn's "Songs without Words": *a, b, a, b, a,* coda. Every return of the principal theme is more elaborately ornamented.

In Op. 32, No. 2, the middle section is heard twice in a harmonic progression from F minor to F sharp minor. Each time the middle section is led to a powerful climax towards the close, intensified by the transposition a half tone higher. This explains the passionate fortissimo entrance of the reprise, whereas originally the main theme sounded "sempre piano."

Op. 37, No. 3, is built after the pattern: *a, b, a, b, a,* coda. At every return of *a* and *b* Chopin introduces harmonic and melodic variations.

piano pieces by Brahms

Masterpieces in the treatment of the song form are found among Johannes Brahms' smaller piano compositions. The four ballads, Op. 10, the eight capricci and intermezzi, Op. 76, the two rhapsodies, Op. 79, the capricci, intermezzi, rhapsodies and ballads, Opp. 116, 117, 118, 119, are the chief works to be kept in mind. Many of these pieces show interesting transformations and elaborations of the form, tending towards the sonata, rondo, or variation form. They would have to be treated under the heading "mixed forms." The reason for these transformations is to be seen mainly in the larger extension desired by the composer in these pieces, especially in most of the capricci, rhapsodies, and ballads.

CHAPTER **XV**

the contrapuntal forms[1]

the preludes of the *Well-Tempered Clavier*[2]

Three classes of preludes have already been pointed out:

(1) The simple prelude in broken chords, in the manner of an improvisation.

(2) The prelude in constant motion, originating from the technical aspects of the instrument, sometimes approaching the toccata type.

(3) Pieces in the style of an invention (cf. Chapter IV). Besides those already mentioned above, the following preludes of the *Well-Tempered Clavier* belong to this invention type:

Part I, No. 12 (F minor), No. 18 (G sharp minor), No. 20 (A minor), No. 23 (B major).

Part II, No. 1 (C major), No. 2 (C minor), No. 8 (E flat minor), No. 10 (E minor), No. 20 (A minor).

Several other classes remain to be discussed.

---

[1] An advanced continuation of Chapter IV.

[2] The following remarks concerning the preludes of the *Well-Tempered Clavier* are not meant to supersede Hugo Riemann's valuable discussions in his *Handbuch der Fugenkomposition*. On the other hand, they are not made superfluous by Riemann. He aims at explaining the emotional contents and the metrical structure; here the attempt is made to supplement Riemann by pointing out the structural ideas on which the Bach preludes are based.

(4) A fourth class of preludes more or less approaches the fugue or fughetta. To this type belongs No. 7 in Part I of the *Well-Tempered Clavier,* consisting of an introduction (whose motif later is used as countersubject of the fugue), exposition of the fugue theme, and a normally worked out fugue with a countersubject. No. 19 (A major) represents an elaborate fughetta on three motifs, in triple counterpoint, with refined use of inversion. Prelude 3 of Part II (C sharp major) introduces a small three-part fughetta as a coda to a piece in type one character (like I, 1, C major).

(5) The great wealth of form in Bach's art is also manifest in a fifth type, representing aria-like concertizing solo or duet with basso continuo: Part I, No. 10 (E minor), like a flute solo accompanied by stringed instruments pizzicato, and a calmly flowing thorough bass, with a brilliant toccata suddenly entering in the second part. I, No. 13 (F sharp major): like an oboe or violin solo, with a delicate, singing tone. Busoni calls attention to the unusual construction of the three-part form, the constant interchange (for the ear), of 12/16 and 18/16 time, brought about by frequent one-and-a-half measure extension, appended to the four-bar phrases. In such places, like measures 5, 6, and so on,

one perceives the above-mentioned coincidence of the ending of one phrase and the beginning of the next one; at this junction the closing note of the phrase is omitted, and the result is an appendix of one-and-a-half instead of two measures. I, No. 24 (B minor): like a duet of two violins in canonic imitations above the continuo. Part II, No. 4 (C sharp minor) shows a highly interesting complication of this constructive idea: in the first half a concertizing duet of the two upper parts above the continuo, in the second half the bass participates in the dialogue, thus producing a terzetto. A modern pendant to this piece (so far as the duet idea is concerned) is found in Chopin's nocturne in E flat major, Op. 55, No. 2.

The arioso-like preludes, No. 12 (F minor) and No. 14 (F sharp minor), belong to a similar type, reminiscent of a violin solo, accompanied by two obligato parts. No. 17 is interpreted by Busoni as two solo voices with a tutti accompaniment, both groups playing partly alternately, partly simultaneously.

(6) A fantasy type of prelude, pieces of highest beauty, in which elements of aria melody and polyphony are mingled. Famous pieces of this type are the preludes in C sharp minor, I, No. 4; in E flat minor, No. 8; G minor, No. 16; B flat minor, No. 22.

The prelude in C sharp minor (I, 4) is a piece of arioso soprano melody of the loftiest nobility. The lower voices, conversing with the soprano in imitation in duet or terzetto, give, so to speak, a commentary to the leading part, pointing to its beauties, enlarging upon them, and intensifying them. But even the soprano part alone, played by a solo violin and accompanied by plain chords, would be impressive: Part I (measures 1–14), starts in C sharp minor, closes in G sharp minor. With Part II (measures 14–39), the texture of the parts becomes denser; modulation touching B major, F sharp minor, prepares an impressively intensified return to the C sharp minor cadence, whose resolution into the tonic is twice delayed by deceptive cadences and by a broadly curved interpolation (measures 30–35). This bending around of the melodic line contributes considerably to the long breath of the melos. The soulful chanting of every single voice, their animated and expressive ensemble are admirable. The skillful use of holding tones helps much; every resting point in the melodic line affords the other parts an opportunity to display their melodic chant. The fantasy element of the piece is noticeable in Part II, with its broad flow of melody and its omission of a reprise.

The entire piece, measure for measure, from beginning to end, flows without any exception from the two motifs *a* and *b,* combined in the first measure:

Measures 1–4 bring *a* and *b* successively; in measures 5–7 *a* is heard alone; starting in measure 9, *a* and *b* are heard simultaneously in various parts; here the complexities of part-leading commence. Later on alternately again, *a* alone, and *a* and *b* simultaneously. In measures 30, 31 in the soprano, *a + a + a + a;* in the lower voice, *b + b + b + b.* Measures 32–35, *a* in the lower voice five times, in the higher voice a slight change of *a* by contraction of the last two eighth notes into one quarter note. Motif *b* is innately appropriate for a cadence and therefore serves for all cadences; the evenly flowing motif *a,* in contrast to *b,* has an intrinsic impulsive power and gives rise to the motion, the flow of the piece.

The E flat minor prelude (I, 8) is a duet in arioso style. Upper and lower voices, supported by chords in the accompaniment, sing a duet on the motif:

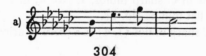

Sometimes this motif appears in its original form, sometimes in melodic amplification and transformation. The cadences of every one of its three sections are especially enhanced in their effect by most expressive melodic ornamentation. One might easily make an extract of the whole piece, reduced to the formula *a* as can be seen here by the little excerpt from measures 12 and 13:

Part I (measures 1–15): E flat minor to B flat minor. Duet, at first simple, is later more and more richly ornamented.

Part II (measures 16–30): Middle section, with the characteristic tendency of these middle episodes to thematic development and free modulation. Culmination of the duet, the two voices in always closer, quicker, and more agitated dialogue. Ornamental cadences, at first in A flat minor, then back to E flat minor, after a dramatically excited cadenza, are brought to a climax in passionately expressive recitative (measures 27–30).

Part III (measures 31–42): Actually only a widely extended E flat minor cadenza, delayed by deceptive cadence. Upper and lower voice in rich melodic ornament. The piece obtains its fantasia-like character by the manner of its ornamentation.

The prelude in B flat minor (I, 22) is closely related to the one in E flat minor. An ensemble of four voices in dialogue on the motif:

with the assistance of a freely treated fifth part, these voices during the pauses of their dialogue also act as filling out chordal accompaniment. In distinction to the E flat minor prelude, however, the motif *a* is not ornamented in the manner of a fantasia, but is retained in its original form from beginning to end. The structural idea is: The theme (at least its first two measures) appears six times in the twenty-five measures of the piece, starting three times on B flat, and three times on F; sometimes it is heard in the soprano, lightly supported by a chord structure; in the middle parts it is woven into the polyphonic texture, and once it appears in the bass.

Part I (measures 1–13): Theme in B flat minor, in the soprano, rising stepwise. Theme in B flat minor, in the bass, in dialogue with the soprano (measure 3). Theme in B flat minor, soprano (measure 7), descending stepwise. Theme in F, in the alto (measure 10), descending. Theme in F, in the alto (measure 12), ascending.

Part II (measures 13–20): Development in dialogue manner, culmination reached in measure 16, then stepwise descent to the organ point on the dominant F.

Part III (measures 20–25): Resting on the organ point F, the theme now in the soprano enters for the sixth time, ascending from F. A second climax marks the intensive culmination of the piece (the fermata in measure 22), whereas the extensive climax was reached in measure 16.

The entire piece is dominated by the diatonically rising and descending line. In motif *a* notice the subdivision into an ascending and descending half. This counterplay of the melodic lines not only dominates the basic motif, but the entire piece. Its idea, in a germinal state, is already indicated in the motif. The soprano is treated as a broad, arioso-like cantilena, partly in thematic, partly in free melodic leading, above the closely intertwined lower voices.

(7) A seventh type of prelude is represented by pieces like II, 11 and II, 17. The structural idea is: characteristic symmetrical structure, frequent returns of the same phrase with manifold variants each time, but strict co-ordination of sections, a kind of rondo, but almost entirely without interludes or transitions.

The prelude in F major (II, 11) is in five sections:
(a) Theme of 16 measures, melody of the arioso type, F major, close in C major.
(b) Repetition of the theme in C major, with variant in the last 6 measures, close in D minor, 16 measures.
(c) Repetition of the theme in D minor, close in A minor, variants, 16 measures.
(d) Free development of the theme as intermezzo, 8 measures.
(e) Repetition of *a* with slight changes, 16 measures, F major.

The prelude in A flat major (II, 17) is a duet, with accompaniment of obligato parts; in four sections:
(a) Theme, 16 measures. In spite of numerous repetitions, the ear does not have the impression of reiteration, but of a broadly curved, beautifully flowing melody in constant development. A flat major, close in E flat. *Vordersatz* (antecedent), 6 measures. *Nachsatz* (consequent), 8 + 2 measures.

306

(b) Repetition of the theme in E flat, *Nachsatz* varied, 6 + 11 measures, close in F minor.

(c) Repetition of the theme in F minor, *Nachsatz* varied—6 + 10 measures, close in D flat major.

(d) Free development of the theme in D flat major, *Vordersatz* amplified to 14 measures, *Nachsatz,* 14 measures. Close in A flat major.

(8) As an eighth type Bach sometimes makes use of a peculiar variation of the three-part song form. The prelude in E major (I, 9) illustrates this type well. It applies the form *a-b-a* with reprise in the subdominant instead of the tonic.

(a) First part, E major with close in the dominant B major (measures 1–8).

(b) Middle part, modulation from B major to the subdominant of E, A major (measures 8–14).

(a) Reprise in A major, closing on the dominant of A, E major, thus returning to the original key at the close of the piece (measures 15–24).

Because part *a* modulates to the dominant, the reprise, in order to retain the effectiveness of the dominant, modulation is moved one dominant backwards, that is, to the subdominant.

Another example for this form is found in the introductory Adagio of Bach's First violin solo sonata in G minor:

(a) First part, G minor modulating to the dominant D major (measures 1–9).

(b) Middle part, D major to C minor (measures 9–14).

(a) Reprise of *a,* but beginning in C minor and closing in the tonic key G minor (measures 14–22).

Also the well-known F major Invention (No. 8 of the two-part Inventions) is built quite similarly.

(9) A whole series of preludes are built on a form like the gigue, like I, 15 in G major; II, 5 in D major; II, 7 in E flat major; II, 19 in A major.

(10) Some preludes approach the Bach sonata form. The prelude in B flat major (II, 21) may well be compared to the first movement of the Italian concerto, or to the sonata-like "Préludes" of the English suites in A minor, D minor, F major. All these pieces have a grand swing in their three-part form, with a middle section corresponding to the "development" part. The B flat prelude is especially interesting on account of the inserted amplifications of phrase and period structure, brought to a climax in the brilliant virtuoso cadenza before the close.

The F sharp minor prelude (II, 14) also illustrates this type.

(11) Finally, there are some preludes in the *Well-Tempered Clavier*

which cannot be classified, because as "free forms" they evolve special constructions for every particular case. These structures are of the highest formal interest because they represent exploration of new, unknown regions, because they illustrate the maxim that every musical idea carries its perfect form within itself, concealed as if within a seed. This form, manifest to the penetrating, probing glance of a real master, may sometimes lead him into new untrodden paths.

The B flat minor prelude (II, 22) develops a theme of five measures in three-part counterpoint. The theme is introduced twice in every one of the four sections, and is followed by a thematic interlude which is omitted only once between sections 3 and 4, but later serves again as coda. Here is an interesting structure, applying the technique of the fugue in expanding a single theme into a well built piece, yet in its essential form very different from a fugue.

the forms of inversion

Inversion forms are a special type of the contrapuntal forms. They make use of double or triple counterpoint, beginning by exposing the theme, and simultaneously one or two countersubjects, and from these motifs building up the entire piece by inversions of the various parts and by different combinations of these inversions. Thematic interludes occur frequently, as do sharply marked cadences in order to indicate clearly to the listener the division of the piece into two or three sections. Models of this very logical type of construction are found in Bach's Inventions.

F MINOR INVENTION

Of the two-part Inventions, Nos. 5, 6, 9, 11, 12 belong to this class. A great masterpiece of this form is found in the noble and moving three-part Invention in F minor (No. 9), whose entire thematic material is exhausted by the first four measures. Not a single one of the thirty-five measures makes use of any other motifs but those stated at the beginning, and the manifold and most expressive combinations of the three motifs are the sole content of the piece. The three motifs are:

Every combination of the three motifs fills out two measures. The structure of the entire piece and the combinations of the three themes (counting from above to the bass below) are as follows:

Part 1: II, I, F minor; II, I, III, C minor; interlude, 2 measures; I, III, II, F minor; interlude, 2 measures.

Part 2: III, II, I (F minor to A flat major); II, I, III (to E flat major); interlude, 3 measures; I, II, III (C minor).

Part 3: Interlude, 4 measures; I, III, II, D flat major; II, I, III, A flat major; interlude, 3 measures; II, I, III, F minor; III, II, I, F minor (coda).

In another sense "inversion" is used in pieces like No. 12 of Bach's "Goldberg" variations, entitled "Canone alla quarta e per moto contrario." Here is a two-part canon, with the answer in inversion. The first measures are:

Another specimen of a very similar type is found in No. 15 of the "Goldberg" variations already mentioned in the chapter "Contrapuntal Forms." The gigues of Bach's piano suites belong also in this class, with their fugal treatment "recte" in the first part, and "inverse" in the second part.

On the whole the methods of the invention are closely allied to those of the fugue, and constitute an important means of fugal style. Also the so-called *Gegenfugen* (counterfugues), from Bach's "Art of Fugue," belong to the forms of inversion.

Especially interesting and thus far not systematically utilized combinations are made possible by the symmetrical inversion. Bernhard Ziehn has established the theoretical basis for this little known speciality of contrapuntal writing. Symmetrical inversion aims at the strict inversion of an entire phrase or piece in several parts. Every ascending melodic progression is answered by the same interval descending, and vice versa; at the same time, however, all parts exchange places so that the soprano, for instance, becomes a bass, the alto a tenor, and vice versa. As the intervals (pure, major, minor, diminished, augmented) are strictly retained in their original extension, the tonality is entirely changed at the inversion, and sometimes quite novel chord structures are the result. Models for this technique of contrapuntal writing are yet scarce. Busoni (in his edition of the *Well-Tempered Clavier*, Part II, pp. 66–70), quotes an organ piece by Middelschulte with its symmetrical inversion. A few measures at least (borrowed from Ziehn) may illustrate the peculiar effects achieved by symmetrical inversions:

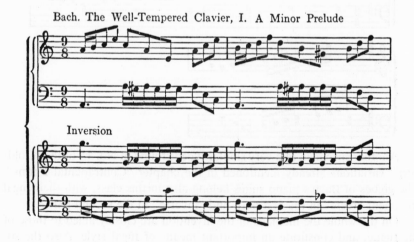

Bach. The Well-Tempered Clavier, I. A Minor Prelude

Busoni's resolution of the second canon in Bach's "Musikalisches Opfer" [3] is a fine model of symmetrical inversion.

A masterpiece unique of its kind is the passacaglia in Act IV of Henry
Purcell's *Dioclesian*. Here the passacaglia consists of a whole suite of various pieces, all written on the same bass theme: (1) Instrumental prelude.
(2) Song for soprano with chorus. (3) Extended interlude of the orchestra
on the somewhat ornamented bass. (4) Duet for soprano and bass.
(5) Chorus. (6) Terzetto (with the bass theme inverted). (7) Second
Terzetto. (8) Third Terzetto. (9) Chorus.

BACH'S ORGAN PASSACAGLIA

Bach's great organ passacaglia in C minor starts with an eight-measure
theme in the bass, to which are joined twenty variations without any interludes, each variation being eight measures long; an extended double fugue
serves as finale.

The theme:

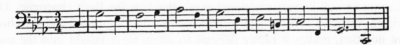

is heard eleven times successively in the bass, either in exact repetitions or
slightly varied as:

---

[3] Breitkopf edition, No. 4940.

After these eleven repetitions the pedal bass pauses, and during the next five variations the theme appears twice in the soprano, once in the alto, once in the manual bass lightly sketched out, once distributed between lower and upper parts.

A new third group commences with variation 16. The theme is heard in its original shape four times in succession in the pedal bass, and finally the magnificent double fugue enters as the crowning summit of the vast structure. From the eight-measure theme the double fugue evolves no less than 124 measures, and can therefore in itself be considered as balancing the entire twenty variations. The rhythmical structure of the single variations is of essential importance, because the coherence and flow, the culmination and the impressiveness of the entire piece depend on its rhythmical vitality; otherwise the monotony of a theme repeated twenty times would be fatal to the piece. Bach starts with dotted eighth rhythms; then he mixes eighth and sixteenth, retains the even flow of the sixteenth notes, sometimes continued in one part as a running counterpoint, sometimes variously distributed among several parts. In the seventeenth variation the velocity has reached its acme with sixteenth triplets; in the last two variations a slight retard is introduced, through combinations of quarter, eighth, and sixteenth rhythms. The purpose of this rhythmical expansion is to reach a ritenuto, an accumulation, concentration, and intensification of sound, as a weighty and impressive close to the variations, and as an effective introduction to the fugue. The fugue itself retains the smooth flow of the sixteenth rhythms throughout. The single variations are frequently coupled together into groups with the same rhythm, like variations 1 and 2; 4 and 5; 6, 7, and 8, 10 and 11; 12 and 13; 18, 19, and 20. The entire work is a grandiose masterpiece of musical construction.

THE BACH CHACONNE

A still more amazing masterpiece of contrapuntal structure (not to mention as well its vast emotional expression), is the Bach chaconne. The original version for violin solo with its necessarily compressed and sketched-out notation, makes it rather difficult to attain clear insight into the construction. Busoni's admirable transcription for the piano makes the composition much easier to understand. Here a theme of four measures is varied no less than sixty-five times. All these dozens of variations follow each other directly, almost entirely without interludes, this time without any broadly worked out fugue as a finale. Yet there is no monotony, but rather the impression of a towering edifice, erected with greatest wisdom and boldness, of a glowing flame of emotion, of a boundless imagination. Expressed in sober numerals this marvelous structure presents itself as follows:

Part I: Variations 1–33, D minor

312

Part II: Variations 34–52, D major
Part III: Variations 53–65, D minor

Part I comprehends the first half of the entire work with almost mathematical precision, whereas Parts II and III together make up the second half, in the ratio 19 : 13, or approximately 18 : 12 = 3 : 2. The ratio of all three parts to each other is about 5 : 3 : 2. The principle of construction is the constant retaining of the harmonic functions of the theme. The bass:

appears in the single variations in at least twenty-five different versions, without a change in the harmonic functions. These variants, a study in themselves, are herewith enumerated, without any attempt at exhaustive completeness:

D, C sharp, D, B flat, G, A, C sharp, D
D, C sharp, C, B, B flat, G sharp, A, D
D, B flat, A, G, A, D
D, G, A, B, B flat, A, D
D, E, D, C sharp, D
D, B flat, C, A, B flat, G, F, A, D
D, G, C, F, B flat, E, A, D
D, C, B flat, A, D
D, C sharp, B, A, D
D, A, B flat, C, B flat, A, B flat, A, G, A, D
D, E, F, G, A, D
D, E, F, G, G sharp, A, D
D, B flat, A, G sharp, A, G, F sharp, G, F, E, F, E, D
D, A, B, C, G, A, B flat, A, G sharp, A, D
D, C sharp, A, B, G, A, D
D, E, F sharp, G, A, B, C sharp, A, B, C sharp, D, C sharp, B, A,
    G, F sharp, E, D, A, D
D, C sharp, A, A sharp, B, G sharp, A, D
D, E, F sharp, G, G sharp, A, D
D, A, G, G sharp, A, D
D, C sharp, B, A, G, G sharp, A, D
D, G, G sharp, A, A sharp, B, G, A, D
D, G, A, B flat, A, G, A, D
D, E, F, G, A, D
D, F, B, E, A, D, G, D, C sharp, A, D
D, A, G, C, F, B flat, G, E, C sharp, G, E, A, D
D, F, G, E, F, D, B, E, C sharp, A, D, and so on

313

Some twenty different rhythmical formulas are used for the sixty-five variations. Generally two or three successive variations are based on the same rhythmical motif, thus broader levels are obtained and excessive variety of rhythms avoided. Whereas every four-bar variation in Part I is a finished little structure in itself, Part II has a predilection for eight-, even sixteen-bar melodic structure, by contracting at least two variations into one larger, coherent melody. In this way Part II takes on an aspect of broader melody in the manner of a trio, contrasting with Part I by its brighter major coloring, its more consoling tone. The entire piece rises and falls like a vast wave, moving toward several dynamic crests, and ebbing away once again. In variation 19 the first culmination is reached. Observe how effectively the ascent is prepared by the gradual change of the note values, from the dotted quarter and eighth at the beginning, to the uniform eighth, to the eighth and sixteenth mixed, to the uniform sixteenth in manifold variants between staccato and legato, to the climax in variation 19 with its tempestuous thirty-second figures. At variation 20 a sudden piano enters, followed by a new gradual culmination, until variation 23 is reached. Variation 24 begins again piano; this is followed by an irresistible forward drive to the close of Part I, culminating in a fortissimo reprise of the theme with added coda of four bars strongly underlining the close. The addition of this coda is the only liberty taken in the strict construction of the entire piece. Part II is led up to a broad and elevated plateau, extending from variation 45 to 53. Here Part III commences, again in sombre minor, meditative, subsiding to the faintest pianissimo (variations 55–59) before beginning the grandiose final climax (variation 65).

In his biography on Bach, Philipp Spitta tries to approach the chaconne from another aspect. His aesthetic interpretation can hardly be surpassed (volume I, page 705, German edition), but his formal analysis appears unsatisfactory. He assumes five different themes, and, with forced ingenuity, explains the whole piece as an alternation or a combination of several themes. The constructive idea, the logic of the structure is obscured by this roundabout interpretation. In following Spitta's indications one is hardly likely to find one's way through the intricate piece, even though he takes great pains to clarify it. The different melodic designs are easier and more naturally interpreted as variations on a constant series of harmonic functions, as has been demonstrated above.

THE SLOW MOVEMENT OF BACH'S PIANO CONCERTO

An interesting variation of the chaconne form is found in the slow movement of Bach's D minor piano concerto. It is built on a bass theme of thirteen measures, recurring five times, not, however, in the same key, as customary, but in different tonalities. Short free interludes take care of the modulations from one key to the other. The free development of the melodic soprano line above the chaconne bass is admirable. One does not have the impression of five variations, but of one extended aria. The plan of construction is as follows:

(1) Bass theme, G minor, orchestra in unison (measures 1–13).
(2) Bass theme, G minor, piano, above it an arioso melody (measures 13–26). Close in C minor. Modulation from C minor to D minor (measures 26–29).
(3) Bass theme, D minor, close in B flat major (measures 30–42). Modulation B flat major to C minor (measures 42–45).
(4) Bass theme in C minor (measures 45–57). Modulation from C minor to G minor (measures 57–61).
(5) Bass theme in G minor (measures 61–74).
(6) Bass theme in G minor (measures 74–86).

FINALE OF BRAHMS' E MINOR SYMPHONY

One of the most eminent modern applications of the chaconne form has been made by Brahms in the finale of his E minor symphony. A theme of eight measures is here varied thirty-one times, with an extended final section appended. The variations are written partly on the bass of the theme, partly on its melody, partly on both bass and melody. The variations, each one eight measures long, follow each other without any interludes; a single interpolation of four measures is made just before the thematically developed, broad coda variation (No. 32). The analysis of the piece follows:

(1) Variations 1–10. Forte, with gradual culmination of the rhythms and of the emotional expression until the climax is reached in variation 10.
(2) Variations 11–16. Piano, in the manner of a contrasting trio, partly in E major, instead of the preceding E minor. This idyllic intermezzo is followed by the sharply contrasted next variations.
(3) Variations 17–22. Forte, growing excitement, until the climax is attained in variation 22.
(4) Variations 23–31. Piano and forte alternating. The triplet rhythm dominates variations 23–28. In this final group there is a reminiscence of (1) in the manner of a sonata reprise. Thus variations 25, 26, 27 correspond to variations 2, 3, 4.
(5) The finale, starting at variation 32, is broadly expanded. After the long, uninterrupted E minor and E major tonality, more distant modulations are used in order to gain a new basis for the tonic E, as preparation for an effective close. Thus No. 32 touches G minor, No. 33 passes through a whole series of distant keys in order to lead over to the E minor cadence.

mixed contrapuntal forms

Mixtures of the fugue with other formal constructions are possible, and occasionally the works of the masters contain such examples, though not very frequently. Thus a combination of fugue and song form or dance form is indicated in the B flat major fugue from Part II of the *Well-Tempered Clavier* (No. 21). The same combination is even more distinctly evident in variations 10 and 12 from Bach's "Aria mit 30 Veränderungen," the so-called "Goldberg" variations. The theme of variation 10 is:

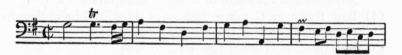

Other examples are: the fughetta from Beethoven's "Diabelli" variations; the D major fugue No. 2 from Mendelssohn's Op. 35. Most of these fugues might also be classified as variations.

The most brilliant example of a combination of fugue and sonata form is Mozart's *Magic Flute* overture. The finale movements from Beethoven's C major quartet, Op. 59, No. 3, and from Brahms' string quintet, Op. 88, illustrate a similar combination.

An ingenious mixture of fugue and variation or passacaglia is found in the G sharp minor fugue (No. 18) from Part II of the *Well-Tempered Clavier*. A lucid analysis of its ten variations may be found in Busoni's edition.

BUXTEHUDE'S FUGUE VARIATION

Another highly interesting mixture of fugue and variation had already been practiced around 1700 by the Lübeck organ master Buxtehude. He uses the theme in two or three variations, each variation being worked out as a fugue; the single variations or fugues are connected by interludes in a virtuoso style, partly thematic, partly free. The whole composition is crowned by a brilliantly treated postlude in finale character, occasionally taking up ideas of the prelude, thus rounding off the piece significantly. Bach thereafter no longer employed this form. It might, however, appear promising enough to deserve some attention again.[4]

An interesting combination of canon and chaconne is found in a composition of the Nuremberg master Johann Pachelbel (manuscript in the Library of the Academy for Church Music, Berlin).[5] Here is found an ex-

---

[4] On Buxtehude's fugue variations see Spitta's *Bach*, vol. I, 261–273, German edition.

[5] Reprinted in G. Beckmann's study, "Johann Pachelbel als Kammermusikkomponist," *Archiv für Musikwissenschaft*, January, 1919.

tended three-part canon in unison (for three violins) built on a basso ostinato of two measures, which is repeated twenty-eight times successively. If one plays only one of the violin parts with the bass, one has a chaconne in twenty-eight variations. It is indifferent which one of the three violin parts one picks out, as all three play the same music, with the exception of the few concluding measures. The unusual elaborations arise from the strict canonic leading of the three parts.

SCHÖNBERG'S DOUBLE CANON

Arnold Schönberg's "Pierrot Lunaire"[6] (No. 18) contains one of the most intricate pieces of the whole of contrapuntal literature. It is a four-part double canon: clarinet and piccolo, violin and violoncello, playing two different canons together. In the tenth measure the canon is turned backwards, in "cancrizans" motion, that is, from this central point all four parts move backwards, playing exactly the same notes as before, only in the reversed direction, until at the close the beginning has been reached again. To this double canon in inversion the piano adds a complicated three-part invention in fugal style, which is developed quite independently, not participating in the inversion of the other parts, not moving backwards, but very decidedly forwards.

the toccata

FROBERGER'S TOCCATAS

Besides the toccata-type explained earlier,[7] there exists a second type of the older toccata. It represents a mixture of toccata proper and ricercar or fugato. The organ works of Froberger, easily accessible in the series *Denkmäler der Tonkunst in Oesterreich,* may serve as examples. Toccata 25 starts in real toccata style with eleven measures of runs and full chords; next follows a fugato of eighteen measures on a new motif in 4/4 time, after which a second fugato of thirteen measures on the same motif, now in 12/8 time in triplets follows. At the close, a free coda of two measures, in toccata manner.

A still more interesting plan of construction is seen in Toccata 22, in C major:

(1) Intrata in toccata style, 12 measures, 4/4 time.
(2) Fugato on a new motif, passing over, at the close, into toccata-like figuration, 28 measures, 4/4 time.

[6] Score published by Universal Edition, Vienna.
[7] See p. 84.

(3) Second fugato on the same motif in 6/4 time, 18 measures.

(4) Coda toccata-like in the sense of Part I, but not an exact repetition, 7 measures, 4/4 time.

The formal pattern here is: a-b-b_1-a.

Sometimes the form is still enlarged by a more extended toccata-like intermezzo, changing the pattern into: a-b-a-b_1-a. Here the toccata-like sections are designated by a, and the fugato sections by b.

BACH'S TOCCATAS

Bach has brought both types of toccata to the greatest perfection in several grandiose structures. Of chief importance are the organ toccatas in D minor and C major and the six piano toccatas. The organ toccata in D minor corresponds to the fantasia-like Buxtehude type, with its onrushing and precipitous passages, its mighty columns of chords, its trills, its pathetic declamation, its frequent fermata, its contrasting sound effects and dialogues. The toccata is welded together with the following fugue, and the fugue closes with a toccata-like fantasia coda. No purposeful constructive idea is evident in the first toccata, which fully deserves the title of fantasia, more so perhaps than any other piece.[8]

The second toccata type, with fugato episodes or even entire fugues interspersed, is seen in Bach's piano toccatas in D minor, G minor, and E minor. They all have several movements. The G minor toccata starts with a toccata introduction; next follow a double fugue, an adagio as intermezzo, and a second fugue, ending with a reminiscence of the introductory toccata.

Forerunners of the fugue in the organ and clavier music of the seventeenth century are the ricercar, canzone, capriccio, and fantasia.

ricercar

The ricercar consists of a series of fugal developments on a theme and on rhythmical variations of the same theme. Froberger's Fourteenth ricercar, for example, consists of three rather extended fugal developments on the theme:

and its variants shown at the top of the next page.

[8] On the toccata in older Italian piano music see: Sandberger *Gesammelte Aufsätze,* p. 169; Shedlock, "The Harpischord Music of A. Scarlatti," in *Sammelband* (1904/5), p. 160, of International Society of Music; Leo Schrade, "Zur Geschichte der Toccata," in *Zeitschrift für Musikwissenschaft* (1926), pp. 610–635.

The three sections are well proportioned: 58, 37, and 42 measures, in the ratio of approximately 3 : 2 : 2. Some ricercar have four or even more developments; sometimes the theme is transformed into another time, from 4/4 into 3/2, or 6/8 or 9/8 time. Ricercar always meant an artificially built piece, full of contrapuntal complexities, as is evident already in the name *ricercare,* meaning to seek (the theme). The earliest classical master of this form was Girolamo Frescobaldi, who was one of the first to apply the structural idea of the vocal motet to instrumental music.

canzone, capriccio, fantasia

Almost the whole of the more developed instrumental music of the seventeenth century makes extended use of the principle of varying a theme rhythmically or metrically and working it out fugally in various ways several times in succession.

The canzone of this epoch can hardly be distinguished from the ricercar. Also the capricci are quite similar to the ricercar; a more explicit, more virtuoso-like development is perhaps the main feature which distinguishes these two from the ricercar. Fantasia, in the sense of the seventeenth century, is also a species of the ricercar. Only rarely do composers take the liberty, in a modest way, to interrupt the strict ricercar structure by "free fantasy" episodes.

BEETHOVEN'S OP. 133

The form of the ricercar has been magnified into gigantic dimensions by Beethoven in his vast fugue for string quartet, Op. 133, which has remained a unique piece in its manner of construction. The fugue is comprised of a series of fugal variation-fantasias, joined together in the manner of a sonata. The formal disposition of the piece is:

(1) Overture, corresponding to a free introduction. The theme appears here as raw material, an unpolished block of stone, stated in various rhythmical versions. The entire introduction is like a general heading, an extract from the three sonata sections, formed by the three fugues. The theme is hinted at in the version of the following allegro, the slow inter-

mezzo, and the finale. Fuga, allegro, corresponding to a first sonata movement. Extended development in the style of a double fugue. In this piece ricercar features are already manifest in the different rhythms, dominating wide stretches; at first the constantly retained triplet rhythm, later eighth and sixteenth intermingled:

though these rhythmical changes are less a part of the themes than of the counterpoints.

(2) Meno mosso e moderato. Corresponding to a slow movement. Here the metrical variants of the theme commence, in accordance with the ricercar style.

(3) Allegro molto e con brio, 6/8 time. The finale. The third fugue on a new version of the theme; before the increased speed of the close, the quick motion is once more interrupted by a return to the meno mosso of the intermezzo. This fugue is subdivided by various rhythmical versions of the theme.

Here follow the three main versions of the theme, together with its countersubjects in the three movements. To these three versions must still be added a number of other melodic and rhythmical variants:

This little known and hardly adequately appreciated work is nevertheless worthy of serious attention, not only on account of its rare form and the almost confusing abundance of contrapuntal combinations, but still more on account of its unique spirit, originating so strange and eminent a piece of music. It seems as if Beethoven had set aside all regard for euphony, for beauty, and effectiveness, and that he was content with letting a motif seek its own way, just like a brook dashing down from a glacier to the valley. A destructive, cruel logic is at work here, intent only on doing what is necessary in every moment, without any adornment. The introductions of the single movements and the interludes are of especial interest because here the constraint of the fugal treatment is left out of consideration, and, so to speak, the absolute musical substance (*Ding an sich*) is shown in its efficiency, the innate urge and will of the motif to be active in a certain direction, in a certain manner. Nothing playful or voluntary is seen here; even the "fantasy" of the composer, in its ordinary sense, is ruled out or rather his fantasy is busy with investigating the innermost nature of the motif and giving it its free course without artificial impediments. Here the logic of steadiness, perseverance, and of change is strikingly brought into evidence. Every change carries its reason with it, manifesting it in harmony, in motif, and in rhythmical structure. "Absolute" music, without any secondary aim, is its firm, immovable maxim, as is the idea of "justice" to the judge. The consequence of this attitude is an almost impersonal, almost hostile objectivity, which convinces, however, by sheer brute fact, and which rejects the temptation of making itself agreeable through amiability or friendliness. No lyricism, no sentiment in the ordinary sense is evident here, but a vast spiritual power, seriousness, and sublimity.

CHAPTER **XVI**

variation form[1]

Richard Strauss' Don Quixote

Modern composers have sometimes made use of variation of the variation form for special reasons. Thus in Richard Strauss' *Don Quixote* are found: introduction, double theme, ten variations, and a finale coda. The single variations are entirely independent, characteristic pieces, reminiscent of the variation form only by the weaving in of motifs of the theme into each variation. Thus the single pieces, descriptive of Don Quixote's adventures, all stand in some common relation to the hero and his servant Sancho Panza. Here is apparent the application of the Wagnerian leading motif technique to the variation form.

D'Indy's "Istar"

Vincent D'Indy in his "Istar" makes strange use of the variation form, in inverted order: the most complicated variations are the first ones; as the work progresses the variations become plainer and more perspicuous, and the theme, played in unison, is heard only at the very end. The explanation is given by the program: The goddess Istar releases her lover, the sun, from Hades. She must halt at seven gates, where each time she is divested of more

[1] Continuation of Chapter VI.

and more of her clothing and her jewels by the guards, until in complete nudity she is permitted to free her beloved.

Max Reger's orchestral variations on a theme by Hiller,[2] Op. 100, vary the theme in a very free manner: the variations are contrapuntal fantasias on motifs of the theme, and more extended than the theme itself. Generally the theme, used as a cantus firmus, is introduced somewhere in each variation. One variation often represents a compilation of several others.

Bach's cantata "Christ lag in Todesbanden"

The idea of leading the theme as cantus firmus through the entire series of variations has already been worked out with the greatest mastery by J. S. Bach. The Cantata No. 4, "Christ lag in Todesbanden" is treated as a series of chorale variations from beginning to end. A short sinfonia is followed by seven chorale verses in variation manner:

Verse 1: Allegro. Four-part chorus with string orchestra obligato. Chorale-fantasia. The cantus firmus in augmentation in the soprano, its single phrases separated by rests. Added to this a thematic texture of the other choral voices and the string orchestra. The piece is crowned by a festive, joyful, pompous alleluia.

Verse 2: Adagio. Cantus firmus as duet, distributed to soprano and alto, accompanied by a basso continuo in restless motion.

Verse 3: Presto. Cantus firmus in the tenor solo, accompanied by a brilliant rapid counterpoint in sixteenth notes in the violins, above a continuo in quarter and eighth notes.

Verse 4: Allegro moderato. Four-part chorus, without orchestra, but with continuo. Complex contrapuntal texture, into which the alto intermittently enters with the weighty tones of the cantus firmus, phrase by phrase.

Verse 5: Andante. Bass solo with string orchestra. The chorale melody, now in 3/4 time, given to the violins, with free interludes plentifully interspersed. The solo voice in free counterpoint.

Verse 6: Duet. Soprano and tenor above the chorale melody, accompanied by a brisk, energetic continuo in dotted rhythms.

Verse 7: The plain chorale melody, for four-part chorus, doubled by the orchestra in unison.

Schumann's "Carnaval"

In his "Carnaval," Op. 9, Robert Schumann has varied the variation idea in an ingenious and imaginative manner. On the title page Schumann wrote: "Scènes mignonnes sur quatre notes." Here a playful idea gave rise

---

[2] See the explicit analysis of Reger's Op. 100 by H. Leichtentritt, *Kleine Konzertführer*, No. 631 (Breitkopf & Härtel).

to a weighty work of art. Just as the theme "Bach" has given rise to many compositions, so the name of a little town "Asch" is here utilized musically as homage to a lady from Asch revered by Schumann.

The "Carnaval" consists of a festive, pompous "Préambule," a free prelude, that has nothing to do with the four-note motif proper, followed by seventeen characteristic pieces on the series A–S–C–H (in English style, A–E flat–C–B) after which a "pause" is introduced—a repetition from the préambule—and as a finale the "Marche der Davidsbündler," starting with the four-note motif and leading back again to the préambule. The variation idea of the seventeen character pieces is seen in the manner in which Schumann bases every one of these pieces on the motif "Asch," with the motif in a different rhythm every time; each piece, however, is built up quite independently on its own varied form of the "Asch" motif. (In the following analysis the German names of the notes have been retained, as it is impossible, using the English designations, to explain Schumann's fanciful ideas.)

Nos. 2–7 and 9 make use of the group A–ES–C–H (A–E flat–C–B).
No. 8 stealthily introduces A–H–C–(D)–ES (A–B–C–(D)–E flat).
Nos. 10–11 make use of AS–C–H (A flat–C–B).
No. 12, "Chopin," uses the notes A–ES–H–C (A–E flat–B–C).
Nos. 13–18 and 20 again make use of A–S–C–H (A–E flat–C–B).

Schönberg's second string quartet

In the slow movement (entitled "Litanei") of Arnold Schönberg's Second string quartet is found a combination of variation form with lyric song as remarkable as it is valuable. The eight stanzas of Stefan George's poem here set to music are shaped into five variations of eight measures each, and a finale on a theme, whose four motifs are taken from the two preceding movements of the quartet.

CHAPTER **XVII**

sonata form[1]

the older sonata form

BACH'S SOLO SONATAS FOR VIOLIN

Of Bach's six sonatas for violin solo, only one half are real sonatas of the older type. The rest must be classified under the heading of suite or partita. Spitta has already called attention to the fact that the older Italians, as well as Bach, always adhered to the idea of the coherence of the three sonata movements, and also that the classical Viennese sonata did not depart from this idea of correlation, though it introduced new forms for the individual movements. Bach begins his sonata with a fantasy-like adagio of the prelude type, leading directly into the allegro; the fugue, adagio and allegro, or prelude and fugue, are welded together into one larger whole. Next follows a slow movement in a very different mood, and the vivid finale aims at a balance between the various moods of the preceding movements. In Bach the sonata elements have their origin in the fugue and in the Italian aria, welded together to produce a new entity, a new style. The Viennese sonata type is derived mainly from dance and song forms. Accordingly, the homophonic style is predominant in the Viennese sonata—in like degree as the polyphonic element in the Bach sonatas. For details, the reader is referred to Spitta's excellent appreciation of the violin solo

[1] Addenda to Part One, Chapter VIII.

sonatas in his biography (vol. I, pp. 685–692 of the German edition). Spitta's remarks on Bach's six sonatas for violin and piano are also most valuable (vol. I, pp. 718–724), as well as what he has to say on the sonatas for viola da gamba and for flute (vol. I, pp. 725–728, 728–731).

the cyclical sonata form

BEETHOVEN'S OP. 106

Beethoven's majestic piano sonata, Op. 106, one of the most subtly constructed and organized works in the whole literature of music, may here be subjected to a thoroughgoing analysis. It may well be that many of the close mutual relations among distant phrases did not enter into the clear consciousness of the composer and were not introduced intentionally. Yet it is no less instructive and interesting to observe even the subconscious activity of an artistic mind so incomparably gifted and trained in organic construction. Op. 106 is built according to what César Franck called his "principe cyclique." Every measure in this sonata is a sprout growing from a few germinal motifs. These originating prototypes are manifest to the expert eye and ear of the trained observer in every particle of this immensely complex and, in its variety, apparently confusing organism. In this respect, Op. 106 is similar to the string quartet in B flat major, Op. 130, which will be closely examined below. In Op. 106 an especially admirable feature is the art with which one particle engenders the other with a compelling logical consequence. Here one can also learn how new organisms through several generations, so to speak, grow forth from the archetypes of the motifs; something similar happens here as in a family where the main branch, after continuing in a straight line for generations, is suddenly freshened by new blood through marriage so that new qualities are added to the old stock.

The germ motifs of the sonata are stated at the very beginning of the first movement. Motifs a and b are subdivided into a number of partial motifs: a_1, a_2, a_3, and a_4. Strictly speaking, even b is only a varient of a_3:

327

The allegro is in sonata form. The exposition of the first theme, with its subsidiaries, fills measures 1–63. The first period (measures 1–16) is dominated by *a* and mainly by *b*. The second period includes measures 17–35. The motif

is derived from a_3. The two-bar motif is continued in one-bar phrases, by division into halves, according to Beethoven's method (measures 24–35). The close of this section, passing over into wider and wider leaps, leads convincingly to the leaping motif *a*, which is resumed in measure 35; again it is cut into halves and continued in one-bar rhythms until measure 45.

Transition to the second theme (measures 39–63) is dominated by two motifs derived from a_3 and a_1:

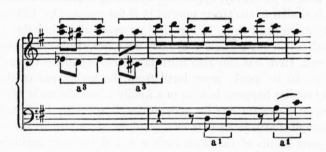

Second theme group, in G (measures 63–100). The first part (measures 63–91) is dominated by two variants of a_3, until measure 75.

328

Measures 75–91 are doubly linked to the foregoing: the eighth-note figures in the right hand are a variant of a_3 with an added eighth note; the half and whole notes of the left hand correspond to the syncopated alto part, measures 70–75. Thus:

and corresponding to this, the bass, in measure 75:

proceeding in like manner, until measure 91. Here the original version of motif a_4 is restored again: 2/4 + 2/8 + 2/4 notes:

Closing section, measures 100–120. (The six measures prima volta before the double bar are not counted.) The massive chords in measures 94, 95 are a remnant of the motif a_4, the eighth-note passage ascending from the bass (measures 86–100) is similarly explained as a variant of a_3, as above in measures 70–75. The theme of the closing section (measures 100–106) is not an outcome of the original motif a, but the answer to the close of the subsidiary theme, measures 96, 97:

The ascending rhythm in measure 100 corresponds to the descending rhythm in measures 96, 97:

The second theme of the closing section (measure 112) is the direct continuation of the phrase closing in measures 110, 111.

Motif b_1 is then appended.

The development section offers no difficulties. The first episode, measures 120–133, is directly joined to the end of the exposition, a parallel to measures 112–120. The second episode, measures 133–177, is a fugato on motif a. Observe how motif a grows from the preceding measures 129–134:

The three repeated E flat notes of motif a sound like a diminution of the three preceding thirds, whose time value is doubled (two measures instead of one), owing to the rests.

The third episode includes measures 177–200. Climax of the fugato, through dialogue of motif a_3 with the eighth-note figure of the fugato, derived from motif b. The peak of the climax of a_3 should be borne in mind (measures 185–197), inasmuch as the fugue in the fourth movement bears a relation to it.

The fourth episode comprises measures 201–227. The coda of the development briefly recapitulating a series of former ideas. After a diminuendo and ritardando in octave leaps (significant for the entire sonata), based on the rhythm a_3, the closing episode of the exposition is heard, now in B major (measures 201–208); this melody is next dissolved into eighth-note figures, reminiscent of measure 50 and following; a reminiscence of the fugato follows, and finally the fugato motif is dissolved into the characteristic leap (this time a leap of a sixth) with which motif a commences, forcefully pressing on in close imitations until the fortissimo is reached with which the reprise enters (measure 227). Also this stretta in sixths points to the fugue finale. The entire episode (measures 201–227) is very instructive: in an exposition, somewhere near the beginning of a sonata, it would have been logically incomprehensible. The succession of the five different episodes cannot be explained by itself, but only through their relation with the foregoing. At the close of the development section, however, such a combination has its well founded logical coherence: it represents a retrospective glance in compressed form at the distances already overcome.

The reprise hardly requires much explanation. The beginning (measures 227–232) shows thematic accompaniment in the left hand (motif a_3). Further on there is an unexpected transition to G flat major which prevails for some time. The second theme now enters, according to the rule, in B flat major. The closing episode is also quite regular.

The coda (measures 352–405), joined to the closing motif of the reprise, approaches once more through a series of sequences, the first theme of the closing group (measures 362–372). After the 6/4 chord a short cadenza is inserted (measures 373–376), leading to a dialogue treatment of motif a_2; a broad tonal level is maintained up to the close. This last episode indulges in quaint play with motif a, tearing it apart in various ways.

The scherzo takes its motif from the close of the first movement:

First phrase, measure 402   Scherzo

a variant of motif a_3. Development of the scherzo motif begins in shortened seven-measure (instead of eight-measure) periods. The structure is divided into $7 + 7 + 8 + 8 + 8 + 8$ measures. By virtue of the seven-measure phrases, the cadences (measures 7 and 14) are made peculiarly impressive to the ear. At measures 18–22 and at the parallel place, measures 34–38, the scherzo motif in quarter notes serves to make the close broader.

The trio in B flat minor (measures 46–115) is derived from the scherzo motif through augmentation:

Scherzo.   Trio.

This trio motif contains the germ of the adagio. The trio has 4×8 measures + 2 measures coda, with the melody alternately in the bass and in the soprano. Next follows, presto, the second part of the trio (measures 81–115). The theme is a broadened version of a:

Structure: 8 + 8 + 8 measures. Next follows an appendix, measures 105–115; again the close of the phrase shows those characteristic octave leaps, plunging down to the lowest depth, and through a prestissimo transition of the scale figure type (cf. page 235), reverses towards the loftiest height, only to hurtle down once more, rushing into the reprise, which until measure 162 is an exact repetition of the first part.

The coda, measures 162–177, again utilizing the octave leaps, takes up the scherzo motif towards the close.

The adagio sostenuto is in large sonata form. The principal theme is derived from motif *a;* it is also closely related to the trio theme of the scherzo:

The first principal theme fills out the first half of the main section (*Hauptsatz*) completely (measures 1–26). A second principal theme is introduced at measures 26–45, with a transition episode joined to it. This theme:

is derived from a free inversion of the first principal theme, as is made manifest by the following juxtaposition:

The development of this phrase makes use of much ornamental figuration of the melody. At measure 39 a new motif is crystallized from the sixteenth notes of the accompaniment. This motif is a free inversion of the figure in measure 47 of the first movement:

The same motif serves as accompaniment figure of the second theme.

Second theme in D major (measures 45–61) which again is a variant of motif *a* and is also closely related to the principal theme of the adagio:

Closing section (measures 61–69). The theme here is also derived from *a:*

The development section (measures 69–88) deals with the first principal theme of the adagio, still further subdividing its motifs into smaller particles.

The reprise (measures 89–155) is a rather exact repetition of the principal section of the exposition, but makes somewhat more lavish use of figuration.

The coda (measures 156–189) ushers in the melody of the subsidiary theme (measure 160) for the third time, now in G major. In measures 166, 167, the constantly repeated F sharp in the soprano should be compared to the beginning of the largo preceding the final fugue. The coda recapitulates the entire thematic material of the exposition, the two principal themes (measures 168, 176) as well as the now still broadened closing theme (measure 179):

The octave leaps of the close also have a thematic significance for the entire sonata:

The largo, the introduction to the fugue, is a piece in free fantasia style, but nevertheless full of intricate thematic relations. The start, with the characteristic octave leaps (variant of the leap of a tenth at the beginning of *a*), is closely connected with the close of the adagio. Toccata-like treatment.

These powerful chords with their vigorous octave leaps enter five times, the entries being interrupted by imitating interludes, passages of various kinds. Especially remarkable is the second passage, since later the fugue theme is derived from it (measure 2):

The first and third interludes (measures 1 and 3) have a thematic relationship, the fourth interlude (measures 9, 10) is more in the nature of an ornamental cadence. In the octave entry (measure 10), the bass clearly shows the beginning of *a:*

These leaps are continued in the bass in the allegro risoluto, below the trill from which the passage issues, leading directly into the fugue.

The theme of the fugue is:

(measure 6 of the allegro risoluto) and is developed from measure 2 of the largo, but had already been foreshadowed in the first movement (measures 1 and 46 and following). The countersubject, entering for the first time in measure 17, again makes use of the octave leap:

In the main the entire fugue obtains its thematic material from the theme and countersubject. This very complicated piece has eight fugal sections, interrupted by interludes as shown in the following outline.

First fugal section, measures 6–31, a normal exposition of a three-part fugue, B flat major.

Interlude (1), measures 31–41.

Second fugal section (measures 44–75), D flat major. By shifting the fugue theme a quarter of a measure ahead, the counterpoint is still more assimilated to the principal motif *a*. See measures 50–55:

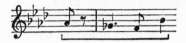

and measures 70–75:

Interlude (2), measures 75–85. G flat major. The three parts are intertwined in elegant canonic imitations.

Third fugal section (measures 85–120), E flat minor. Theme in double augmentation. Compare measures 109–120, the accumulated imitations of the first measure of the fugue theme, with the similar fugato episode in the development section of the first movement, measures 213–227.

Interlude (3), measures 120–142. Intricately woven from the same motifs as the second interlude, only worked out more extensively.

Fourth fugal section (measures 143–165). Theme *inverse*, that is, in cancrizans or crab-wise inversion, read backwards, a remarkable example, in classical music, of this rather rare and artificial inversion:

Starting at the close of the last measure and reading backwards, one restores the original version of the theme. There is a curious change in the character of the theme. The entire episode, piano and cantabile, proceed smoothly flowing.

Interlude (4), measures 165–186. Crescendo up to forte and fortissimo. Play of the thematic scale figures throughout all three parts. The full

335

energy of motion is reached again after a magnificent, vigorous D major cadence (measures 182–186) at the entrance of the next section.

Fifth fugal section (measures 186–224). The theme at first *recte,* in its original form, with new counterpoints in constant motion, afterwards *inverse,* turned upside down, with the likewise inverted two counterpoints of the first episode (measure 198), still later twice more inverted, with new counterpoints (measures 206 and 219).

Interlude (5), measures 224–239, on the trill and the sixteenth-note figure from the theme, at the close in utmost concentration of energy, leading to the dynamic climax of the entire fugue. Compare this place (measures 233–239) with the similar trill and leap episode, measures 109–120, and with places in the first movement, measures 31–35, 190–200, 213–227. Culmination at the powerfully worked out A major. After the chord beats in fortissimo, a long pause follows the main caesura of the entire piece.

Sixth fugal section (measures 240–284). Sharp contrast of sound, owing to the entrance of a new, calm theme in even quarter notes, which at first is developed in three-part writing and later combined with the first three measures of the fugue theme (measures 269–284). The beginning of a double fugue, which, however, is not continued further. No special interlude follows this sixth episode. Considering the fragmentary state of the double fugue, one might conjecture whether this entire episode would not better be considered as an interlude.

Seventh fugal section (measures 284–324) follows immediately, which compensates for the sketchy character of the sixth section by an overflowing wealth of material, comprising almost two sections. Here the strettas commence in especially complex and artificial treatment, twice *recte* and *inverse* (in straight motion and in inversion) at the same time (measures 284–290, 290–296). An interlude is inserted within this episode, a three-bar sequence, in three different transpositions (measures 298–300, 301–303, 304–306), with one measure added for the purpose of transition (307). Next follows the second half of the fugue theme, with the original counterpoints (measures 308–311, 312–315) worked out twice in strict fugal style, to make up for the fragmentary double fugue treatment of the same theme in the sixth section. Harmonically this section is important because, starting in the middle of the sixth section, the harmonically rather extravagant piece works its way back to the tonic key of B flat major, decisively aiming at the tonic, especially after measure 308 (organ point on F). A short interlude leads with ever growing agitation (measure 315–323) to the next section.

Eighth fugal section (measures 324–357). The theme at first appears in F major, in its original form, only with the sixteenth-note figures distributed in both hands. Next follows a combination of the theme, *recte* and *inverse,* at the same time in the first half. After this a somewhat free three-part stretta enters (measures 339–349), followed by the theme in the highest soprano register. This section, drawing to a close, is suddenly and most effectively interrupted by a cadenza (measures 357–374) tending to retard the tempo, rhythm, dynamics, and harmony. This cadenza may be considered a part of the coda.

The theme of the coda keeps repeating in pianissimo, in the sinister key of E flat minor, above the soft drumlike tremolo of the lowest basses. In the chains of trills in double sixths the plastic form of the motifs gradually vanishes, until at last only the germ motif of the entire sonata, the upbeat:

is left. The adagio measures 371–373 are also to be interpreted as upbeat formations:

The third quarter of each measure is thus joined in a peculiar relation with the preceding two quarters as well as with the next measure. From this adagio the rapid sixteenth-note passage of the fugue theme at first emerges softly, then rushes down rapidly in a tremendous crescendo to the lowest depths of the bass and finally comes to a close in the shrill, metallic trills and the mighty leaps at the end. This close, in its 3/4 time notation, is veiled in its meaning. It becomes clear in its thematic context only when one mentally transposes these measures into 4/4 time, as follows:

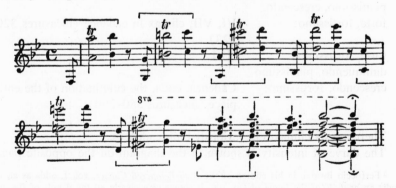

Every one of these sections has its own tonality, a device which is something quite novel in fugue composition.

I. B flat major, F major, B flat major.
    Interlude (1), B flat major to D flat major.
II. D flat major, A flat major, B flat minor.
    Interlude (2), G flat major, D flat major to E flat minor.
III. E flat minor, B flat minor to A flat major.
    Interlude (3), A flat major, F minor, B flat minor, G flat
    major to B minor.
IV. B minor, D major, B minor.
    Interlude (4), D major.
V. D major, G major, D major, E flat major.
    Interlude (5), E flat major to D major.
VI. (VII). D major, B flat major, F major, B flat major.
VIII. F major, B flat major. Coda, E flat minor, B flat major.

The fluctuation of the dynamic scheme might be sketched out as follows
(Roman numerals refer to the fugal sections; Arabic to the interludes):

mezzo forte:	I, 1, II, climax (measures 70–75), cadence in G flat major
piano, crescendo, forte:	2, III, climax (measures 107–115), then follows diminuendo
piano, crescendo, forte:	3
piano:	IV
crescendo, forte:	4, climax, D major cadence (measures 182–187)
forte, fortissimo:	V, 5, highest culmination in measures 232–238
pianissimo, crescendo, forte, fortissimo:	VI, VII, climax in cadence (measures 320–323)
forte, fortissimo: diminuendo, pianissimo crescendo, fortissimo:	VIII Cadenza, coda, the culmination of the entire piece (measures 380–390)

There are six climaxes in variously built cadences.

The curve of intensity is shown in the diagram on the opposite page.[2]

[2] Ferruccio Busoni, in his edition of the *Well-Tempered Clavier*, vol. I, adds as an appendix an analysis of the fugue of Op. 106. It shows very clearly all the details of the contrapuntal complexities, more so than the present analysis which aims at pointing out the structural ideas rather than all the structural details. Attention may also be called to Riemann's thorough analysis in vol. III of his work on the Beethoven sonatas (Max Hesse, Berlin).

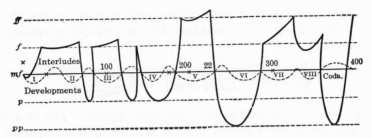

BEETHOVEN'S OP. 130

With extraordinary mastery, novelty, and ingenuity Beethoven builds up his grandiose string quartet in B flat major, Op. 130, from a few motifs, all of which make their appearance at the beginning of the first movement. They are the following:

First movement. Simple exposition of the four motifs, *a, b, c, d.* Measures 1–16; *a* in measure 1, *b* in measure 7, *c* and *d* mostly combined with each other, measures 15, 16. The first three motifs can even be reduced to a common ground or germ motif, the descending scale, which is made apparent by the brackets in the example above. The movement is constructed in sonata form. First theme (*Hauptsatz*): measures 1–37, composed of the four motifs, especially *c* and *d.* Transition, measures 37–55. Motif *b,* measures 37–40, motif *c,* measures 40–44. The following four measures in eighth notes are a more concentrated version of measures 43 and 44. Variant of the descending scale motif in measures 49, 50, in the inversion ascending, measures 51, 52. Motif *c,* measures 53, 54. Transition to G flat major by unison scale passages, without regular modulation. Second theme (*Seitensatz*), G flat major:

339

A variant of motif *a,* both parts of this motif exchange places, the first half being placed after the second half. Measures 64–70, an episode on a fragment of *c:*

Measures 70–86 developed from *c;* the motif appears at first in a broad legato with new counter melodies, afterwards cut up into fragments and thrown from one instrument to another in vivid dialogue. Closing theme (*Schluszsatz*), measures 87–93, the first three measures derived from *c,* the last four based on a fragment of *a:*

The development section is rather brief (measures 93–132), no doubt because the entire exposition section had already anticipated much of the development by its subtle thematic treatment. Measures 93–95, motif *a.* Measures 96, 97, motifs *c* and *d* together. Measures 97–104, motifs *a, c, d,* and a fragment of *a.* This fragment marks the close of the episode; the three, later the two last tones of *a* serve as the rhythmical formula of the accompaniment for the remainder of the development section:

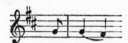

Measures 104–118 contain an intricate texture of motif *a* (in a new variant, approaching the second theme), and motifs *c* and *d* based on the above-mentioned rhythmical formula:

Measures 118–122, dialogue of first violin and violoncello on motif *d;* measures 122–132, dialogue of first violin and cello on the new variant of the second theme and motif *d.*

The reprise, measures 132–213, corresponds in general to the exposition section. The second theme now in D flat major, turning towards the tonic B flat.

The coda, measures 214–234, corresponds to the beginning of the movement. Ingenious play with the motifs *a, c, d*. Measures 223–226 on the rhythm:

derived from *d*. The entire movement contains literally not a single measure which does not have its origin in one or several of the four ground motifs.

Second movement, presto. Large three-part song form with trio. The principal theme of this scherzo has a double relation to motif *a,* in the first, as well as in the second violin:

This is a transformation of

from motif *a*. The lower part brings the germ motif of the entire quartet, the descending scale in augmentation. The entire first part of the scherzo is dominated by these two motifs. The trio theme:

is derived from the first scherzo motif of the first violin, with a new arpeggio-like introduction added. The ingenious and masterly thematic return to the reprise has already been recognized as a model of its kind (see page 235). A comparison of the reprise with the first section reveals no essential changes. The last ten measures, the coda, show a transposition of the two scherzo motifs, the motif of the first violin is now given to the viola and the motif of the second violin to the first violin; shortly before the close the second violin comes to the fore again.

Third movement, andante con moto. A very complex structure in a kind of free sonata form. An analysis follows:

Exposition: Principal theme, measures 1–10, D flat major. Transition, anticipating thematic development of the principal theme, D flat major, touching F minor, B flat minor to A flat major, measures 10–26. Second theme in A flat major with close in D flat major, measures 26–33. A closing section is lacking.

Development section very brief, derived from the second theme. Measures 33–39.

The reprise, measures 39–67. Second theme now in the tonic D flat major, with close in G flat major.

The coda more explicit, to make amends for the brief development, measures 67–88.

The first three measures show motif *a* in free transformations; the real theme of the movement in the tenor, below another version of motif *a* in the upper part:

New transformation of the principal theme in the transition episode, measure 11:

Beginning with measure 17, variants of motif *d* make their appearance

Measure 17

Measure 18

Measures 22, 23

in the second and first violin, as accompaniment of the principal theme in the cello. The second theme (measure 25) is derived from motif *d:*

The accompaniment motif at the start of the reprise, measures 38–44, also derives its rhythm from motif *d:*

The reprise corresponds rather exactly to the first part.

The coda intricately weaves motif *a* through all four parts:

Measure 68

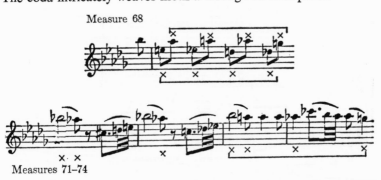

Measures 71–74

Here the motif: B flat, A, A flat, G, is seen, exactly as at the beginning of the first movement and of the andante. Measures 81–84 softly anticipate the next movement, "alla danza tedesca." Compare the motif in thirds, measure 81:

with the danza:

Fourth movement, "alla danza tedesca." In large three-part song form with coda. The main theme is composed of variants of motifs *d* and *a*. In the middle section motif *d* is still more distinct, now combined with motif *c;* both motifs dominate the entire middle section, from measures 25–80:

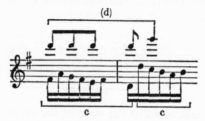

The coda, measures 129–150 breaks the theme into tiny fragments and allows motif *a* to enter quite unexpectedly:

Fifth movement, cavatina, adagio molto expressivo. Songlike, with a double theme. First theme in E flat major, measures 1–23. Second theme in E flat major, measures 23–40. Middle section, C flat major to E flat major, measures 41–50. Shortened reprise, measures 50–66. The principal theme is a variant of *a* in inversion:

The second theme is even more similar to *a:*

The middle section contains distinct allusions to *d* and *a*. Measures 44 and 46:

Finale, allegro. A rondo combined with sonata features. The principal theme is composed of *b, c,* and *d:*

The other themes and interludes are almost entirely derived from the four motifs. The first interlude (measure 18):

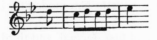

has its origin in the first measure of *b:*

Further on occur the much used motifs (at first in measures 51, 55, 67):

Measure 75, bass viol

Measure 104, two violins

Measure 132ff.

Whatever new ideas appear in this movement besides these four ground motifs, are always brought into some sort of relation to them, with the result that these new episodes, too, are organically connected with the fundamental thematic substance of the piece.

Beethoven had originally intended to make the "Grosse Fuge," Op. 133, the finale of this B flat major quartet, instead of the rondo finale just analyzed. The thematic relations of Op. 133, however, seem to point much more to the quartets in A minor and C sharp minor, Opp. 132 and 131, than to the B flat major quartet.

CÉSAR FRANCK'S VIOLIN SONATA

César Franck's violin sonata in A major represents a happy and masterly application of the sonata form, in the sense of strictly organic development.

The first movement, allegretto ben moderato, is written in an abbreviated sonata form:

Exposition, consisting of first, second, and third theme.

Reprise, consisting of first, second theme, and coda in place of the third theme. The usual development section in the middle is left out altogether.

The germ of the entire sonata is the main motif:

of which the entire first theme group is formed. The second theme:

though used as an independent melody, may, nevertheless be derived from measures 23 and 24:

The closing section, measures 46–61, goes back to motif *a*. The reprise with the usual changes is followed by the coda, which again is based on motif *a* alone. It is a peculiarity of this sonata that the single movements not only grow from the same germ motifs, but that even the newly added counter melodies in the various movements are made to have a mutual relation.

The second movement, an allegro in sonata form, derives its principal motif from *b,* and the second part of its theme from those chromatically descending six last measures of the first movement where they are thematically unimportant. Compare the second movement (b_1) principal theme with the first movement:

twice repeated in sequences, starting from C sharp and E, followed by the closing phrase:

Closing measures

347

A secondary motif of the first movement here gains importance for the principal theme of the second movement. The second theme (*Seitensatz*) has its origin in a transformation of *a:*

In the continuation:

the partial motif a_2 becomes important. The phrase:

is derived from the first measure of b_1. The development section commences at "quasi lento." It is dominated by a new form of b_1:

to which are joined all the other motifs of the second movement. The archaistic, solemn chord progression b_2 becomes the germ of the third movement, the recitative. These few motifs suffice for the remainder of the long, passionately progressing and broadly constructed movement.

The third movement, recitativo-fantasia, is still more admirable in its fine thematic structure. Down to its smallest details and figurations, the piece is thematically strictly built, yet so ingeniously does it vary the motifs taken over from other movements that not for a moment is the impression of strain produced or of carrying on until exhaustion, a danger which always accompanies the application of the "principe cyclique." The movement is written in a three-part fantasia form:

First part, measures 1–31. The piano commences with the phrase:

348

which is a direct continuation of motif b_2 of the second movement. After four measures, the violin solo enters in recitative with a phrase quite important for the continuation of the piece; in spite of its new impression it contains a relation to b_2, and at the close alludes to the germ motif a_2:

In the next two phrases of the piano a is heard in measures 11 and 14:

The start with the ascending third, characteristic of the whole piece, is also seen in the following phrase of the piano, measure 17, directly connected with the corresponding measures 13 and 16.

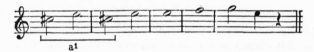

Next follows a repetition of the first ten measures of the piece, now transposed to the dominant D minor. Immediately after this episode the next part enters.

Second part (measures 32–52). It is at first dominated by a figuration of the violin, intertwining the motif a_2:

There is growing agitation for thirteen measures. The fortissimo is prepared by a new third entry of the initial phrase c. The climax is reached with a phrase recurring three times in different keys—compounded of motif a_2 and a variant of b_2:

This passionate outburst is immediately followed by the next part.

Third part, measures 53–117. It begins with an effect of sharp contrast: pianissimo in calm response to the preceding agitated fortissimo. Connection with what has preceded is manifest by the opening measures growing directly from motif b_2 of the closing measure of the second part; this time the motif is doubly and triply augmented. Moreover, the piano here resumes the phrase d from the first part, measures 8 and 29:

A few measures later (measure 59), the last motif of importance for the construction of the sonata enters, namely the phrase:

which in reality is a transformation of motif c. Further on a climax is in preparation; this climax again shows an interesting relation between principal and secondary motifs. Measures 71–79 in the bass are based on a new transposition of the four-note motif b_2 now on the notes F sharp, C sharp, A, G sharp. In addition to this, the violin, as principal voice, plays a phrase from the second movement (measures 135 and 136), which had served there as counterpoint to the motif b_1. Again a secondary motif of one movement is made the principal motif of another movement. Compare the second movement (measure 135) with these measures:

Second movement

350

Third movement

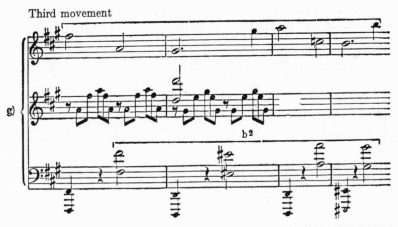

Again there is a return to pianissimo. Once more the various motifs pass in array over the thematic triplet accompaniment *e,* at first *f* (measures 81–92), then *a* (measures 93–100), finally *g,* mounting to the strongest outburst, fortissimo (measures 101–110). The "molto lento e mesto" is followed by a coda of seven measures, resuming measure 17; at the same time the violin in the last three measures clearly points to the following finale. The entire movement cannot be assigned to a definite formal pattern. But in spite of its freedom of structure, it is nevertheless most logically developed and admirably solves the problem of how an entire piece may be evolved from a given germinal substance, a given basic idea with logical consequence, and how it should seek the form appropriate to its situation.

The finale, allegretto poco mosso, is likewise very original and interesting in its form. One might call it a canon with free interludes, after the analogy of a fugue, in which the various fugal episodes are bridged over by interludes. An interesting variation of the rondo idea could also be assumed. The plan of construction is as follows:

(1) Canon between piano and violin, A major (measures 1–37); interlude on motif *f* with return to the canon theme (measures 38–78).

(2) Canon in E major (measures 78–99). Interlude on motif a_1, apparently leading back to the canon theme (measures 99–133). Instead of the expected canon an intermezzo of dramatic character (measures 133–184) enters, an agitated dialogue between a fragment of the canon theme and the episode *g* from the third movement, worked out particularly in the remote keys of A flat minor, D sharp minor, B flat minor, and F minor, brought to a climax in C major, with motif *f* from the third movement against the descending bass octaves. After that, diminuendo and return to the next canon.

(3) Canon reprise in A major (measures 184–236); coda (measures

236–243). The canon theme, a variant of *a*, is a response to the closing measures of the recitative. The close of the recitative and the canon theme:

DEBUSSY'S STRING QUARTET

One of the most fascinating works of art in accordance with the demands of the "principe cyclique" is the string quartet, Op. 10, of Claude Debussy.

The principal motif *a*, from which all four movements are more or less derived, is stated at the very beginning:

The first movement in sonata form, besides making use of the principal motif, also employs several other motifs (*b, c, d*) similar to each other:

of which only *a* and *d* are of importance for the development of the movement.

The second movement, a kind of scherzo serenade, is completely dominated by the principal motif *a* in the following transformations:

as an ostinato-like middle part. After twenty-one repetitions of the phrase in the viola, first violin, cello, a melodious trio enters, with the following transformation of the motif *f:*

After a return to the now abbreviated ostinato episode, there follows a thematic, recitative-like introduction (*g*):

which again yields its place to the broad trio version of the motif. Next follows an extended coda on the motifs *h* and *i.*

The third, slow movement, has a principal theme (*k*) derived from motif *d* of the first movement:

It dominates the entire first part. Next follows a somewhat more vivid intermezzo; its first motif (*l*) represents a variant of measure 2 of *k:*

In the further development of the piece, a variant of *a* and *g* makes its appearance (*m*):

After a reminiscence of *l* the coda briefly touches *k.*

The finale begins by introducing three variants (*n, o, p*) of *a:*

The main section now follows, sonata-like in character, with two entirely new themes, *q* and *r,* of which *r* is an offspring of *q*. Only in the development section are these new themes brought into relation to the principal motif *a:*

Motif *a* in its manifold variants dominates the entire movement, sometimes in broad melodic lines, in augmentation, at other times in diminution, as an ostinato middle part. Every few measures the motif emerges out of the mesh of voices in some new disguise; it then dances its nimble way through the coda:

CHAPTER **XVIII**

free forms[1]

Tristan und Isolde: prelude

The prelude to Wagner's *Tristan und Isolde* presents certain difficulties of analysis because the intentional avoidance of full cadences, which are replaced by deceptive cadences, obscures the structure of the piece for the listener. The result is the so-called "unending melody," which as a stylistic element has perhaps never been employed with greater mastery than in this piece. Compared with the forms based on division by means of cadences, this piece is distinguished by the absence of all "transition groups" leading over from one theme to another, as occurs in the sonata and the rondo. The strictly thematic melos does not stop for even a single measure; it entirely scorns introductions and transitions before the entrance of certain melodic phrases. The ear hears an unbroken chain of melodic phrases; it perceives only a difference in intensity, in color, in accumulation of sound, but not a difference in melodic character. Nevertheless, the inquisitive mind can perceive the planned structure of the piece. Its first two measures state two closely related and yet essentially different motifs, exhausting the entire thematic material for the 110 measures (see page 356).

[1] See Part One, section on overture, Chapter VIII.

Motif *a,* with the leap of a sixth, followed by a chromatic descent; motif *b* chromatically ascending. Motif *b* is later heard in two variants:

and

An analysis of the structure follows:

A.	Exposition	Measures 1–17	
B.		Measures 17–24	
C.		Measures 25–44	
D.	Development and Climax together with Reprise	Measures 45–62	(corresponding to C, but differently continued, leading to the climax)
E.		Measures 63–74	(the climax is being prepared once more)
F.		Measures 75–83	(first climax overtopped by yet a second peak, measures 82, 83)
G.	Coda	Measures 84–110	(descent to pianissimo)

Notice the period-like correspondence of parts C and D to the very original use of the reprise: Measures 66–71, 75–78 correspond to measures 1–12, 17–21, but they lead up to an outburst of the highest ecstasy, whereas the earlier measures start softly, filled with longing. Also E and F have a certain correspondence to A and B. Furthermore, the coda G is an even more precise reprise of the introduction A with but slight variants. A striking feature is the phrase (measures 17–21), which returns three times in identical form in different places, but each time with greater passion and forcefulness: measures 33–36, 58–62, 74–77.

These repetitions occur at exactly equal distances: measures 17, 33, 58, 74, in symmetrical disposition, sixteen, twenty-five, and sixteen measures from each other, in addition to which there are the seventeen measures which precede the first appearance of the phrase. Almost arithmetically exact multiples of eight measures are manifest here: sixteen, sixteen, twenty-four, and sixteen measures, an architectural idea, like a conspicuous ornament which is built into a façade at regular distances. Moreover, the dynamic element in this piece is used more intentionally and more frequently than usually, not only as a coloristic effect, but also as a constructive, formal element. The surging and ebbing motion, manifest already in the elementary motifs of the first two measures, is the real dominating motif of the entire structure. Of these, the surging motion receives preferential treatment. Compared with it the ebbing away gives the impression of a short breathing pause before the still stronger onslaught to follow. The aesthetic balance is brought about in the coda: after the most powerful outbreak, a sudden collapse follows; the entire coda is dominated by diminuendo. The curve of intensity of the piece (disregarding for the sake of clarity slight deviations, passing sforzati) would look like this:

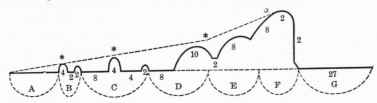

at * the episode *c* enters four times with growing intensity.

The mutual relations of the single sections may be made evident by the following:

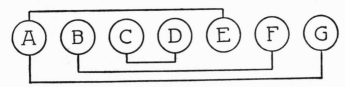

AG, AE, BF, CD belong together in one way or another. The entire piece represents a short exposition, followed by a long development section, led to the highest climax with interruptions. In this development the same melodic episode appears four times at exactly equal distances. A slightly

357

sketched-out reprise is worked into the climax. The development in itself is also symmetrically constructed (CD). The coda corresponds to the introduction, somewhat extended, its energy spent as it comes to the close. Though the piece appears to be very novel and thoroughly original, it nevertheless makes use of many traditional and well tried means, such as two-bar phrases, frequent sequences, cautious modulation. Besides the main tonality A minor, the piece employs only the closely related keys C major, E minor, A minor, F sharp minor.

In one way or another two older (though in sentiment entirely different) masterpieces may be considered precursors of the *Tristan* prelude. They are the A major prelude, No. 19, of the *Well-Tempered Clavier,* volume II, and the first movement of Beethoven's piano sonata, Op. 101.

Bach: A major prelude

The lovely and peaceful A major prelude resembles the *Tristan* prelude in the constant flow of the motifs, in the constant softly rolling waves, one wave continuously overtopping the preceding crest.

Beethoven: Op. 101

The first movement of Beethoven's A major sonata, Op. 101, has as its principal, indeed as its only distinct motif, a phrase resembling Wagner's motif in its ascent and simultaneous chromatic descent in the tenor. Here also contrasting, different themes, running-passage transitions are avoided, and the piece is dominated by uninterrupted, "eternal," and strictly thematic melody. The blissfully idyllic and intimate piece nevertheless shows striking similarities of technique to those of Wagner's prelude, aglow with sensuous passion. These similarities are manifest in the exposition and in the two climaxes in the middle and towards the close.

All three pieces by Bach, Beethoven, and Wagner have, as a striking coincidence, 6/8 and 12/8 time and the tonality of A in common.

CHAPTER XIX

concerto form[1]

Bach: piano concerto in D minor

The form of the concerto has been treated with especial variety and refinement by J. S. Bach. Around 1700 the Italian concerto form was comprised of three movements, of which the outer two were lively and the middle section slow. Bach's piano concerto in D minor, the piano arrangement of an older, lost violin concerto, offers an easily accessible example of the Italian concerto form.[2] This type of form, as analyzed here, has validity for the older violin concerto as well. The first allegro immediately presents the characteristic feature of concertizing treatment in the successive statement of tutti and solo ideas: two different but not contrasting phrases, as the solo is simply the continuation of the tutti. In fact, the entire movement is based on a single principal theme; the formal idea consists in presenting the theme turned about in various directions and illuminated from different angles. Clearcut construction, carefully planned modulation are important factors here.

[1] See Part One, Chapter VIII.
[2] This analysis is based on Busoni's adaptation of this concerto for the modern piano. The arrangement is as faithful to the Bach spirit as it is effective in its own right.

The structure of the movement is:

(a) Tutti (D minor), measures 1–6.

(b) Solo intrata (A minor), measures 7–12.

Tutti and solo on theme a (D minor modulating to A minor), measures 13–21.

Solo, free continuation of b (A minor to F major), measures 22–40.

Development of a (F major, D minor, A minor), measures 40–62.

Intermezzo in free fantasy (A minor, E minor, C major), measures 62–91.

New free development of a (C major, G minor, brilliant cadenza of the solo piano inserted, again G minor, back to D minor, finally to B flat major). This episode brings culmination, climax, free reprise, and combination of a and b all together (measures 91–135).

Thematic development of motifs from a (B flat major, G minor, to A minor (measures 136–150); transition to the closing section, commencing in the manner of an effective solo cadenza with an extended organ point on the tonic D, continued in rich figuration of the piano, and culminating in a weighty reappearance of the principal motif a. D minor is predominant, with few passing transitions to other keys (measures 150–180).

The similarities to the sonata form and also the differences between both forms are evident here. The similarities are: thematic development, three-part form of the entire piece, with distinctly indicated reprise. The differences are: only one principal theme, no contrasting second theme.

The slow intermediate movement is treated in detail in two chapters of this book. Its construction makes it a variant of the chaconne form; in regard to melodic structure it belongs to the fantasia-like pieces in free form.[3]

In its form the finale approaches a very freely treated fugue, whose theme, however, is played in its entirety by the orchestra only, six times in all.

Measures 1–13 in D minor.

Measures 29–41 in A minor.

Measures 61–72 in D minor.

Measures 106–118 in G minor.

Measures 153–165 in G minor.

Measures 238–248 in D minor.

In its dialogue with the orchestra, the piano is treated in concerto style; while the orchestra states or reiterates the theme, the piano occasionally

[3] See pages 315 and 374.

plays along, adding new, interesting counterpoints, filling out, strengthening the sound, or adding a decorative element. At other times it retires more or less into silence, while the orchestra alone is playing. The piano's real field of action lies in the very extended interludes between the six entries of the main theme, in which it concertizes in animated rivalry with the orchestra, in free thematic fantasia, in playful, brilliant dialogue, in constant flow and motion, until the brilliant, most effective cadenza is reached with which the last interlude crowns the entire structure in splendid culmination.

J. S. Bach: six Brandenburg concerti

The Brandenburg concerti got their name from the fact that they were written for a prince of the House of Brandenburg who had given Bach an order for several orchestral works. They were finished in Cöthen, and in 1721 Bach sent the beautifully written autograph scores to Prince Christian Ludwig, who maintained a good orchestra.

These six concerti belong to the species of the *concerto grosso,* a favorite form of orchestral music from about 1700 to 1750. Corelli, Vivaldi, Handel, and Bach were the leading masters in this form. Its constructive idea consists in a contest and a dialogue between a small group of solo instruments (the so-called "concertino," the "little concerto") and the "concerto grosso" ("the big concerto"), that is, the full orchestra. The resulting contrasts of sound and the more or less vivid repartee between the various instrumental groups offer many interesting problems and opportunities for impressive effects. In the application of these basic constructive ideas, Bach showed a very independent mind. His Brandenburg concerti show more deviations from the typical form than is found in the concerti grossi of any other master. They differ not only from the generally acknowledged models of the species, but also among themselves, each one establishing a new, characteristic type, different from the other five companions.

CONCERTO NO. 1 IN F MAJOR

This concerto is written for two horns, three oboes, bassoon, a "violino piccolo concertato," two violins, viola, violoncello, and basso continuo. The "violino piccolo," a now obsolete instrument, was tuned a third higher, and its part was correspondingly transposed. At present the ordinary violin is used for the solo episodes.

The first movement, a brisk allegro, develops the concerto idea by the dialogue of the three groups of woodwinds, strings, and horns, from time to time interrupted by a vigorous tutti. It consists of seven sections:

(*a*) (measures 1–13). Exposition of the thematic material, in a tutti section. In measure 1 the fanfare motif of the violins and horns and the merry countermotif of the oboes in sixteenth notes serve as thematic material for the entire first movement.

(b) (measures 13–27). Concerned with a thematic development of the motifs just indicated, in a more transparent, lighter setting, for little groups of instruments, in vivid repartee, with brief tutti mixed in. The keys touched are F major, C major, G minor, B flat major, D minor.

(c) (measures 27–43). New concertizing development, passing on from D minor to F major and C major.

(d) (measures 43–52). Continued development, C major to A minor and G minor.

(e) (measures 53–57). Dialogue of the solo instruments, horns, oboe, violin. G minor to F major.

(f) (measures 57–72). Repetition of section b, with some variants.

(g) (measures 72–84). Repetition of section a.

Spitta, in his monumental book on Bach, calls attention to the reversed order of the episodes in the recapitulation, the first section corresponding to the last one, the second to the one before the last. This structural arrangement a b c d e b a hardly ever occurs in modern music.

The center of the entire piece of eighty-four measures, the episode, measures 36–43, exactly in the middle, is underlined by an episode of almost romantic harmony, passing from C major back to C major with surprising chord progressions, spiced with suspensions and chromatic tones.

In section f the repetition of b is not complete, but is broken off at measure $62 = 17$, and continued with the romantic episode measures $36–43 = 64–72$, transposed a fourth higher, and thus still overtopping the central climax by a final climax.

The second movement, adagio, is a profoundly touching, elegiac fantasy, in chamber music style, on a richly ornate theme of four measures in D minor, played by the solo oboe and accompanied by the strings. Besides the oboe, the violin solo and the basses are the interlocutors of this impressive dialogue.

The theme is taken up by the violin in G minor (measures 5–8), next by the bass in C minor (measures 9–12), the oboe and violin, in canonic imitation (measures 12–20) in A minor. The next episode begins with the theme in D minor in the bass (measures 20–23), followed by a new canonic imitation in the violin and oboe (measures 23–31), passing over to G minor before the return to D minor. For the last time, the theme is heard in the bass (measures 31–34). The oboe closes the strange fantasy with an expressive cadenza (measures 34, 35), followed by a few measures of coda, reminiscent of the medieval *hoquetus* or hocket effect, those little sighs, interrupted by rests, answering each other in the three groups of oboes, strings and basses. Beethoven has made use of a similar episode of sighs and sobs at the close of the "Coriolanus" overture and of the funeral march in the "Eroica" symphony. Throughout the piece the accompaniment indulges in those sighing, hocket-like figures.

The third movement, allegro, in F major resembles the first movement in its structure, with the reverse order of the repetition of the first two sections towards the close of the piece. The dialogue of the several groups is made more distinct and impressive by the constant interchange of forte and piano, that is, by tutti and solo episodes, by the insertion of a brief adagio (measures 82, 83) in the midst of the allegro. In this piece the character of a solo concerto is much more pronounced than that of a concerto grosso. The solo violin dominates the field in all the solo episodes:

(*a*) Tutti, forte (measures 1–17), F major.
(*b*) Solo, piano (measures 17–40), F major to C major.
(*c*) Tutti, forte (measures 40–53), C major.
(*d*) Solo, piano (measures 53–63), C major, D minor, A minor.
(*e*) Tutti, forte (measures 63–70), A minor.
(*f*) Solo, piano (measures 70–84), G minor.
(*g* = *b*) Solo, piano (measures 84–108), F major.
(*h* = *a*) Tutti, forte (measures 108–124), F major.

The entire piece is based on only one theme, a jolly, rollicking melody, with its fanfare-like attack of the strings and the jocose answer of the horns, sounding like merry and boisterous laughter (measures 1–6). The solo violin takes up the same theme, embellishing it with full chords and some display of virtuosity. At measures 30–40, the contest of the horn with the solo violin is of special interest; a little later (measures 54–63), the oboe tries to vie with the solo violin in an ambitious little duo, followed by the horn a second time. The entire concerto might be closed with this allegro, which has a decided finale character. Bach, however, appended (perhaps for a special occasion) two charming little dance pieces, a minuet and a polacca.

The menuetto with trio, and the polacca, also with a trio, are pieces of that graceful rococo type adorning his harpsichord suites. There is, however, nothing of a concertizing character in these dances. The menuetto employs the full orchestra all the time. The first trio, for two oboes and bassoon, a real "trio" in the old sense, brings in a delightful contrast of sound. The polacca in 3/8 time, written for the string quartet, also dispenses with concertizing traits, keeping all instruments busy all the time with hardly any pauses.

The second trio, for two horns and oboe as bass, has an odd charm, not only because of its melodic beauty, but also because of its rare combination of instruments.

CONCERTO NO. 2 IN F MAJOR

This concerto is written for four solo instruments: trumpet, flute, oboe, violin, and the string orchestra with thorough bass. All four solo instruments are soprano instruments of about the same range. They compete and concertize with each other, by taking up in turn the same motifs, varying them each in its particular way.

The first movement is a joyful, brisk allegro. It starts with a brief tutti (measures 1–8) which contains the entire thematic material of the movement. In fact, the very first measure suffices for Bach's art of evolving a whole piece from a brief impetus. Here are seen the fanfare motif of the trumpet, dominating the entire first tutti, the more finely articulated and a little more complex countermotif of the violins, also of the fanfare type, and the third countermotif, the rapidly running passage in sixteenth notes, played at first by the basses, and passing up into the soprano region in measure 3. This first tutti serves as a sort of ritornello or refrain, recurring three times in the course of the movement, with some variants, at the beginning, in the middle, and at the close of the piece (measures 1–8, 45–48, 102–105, and 112–117). Between the ritornelli the solo instruments concertize with each other as well as jointly with the orchestra. Thus, after the first tutti, the solo instruments enter by couples: oboe and violin (measure 13), flute and oboe (measure 17), flute and trumpet (measure 21), these entries always separated by a short tutti outburst. At measure 29 the four solo instruments are assembled for the first time in a brilliant quartet, soon joined by the orchestra, now not merely accompanying, but adding independent parts. A splendid display of polyphonic writing from four to eight parts fills out measures 29–58.

Towards the end of this section (measures 45–48), the ritornello makes its appearance for the second time, now played by the solo quartet and accompanied by the orchestra, all in charming pianissimo. At measure 49 a surprising new continuation is heard with unexpected chords, piano and forte alternately in every measure. This almost romantic, chromatic intermezzo finally lands in B flat major (measure 58), after a chain of interesting modulations. It underlines the exact middle of the entire piece, with its 117 measures. What follows is a recapitulation of the musical substance, made novel, however, to the ear by many ingenious changes. This recapitulation starts in B flat major. The solo quartet has a free field in its concertizing intermezzo, measures 59–66. Here the orchestra enters again, and in the remainder of the piece the solo quartet and the orchestra combine their resources to achieve a brilliant and effective final climax. At measures 71–76 the romantic, chromatic intermezzo is heard again, now headed in the direction of G minor. The incessant motion of the sixteenth-note passages produces a strong tension, almost of a dramatic kind. At last (measure 102) the ritornello bursts out in radiant fullness of sound, followed by another reference to the chromatic intermezzo, measures 106–113, immediately preceding the brilliant close with the second half of the ritornello, measures 114–117.

The second movement, andante, is a piece of pure chamber music. Flute, oboe, and violin (without the trumpet, unfit for the elegiac character of the piece) play a trio, a marvel of free polyphony, accompanied merely by the thorough bass. Here is a unique mixture of fugue, canon, and aria. Or one might call the piece a three-part invention. It has only one theme, stated at the very beginning, measures 1–7. All three solo instruments vie with each other in singing the elegiac theme, with its sighs, its quavers, its lamenting leaps. Every single measure of the piece is filled with the motifs of the theme. No new countermotif diverts the attention from the intensive expression of the plaintive melody. In fugal and canonic imitation, in free dialogue, the three instrumental parts are closely intertwined. If one would leave out of consideration all these imitations, all this dialogue, and pay attention merely to the main melodic line as it passes from one instrument to the other, one would hear a most beautiful aria.

The piece with its sixty-five measures is very symmetrically divided into three almost equally long sections:

(a) Measures 1–23, D minor to A minor and C major.
(b) Measures 23–43, C major to B major and G minor.
(c) Measures 43–65, G minor to D minor.

The first two sections contain several outbursts of passionate grief (measures 20–23, 26–29, 32–34, 38–40), whereas the last section is filled with sighs and sobs. The accompaniment is based on a bass line running continuously, without the slightest interruption, on an evenly measured figure of six eighth notes. The harmony abounds in colorful and most expressive chord effects through chromatic notes, uncommon use of passing and changing notes, and suspensions.

The finale, allegro assai, F major, is a brilliant fugue on a jubilant, bright, and vivid theme. Its very start, in the trumpet, with its sparkling little trills, its firm rhythm, its jocose leaps and fanfares, is truly electrifying. Its counterpoint, in the bass (measures 1–6), is the constant companion of the theme, and is coupled with it at every appearance, in double counterpoint, appearing either above or below the theme. The fugal portions are generally allotted to the solo quartet and the thorough bass, whereas the full orchestra is reserved for the interludes.

CONCERTO NO. 3 IN G MAJOR

This concerto is written for three violins, three violas, three violoncelli, and thorough bass. A concertino of solo instruments does not occur in this work. The concerto style consists here in the constant dialogue of the three groups of string instruments—the high, medium, and low group—with the tutti, and the contrast of sound colors. The massive, dense, full, and strong tutti is generally content with four-part writing, whereas the dialogue of the three groups varies from thin, transparent three-part writing to a powerful ten-part combination, including the cembalo part of the thorough bass.

The first movement, allegro moderato, is based throughout on one principal motif which dominates the entire piece with its ever recurring rhythms of eighth and sixteenth notes. No contrasting second theme interrupts the even flow of these rhythms. All necessary contrasts are amply supplied by the ingenious variety of the dialogue, by the constant alternation of forte and piano sections. With its 136 measures, the piece develops into a very impressive moto perpetuo, a hardly surpassable model of the motoric style of radically modern music. Melodious singing as well as contrapuntal elaboration are both excluded without detriment to the effectiveness of the piece. Tutti and soli sections are perfectly balanced, with exactly the same number of measures for each, $68 + 68 = 136$ measures. This equality, however, is obtained by the sum total of unequally long phrases, thus avoiding monotonous symmetry. In modulation, also, Bach is very economical. Only the principal key G major and its nearest relatives, D major, B minor, E minor, A minor, G minor, C major, and C minor are used.

The customary slow movement is absent from this concerto. Two long sustained adagio chords—which may be a little expanded "ad libitum" into a florid cadenza of one or two violins—are merely the introduction of the allegro finale. (Dr. Serge Koussevitzky, in his performances, replaces these chords with the introductory sinfonia from Bach's Cantata No. 4.)

This next vivid and brisk movement, in 12/8 time, in dance rhythms, resembles a gigue. Its entire thematic material is contained in the first measure. The two motifs of sixteenth notes and triplets, *a* and *b,* suffice for a most ingenious contrapuntal play throughout the forty-eight measures of the movement, which by repetition of each of its two sections is extended to $48 + 48 = 96$ measures. The triplet motif *b* often gets the effect of a brilliant trumpet fanfare. Motif *a* is constantly led through the parts in elegant imitations, sometimes in inversion, or *recte* and *inverse* at the same time (see measures 3, 19, 22, 42). The triplet fanfare, as countermotif, is the constant companion of the rapid light-footed sixteenth-note figure. The ever-changing combinations of these two motifs constitute the entire contents of this joyful piece.

CONCERTO NO. 4 IN G MAJOR

This concerto is written for violin, two flutes, and string orchestra. Of all the six Brandenburg concerti, it comes closest to the Handelian type of the concerto grosso. The three solo instruments are treated here either as a "concertino," opposed to the tutti as a group; or concertizing among themselves; or, in places, approaching a solo concerto.

The choice of the gentle, pastoral flutes has influenced the character of the music, or one might say, vice versa, the idyllic music called for the flutes as the proper instrumental medium.

The first movement, allegro, G major, is evolved from the principal or rather the only theme of the piece, measures 1–16. Its three characteristic features serve throughout the movement as motif from which the music is spun out. They are:

(1) The undulating arpeggio figure of the flute (measures 1–2).
(2) The melodious singing of the two flutes, in parallel thirds (measures 3–6).
(3) The more energetic marcato figure in sixteenths, in scale runs, or with repeated notes, generally given to the violin (measures 13–14).

The form of the piece resembles the structure of the first Brandenburg concerto, with the inverted order of the sections at the recapitulation. The formula of the structure is *a–b–c–b–a:*

(*a*) Measures 1–82.
(*b*) Measures 83–157.
(*c*) Measures 157–235.
(*b*) Measures 235–345.
(*a*) Measures 345–427.

Most of the time Bach vies here with the Italian opera composers, Scarlatti, Pergolesi, Hasse, in sweet melodious charm; yet he mixes in a good portion of virile energy to prevent the impression of too much softness.

The concertino group starts the piece, lightly supported by the orchestra (measures 1–14). The first tutti (measures 14–23) adds a contrast of joyful energy.

Soli and tutti continue alternately, until at measure 83 section *b* is reached. Here a novel feature makes its appearance: the solo violin dominates most of the time with brilliant passage work, followed by a new tutti, terminating the section (measures 147–157).

Section *c* has the function of a trio-intermezzo. It is reserved almost exclusively for the concertino group. In the graceful play of the two flutes (measures 167–188), the violin participates with capricious and elegant slides and rapid runs in thirty-second notes (measures 185–208). Again a resounding tutti closes the section (measures 226–230). What follows is a recapitulation of sections *b* and *a* in reversed order. This recapitulation, however, is varied most ingeniously in harmony, in melodic curve, thus impressing the listener more as a continuation than a repetition.

The second movement, andante, in E minor, has the character of a short intermezzo between the extended outer movements. The piece is evolved from one motif (measures 1–7). Measure 1 contains the entire thematic material: the melodious little sighs of the flutes and violins, and the wide steps of the bass. The melody is expanded in the manner of an aria in every symmetrical structure, but without any fixed formal type. With its constant alternation of forte and piano—the phrase of the tutti is repeated in echo by the concertino—with its touch of delightful sentimentality, its agreeable sighs, and elegant chromatic progressions, this melodious andante anticipates the so-called "gallant" style that came into vogue after Bach's death. The chromatic sequences in measures 13–18, 39–45, 60–66 remind one of many a Mozart piece, in their refinement of line, sound, and sentiment. The piece lacks a real close. With a little cadenza of the flute and with a half-close prolonged by a fermata, its last part leads over without stop into the finale.

The third movement, presto, G major, is a spirited and broadly extended fugue. It is first developed by the string orchestra as a five-part fugue with a splendid fullness of sound. In general, the fugal portions are played by the orchestra, whereas the interludes, much thinner and more delicate in sound, are given to the trio of solo instruments. Thus a very effective contrast and dialogue effect is obtained. This first interlude of the violin and the two flutes occurs at measures 41–67. Here even the basso continuo is omitted.

The second fugal development starts at measure 67, with the theme in the basses, a rolling figure of eighth notes as counterpoint. The second interlude (measures 87–127) accentuates the concerto character. It consists of a brilliant solo of the violin, the free fantasy, cadenza of a virtuoso. At its culmination the fugue theme sneaks in softly, almost unnoticed in the accompaniment (measure 105) in canonic imitation (stretta), then disappears again, leaving the violinist as protagonist for a while, until at last (measure 127) the orchestra takes the lead again. Once more the fugue returns in a powerful tutti (measures 127–152), rising to a climax and passing over to the key of B minor. Here the concertino also participates in the fugal development, emerging from the orchestra at measure 159, when the two flutes, together with the violoncelli and the thorough bass, enjoy themselves in a sportive interlude (measures 159–175). A little later the concertino trio has two little episodes all to itself (measures 183–189, 197–207), answered by the fugue theme in the orchestra, which, gathering all its forces, brings the fugue to a brilliant and joyful close (measures 207–244).

CONCERTO NO. 5 IN D MAJOR

The concerto No. 5 in D major is the most brilliant and effective work of the lot. It is a real triple concerto, for piano, flute, and violin, with the accompaniment of the string orchestra and the basso continuo.

In the first movement, allegro, the three solo instruments dominate to such an extent that not much is left for the orchestra but an unpretentious accompaniment. Whenever the orchestra tries to start a more elaborate tutti, it is cut short by the élan with which the solo instruments impatiently enter. The constructive idea is to build up the piece with two different motifs, one for the tutti, one for the soli. Consequently the dialogue is concerned here not only with the concertino and the concerto grosso, but also with different motifs for the soli and the tutti. The concertino is especially favored by a more ornate and finer articulated rhythmical treatment and through the brilliant display of virtuosity in the cembalo obligato. Here follow the two motifs (tutti: measures 1–5; solo, measures 9–12):

After the initial statement of the tutti theme, the solo group predominates. Repeatedly, the tutti theme tries to assert itself (measures 10, 13, 19, 29), but is immediately interrupted by the solo instruments. An interesting thematic conversation between soli and tutti starts at measure 35. At measure 42 the soli take the lead again, several times interrupted by a modest remark of the tutti (measures 44, 58). At measure 71 an intermezzo episode with entirely new thematic material is inserted (measures 71–75).

With its intimate lyric dialogue of the solo flute and violin, its delicate, calm figuration of the piano, its pale pianissimo background of the string orchestra, its F sharp minor color, these thirty measures (71–101) have a fascinating romantic character. At measure 101 the concertizing play of the tutti and soli motifs is taken up again with an abundance of new combinations. Here the center of the piece is reached. From the dominant tonality, A major, the music soon finds its way back to the tonic D major (measure 121). At measure 139 the piano, lightly accompanied by the orchestra, starts a brilliant improvisation, merging at measure 154 into a virtuoso cadenza, which with its seventy-five measures occupies one third of the entire movement. The same tutti ritornello with which the piece had commenced brings this combination of a concerto grosso and a piano concerto to a brilliant and effective close, immediately following the cadenza.

The second movement, affettuoso, is a trio for the solo instruments exclusively. This melancholy and at times even pathetic piece impresses the listener by its touching expression as well as by its exquisite beauty of sound and construction. Its plan is novel and ingenious. The piece is divided into four sections or stanzas. Every stanza commences with a duet of the closely intertwined flute and violin. After four measures the piano takes up and continues the richly ornamented arioso effusion into which flute and violin drop short phrases in faint echo.

First stanza: Duet in B minor (measures 1–5), followed by piano solo with echo of flute and violin, passing over from B minor to D major (measures 5–10).

Second stanza: Duet (measures 10–14), D major. Piano solo with echo of flute and violin, D major to F sharp minor (measures 14–20).

Third stanza: Duet (measures 20–24), F sharp minor. Piano solo with echo, G major to B minor (measures 24–30).

Fourth stanza: Duet (measures 30–34), E minor to G major. Piano solo with echo, G major to B minor (measures 34–40).

Coda: In trio style, B minor (measures 40–50).

Notice the symmetrical construction: five sections, each consisting of ten measures.

The third movement, allegro, is a spirited piece of music in the form of an extended da capo aria of the type *a–b–a:*

(*a*) The first part (measures 1–78) starts with a fugato on a theme sparkling with vitality, energy, and good humor. One must call it a scherzo theme. It is developed in fugal manner at first by the three solo instruments (measures 1–11). A little later the orchestra participates in the jocose contrapuntal play (measures 29–78), the piano adding ornamental marginal remarks by rapid runs and capricious passages (measures 42–48, 58–63).

(*b*) The middle section (measures 79–232) is the concertizing part, in the proper sense of the term, as opposed to the purely contrapuntal section (*a*). A new melodic idea is here opposed to the fugato theme, from which it is derived (starting at measure 79).

A delightful concertizing play results from the graceful dialogue of these two charming and melodious companions, or from the occasional accumulation of all the parts. Strange to say, Bach avoids the seemingly natural contrapuntal combination of the fugue theme with this new idea. Perhaps he wanted to give this intermezzo, rocking on graceful triplet figuration, a singable, calm, serenade-like or canzonetta character, in order to make the contrast to the polyphony of section (*a*) stand out more plastically. The tonalities B minor, F sharp minor, and A major dominate part (*b*).

(*a*) The third section (measures 232–310) is an exact repetition of the first section (*a*). Notice the almost arithmetically exact proportion of the three sections: $78:154:78 = 1:2:1$. Part (*b*) is as long as the two (*a*)'s together.

CONCERTO NO. 6 IN B FLAT MAJOR

This concerto is written exclusively for the lower instruments of the alto, tenor, and bass range. In this ensemble of two violas, two violas de gamba, violoncello, and thorough bass, the higher octaves are entirely absent, save for an occasional touch in the accompanying cembalo.

The first movement, allegro, is in the main a duet of the two violas as concertino group. The other instruments accompany, either simply filling out the harmony, or in places entering into a thematic dialogue with the violas. Thus sometimes the duet is changed into a trio or quartet. The piece commences with a tutti dominated by a broad theme of the viola, of a preludizing character, passing through the entire range of the instrument in surging lines. The effect of this splendid "arpeggio" theme is still enhanced by the second viola, following on the heel of the first viola in canonic imitation (measures 1–5). After sixteen measures this principal theme, supported by simple harmonies of the other strings, is brought to a full close. Here the first intermezzo of the soli enters with a new theme (measures 17–19).

This exhausts the thematic material of the piece. The structural idea aims at making the tutti duo stand out effectively six times in varying keys and inserting polyphonic intermezzi between the different entries. The duets and the intermezzi each retain their individual theme. Here follows the outline of the structure:

(*a*) Measures 1–16, tutti, canonic duet, with plain chord accompaniment (B flat major).
(*b*) Measures 17–24, dialogue of the soli (B flat major to F major).
(*c*) Measures 25–45, duet and tutti, followed by trio and quartet (F major, B flat major, C minor).
(*d*) Measures 46–52, duet (C minor).
(*e*) Measures 52–72, quartet and trio (C minor–G minor).

371

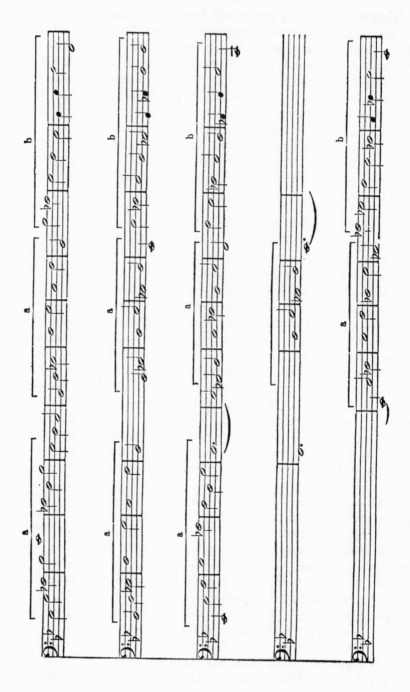

(*f*) Measures 73–85, duet, followed by trio (G minor–E flat major).

(*g*) Measures 86–95, duet (E flat major–F major).

(*h*) Measures 96–114, quartet (F major–B flat major).

(*i*) Measures 114–130, duet with tutti (B flat major).

The second movement, adagio ma non tanto, shows ingenious bass leading and an interesting variation of the chaconne idea. The first part contains a fugato in the higher instruments above a double basso ostinato motif in changing keys. A sketch of the bass leading is shown on page 372, with the two motifs (*a*) and (*b*), in which the tonalities, small variants, and the plan of the structure are clearly seen. This is followed by the fugato theme in the bass; this fugue and chaconne fantasy is brought to an unusual close in G minor with a half-close on the dominant D major.

The third movement, allegro, in 12/8 time, in the character of a gigue, shows the three-part da capo form: *a–b–a*

(*a*) Measures 1–45.

(*b*) Measures 45–65.

(*a*) Measures 65–109.

In all three parts tutti and soli alternate. The constructive idea consists in effectively bringing out the principal theme four times, always in B flat major: measures 1, 38, 66, 103. Concertizing polyphonic intermezzi are interpolated. The piece is written in a mixed form of aria, rondo, and concerto allegro.

CHAPTER **XX**

fantasy[1]

The small two-part song form, generally founded on a single theme (notwithstanding its middle section) finds a companion in still another more complex form which also derives its entire contents from a single theme, without employing the contrast of a new, second theme. This class includes fantasia-like pieces of richly ornamented arioso-like melody, pieces like the already analyzed preludes in C sharp minor, E flat minor, B flat minor from the *Well-Tempered Clavier,* and the slow movement of Bach's cembalo concerto in D minor. In distinction to the song form, little use is made of songlike, periodic, symmetrical melodic structure and also much more freedom is granted to modulation; the entire melodic contour often branches out in a broad, sweeping arc, without regard for the recapitulation of the initial melody at the close of the piece. In spite of all these liberties, there may be close coherence of motifs. An especially interesting feature in the above-mentioned Bach concerto in D minor is the combination of utmost freedom of the melody with strictest leading of the bass.

andante from Beethoven's piano concerto in G major

Another piece of this type is the Andante from Beethoven's piano concerto in G major. One might call it an instrumental arioso, a form intermediate between recitative and aria. Recitative has lent the piece its dia-

[1] Continuation of Part One, Chapter VIII.

374

iogue, the dramatic opposition of piano and orchestra, and from the aria it has taken its symmetrical structure, the coherent melodic line, at least in the first part; the second part passes over into ever freer fantasia, into ornamental cadence. Mark how this cadenza serves for a most soulful kind of expression, at the same time revealing a refined sense for coloristic and pianistic treatment. Never has the trill—the pianistic expression of tremor in the voice—been more poetically used. No less admirable and convincing in expression is the gradual retardation and the final cessation of the trill, its expiring breath in ever longer time values: sixty-fourth, thirty-second, sixteenth, eighth notes, down to the quarter notes at the close.

arioso in Beethoven's later works

Such arioso pieces in many varieties are not infrequently found in Beethoven's later works. They often serve as slow introductions of independent character to a finale movement. Examples are found in the adagio of the piano sonata, Op. 101, the adagio from Op. 110, entitled recitative and arioso. The largo and allegro introducing the fugue in Op. 106 has more of a fantasia or toccata character.

Some fantasia-like pieces, shaped by a master's hand, are worthy of special attention, because in them the formal, shaping force of the motif, the possibilities of new, not stereotyped construction, and the organic growth from a germinal motif become manifest. Just as a seed gives rise only to a plant of its own species, so every musical idea demands in the strictest sense a shape and continuation of its own kind. The feeling for this kind of development represents a considerable part of the musical creative power in a composer. This instinct can be strengthened and trained; it cannot, however, be taught. The young artist gifted with this insight will be greatly benefited by observing how the great masters occasionally take no heed whatsoever of normal procedure and established formal types, but let a musical idea, emanating from a certain emotional mood, find its own way in a fantasia-like manner, free from all formal conventions. It is quite significant that the academic theory of art is prone to consider such structures, often splendidly natural in growth, as "formless," because unconventional. Pieces of this type are Bach's organ fantasias and toccatas, the "Chromatic" fantasy, a series of slow introductions in the symphonies, overtures, quartets, sonatas of Beethoven, the introduction of the finale in Brahms' First Symphony.

Bach's chromatic fantasy

Bach's "Chromatic" fantasy [2] comprises eighty-two measures, which are distributed among the four sections of the piece as follows:

[2] The present analysis is based on Busoni's edition (Breitkopf & Härtel).

(a) Toccata-like intrata, measures 1–33.
(b) Chorale (arpeggiando), measures 34–49.
(c) Recitative, measures 50–77.
(d) Coda, measures 78–82.

Among these four different ideas it can be observed that every one calls forth the following section with logical necessity. Hence the unity of the entire piece, in spite of its unusual structure which does not conform to any conventional type.

The nucleus of the entire piece, the originating center, is the rapid run in its upward and downward sweep at the beginning of the toccata. It suggests the image of a swiftly rushing torrent of water, in constant flux and reflux; no firm ground, no sustained low basses; everything in high position, fluctuating up and down, to and fro. The restlessness is softened by the constancy of the tonality, in the main, D minor, with only a few deviations. This flood of restless sound, expanding in a broad tonal level despite its turbulence, finally spends its force, and the ear demands a change which is brought about in the chorale (b); in place of the high, swiftly moving figures, one hears low basses, sustained, solemn, reposeful melody, and the steady tonal harmony suddenly yields to sharp chromatic shiftings towards distant keys.

The arpeggiando of the accompaniment achieves a certain coherence with the swiftly undulating figure of the toccata. In the midst of the chorale (page 15, measures 1, 2, 3), the steady chorale melody trickles out at one place into a recitative-like run—the germ for the following part (c), which now enters as a recitative, after the close of the chorale in A minor. The chorale had been rather free harmonically, but strict and steady in rhythm. The recitative brings a welcome continuation and contrast at the same time: rhythms of utmost freedom, and harmonies wandering off still further in bold chromaticism. At the same time this recitative spins connecting threads back to the brilliant runs of the toccata. The coda (d), in an exhaustive close of the recitative, terminates the entire piece in its wonderfully vanishing sound, at the same time casting retrospective glances at the toccata as well as at the chorale.

Bach, organ fantasy, G minor

Bach's organ fantasy in G minor (widely known by Liszt's transcription for the piano), is, together with the "Chromatic" fantasy, a chief example of "rhetoric" music in opposition to "singing" music. These declamatory rhythms are much more complex than the rhythms of singing music. They have retained much of the emotional contours in their sudden jerky transitions from gliding to jumping; from smooth, level surfaces to jagged outlines; in their heaping up of heavy accents, their mixture of rapid runs and passages with massive, full columns of chords, their broadly curved lines, suggestive of hurling motion, of towering contours. To this is added a harmony of glowing colors, of dramatically exciting, propelling effect in its chromatically shifting progressions. It is not surprising that the forms of "singing" music, intent on symmetry, clarity, and roundness, with their more intimate nature, should be foreign to this declamatory style, which has to solve the problem of finding its own, appropriate form.

The structure of the fantasy is as follows:

(a) Toccata-like introduction, measures 1–8.

(b) Interlude in imitating style in five-part writing on the motif:

(which had already occurred in (a) as a phrase of secondary importance), introduced by the chord rhythm:

(also heard in (a), though somewhat hidden), measures 9–14.

(c) Toccata-like development of motif (*b*), measures 14–20.

(d) Free continuation in tutti manner of motif (*b*), in crowded succession of entries, measures 21–25.

(e) Renewed development of (*a*) in imitations, measures 25–31.

(f) Sequence-like chord progression on the bass figures in eighth notes already used in (b) and (e), a variant of motif (*b*), measures 31–35.

(g) Parallel to section (d) in a different tonality, ending in a richly ornamented cadence (with complications of harmony, rhythm and melody), again utilizing motif (*a*) and section (a), measures 36–44.

(h) Coda, with retrospective glances at (b) and (a), measures 44–49.

The whole of this magnificent fantasia is admirably developed from the first idea (measures 1–3). The piece is framed in by the widely ranging, fantastically curved lines of the introduction (a) and the coda (h), whereas the main part of the piece, in contrast to the outer wings, is based on the steady eighth-note rhythms, interrupted in but a few places by the toccata rhythms of (a). The progression of tonalities, apparently subject to fantastic caprice, swings to and fro like a pendulum from the fixed pillars of the related keys of G minor, D major, A major, to widely distant keys, yet always

led back, as if by magic attraction, to the dominant tonalities of G and D.
A more precise investigation reveals its systematic organization. Beginning
with measure 14 one observes a stepwise ascent of keys: A minor, B minor,
C minor, D minor, to E flat minor in measure 21. In the next measure, the
bass starts an upward chromatic progression from B flat (dominant of
E flat minor) to C flat, C, D flat, D, E flat.

After this episode, there is still further ascent to F minor and G minor.
At this point the center of the intricate harmonic motion is reached, the
tonic key returns. A halt is made in the upward moving development. The
corresponding parallel episode starts in measure 31, where the sequence of
tonalities reveals a doubly intertwined descent, in stepwise progression:

G, C, F, B flat, E flat, A flat, D flat.

Starting in measure 37 the pedal tones move in a new chromatic ascent:
B, C, C sharp, D, D sharp, E, E sharp. The sketch below indicates the
scheme of modulation through the entire piece in its sections (a) to (h),
and clearly demonstrates the constructive power of tonality in contradistinction to the deviations.

Introduction, G minor.

D major–A major.

A major (B minor, C minor), D.

D major (E flat minor, F minor), G major.

G major (F minor, C minor, G minor), D major.

D major (Sequence, G, C, F, B flat, E flat, A flat, D flat), E minor.

E minor (C minor, D major), G major.

Coda, G minor.

CHAPTER **XXI**

(*To Otto Klemperer*)[1]

anton bruckner: the eighth symphony

Only a few years have passed since the musical world has begun to be conscious of Anton Bruckner's greatness, and this great master of symphony has been accorded the place due to him. Within the last twenty-five years an extensive Bruckner literature has been published, crowned by the exhaustive two volumes of Ernst Kurth, entitled, *Anton Bruckner* (published by Max Hesse, Berlin). In spite of the detailed analysis and excellent critical inquiries contained therein, the present study attempts once more to inspect one of Bruckner's most grandiose symphonies exhaustively, in all the details of its structure. The reason is that E. Kurth's profound interpretation from the philosophical and aesthetic point of view still leaves important questions to be answered as regards the technical, structural features of the symphony. The analysis of the Eighth symphony here presented will, I confidently hope, strictly prove how many original, novel problems are contained in Bruckner's art. It will show that Bruckner's art of formal construction is worthy of the most minute attention, and that the study of his scores can give us most valuable new insight into the problem of form.

[1] This essay is dedicated to Otto Klemperer, in grateful recognition of the enlightenment issuing from his magnificent interpretation of this Bruckner symphony.

379

first movement, allegro moderato

The construction is very clear and impressive. The piece is written in sonata form, with three themes and a coda as exposition, a middle development section, and a reprise of the first part, again with a coda.

Subdivisions and proportions of the piece are as follows:

Exposition

First theme:	(22 + 28) = 50 measures	(measures 1–50)
Second theme:	(22 + 24) = 46 measures	(measures 51–96)
Third theme:	(12 + 20) = 32 measures	(measures 97–128)
Coda:	(12 + 12) = 24 measures	(measures 129–152)
	152 measures	

Development

First theme:	(16 + 24) = 40 measures	(measures 153–192)
First and second	(12 + 20 + 24) = 56 measures	(measures 193–248)
themes:	(6 + 8 + 8 + 8 + 4) = 34 measures	(measures 249–282)
	130 measures	

Reprise

First theme: (8 + (4 + 3) + 13) = 28 measures (measures 283–310)
Second theme:

  (3 + 3 + 4) + (4 + 6) + 10 = 30 measures (measures 311–340)
Third theme:

  (8 + 4) + 8 + 8 + 16 + 8 = 52 measures (measures 341–392)
Coda: 8 + 8 + 8 + 1 = 25 measures (measures 393–417)

  135 measures

Total: 417 measures

First theme

EXPOSITION, FIRST THEME

First section (measures 1–22). After two measures the "germ motif" of this movement emerges from the soft tremolo on F, in three octaves:

at first sounding the fundamental note F, then the neighboring G flat, and after long hesitation returning to F, before the plaintive melisma of the fourth measure unfolds itself. It seems quite remarkable that the first fifty measures of this C minor movement touch the tonic C only twice, and then very lightly, so that one cannot recognize the C minor tonality earlier than in measure 22. The exposition of the first theme demands five phrases of four measures each (the long rests included), ascending gradually from the bass, against a slow, chromatically ascending tremolo in the upper parts.

The pauses between these bass entries ascending with abrupt, jerky motion in four planes of sound, like terraces, are filled out in dialogue manner by short questions and answers of the woodwind: the first question of the clarinet timidly expanding towards the still distant "dominant" region G–D, the later wind entries answering with the prolonged wail of measure 4. In measure 18 the bass line has ascended into the soprano region of the violins which now quite logically take up the thread, gradually bringing the music to a forte; after which they gently descend again, rounding off the melodic line in piano and terminating it in measure 22.

The second section of the principal theme (measures 23–50) is a somewhat varied repetition of the first phrase, more emphatic, carried much higher by a stronger impulse, more forcefully modeled, more massive in sound, more luminous and bright in color. All the more mysterious and threatening is the piano and pianissimo, suddenly following this fortissimo. This piano, with the chromatic wail, effects the transition to the second theme in G major, entering in measure 50. Alternately in high and low position this wail is heard five times on the same four-note phrase. Also in this section the triad of C minor is heard only once in its function as tonic, in measure 41:

SECOND THEME

The manner in which the second theme (measures 51–96) grows forth from the first theme is made clear by the preceding example. The ascending quintuplet in measure 51 (a favorite figure of Bruckner, by the way), so characteristic a feature of the new theme, is the answer to the descending quintuplet group at the climax of the first theme; the origin of this quintuplet is seen in the transformation of the first theme in measure 10.

In its first section (measures 51–72), the second theme also shows an ascending tendency, similar to the first theme. It is built up in eleven two-bar phrases, towards the end (measures 67–70) impatiently hurrying to the climax, corresponding to the culmination of the first theme (measures 40–43), only more radiant, brighter in the light of the sharp major keys. After brief descent and diminuendo, the second section starts, again in G major (measures 73–96). Commencing in the same way (measures 51–54 = 73–76), the melodic line is now shaped differently: no impetuous urge towards a steep summit, but everything kept to a middle position, with short crescendi, alternating with sudden piano. In measure 89 profound darkness falls, ushered in by the chord of the seventh in the tubas. The oboes, with an apparently new melody, take up the melodic thread, at the same time preparing the third theme which enters eight measures later, and thematically continuing the transformed second theme in the trombones (measure 81). One may consider measure 89 directly as contrapuntal countersubject to measure 81:

Measure
89

81

Bruckner gives us only an intimation of this combination without actually using it, thus appealing to our subconsciousness. The "germ rhythm" of the first theme becomes active once more in the structure of the music, once (measures 81–83), forte in the basses, the second time in piano, vanishing in the ethereal sound of the flutes. The subtle concatenation of the various themes in this movement is continued in the next theme.

THIRD THEME

The third theme (measures 97–128), in its continuation, manifests relations to the second as well as to the first theme. The beginning of the third theme (measure 97) was already prepared in measure 89:

Measure

In both places a very similar sextuplet figure is employed as rhythmical countersubject, acting as a more animated version of the quintuplet figure in the second theme. Starting at measure 100, a rapid culmination is prepared, a compound of two different elements, the sextuplet rhythms and the resounding, broad downward plunges of sevenths (measures 103–108), already preformed in the descending seventh of the second theme, in measure 52:

Measure
52

Measure
103

With measure 108 this climax is over. A new episode starts pianissimo, with allusion to the first theme, beginning with measure 110:

First theme

Measure 110

Commencing in E flat minor, a new powerful climax is prepared, slowly mounting by chromatically ascending basses, and culminating in brilliant E flat major fanfares of the trumpets (measures 125–127). This eruption of radiant brightness is followed by a plunge into the opposite extreme.

CODA

The coda (measures 129–152) commences pianissimo, with the impression of a vast empty space. Below the soft tremolo of the high violins, the "germ rhythm" is heard again in a timid dialogue of basses and flutes, soon leading in the first theme, which in the manifold murmurings of its last phrase (*b*) gives the impression of a dense, ominous mass. The first theme, in double enlargement, vanishes after this episode, sung tenderly again and with consoling accent in E flat major by the horn and oboe: the chromatic wail has been transformed into a gently descending figure.

DEVELOPMENT

The development section (measures 153–282) is built up in three episodes or terraces.

The first terrace (measures 153–192) deals with the first theme and is subdivided into two smaller sections. The first section (measures 153–168), in E flat major, directly follows the preceding coda, continuing it in pianissimo. Surrounded by the tremolo of the high strings, the first theme soars on, twice sung by the graceful oboe in dialogue with the tubas from below, opposing their soft, sonorous fullness with the high-soaring oboe tone, subduing and darkening it to E flat and B flat minor. This episode, replete with calm, lasting for nearly thirty measures, must now be gradually set into motion again. For this purpose the pizzicato figure of the violas and celli are introduced in measure 167, at first appearing quite insignificant. Gradually, however, there is evolved from the figure a propelling momentum, causing a stir in the basses, growing from pianissimo to fortissimo, passing over in measure 187 from 4/4 into the quintuplet figure, which in measure 193 leads over to the second theme with its quintuplet rhythm. The first theme spins out the melodic thread, at first in inversion (measures 169–172), in the violins, woodwind, horn, later in inversion and augmentation (measures 173–178), played by horns, tubas, and trumpets:

Inversion and augmentation

This complex of sound is repeated once more in similar manner, with the necessary variants of harmony and tone color, measures 178–192. Twice the wave of sound rises from pianissimo to fortissimo, sinking back again into pianissimo. F major, D flat major, A flat major, C major, E flat major, D major, B flat major, G flat major, D flat major are touched.

The second terrace (measures 193–249) commences in G flat major with the second theme, also inverted, prepared rhythmically by the quintuplet figure, touching G flat major, A major, B flat minor, C minor. A broad C minor level (measures 200–212) serves as the start of a slowly growing climax. To the quintuplet rhythm in the ever-ascending strings is added, alternately in basses and horn, the germ rhythm of the first theme. In measures 216–229 there follows a new higher lying B flat minor level, parallel to the C major level, finally leading to the eruption of the long prepared climax. The second theme resounds in fortissimo in the high instruments, combined with the first theme in the basses; both themes are written in augmentation, the second theme, moreover, in inversion:

Second theme in augmentation and inversion

First theme in augmentation

This complex of sound is likewise repeated twice successively. A twin summit rises in measures 235–239, a minor third higher; in between them lies a saddle-shaped hollow (measures 230–235), leading over from the F minor and B flat minor harmonies into the regions of A flat minor and D flat minor. Once more a short valley spreads over to the E flat major region (measures 240–244) before the third and highest summit towers majestically (measures 245–249), oscillating between E flat major and C minor. This place, starting at measure 193, is one of the most astounding masterpieces of the art of climax. Its proportions, symmetries, parallelisms, dynamic and sound contrasts are chosen with highest art, and all together they produce a linear and tonal event of quite extraordinary power and impressiveness. The following linear sketch is an attempt to make this manifest:

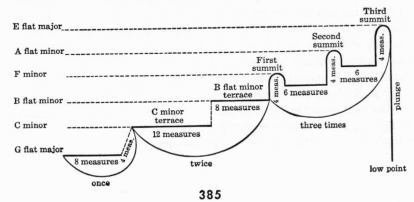

Notice the proportions of the single parts: 12:20:24 equals 3:5:6, also to the increase of the symmetries: the G flat major episode appears only once, the surface structure C minor, B flat minor is heard twice, the summit episode three times.

The effect of this climax is, however, brought to completion only in the following third terrace episode (measures 249–282). In a mighty plunge, the low point of the entire movement is reached immediately following the culmination. For six measures (249–254) there is lonely, dreary silence: on high the flutes play the quintuplet rhythm of the second theme in augmentation, below the basses linger on the chromatic wail of the first theme, and as a connecting link only the low, awesome tremolo of the kettledrum is heard. In the next phrase a new stir of motion is added (measures 254–261), the pianissimo tremolo of the violas and the basic rhythm in the trumpets. This entire section is based almost entirely on rhythm and dynamic effect, with the melodious element kept in the background. After the four rhythms of the first and the second themes have been combined, there follows in measures 262–278 a dynamic climax on the wail of the first theme, in 2×8 measures, the quintuplets of the second theme disappearing at the same time. At the forte in measure 272 the trumpets come in again with the germ rhythm. Starting here the "wail" has been intensified and condensed to a four-bar phrase of great melodic and rhythmical power. Here we meet one of those quaint, fanciful Brucknerian "veiled" unisoni— veiled by the simplified wind figures. The four-bar phrase turning downwards in spiral convolutions appears four times, in diminuendo (measures 271–282). The end of the development section is reached. The pocket score edition of this symphony errs in marking these measures, 262–279, as a permissible cut. On the contrary, this episode is an admirable organically constructed and indispensable preparation for the reprise.

THE REPRISE

The reprise (measures 282–393) begins apparently in a very distant tonality. True enough, the first theme, recited by the oboe, is written in the principal key, C minor. The harmony of the other parts, however, very ingeniously maintains the key of D flat major simultaneously with C minor. Thus curiously attractive cross-relations and frictions of tonality are produced, G and D against G flat and D flat, a polytonal effect anticipating harmonic methods of the twentieth century. In the D flat counterpoints, the four-bar wail from the close of the development section is continued into the reprise, like a seam connecting the two phrases, as we can see in the example shown at the top of the opposite page.

The tonic C minor becomes clearly manifest only in measure 298, when the violins on A flat take up the close of the first theme, after the first three measures of this theme have been heard in several versions four times, played by the oboe, clarinet, trumpet. Compared with the corresponding portion of the exposition, the reprise of the first section, with twenty-eight instead of the former fifty measures, is reduced to approximately one half. This time the second climax of the main theme (measures 23–50) is lacking, and also the transition to the second theme (measures 303–310) sounds different, less mystic, but more delicate and intimate in effect. Also the second theme (measures 311–340) is shortened in the reprise, with thirty measures compared to the former forty-six. The original four-bar version of the theme is now replaced by a three-bar structure (measures 311–316). In three perfectly symmetrical phrases of ten measures each, this episode is rounded off in utmost brevity, touching many keys from its initial B flat major to its close in E flat major and C minor.

The reprise of the third theme is considerably amplified with fifty-two measures compared to thirty-two in the exposition. This amplification is caused by the preparation of a vast climax, representing the culmination of the entire movement (measures 368–385). The four-bar fanfare in E flat of the corresponding place (measures 125–128) is here replaced by an extensive, powerful C minor cadence, expanded to eighteen measures. All through this wide expanse and still further on, the basic rhythm continues hammering on the constantly retained C of the horns and trumpets, as middle part of the changing cadence chords. The most magnificent eruption of sound is reached in measure 381, not, however, victoriously, triumphantly on the tonic C minor triad, but on the subdominant harmony of F sharp, A flat, C, E flat, which here has a rather threatening, terrifying effect. The entrance of the tonic takes place quite unusually in a rapid diminuendo of

the chord of the sixth and fourth: G, C, E flat, gradually casting off all instruments of the orchestra, until only the germ rhythm of the horns and
trumpets remains alone with the tone C, vanishing in pianissimo, and the
kettledrum, lost in desolate loneliness. The tonic C, thus introduced, has
nothing liberating or comforting in its effect, but rather gives the impression
of something tragic, terrible, paralyzing all vitality. And indeed the amazing
coda (measures 393–417) confirms in the most touching manner the impression of stupor and of ebbing life. On the pianissimo organ point C, the
violin and clarinet, as if in inconsolable resignation, call to each other in
dialogue, repeating the four-bar main theme, the violin three times, the
clarinet in inversion twice. Then the vitality seems exhausted. Only a thematic fragment of one measure can still be emitted; the rippling sound waves
of the violins become tinier and ever softer, until finally all motion has
ceased, and vanishing life comes to a final standstill in the viola.

second movement, scherzo, allegro moderato

The second movement is written in the traditional classical scherzo
form: first part, trio, and return of the first part, after the pattern *a–b–a*.
  (*a*) First part (measures 1–195):
    a. Main section, measures 1–64.
    b. Middle section, measures 65–134.
    c. Reprise of the main section, measures 135–195.
  (*b*) Trio: (measures 1–93).
    a. Main section, measures 1–44.
    b. Middle section, measures 45–60.
    a. Main section, measures 61–93.
  (*a*) Repetition of the first part, measures 1–195.

THE FIRST MAIN PART

  (*a*) The two contrasting elements of sound, whose activities determine
the musical contents of the piece, make themselves felt from the very beginning. A light, fluttering, whispering, obliquely rising and falling figure in
eighth notes is opposed to a firm-legged, broad, sturdy, and primitively obstinate phrase of the lower parts, which Bruckner himself has dubbed *Der
deutsche Michel* (the German Michael). This ostinato phrase of four-bar
length, with its leaps of a third, a fourth, and an octave, represents the type
of the carillon bell tunes, with their plastic impressiveness and elementary,
natural sound effect, but without any great amount of emotional expression.
  The music begins on the dominant harmony; the tonic enters only in
measure 3. While the first motif is heard continually, almost without the

slightest interruption, the massive four-bar second motif comes in only intermittently, in the principal section five times in the following keys:

C minor, measures 3–6.
{A major, measures 33–36.
{E major, measures 37–40.
{A flat major, measures 49–52.
{E flat major, measures 53–56.

First motif

Second motif

The interval between the first and the second entrance of the four-note second motif (measures 7–33) is bridged over by a continuation of the first motif, in sequences of 2 + 2 measures, later of one measure, mounting upwards in chromatic progression from C to D flat, D, E, F, G flat, A flat, B flat, C flat in the basses, with continually increasing dynamic strength. At the forte, C flat major, the second motif comes in again in measure 19 with the trumpets in a one-measure version, until the climax is reached with fortissimo in measure 23. After a rapid diminuendo, the second motif reappears, now but half as long, in two-measure phrases, rising chromatically and sequentially (horns, oboes, clarinets in dialogue), with constant crescendo up to the A major entry of the trumpets, celli, horns in measure 33, and finally to the climactic E major entry of the basses and tuba, in measure 37, fortissimo. The key of E major, far distant from the principal key of C minor, is led back to the flat keys again in an eight-bar diminuendo on the E flat major harmony, and now, as a parallel to measures 33–40 with their A and E major tonalities, the "German Michael" returns to his home regions in measures 49–56 with A flat and E flat major. A resounding E flat chord, continued through eight measures (measures 57–64), brings the principal scherzo section to a close. Its sixty-four measures are built up symmetrically throughout, not in the monotonous arrangement of 8 × 8 measures, but with a two- and a six-bar group intercalated. The following sketch shows the grouping of measures, the symmetries and parallelisms:

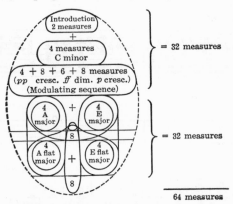

THE MIDDLE SECTION

The middle section (measures 65–134) represents a more delicate inter-mezzo of a pastoral, idyllic color, in the manner of a development section. The structural plan is $(8 + 8 + 8 + 6) + (12 + 8 + 12) = 70$ measures. The entire development is of a piano and pianissimo character, with only a few occasionally stronger accents. No climax is aimed at here, but only color contrasts. The first three eight-measure phrases (measures 65–88) are variants of the same thematic idea in different keys, A flat minor, C minor. The first motif, hurrying through the string group, is joined here by the second motif in the woodwinds, now in delicate contour, circling high up through the flutes, oboes, clarinets. The light foundation of this airy sound structure is entrusted to the kettledrums, introducing every phrase with E flat, F sharp, G. The six-bar phrase, measures 87–94, is an extension and accentuation of the C minor cadence. In the second part of the development, now commencing, the first motif no longer has a part assigned to it. The woodwinds on high play the second motif inverted, above the rocking C minor accompaniment of the horns. The parallel passage in the strings enters at first in C minor, later in F minor (measures 103 and following). Once more the woodwinds answer with the sequence on the second motif, slowly sinking down to the kettledrum roll on C, appearing to aim towards F minor in the closing phrase, measures 127–134, but deflected to C minor at the reprise, starting in measure 135.

The transition to the reprise (measures 123–135) is of special artistic refinement, with the tonic and dominant organ point C, G in the kettledrum and horn, the echo-like string pizzicati after the beat, continued at the climax by the flutes, and with the now logically convincing entry of the main first motif in the violins:

THE REPRISE

The reprise (measures 135–195) at first repeats the main section exactly until measure 175, afterwards gliding through slight changes of harmony, not as before to E major, but to D flat major. Correspondingly, the last two entries of the "German Michael" (measures 183, 187), now in F minor and C major, bring the entire scherzo to a triumphant close. The order of keys is now: A major, D flat major, F minor, C major.

THE TRIO

The trio is written in the usual large three-part song form. In its entire plan and extension, it far transcends the usual slow intermezzo in the trio. It has an outspoken adagio character. The emotional content of the piece is characterized by intimate contemplation, gradually growing to ecstasy. A broad cantilena, from beginning to close almost unimpeded by contrapuntal elaborations, is essentially homophonic in style, though of course adorned by expressive melodic secondary parts.

The first part (measures 1–44) is built quite regularly in 11 × 4 measures. It represents a large melodic "wave" (according to E. Kurth's terminology), starting calmly and expanding its motion more and more, with its culmination in the E major phrase, starting in measure 25. The ebbing off of this broad E major wave is seen in the most beautiful manner in measures 37–44, with its broad expanse of E major, radiant in effect, compared to the soft, subdued A flat major of the beginning. Between the first tonality of A flat major and the culminating tonality of E major, there is an abundance of modulating connecting links. The roving harmony acquires systematic order when one gives due attention to the bass leading between A flat major and E major, which (with insertion of a few vagrant auxiliary tones) is in the main based on the ascending scale:

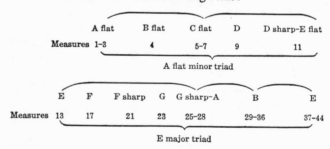

The short middle part (measures 45–66), entirely in piano and pianissimo, leads back in its (4 × 2) + 4 + 4 = 16 measures from E major to the principal tonality of A flat major, touching the keys of B minor, C major, C minor, E flat major, A flat minor, A flat major. Nothing, however, can be noted here in the nature of a "development" or of a tendency towards a climax, which usually occurs at such places; one perceives only the last, faintly vanishing waves of the preceding forceful expansion of sound, reflections of the former motifs.

The reprise (measures 61–93) commences with an almost exact repetition of the first eight measures, but modulates from A flat major to the E major tonality (measure 81), significant for this piece, by way of a different progression, now touching A major and C major, in $3 \times 4 = 12$ measures, as compared with the $4 \times 4 = 16$ measures of the corresponding place in the first part. The E major climax (measures 81–84) is now limited to four measures, as compared with the broader level of twelve measures before. The horn melody, closing in E major, is now heard in A flat, instead of E major. All in all, the reprise is shortened by twelve measures, compared with the first part.

third movement, adagio

The adagio, one of the longest pieces of its kind in the entire literature, demands, for that reason alone, for conductors, players, and listeners, a clear insight into its formal ideas and coherence. Otherwise one easily loses one's way in these vast stretches of sound and one risks sinking down, so to speak, exhausted in the middle of the road, without really enjoying the sublime beauties rewarding the exertions of so toilsome a pilgrimage.

The piece is written in a sonata form of vast dimensions, with various deviations from the normal type. The exposition deals with four themes, an unusual abundance of thematic material. Of these, the first two themes are even repeated in variations. The development section occupies itself only with the first, third, and fourth themes; the reprise omits the fourth theme, bringing only the first, second, and third themes. The coda, finally, makes use of the first theme only. The architectural ground plan of the piece would look as follows, with *a, b, c,* and *d* signifying the four themes.

$\| : a \ b : \| c \ d$ (exposition)

$\quad a \qquad c \ d$ (development)

$\quad a \ b \qquad c \quad$ (reprise)

$\quad a \qquad\qquad$ (coda)

a is treated five times, *b* three times, *c* three times, *d* only twice.

EXPOSITION

The exposition (measures 1–94) is constructed as follows:

(*a*) First theme (measures 1–20), 2 measures introduction + 18 measures (D flat, A, D flat major).

(*b*) Second theme (measures 21–28), 8 measures (G flat major, B flat minor, F flat major to F major).

(*a*) First theme (measures 29–38), 10 measures, varied repetition (D flat major to E flat major).

(*b*) Second theme (measures 39–46), 8 measures, varied repetition (A flat major to G major).

(*c*) Third theme (measures 47–66), 20 measures composed of 10 measures (E major to F minor) + 10 measures (E major to B minor).

(*d*) Fourth theme (measures 67–81), 15 measures (C to G flat major), gradually passing back to the third theme.

Coda (measures 81–94).

FIRST THEME

The first theme is closely related to the principal theme of the first movement, as is manifest by the following coördination of the two themes. One may call the adagio theme an expansion of the allegro theme, which is contained in it almost note for note. Yet one can hardly speak here of an intentional transformation of the former theme; more probably the unconscious working of the mind, nonetheless admirable in its organic method, is responsible for the result.

Main theme of the first movement:

Main theme

The first theme in its totality shows the bar forms,[2] demonstrated by A. Lorenz in his study of Wagner. Its two parallel *Stollen* and the *Abgesang* are clearly seen in the two corresponding phrases in measures 3–10 and 11–17, and the close of the section, measures 18–20. The entire melody has an ecstatic impulse expanding upward. From the beginning in D flat major, the melodic line rises heavenwards with gestures full of longing, the harmony brightens on the constantly retained organ point D flat or the enharmonically equivalent C sharp, and changes over from the dark flat keys to the brighter sharp keys, culminating in a radiant A major light. Thematic relations to the preceding movements are also evident during the further course of the music: measures 8 and 10 are very similar to the first

[2] See page 148.

measure of the scherzo; the ecstatic close in measures 15–17, with its steep ascent in the chord arpeggio and its quintuplet passage at the close, is one of Bruckner's favorite figures. We meet with similar passages in the first movement, measures 67–72, and in the trio of the scherzo, measure 25. In a sudden downward plunge from the radiant A major summit, the melody (measure 17) falls down three entire octaves, at the same time returning to the mystic awe of the D flat major beginning. This closing phrase has a distinctive trait by virtue of the manner in which the final cadence (measures 19, 20) is deflected from the clear D flat major of the upper voice to the dominant of G flat major, through the addition of the minor seventh C flat; thus the closing chord is no longer a D flat major triad, but the dominant seventh chord D flat, F, A flat, C flat, leading on to something new.

SECOND THEME

Through the effect of this dominant harmony, the second theme, now entering in G flat major (measure 21), is more related to the first theme than opposed to it. This new eight-bar theme (measures 21–28) is solemn, chorale-like in character, with the same upward soaring tendency as the first theme. Starting in G flat major, the chorale melody touches the B flat minor sphere, closing on its dominant F major, after deviations into regions of F flat major, D flat minor, and E flat major.

Next follows a somewhat varied repetition of both themes, reduced from 28 to 10 + 8 measures, both themes now closing a tone higher than before, namely in B major, in the dominant of A flat major, and in G major (measures 33–37), instead of the previous A major, the dominant of G flat major, and F major. The starting point, D flat major (measure 28), remains, however, the same as before.

THIRD THEME

The third theme (measures 47–66) is mainly sung by the broadly declaiming violoncello. Its structure is: (8 + 2) + (8 + 2) measures, a twenty-bar period. The consequent (*Nachsatz*) repeats the antecedent (*Vordersatz*) of the first half, note for note, but enriched by new countermelodies of the flutes and the solo violin; in the second half (measures 51, 61) a change occurs through different modulation so that the theme closes the second time an augmented fourth higher. The plan of modulation is:

Antecedent (measures 47–56): E major, B major, F minor.
Consequent (measures 57–66): E major, B major, B minor.

FOURTH THEME

The fourth theme (measures 67–81) commences as a solemn hymnal chant of the tubas, its mild darkness irradiated by an aureole of shimmering light in the soft tremoli of the high strings. Just as this theme appears as the final goal of the third theme, which strives towards it with longing aspiration, so it is merged again into the same third theme, which after distinct allusions to its structure (measures 71 and following), shines in mild light in the C flat major (measure 77) entry. The modulation of this episode leads from C major to G flat major, on the way touching D flat major, E major, once more C major, E flat major, and C flat major. Counter melodies singing in the oboes and clarinets contribute to an ecstatic C flat major eruption of the third theme (measure 77) in which the entire episode culminates.

CODA

After the calm, mild G flat major cadence there follows (measures 81–95) a kind of coda of the exposition, leading over to the beginning of the development (measure 95) section. The newly entering 3/4 time, together with the effect of the high woodwinds, produces the impression of heavenward soaring. In its thematic texture this episode is a combination of three motifs; the first two motifs are derived from the third theme, the last motif has a relation to the first theme, preparing its return in the development section: motif (a) is derived from the first measure of the third theme (measure 47). Motif (b) makes use of the descending eighth-note figure of the same theme, appearing for the first time in measure 53. Motif (c) is an easily recognized variant of the first theme, measure 3:

Measures 83, 84

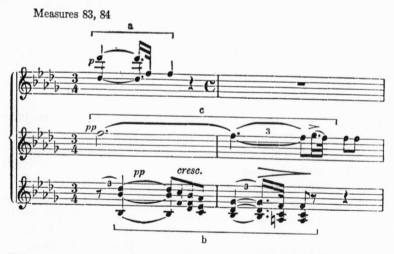

This concatenation of the three motifs is worked out in 4 × 2 measures, radiating its sounds into ever brighter and brighter regions of the tonal atmosphere. Next follows (measures 91–94) the necessary counterbalance: in middle position, with broad and full sound, the strings take up motif (b), modulating in crescendo to the principal tonality of D flat major, in which the development section is written.

THE DEVELOPMENT SECTION

The structure of the development section (measures 95–184) is as follows:

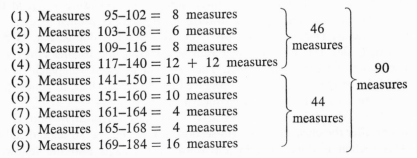

(1) Measures 95–102 = 8 measures
(2) Measures 103–108 = 6 measures
(3) Measures 109–116 = 8 measures
(4) Measures 117–140 = 12 + 12 measures   ⎱ 46 measures
(5) Measures 141–150 = 10 measures
(6) Measures 151–160 = 10 measures
(7) Measures 161–164 = 4 measures   ⎱ 44 measures
(8) Measures 165–168 = 4 measures
(9) Measures 169–184 = 16 measures

⎱ 90 measures

The first section (measures 95–102) commences in the principal tonality of D flat major, in 4/4 time, with a recapitulation of the principal, first theme, accompanied by the syncopated figure of the strings, already heard at the beginning of the movement. The broadly singing violins are answered by the horn, imitating the rhythm of the theme; at the same time, however, pointing back to the horn phrase of the coda just heard (measures 81–87), and thus making the connection with the preceding episode still closer. The entire section rests on the organ point D flat, modulating to F minor in the last two measures of the higher woodwinds.

The second section (measures 103–108), starts with the first phrase of the principal theme in F minor, played by the violins, reëchoed in imitations by solo violins and horn, resting on the darkly luminous substructure of the long tuba chords. A flat minor and E flat minor follow. Again, as in six measures earlier, the high woodwind instruments close the section.

The third section (measures 109–116) and the fourth section (measures 117–140), coupled together, build up to a magnificent climax, which is suddenly converted into an anticlimax, in measure 129. The first principal motif is heard four times chromatically ascending in the basses with new countersubjects of the first and second violins broadly unfolded in contrary motion. Starting in measure 117, the basses and the upper parts converge with ever-increasing power on the middle parts, retaining the syncopated rhythm of the commencement. At the climax (measure 125) the accumulated mass of sound assails with tremendous force the B flat major chord, firmly braced in rigid opposition. The power of the onslaught, however, is wrecked by this unshakable rock. At the culmination (measure 125) the basses are already hesitating, their force gradually losing itself on the organ point F. The anticlimax (measures 129–140) is prepared with convincing logic. It consists in the vanishing of the violins (in contrary motion) into loftiest heights, in the complete shutting off of power from the depth, the bass region. The thematic material of this anticlimax casts significant backward glances at two corresponding places (measures 101, 102 and 107, 108). In double augmentation and simultaneously in free canonic imitation, both flutes and oboes take over this soaring motif (measure 135), at the same time already turning back towards the descent, continued by clarinets and bassoons (measures 139–140). On the chord E double flat, G flat, A flat, C flat, this amazing idea vanishes, leaving the listener entirely in uncertainty what next to expect. The first half of the development is finished. Its forty-six measures are followed by the second half, in almost perfect symmetry with its forty-four measures.

The fifth section (measures 141–150) falls surprisingly into E flat major after the close of the fourth section, whose aim was so unpredictable. This section is dominated by the third theme, as is also the following section.

The sixth section (measures 151–160) is coupled with the preceding section. The third theme appears twice, each time beginning in E flat major (celli and violas), but closing with a deviation, the first time to E minor (measure 149), the second time to B flat minor. Here is an exact repetition of the third theme from the exposition, transposed a half tone higher. This repetition is enriched by a newly added web of countersubjects. Again one hears strange passages, freely soaring in the altitude (measures 149, 150 and 159, 160), now occurring for the eighth time in this movement. It is also remarkable that in measure 151 the theme in the bass is accompanied by its inversion (as seen in a mirror) in the highest position. Also the dark, mellow fullness of the tuba and trombone chords (measure 151) prepares the ear for the entrance of the fourth theme in C flat, filling out the short seventh section.

The seventh section (measures 161–164) has four measures only. The solemn, mystic sound effect of this C flat episode with its dark splendor of magnificent opaque sound is changed in the next.

The eighth section is characterized by an invasion of bright C major light at the renewed entry of the third theme, now brought to a rapid climax. From measures 159–165 there follow B flat minor, C flat major, C major. The C major climax, again turning towards pianissimo, closes with a G major cadence (measure 168).

In the ninth section (measures 169–184) there occurs that curious final episode of the development, one of the most original manifestations of Bruckner's art. A new anticlimax makes its appearance here, a structure of crystalline clearness and transparency, combining utmost delicacy of sound

398

with utmost emotional intensity in every tone. The longing effect of the chords of the ninth, eleventh, thirteenth (G, B, D, F, A, C, E) becomes touchingly manifest here. The first violin designs the delicately curved, profusely articulated, sharply pointed melodic main line (derived from the third theme). The cello answers in dialogue, with a phrase (measure 170) distinctly reminiscent of the first theme, rising gradually into the highest octave, always in pianissimo, and yet saturated with the nervous tension, the emotional intensity of those high sounds. Joined to this dramatically tense duet of high, soft tones is yet a second duet of faint, dim colors: pizzicato basses in dialogue with the thin, pointed pizzicato sixths of the second violins and violas, with a softly held chord of the clarinets as a delicate connecting link.

In the second half of this return (measures 177–184), the long retained chord of the dominant thirteenth in C major (G, B, D, F, A, C, E) is quite unexpectedly succeeded by the chord: G flat, B flat, D flat, F, which, by the added A flat in the bass, is characterized as an authentic dominant function of D flat major, the main tonality of the entire piece. Admirable art is manifest in the manner in which this delicate web of tones is made to disappear completely. At first the basses and clarinets cease playing (measure 177). Through its double augmentation the melody of the violin loses its profusely articulated contour; only the seventh, G flat–F, sharply pointed like a needle, remains; a little later the violin also disappears, and finally there remains only the monologue of the cello, encircling its own highest D flat in softest pianissimo, as in an ecstasy of pain, after the pizzicati of the bass and of the middle parts have already fallen silent. With a mute fermata (measure 184), this marvelous transition anticlimax reaches its end in a faint, barely audible breath.

REPRISE

The reprise of the first part is evidently a reprise in the sense of the sonata form, but at the same time contains quite distinct deviations from that formal pattern. These deviations are especially manifest at the reprise of the first theme, which in the immense amplification of its exterior form and in its emotional intensity is now extended to sixty-two measures (185–246) as compared with the thirty measures in the first part. The exposition, half as long, strikes a note of expectancy, whereas the reprise brings fulfillment, in a literal sense of completeness and perfection, an intensity and ecstasy going to the extreme limit of its aesthetic possibility: a few measures more and the impression is in danger of being converted from the sublime into a theatrical and boresome gesture. The sureness with which Bruckner avoids transgressing this dangerous borderline gives eloquent proof of his superior formal art. But a few measures less would equally result in a false perspective of these complexes of climaxes, surmounting each other, and thus would considerably damage their impulse and expressive power.

The entire vast section of sixty-two measures is filled with a sixteenth-note triplet figure, almost exclusively in the strings; ranging from a faint trembling of inner excitement (measure 185) to a stream of sound flowing in broad tonal waves—with many intermediate stages of crescendo and diminuendo, in numerous variants, strangest of which is seen in the trembling and flickering of the figure in measures 223, 235.

The first section (measures 185–197) corresponds in its leading of the melodic line (second violins, clarinets) to the parallel measures 3–15, with C major as its goal instead of the former A major. A devotedly soft, singing countermelody of the first violins is now added, filling out the pauses of the principal theme with which it is in dialogue. The already mentioned sixteenth-notes triplet figuration of the viola also participates. A constant swelling and ebbing fills this episode with a final increase in dynamic intensity, reaching the first fortissimo with the C major chord at the beginning of the next section.

In the second section (measures 197–205), the sixteenth-note triplet figuration passes over into the higher strings (first and second violins, violas). With its waves of sound, it overflows the solemn chorale of the second theme in the low brass choir, to which a new countermelody responds in the horn, with an energetic phrase in sharply marked rhythm. This four-bar phrase is heard twice, the second time transposed a third higher. Here the first culmination is reached (measure 205). The tonality of these chorale phrases cannot be defined since deceptive cadences at the decisive points prevent any clearly marked tonality. The ear gets a certain support by the chord columns of C major, B flat minor, E major, B major, and again B flat minor.

The third section (measures 205–211) contains the second culmination. The entire string orchestra, fortissimo, spreads its waves with the sixteenth-note triplet figure surrounding the principal theme, blasted out by the trombones, trumpets and woodwinds. The modulation proceeds from B flat minor to A flat major. Again, however, a deceptive cadence delays the expected A flat tonality, and with a surprising leap to E major and a sudden piano, the climax is cut off.

The fourth section (measures 211–226) introduces—contrary to the reprise idea in the formal sonata pattern—a piece of free fantasia, with thematic allusions (compare measures 211 and 7, 210 and 16) only very sparingly intercalated. Yet the inner logic of this fantasia structure is convincing, since it shows the way to that overpowering ecstatic summit to which the ear of the listener is led in so exciting a manner. Again the sixteenth-note triplet figure fluctuates here, softly starting in the violas, and gradually growing in intensity of sound.

At measure 215 the thematic allusions disappear, and there remains only a play of faintly fluctuating rhythms in half, eighth, sixteenth notes. This soft, undulating motion gets a definite direction, an aim and a plastic form by the gradually growing chromatic ascent of the basses, at first in half notes, later in double-dotted rhythms

in slow crescendo and accelerando. When forte is reached (measure 223), there commences a strangely fantastic play of contrasting rhythms. The sixteenth-note triplets flicker and tremble in the high octaves, in staccato tremolo of the flutes and clarinets; the bass in its double-dotted rhythms firmly strides upwards in half-tone steps; the violins throw in a playful figure in eighth notes adorned with trills; the horns march on "choraliter" with even quarters; the trumpets start with whole notes, plunge into great excitement, however, at measure 225, with their strongly accentuated eighth-note figures with quarter rests, to which the oboes respond. With the approach of the fortissimo there is an uproar of waving motion, of trembling, stammering, flickering. Suddenly, however, the tension ceases in diminuendo, with a rigid stop of a fermata (measure 226).

In the following fifth section (measures 227–246), the exciting, fantastic play of the rhythms is repeated in a new variant—quarter-, eighth-, sixteenth-note triplets, syncopated rhythms, fragments of passionate song in the first violins (measure 229), allusions of the celli to the first theme (measure 227), trills and high sparkling tones, provocative trumpet signals (measure 236), irresistibly forceful ascents of the basses and trombones in eighth notes. All this together results in a sound of intoxicating, ecstatic, impulsive power. After the allusion of the basses (measures 237, 238) to the thematically important motif from measure 7, the magnificent climax finally comes to a veritable explosion with a flood of dazzling brightness at the E flat major chord (measure 239), and here one feels that something inconceivably grandiose has happened, and the long accumulated excitement finds release in a liberating, immense cry of ecstasy. What follows is the indispensable gradual preparation of the final restful end.

The close of the first theme with its significant quintuplet figure (measures 240–244) passes through the entire orchestra in double augmentation, emerging from the radiant E flat major as if carried to bright light from the darkness of the depths. Once more a striking outburst is heard at the deceptive cadence B flat major-C flat major (measures 242, 243), and then this musical vision of heavenly light has finally vanished. The few closing measures and the transition to A flat major correspond exactly to the parallel place in the exposition (compare measures 244–246 and 18–20).

The sixth section (measures 247–254) is a condensed reprise of the second theme in A flat major, with its chorale-like ascent, the magnificent broad harmonies, the scintillating harp arpeggios and the solemn C major close.

The seventh section (measures 255–258) too, with its four measures, is merely a reminiscence of the third theme, coupling together the beginning and close of this theme and omitting the nearly thirty intervening measures including the fourth theme contained within them. The newly introduced countermelody of the clarinet (measures 256–258) is thematically important for the coda:

Motif (a), significant during the entire movement, was heard for the first time in measure 7. A little later, in measures 53, 54, the same motif (a) appears in a new version, also introducing motif (b) with the sixteenth notes.

CODA

The coda (measures 259–291) is divided into $12 + 12 + 9 = 33$ measures. It represents a calm, broad exhalation of the tonic D flat major triad, heard constantly in the low strings in the syncopated rhythm which had been so significant from the very beginning. Above this softly modulating D flat major substructure, occasionally interrupted by rests or replaced by an A flat 6/4 chord, the first theme sings its principal motif in dialogue with the above-mentioned coda motifs (a) and (b). The blissful sounds of this sublime coda are animated by little crescendi. Only once, at the subdominant turn D flat, F, A flat, C flat towards G flat major (measures 277, 278) is a stronger agitation noticeable, merging very soon, however, into the infinitely blissful peace of the close.

fourth movement, finale

The finale, marked *feierlich, nicht schnell* (solemn, not fast) is written in a sonata form of vast proportions. Its 706 measures are distributed among the large groups as follows:

(1) Exposition, measures 1–208.

(2) Development, measures 209–432.

(3) Reprise and coda, measures 433–706.

The exposition of the three usual themes (measures 1–208) is planned as follows:

(*a*) Group of the principal theme, measures 1–68.

(*b*) Second theme, measures 69–128.

(*c*) Third theme, measures 129–208.

PRINCIPAL THEME

The principal theme is built up in three terraces. Only at the third terrace, in 3/2 time, is the tonic C minor reached. What precedes is modulation into the principal key from a distant starting point outside the key.

The first terrace (measures 1–16) is filled out by two different linear structures. At the very start the strings, galloping wildly, emit sounds as though by blows of a whip. These violent beats are, from a formal point of view, merely the framework into which the brass orchestra triumphantly blasts the first theme proper. The framework and the theme itself are strange enough in their mutual relations. The following extract, reduced to the simplest possible components, shows these relations:

Within the framework of the string orchestra the sixteen measures are subdivided into 4 × 4 measures. The caesuras of this line do not, however, coincide with those of the brass theme, whose fourteen measures are subdivided into (3 × 4) + 2. The two redundant bars are to be explained as one measure extension at the beginning and one measure at the close. The theme is intensified in expression as it progresses from a broadly extended, solemn beginning to jubilant, rapid fanfares in the second part.

The second terrace (measures 17–30) is an exact, sequence-like repetition of the first one, transposed a whole tone higher. The only difference is the omission of the two introductory measures of the string orchestra. The modulation wanders about apparently aimlessly, searching in a wide circuit, starting in F sharp major, and touching D major, B flat minor, G flat major, E flat minor, D flat major, then one tone higher, A flat major, F flat major, C minor, A flat major, F minor, E flat major, until finally the ascent has reached the third terrace.

At the third terrace (measure 31) the high plateau of the tonic C minor has at last been gained. At the same time, however, the onward drive of the principal theme, thus far energetic and powerful, is now changed into the opposite. From the C minor goal now reached, the theme turns downwards, descending step by step in marchlike manner, and losing more and more of its plastic firmness, until finally, after a long diminuendo, its savage, spiteful force has dwindled away to almost nothing. The method of this anticlimax is as original as it is surprising in effect. A bell motif, with the intervals of the fourth, fifth, and octave, typical for the carillon motifs, makes its first appearance in the woodwinds and strings in measure 33, and now reduced to the leap of a fourth, dominates the entire diminuendo, beginning at measure 41. The pealing bells seem to break the power of the formidable, savage strength of the beginning. The solemn, ecclesiastic litany stands out more and more serenely and peacefully in ever softer colors. After the blaring trombones have left the field of action, trumpets and horn cease playing in the following phrase. High up the oboes, clarinets, and violins in pianissimo suggest shimmering brightness; next the solemn tubas enter with their soft, broadly extended level of sound. A pious mood prevails; in mild prayer the C major resounds even as in the vast spaces of a Gothic cathedral. The following extract will illustrate the peculiar linear and harmonic procedure of this section:

Masterly skill is also manifest by the manner in which the remote C flat major is inserted into the C major level, breaking its monotony and at the same time intensifying the solemnity.

THE SECOND THEME

The second theme (measures 69–128) is more restful in character. One hears solemn, mild chorale chanting in dialogue, as if alternating between chorus and solo voices, with a few echo measures interspersed. The subdivisions are: $10 + 10 + 4 + 6 + 6 + 9 + 3 + 12 = 60$ measures.

The first section (measures 69–78) consists of a four-bar phrase of solo type, answered by a four-bar phrase of the full chorus. A two-bar transition motif of the basses is inserted between the two four-bar phrases, serving both to separate and connect them, thus extending the phrase to ten measures. A flat major and C major, as dominant of F minor, bound this ten-measure phrase.

The second section (measures 79–88) is a somewhat varied and intensified repetition of the preceding organ and choral episode, this time starting in A flat major and terminating in D flat major.

The third section (measures 89–99), again a ten-measure phrase, is comprised of a four-bar phrase of the strings (A flat major to C flat major),

a five-bar chorale of the tubas as answer, into which a litany-like closing phrase of the clarinets and horns is inserted, with an echo of flutes and clarinets as the finishing touch:

The fourth section (measures 99–104) is a sequence-like repetition of the tuba chorale, the litany and the echo, a tone higher, passing from

C sharp minor to E major. By this repetition the relation of section 4 to 3 is the same as of section 2 to 1.

The fifth section (measures 105–113) takes up motifs of section one, continuing in ascending sequence the first two-bar motif (in the celli), passing from A flat major to C flat major and D major. The transition motif mentioned in section 1 is here ingeniously employed as continuation of the violin melody connecting section 5 with the next section.

The sixth section (measures 113–128) is subdivided as follows: 4 (transition motif) + 4 + 4 + 4 measures. The entire section serves as answer to section 5. The second violins (measures 117–127) play the chorale melody; the first violin adds a free countermelody, which, thanks to the transition motif, forms a magnificent, broadly curved and uniform arch with the chant of the first violins in section 5. The modulation leads from G flat major to E flat minor and to the dominant, B flat major. At the point where B flat major is beginning to disappear (measure 125), the kettledrum enters with that motif of fourths, which serves as the main building stone of a new melodic structure.

THE THIRD THEME

This new melodic structure is the third theme (measures 129–208). Its subdivisions are: $(16 + 8) + (8 + 8 + 8) + (8 + 8 + 16) = 24 + 24 + 32$ measures.

The first section (measures 129–144) brings one of those veiled unison-themes, so characteristic of Bruckner. The wind instruments double the marchlike figure of the strings in simplified manner, contracting several quarter notes to half or dotted half notes. Thus march and chorale character are combined in the same notes. The tonality is E flat minor with D flat, equivalent to the Aeolian scale.

The second section (measures 145–152), only eight measures long, corresponds fairly well to the first part of the preceding section, with a more intensive close the second time, modulating from E flat minor to B flat and F minor. Thus far the chorale tune and the brisk march rhythms had been of equal importance.

In the third section (measures 153–160), the march rhythm is entirely abandoned and the solemn chorale, supported in the bass by the trombones and tuba, remains alone. E major to C sharp major, and A minor to A major mark the modulation of the two four-bar phrases of this chorale structure. In its descending melodic line it has a close relation to the end of the first theme (measure 32), as also to the chorale episode of the second theme (measures 75, 85, 93).

In the fourth section (measures 161–168) the march rhythm again joins the chorale, soaring down from lofty heights, touching D minor and F major.

The fifth section (measures 169–176) lets the violins rise in animated song above the march rhythm of the basses, but does not long continue this lightly indicated mood. After a few measures pianissimo enters, the singing ceases, everything seems as if hypnotized by a new event developed with highest tension and growing increasingly more powerful, touching G flat major and A flat minor.

In the sixth section (measures 177–184) the entire wind and brass orchestra enters in B flat major with a distinct allusion to the principal theme of the first movement, with its characteristic double dotted rhythms, all this combined with the march rhythms pervading the entire string orchestra in four octaves.

In a powerful crescendo the seventh and eighth sections (measures 185–192, 193–208) continue the same idea until a veritable explosion of sound is reached: a musical scene of elementary force and sinister, threatening grandeur. This vision vanishes as quickly as it appeared. After the strongest fortissimo (measures 203, 204) great silence suddenly ensues, a frightful emptiness. Only the kettledrums and the strings pizzicato continue the march rhythm a few measures further. The march recedes further into the distance. The grandiose exposition of this finale is brought to a close with the kettledrums sounding B flat, after the organ point B flat, D, F has constantly dominated the entire last part, from measures 177 to 208.

DEVELOPMENT

The development section (measures 209–432) aims at two culminations: at measures 317–338, almost exactly in the middle of the entire development section, and at measure 433, where the reprise starts. The tonal idea is quite similar in both cases: a slow dynamic ascent from pianissimo to fortissimo, beginning hesitatingly and gradually gathering force. Of course, the thematic contour of these two sound waves is altogether different, no trace of "repetition" is to be found. One gets the impression of seeking, of striving to reach a goal. The first time the aim has not been fully reached; a second ascent is attempted, on a different path, leading to the actual summit.

The first culmination (measures 209–371) is the result of a whole series of smaller, completely rounded episodes. In the first phrases the tension of silence is repeatedly utilized: a fragile texture, full of pauses, mainly in piano and pianissimo; the latent energy makes itself felt by sudden jerks, a small crescendo, a short forte, a sudden sharp accent.

Episode 1 (measures 209–216) lets the march rhythm of the third theme disappear on the E flat major chord of the strings. The horns add reminiscences of the dotted rhythms of the first theme, flutes and clarinets in echo in the highest octaves.

Episode 2 (measures 217–224) contains the same thematic structure, now in C minor.

Episode 3 (measures 225–232) contains the chorale intermezzo of the third theme (measures 153–160) in two four-bar phrases, calmly and broadly sung by the string choir. The modulation passes from E flat major to C major, from A flat minor to A flat major. At the sombre D flat minor chord, pianissimo suddenly enters. In this pianissimo the strings gradually vanish during the following episode.

Episode 4 (measures 233–246). Above these dim cathedral sounds, these long chords of the strings and soft rolls of the kettledrum, vanishing in the depth, three flutes in brightest coloring play the first theme of the finale in E flat. The clarinet enters, while the strings drop out.

In the next episodes, 5 (measures 247–258) and 6 (measures 259–279), various groups of instruments alternate. The high flutes and clarinets are followed by the strings in the middle register, with the descending chorale theme in the cello (measures 247–250), then the higher woodwind group answers with the ascending version of the chorale theme, in canonic imitations; next the horns and trumpets enter, and finally (measure 259), the strings reappear with the inverted ascending chorale theme in the basses. The violins sing a calm, broad countermelody, related to the second theme (measure 69). After a quick crescendo to fortissimo, a descent to piano follows (271–278). "With ecstatic motion" (*Ekstatisch bewegt*), as Bruckner prescribes, the violins soar downwards, resting for a short time on the B flat major chord.

Episode 6 treats the exact inversion of the third theme in 4 × 4 measures with a free thematic continuation, starting from E flat major, touching A flat minor and other related regions, and finally playfully rocking aloft to and fro four times on the diminished seventh chord of E flat (D, F, A flat, C flat). Again E flat minor is reached, this time, however, in episode 7, in firm concatenation of the third marchlike theme with the second part of the first theme (in the brass):

Episode 8 (measures 303–310) corresponds to measure 285 and following. This time, however, the sequence employs the march motif *recte,* whereas before it had been used *inverse.* This episode in the high range is followed by the next episode.

Episode 9 (measures 311–317) contains the third, marchlike theme, played by the celli and bassoons, changing in tonality from C major to C minor and F minor.

A crescendo leads to the first culmination, reached in episodes 10 and 11 (measures 317–326, 327–339). Episode 10 is a freely treated parallel to episode 7, with the same combination of the first and third themes, now in F minor. This time, however, the third theme is no longer heard in its entirety, but is only hinted at by its march rhythm. Episode 11 freely continues the brass melody of the first theme in fortissimo, constructing it as a magnificent arch, only to break off suddenly in the splendor and fullness of its sound, when G major has been reached (measure 339).

The second part of the development section begins here. Bright sound soars in a free ether, with rounded rhythms and without the sharpness of strong marcato accents. A gently flowing sextuplet figure of the clarinet, later taken over by the horns, serves to hold the transparent structure together for a considerable stretch.

Episode 1 (measures 339–345) allots the unexpectedly entering initial measures of the first theme to the second violin, against which the clarinet plays the above-mentioned sextuplet figure, and the first violins a new countermelody; in the lower register the timpani give forth faint rolls.

The radiant, luminous sound combination:

Clarinet

First part of first theme

beginning on G and closing on A is repeated in episode 2 one tone higher (measures 345–351), transposed from A to B major, in different orchestration, for the woodwinds only.

Episode 3 (measures 351–361) places the melody yet a tone higher, starting on B; a high string trio with the clarinet sextuplets. The sequence is somewhat complicated by the canonic imitation of the first theme in the viola.

In the following episode, 4 (measures 362–380), the texture of the parts becomes denser and darker. A fragment of the first theme is heard *recte* and *inverse* at the same time; free parts in the characteristic rhythms of the same theme are added as counterpoints; the horn sextuplets bind the texture in the middle region:

Ascending in thirds in somewhat sequential treatment, this idea is repeated thrice: the first time on B flat, the second time on D flat, the third time on F, the upper parts being changed accordingly. After measure 373, the four-bar sequence is reduced to a two-bar sequence, which, ascending a whole tone three times, rises again from the darker, lower regions to the luminous heights. At measures 379–380 this radiant expansion (through the wood-wind sextuplets) is especially emphasized on the chord:

$$\begin{cases} \text{B F A flat E flat A flat} \\ \text{B F A flat} \quad \text{D} \quad \text{A flat} \end{cases}$$

Episode 5 (measures 381–394) goes back again to the first part of the first theme, in the horns, to which it opposes a counterpoint of the violins containing the descending chorale in diminution, but, in its first phrase, 1/4 + 2/8, also reminiscent of the rhythm of the march motif:

The surprising turn of C major and A minor to the mild, dark keys of D flat and G flat major and back to C major (measure 387), finds its continuation in the chords of the trumpets and horns (measures 388–394), with the final close in E flat major.

The same thematic material in a new version dominates episode 6 (measures 395–406). The climax already prepared in episode 1 (measure 340) is based more on emotional tension than on dynamic accumulation of sound. It is very remarkable that for nearly one hundred measures, from measure 340 to the beginning of the reprise (measure 433), the entire musical procedure takes place in the upper regions only, that the basses are silent all the time.

The twelve measures of this episode are comprised of a 3 × 4 bar sequence: the broad beginning of the principal theme, the solemnly expanded two chords in the woodwinds, violas, celli to which is opposed the counterpoint of the violins, remembered from episode 5, the chorale theme in diminution, heard three times in progression from E flat major to C minor, D flat major to D flat minor, A flat major to F minor.

Splendid harmonic effects fill the following episode 7 (measures 406–418). F minor (measure 406) is followed immediately by A major and E major, C minor, G major, E flat minor, B flat major, G flat major, D flat major, A flat minor, B flat major, in easily recognized harmonic sequence: progressions of thirds and of fifths interlaced. Horns, trumpets, and trombones are combined in this splendid tonal structure. The violins adorn this pompous cathedral-like music with those graceful figures which have been employed since the fifth episode (measure 381), and at every third measure the woodwinds throw in that carillon motif, which had already shown its effectiveness at the beginning of the movement (measure 33), in harmonic progression, starting from A, C, E flat, G flat. The tension produced by the last episodes after measure 339 is attributable in no small degree to the great art with which the goal is veiled by means of modulations and chord

A major   E major

progressions. The ear is never certain where the effective harmonic progressions are tending to, and is led from surprise to surprise, until finally at the commencement of the reprise the view suddenly clears up with astounding impressiveness, and the goal lies before one in dazzling brightness. The beginning of this episode is quoted here, beginning on page 414. Notice how the dynamic ascent starting in measure 410 is again interrupted.

Episode 8 (measures 418–430) is filled out by a piano and pianissimo of strangely exciting, mysterious effect. One hears little thematic fragments, floating so to speak in the vast space of sound, a dim series of sequences (measures 418–422), leading from B flat major to E major. Then the flutes sustain the high E for eight measures in that rhythm so characteristic of the entire finale, as well as of the first movement:

The first violins double this E in lower octave with the provoking appoggiatura rhythm:

from the beginning of the finale; oboes and celli in sequence descend stepwise in oblique motion towards the high organ point. The violins and violas, with their thin, pointed figures run in among them in the rhythm retained through fifty measures. All this takes place in utmost pianissimo, with extremely attenuated sound. Thereupon, after the A minor tonality has been reached (at measure 430), trumpets and timpani suddenly hurl into the surging mass that ominous F sharp from the savage appoggiatura rhythms of the beginning.

REPRISE

The reprise enters, but not directly into the principal key of C major. As with the exposition, the reprise commences far distant from the main tonality, in F sharp minor and D major. Only considerably later (measure 469) is C major reached, thus closing the vast arch, whose next to the last pilaster had been the anticipated C minor in the middle of the development section (measures 311–338). Compared with the exposition, the reprise shows manifold deviations. The construction of the theme is different. The whistling appoggiatura figure of the basses and woodwinds, framing the theme, now sounds even more savage than before. Violins and violas throw in an accompaniment figure of wild, almost wrathful energy, thus greatly increasing the intensity of expression, in addition to serving its purpose of filling out the accompaniment. The figure is derived from a significant pattern in the second part of the development section (measures 381–433), but also has a resemblance to the carillon motif that had been so effective in the exposition (measure 33). The following sketch shows these relations and at the same time the relationship with the third theme (measure 130):

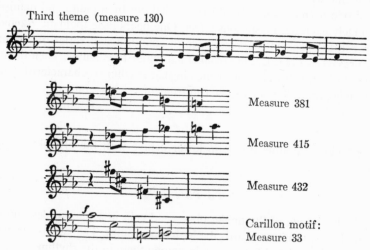

Third theme (measure 130)

Measure 381

Measure 415

Measure 432

Carillon motif:
Measure 33

In the exposition, the ascent of the theme had come to its termination on the second terrace (measure 31), and had begun its descent immediately upon reaching the third terrace (measure 32). In the reprise the theme shows no descending tendency at all. The descending motif (measures 31–35) does not reappear in the reprise at all, after having extensively dominated the first part of the development section (measures 295–338). The impression of an uninterrupted triumphal ascent is evoked by the reprise in a truly dazzling manner (measures 431–474). All melodic lines are boldly and steeply pointed upwards. Each of the three eight-bar terraces, parallel to one another at the distance of a fourth, mounts an octave upwards. The third terrace, with a prolongation of two measures, is crowned by the four-bar fanfare figure. Next follows a new slow ascent, at first in two-measure, later in one-measure phrases, until finally, when the C major summit has been reached, the grandiose melodic line is brought to its close in 3 × 2 measures.

In measures 462–469 a very original and quite unusual means of attaining the climax demands attention; the continued alternation of "very broad" 4/4 time and quick alla breve time, 2/2. This retardation and acceleration gives the impression of exhaustion at the ascent to a summit, an exhaustion that can be overcome only by highest concentration of will power, after repeated relapses. In this realistic allusion to climbing one recognizes the son of the Alpine country. The extract on page 418 will make manifest the plan of this grandiose construction, with its symmetries, correspondences, progressions, and interruptions. The following graphic sketch will give a still clearer idea of the wonderful linear conception of this episode:

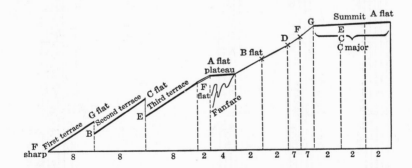

In the exposition the second theme had entered after a gradual diminuendo, after a complete disappearance of the first theme. In the reprise, however, the approach to the second theme is conceived quite differently. It enters after a powerful triple fortissimo (measure 495), proceeding from pianissimo (measure 474) to a first fortissimo, followed by a new pianissimo (measure 509) and a still more powerful new crescendo.

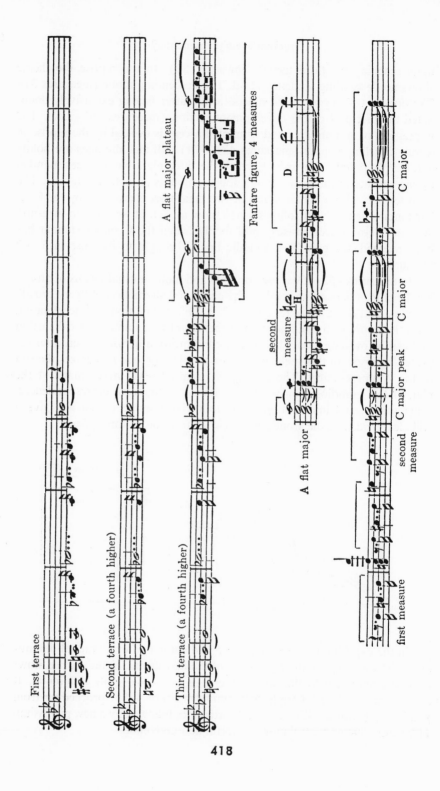

First terrace

Second terrace (a fourth higher)

Third terrace (a fourth higher)

A flat major plateau

Fanfare figure, 4 measures

second
measure

D

H

A flat major

C major peak

C major

C major

second
measure

first measure

TRANSITION TO THE SECOND THEME

This quite new, much broader transition from the first to the second theme is subdivided into the following sections:

(1) Measures 474–494, crescendo from pianissimo to fortissimo.

(2) Measures 495–512, diminuendo from fortissimo to pianissimo.

(3) Measures 513–536, crescendo from pianissimo to fortissimo.

(4) Measures 536–544, transition to the second theme.

Section 1 (measures 474–494) continues the rhythms of the wind instruments of the preceding section, now given to the string basses, with a sudden pianissimo opposed to the fortissimo of the close. The bass figure moves upwards in corkscrew manner chromatically step by step, at first in two-bar groups, then in one-bar phrases. The horns respond to the basses with the same motif; to this dialogue is added yet another between the first and the second violins, based on the same motif in eighth notes, already active from measure 463. This mass of sound, pushed slowly upwards, gains in fullness and strength with every step, until the powerful culmination is reached.

Section 2 (measures 495–512) is filled out by the ebbing off of the vast sound wave after its initial culmination of section 1. With every two measures it sinks a whole tone downwards, always continuing the rhythmical motif:

$$\flat | \downarrow.. \ \flat \downarrow.. \ \flat | \downarrow.. \ \flat \downarrow.$$

taken over from the preceding section. A broad diatonic level expands from E flat major to C minor. At measure 509, the entire previously accumulated energy has already disappeared; a tiny half-tone motion in faintest pianissimo indicates the low point.

Again the sound wave rises in section 3 (measures 513–536), once more utilizing the same rhythmical motif (now only the most primitive allusion to the principal theme). In mysterious calmness it sets out very slowly and then, quickly gathering power, lifts itself higher and higher with threatening gestures, in steeply pointed figures, and finally seems to muster all its might for a deadly blow (measures 532–536). At this moment, however, the mood unexpectedly changes with telling effect. The pious chant of the second theme, entering in measure 544, wards off the power of the assault.

In the eight measures of transition in section 4 (measures 536–544), the second theme works miracles by its closeness alone, even prior to its actual appearance. With gentle, soft harmonies the horns pacify the elementary pressure of the double-dotted rhythms, pointing back again to the principal

419

theme of the first movement. This horn episode (measure 540) is a parallel to a quite similar horn episode at the start of the development section (measures 209–217).

After this introduction, as unexpected as it is impressive, the second theme makes its appearance in A flat major (measures 544–577). Bruckner pays no heed here to the convention and brings back the second theme in the reprise in the same key as in the exposition, namely A flat, instead of changing its key to E flat, for instance. The following measures are an exact repetition. Measures 544–562 correspond exactly to measures 69–87, only in more intensified and sonorous orchestration. A little cut is made here, measures 89–92 being omitted in the reprise. The following chorale of the tubas, however, is also repeated literally: measures 564–573 correspond almost exactly to measures 93–103, the only differences being a new counter melody of the flutes in the reprise and slight changes of orchestration.

Some editions of the score indicate a cut here, extending from measures 520–578. After the preceding explanations, it is evident that this cut, removing the last climax and the second theme, has no justification since it damages essential features of the construction.

Bruckner himself, however, has dropped the magnificent close of the second theme group from the reprise (measures 105–128).

THIRD THEME

Immediately following the E major chord, vanishing in a prolonged echo (measure 577), the third theme enters in C minor above the pedal point G of the timpani. This theme also is now treated differently than it had been in the exposition. Now it represents a dominant upbeat to the majestic coda commencing at measure 644. This expanse, from measures 578–644, consists of a development of the third theme and an entry of the principal theme of the first movement, both on the dominant pedal point G, resolving to the tonic C minor in measure 644. The organ point is interrupted at measures 598–613 for a short time only.

The first episode (measures 578–598) is subdivided into 12 + 8 measures. The march rhythm of the third theme predominates. To the already well known march melody new counterpoints are added, in restless syncopated rhythms, suggestive of inner excitement. The tonality of the several four- and six-bar phrases keeps changing from C minor to F minor, E flat major, G minor, G major, all this on the dominant organ point of the timpani and basses on G.

In the third episode (measures 614–700), the dominant organ point G re-enters. Trombones and trumpet blast forth the principal theme of the first movement into the foaming sound mass of the strings and woodwinds. Immediately after this explosion, the power of the motion is gradually relaxed. A long diminuendo occurs, always on the organ point G, fragments of the motifs are thrown in, the rhythms lose their sharpness. The tension is more and more relaxed, until only the kettledrum remains with the germ rhythm characteristic of the entire symphony:

$$| \, \text{♪}\text{♩} \, \text{?} - | \, \text{♪}\text{♩} \, \text{?} - |$$

There is a pause for the entire orchestra, and at last the gigantic dominant upbeat is brought to a close.

CODA

The coda (measures 544–706) enters, and with it the tonic key C minor. A magnificently constructed climax is erected, starting from a calm pianissimo. Its subdivisions are: $(3 \times 8) + 8 + 8 + 10 + 13$ measures.

Section 1 (measures 644–651) brings the four-bar beginning, the initial phrase of the first finale theme in repetition. The violins hover above this horn motif with a gently flowing figure in eighth notes, the kettledrum adds the germ rhythm with the appoggiatura. The repetition of this phrase (measures 648–651) is varied by a new counter melody of the tubas, in which a characteristic motif from the principal theme of the first movement, this time in augmentation, is recognized. (Compare first movement, measure 4.)

Section 2 (measures 652–659), the parallel to section one, is a slightly intensified repetition, a fourth higher. The sound of the newly added tuba quartet gives this section its peculiarly dark, soft, subdued color.

Section 3 (measures 660–667) repeats the preceding section once more, again a fourth higher, in the luxurious fullness of the large orchestra.

The first three sections taken together represent a very effective chorale-like structure, in spite of their similarity. Enough variety is produced by the gradual progression towards the higher octaves, the growing fullness of sound, the impressive new counter subjects of the tubas, and the upward rising, light, and soaring figures of the violins. Consequently, the similarity of the groups, with their frequent repetitions, is not felt as monotony, but as concentration.

The tendency to a climax, constantly manifest until measure 667, is interrupted in a very ingenious manner by section 4 (measures 667–675), which, in sudden harmonic shift from G flat major to D minor, treats the second phrase of the first finale theme, now in piano, played by the woodwinds, continued by the trumpets in crescendo.

Section 5 (measures 675–693) commences with the full orchestra, the tutti being further augmented by the addition of a crescendo and fortissimo. The nucleus of this section is the third phrase of the first finale theme, in the trumpets and woodwinds, with the new brilliant and pompous figuration of

Construction of the coda

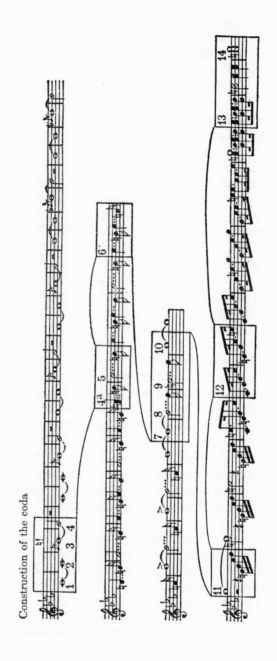

the violins in eighth notes. In the blare of horns one recognizes the "German Michael" motif from the scherzo. Starting in measure 685, the fourth and last phrase of the finale theme makes its appearance, the trumpet fanfares.

CONSTRUCTION OF THE CODA

Here the constructive plan of the coda becomes manifest. The first finale theme is cut up into its four phrases, and each phrase is treated separately in one or several sections, with free use of repetitions, sequences, extensions. This very original and novel manner of recapitulating a theme is illustrated by the melodic extract of measures 644–693 on page 422.

If one takes the fourteen measures from their context of fifty measures, as indicated by the continuous numbers 1–14, and if one plays these measures successively, one obtains the principal theme of the finale in C major note by note, with virtually no change (except for measure 3, where E flat must be replaced by E natural).

After this truly grandiose, triumphant reprise of the finale theme, there remains only the constructive necessity of bringing the tonic to a sufficiently strong close, to a degree and with a tonal quality commensurate with the gigantic proportions and the emotional contents of this symphony.

This is done in the closing section (measures 694–706) in thirteen measures on the C major chord, without the least change of harmony. But this C major is built up most ingeniously. In it are combined the principal motifs of the first, second, and third movements. The finale theme is absent here because it had just been brought to the most grandiose perfection imaginable. The ecstatic figuration of the violins, moreover, is a reminiscence of the trio of the scherzo (measure 38), in the chord of the ninth: G, F, A. The following extract will illustrate this combination:

The transformation of the chromatic theme of the first movement into the clear diatonic progression of the close is significant for the ethical idea, the content of the symphony: a striving away from dark passion towards vanquishing of despair, towards purification by faith, in short, the triumph of faith. This victory of the soul over matter is represented in various forms: devout veneration, confidence, consoling peace. Joyful confession, jubilant joy in life, enthusiastic ecstasy is the emotional content of the various movements, considered in their essential traits. The musical portrayal of the psychic conflicts, the obstacles to be surmounted on the road towards this goal, is the real content in the symphonic elaboration of this grandiose score.

CHAPTER **XXII**

arnold schönberg: opus 11
and opus 19

three piano pieces, Op. 11

Arnold Schönberg's art has excited the attention of the musical world for decades. It is so complicated, so difficult to understand and so obscure and perplexing even to most musicians that it demands a searching analysis of the formal ideas which dominate it. The three piano pieces, Op. 11 (Universal Edition, Vienna), have from the start created a sensational impression of unfamiliarity, and certainly players as well as listeners are even now quite generally at a loss as to how to appreciate this curious music, even in its technical methods, quite apart from its aesthetic value.

Thus far only a few attempts have been made to investigate Schönberg's novel technique thoroughly in all its details. The present attempt at analysis disregards the question of aesthetic values, and is merely concerned with whether it is possible to discover a rational constructive idea in these pieces, a clear formal plan. These piano pieces have often been criticized as constructions which mock the laws of reason, the demands of the ear, as, in fact, "nonmusic," to which the usual reaction has been amused laughter and sneers.

425

The following analysis will prove that these pieces are constructed not only sensibly, but strictly, logically, and concisely. The road to this understanding is, however, laborious, because Schönberg does his utmost to disguise plain progressions and chords and to make them appear strange and enigmatic.

The first step in the analysis will be to recognize the leading melody in its coherent line: Schönberg is fond of letting his intervals move in wide leaps, often into distant octaves. In No. 1 of these pieces, measure 12, for example, an ordinary chromatic run:

looks thus in his notation:

A commonplace appoggiatura effect is disguised by him in curious fashion by shifts in octaves. Thus, for instance, the following extremely "modern" and "atonal" phrase resumes a simple and sensible appearance as soon as one transposes the artificially shifted octave leaps back to their starting point. The result is a plain appoggiatura effect in the right hand, accompanied by a chromatic scale in the left hand:

Measures 36ff.

Reduced to plain, unbroken leading of the melodic line, it looks as follows:

Schönberg here displaces the various melodic tones in a manner similar to the shifting of rhythms in American jazz. Once such disguising mannerisms, quite frequent in Schönberg's music, have become manifest, his melodic style loses much of its enigmatic look.

OPUS 11, NUMBER 1

The principal melody of No. 1 must first be transcribed note for note into a plain, unbroken melodic line (see page 428). It will immediately be seen that the "novelty" of this music is very much reduced to ordinary standards by such a transcription. The melody is easily understood; it hardly differs from the Wagnerian Tristan melos. Moreover the supposed "atonality" is totally absent from the melody, which is actually constructed according to the best traditional maxims of the art.

This "atonality" is falsely alleged by the chords of the accompaniment, the counterpoints with their unexpectedly entering "dissonances." One should not allow oneself to be bluffed by these curious chords, apparently not belonging to any key at all; one should take pains rather to understand the "tonality" of the main melody. Then one should answer the question, whether a plain chorale melody in G major becomes less G major, if one accompanies it with strange, distant, "false" sounding chords. Just as little are Schönberg's curious chords able to change the clearly pronounced tonality of his melody. The various sections of the melody may be of different tonality, as is often found in classical and romantic music. In order to make the tonality of the single sections still more evident to the eye, I have taken the liberty of rewriting Schönberg's notation in three or four places by enharmonic change, which does not alter the sound. In measures 50 and 61, for instance, I have written A flat instead of Schönberg's G sharp, and so on.

In order to understand clearly the structure of the piece, one must not only consider the main melodic line, but also its thematic material, which is fully and exhaustively presented within the first eight measures. The piece is built up of four motifs (see page 429).

428

Motif (a) is the always recurring main melodic motif.

Motif (b) is a sort of inquisitive sigh, an ascending third, responding to the first measure of (a) with the descending third.

Motif (c) is a winding little chromatic figure of painful expression. Its harmonic relationship would be clearer if one would read: C, A sharp, B, instead of C, B flat, B natural. Likewise, if one reads C sharp in the third measure instead of D flat, the alto part of the first eight measures appears distinctly in B minor.

Motif (d) is a figurated B minor chord of the sixth, rising in arpeggio in five eighth notes. This motif, in diminution to thirty-second notes, is on several occasions responsible for those strange, scurrying transitions (as in measures 12 and 13, 39–41, 50–52), the first two of which fill out pauses of the melodic main line.

Upon examining the sixty-four measures of the piece in the simplified melodic sketch, one perceives clearly that the traditional eight-bar construction is dominant. Only in two places—analogous to the classical models—is the eight-bar symmetry interrupted: exactly in the middle, at measure 32, the eight-bar phrase has been extended to nine bars. To balance this lengthening, the last section has only fifteen measures, instead of the normal sixteen measures. "Papa" Haydn practiced these metrical artifices two centuries ago.

A closer investigation of the several sections follows here:

Section 1 (measures 1–8) is composed of the four motifs (a), (b), (c), (d). Of atonality there is no trace. One might possibly speak, however, of polytonality, of different tonalities heard simultaneously. The principal melody (a) has the Phrygian tonality, E, F, G, A, B. The alto part has already been identified as B minor. B minor is evident also in the tenor if one reads E sharp and G double sharp in measures 2 and 3 instead of F and A. These new enharmonic equivalents can then be explained as a sort of prolonged changing notes, appoggiaturas to F sharp and A sharp in measures 4 and 5, representing the dominant chord of B minor. The bass, not thematically, but freely constructed, acquires tonal coherence if one reads, with enharmonic changes: F sharp, A sharp, G sharp, C sharp, B sharp, G sharp, belonging to a C sharp tonality.

The total result is: a main melody in the Phrygian scale, accompanied by B minor and C sharp minor (melodic). The real disturber of the peace is the G sharp in the bass. One needs only to replace it by G, in order to see how all four parts are quite peacefully in agreement within the frame of traditional tonality, in the sense of G major. The final result in the Schönberg version is a G major, disturbed by a G sharp. It will later be shown how an apparent polytonality in the single parts still may result in one main tonality of the ensemble.

Section 2 (measures 8–16). Motif (a) in measures 9–11. In measures 12, 13, 14, motif (d) in fantastic disguise (the arpeggio of thirds replaced by an arpeggio of fourths, the eighth notes by thirty-second notes). After disemburdening the melodic kernel of its densely veiled figuration in measures 13 and 14, it appears as follows:

All these phrases are recognized as variants of motif (c). Measure 15 shows augmentation of measure 13.

In the melodic line, G major is prevailing, with shifting by sequences, measures 13, 14. This plain, positive fact is veiled by the iridescent flageolet of measures 14–17, shimmering in tonally indefinable hues. The leaps of a ninth, measures 12, 13, are easily understood by transposing them back into the same octave, resulting in the simple figure:

which, by the way, is thematically unimportant, a secondary motif to be played pianississimo, as rightly prescribed.

Section 3 (measures 17–25) commences, like sections 1 and 2, again with the main motif (a), now shortened from three to two measures (17, 18). In the remaining measures 19–24, the motifs (b) and (c) occur alternately. The tonality of the melodic line is G minor, with chromatic changing notes thrown in. The bass mixes in A major, clearly evident, if one reads with enharmonic change:

Thus we see G minor in the soprano and A major in the bass simultaneously, but so evenly balanced that neither key prevails, but both stand next to each other unmixed, without producing, as in section 1, a new third tonality as final result.

Section 4 (measures 25–33) is an eight-bar phrase prolonged to nine measures. In measures 25–27 motif (a) is prolonged at the beginning by an eighth note, in stretta through three parts. The added eighth note at the start has the purpose of making better connection with the eighth-note figure in measure 24. In measure 28 motif (d) in thirds (soprano) and fourths (bass). Measures 29, 30 the descending third from the first measure of (a); measures 30, 31, 32 motif (a) in its entirety, leaping from the soprano into the bass. Measure 31, the center of the entire piece, is marked with mathematical exactness, by a one-bar prolongation of the eight-bar phrase, as well as by the anticlimax, the low point of the entire piece (pianissimo, lowest basses). Melodically, measure 33 is a shortened echo of the two preceding measures. The sixteenth-note figure of the lower parts (measures 29, 30) is gained from motif (a) by elision, as can be clearly seen in measure 31, where motif (a) enters. The tonality of the melodic line is a modified A minor, based on the scale: A, B flat, C, D, E, F sharp, G sharp, A, with slight chromatic alterations here and there.

The last measures, from the end of 30 to 33, one might consider, together with the accompaniment, as G minor, until the resolution into the tonic G enters, in the echo-measure 33. By enharmonic change of the notes D flat and C flat into the equivalent notes C sharp and B, at the places marked with an asterisk, the G tonality becomes evident, and here again the observation is confirmed, that a melody of clearly defined tonality can, by the nature of its accompanying harmonies, accept another tonality in polyphonic setting. This seems to be one of the essential principles of polytonal harmony. In the following examples, Schönberg's C sharp is to be considered a freely entering leading tone to D, the dominant of G minor, without, however, being actually followed by the expected resolution to D. The bass harmony A flat–E in measure 32, which seems to contradict the G minor, is explained as an anticipation of the passing A flat in the following measure:

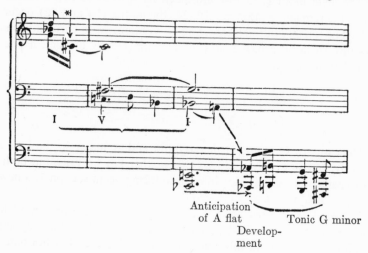

Anticipation of A flat   Tonic G minor

Development

Section 5 (measures 34–41). The main melody brings motif (a) twice (measures 34–38), followed by the motif of thirds (b), in measure 38 (B–D), the descending second from the close of (a) in measure 39 (B flat–A). Measure 40 contains the arpeggio of the motif (d) in inversion, descending. In measure 41 the leap of a third in motif (b) occurs again: D, F sharp, twice, passing over from the left into the right hand. The left hand brings chromatic scale figures in measures 35–38, in measure 38 motif (b) with appoggiatura. Measure 39 contains motif (d) in the version of fourths. The alto in measure 38 twice plays the chromatic motif (c). The tonality of measure 34–35 is B flat minor, in measure 36 and 37, 38, G major or C minor follows, in measure 40 and 41, G minor, but in adventurous disguise. Measure 40 loses its prickly look and is turned into

432

a tame, familiar chromatic progression by the following transcription:

Here one may also easily perceive the interlocked motifs (d) and (c), at the places marked by the asterisk and the square brace.

Section 6 (measures 42–49) leads the descending motif of thirds (a) in a broad melodic curve downwards and up again. In the middle voice for the right hand, measures 42, 43, the chromatic motif (c) appears in sixteenth notes. The tonality is A minor, with a transition to D minor in the middle, measures 44–46. Wagnerian chromatic harmony (*Tristan,* prelude to Act 3) has left distinct traces in this section.

Section 7 (measures 49–64) contains the culmination of the entire piece. It starts with an impetuous run, accelerando and crescendo (measures 49, 50) in its sixteenth-note figure, the arpeggio motif (d) is found in a new transformation: the leaps of thirds have now been changed into vigorously marching, aggressive leaps of sevenths. After this very effective preparation, the principal motif (a) is now heard, in the highest reaches in fortissimo, accompanied by motif (d) in the left hand, now martellato, in leaps of fourths. The rest of the piece is filled out by a descent of great linear beauty, beginning after the culmination reached in measure 50. Motif (a) descending at first in the soprano, and later, after measure 57, descending more and more in the bass, in shortened rhythms. The other three motifs in the lower parts. In measure 54 the bass has the arpeggio motif; in measures 55–58, the leap of a third, motif (b) with its accent of question or calling; in measures 56, 57 the chromatic motif (c) is hammered out by the thumb of the right hand.

The tonality of the main melody in the first phrase (measures 50–52) is C sharp minor, with the notes G sharp, E, D sharp, C sharp, B sharp (the last four notes enharmonically changed). This C sharp is veiled by the accompaniment, especially the eighth-note figure of the right hand. This figure is a plain C sharp minor, blurred by deliberate alteration of various intervals. Here follows the transformation into pure C sharp minor, achieved merely by alteration of a few notes, D sharp and F sharp instead of D and F, and so on.

433

The "false" notes introduced by Schönberg through alteration become legitimate, however, by the logical progression of the major third parallels, impossible without those "false" notes. The total impression must nevertheless be called C sharp minor. Neither the "false" notes, the parallels of thirds, nor the quickly darting, still "falser" arpeggios of the basses, can shake the predominance for the ear of C sharp minor.

The second phrase (measures 53–55) is dominated in the soprano by an E tonality, approaching the Phrygian scale: E, F, G (G sharp), A, B. In the following measure 55, the Phrygian mode is changed into C sharp minor by the added bass notes D flat–F flat = C sharp–E. Measures 56–58 are unmistakably C minor, dimmed through intentional alteration of G–B into G flat–B flat.

In measures 59, 60, D minor is understood on the dominant organ point A. The dominant triad of D minor is disturbed by the sustained tone D in the middle voice, an old effect of anticipation, known to Haydn, but taking on the appearance of novelty and strangeness in the Schönberg piece by the unusually long duration of the anticipation. A second disturbance of the dominant sound is brought about by the foreign note G sharp held in the left hand. This G sharp in its turn anticipates by several measures the same G sharp with which the next phrase (measures 60, 61) begins.

In spite of all these disturbances, the tonality remains D minor to the end. Even the close on E flat in the bass (measure 64) is not contradictory to D minor. The E flat is a passing note between the scale tones E and D. The piece, however, breaks off on the passing note, E flat, ignoring the tonic D which is replaced by the rest of a quarter note. Moreover, the tonic harmony D–A is contained in anticipation in the chord of the right hand above the E flat (measure 64), since the G sharp is leading tone to the dominant A, which again is passed over in silence and replaced by a rest. In such sound structures the impression of "atonality" is brought about by shifting the chord notes from their normal place to other points, sometimes in advance (anticipation), sometimes backwards (suspension), and sometimes in anticipation and suspension simultaneously, with the addition of free alteration and unresolved changing notes. The close of the piece is given here in a D minor version, according to the strictest rules of pure writing. This D minor is obtained only by omitting the foreign anticipatory notes, D and G sharp, and by filling out the pause at the close.

arnold schönberg

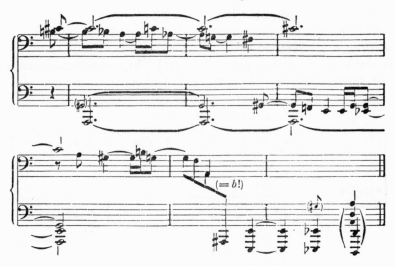

According to the results of the preceding analysis, one might come to the following final conclusions regarding this Schönberg piece:

It is written in a stanza-like form, in the manner of the contrapuntal inventions. In seven short stanzas or sections of generally 8, once $(2 \times 8) - 1 = 15$ measures, the same four motifs are treated, each time differently. Contrapuntal fantasies on four motifs. Central point, low point, culmination, climax, descent are marked and made impressive to the ear, according to the accepted rules of the art. After cutting out all obscurations and disturbances, one can finally obtain a clear view of the tonality, which is changed several times in the seven sections: G major, G minor, A minor, D minor prevail, and secondarily A major, B flat minor, C minor, C sharp minor, and the Phrygian mode. What seems new and confusing in the piece does not lie in the plain and clear formal treatment, nor in the plastic and impressive motifs, nor in the polyphony, but merely in the veiling, obscuring, and also in the amplification of the tonal harmony. Simultaneous progression of several tonalities (polytonality) is manifest. Of "atonality," however, only those will speak who are not able to disentangle Schönberg's confusing discords and reduce them to their traditional tonal basis.

OPUS 11, NUMBER 2

This piece differs considerably from No. 1 in its constructive plan. It has neither the subtle contrapuntal art of the former piece, nor its invention form. Here a three-part song form is evident, after the traditional pattern a–b–a.

435

First part, *a,* measures 1–15.
Middle part, *b,* measures 16–54.
Reprise, *a,* measures 55–66.

Here also a melodic extract will prove useful. The entire thematic material consists of melodic motifs (a) and (b), and accompaniment motif (c):

Motif a)

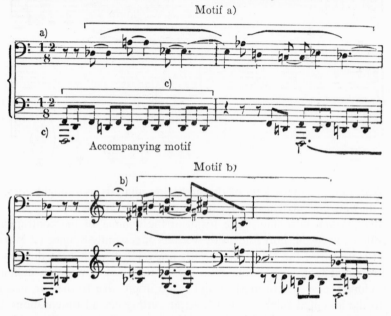

Accompanying motif

Motif b)

First part (measures 1–15). Measure 1, introduction, establishes the accompaniment motif. The melody is subdivided into four phrases: 4 + 4 + 4 + 2 measures.

Measures 2–3 contain motif (a).
Measures 4–5 contain motif (b).
Measures 6–9 contain motif (b) in a new continuation.
Measures 9–13 contain motif (b) in augmentation.
Measures 13–15 contain motif (a).

The entire first part in itself is also constructed in a three-part song form *a-b-a,* corresponding exactly to the minuet or scherzo pattern of the classics. In its melodic line, the upper voice shows nothing unusual or new. Considered in itself, it is written in the key of C sharp or D flat minor, after a few enharmonic changes have taken place. Even the D major episodes in measures 3, 4, and 9, 10 can be easily explained as Neapolitan sixth harmony in C sharp minor. In measures 10–13 there is a deviation into the A tonality, either A major or A minor. Measures 13–15 return to C sharp or D flat minor. The strange effect lies in the conflict of

436

these C sharp minor–D major–A major–C sharp minor lines with the D minor ostinato of the accompaniment. In other words: C sharp minor against D minor. The two tonalities do not result in a third tonality, but run alongside each other without merging. The strange harmony of motif (b) in measures 4, 9, 10, with sharps in the right hand, flats in the left hand, can be explained as collision of D major and D minor chords. Similarly, A major is mixed with D minor in measures 11–13. The curious harmony of measure 13 can be explained as the tendency of two entirely different chords toward a third chord, with a resolution common to both, but which is passed over in silence. The chord B flat, F, C and the chord G, D flat, A flat = G, C sharp, G sharp, can both be quite naturally resolved into the D minor triad which, however, Schönberg omits:

One may state the following rule as a chief principle of polytonal harmony:

Two chords, consisting of any intervals whatsoever, which can be resolved into a common third chord, harmonize together.

The conflict between C sharp minor and D minor is momentarily decided in favor of D minor in the third quarter of the sixth measure. As a compensation, D flat = C sharp major triumphs in the third quarter of measure 7, but also for a moment only. The third moment of compensation, once again in favor of D minor (in measure 13) is passed over in silence by a pause with fermata. At the close of the first part, at measure 16, C sharp minor and D minor come to a close each on its own tonic, without becoming reconciled.

The middle part, b (measures 16–55), is divided into two sections of twenty-four and sixteen measures, quite normally $(3 \times 8) + (2 \times 8)$ measures. The motifs (a) and (b) in new variants constitute all the thematic events, in the sense of "thematic development," in the style of the older sonata technique. Cutting out the main melodic line, one obtains a number of melodic phrases which offer no difficulties of comprehension. They are as clearly defined in their melodic line as in their tonality. Ambiguity and complication arise here mainly through the accompaniment.

Section 1 (measures 16–19) consists of two parallel phrases. Measures 16, 17 begin in D minor (with the Neapolitan sixth E flat) and modulate to

G major. The strange harmony may be resolved into a quite intelligible tonality, if one transposes the C sharp of the bass in measure 17 a half tone up to D, and if one transposes the bass figures in measure 16 out of their two octaves into only one octave. The result would be a translation into the harmonic idiom of the Wagnerian style, with the following tonally simple harmonic structure:

Schönberg thus writes a modulation from D minor to G major, richly adorned by chromatic passing notes, disturbed by the foreign bass tone C sharp = D flat, instead of D. His procedure here, in fact, is to dim the tonality by willful alteration and introduction of a foreign tone at many important points.

The eccentric harmony in measures 18, 19 may be similarly explained. Upon comparing Schönberg's original version with the following transcription, which might stand without the least change in *Parsifal,* one would recognize how trifling differences are able to change harmonically normal progressions into something "atonal," inexplicable by the rules of tonal harmony, as is generally believed. These differences are the following: in measure 18 Schönberg makes the chord B, D, G in the bass enter one eighth note too early; in the same measure the resolution to E of the last E flat in the bass is swallowed up by the eighth rest; in measure 19 (third eighth of the right hand), a sixteenth passing note B might still be added as a passing note to B flat; in the same measure the last bass note G enters one eighth note too early and would have to be replaced by a G sharp; and finally, the pauses in the accompaniment at the close again swallow up the G minor half-close leading normally to D. A few little touches such as these, putting in omitted resolutions, indicated by rests, or adding omitted passing tones, slight shiftings at the change of chords, and enharmonic change, transform the atonal phrase into something tonally comprehensible (p. 439). The transcription is given with slight retouches at x, indicating passing tones or chords added, at filling out of pauses through omitted resolutions.

Here we see a prolonged modulation, starting from the dominant ninth chord of E flat minor, passing to A major and finally to D major, as half-close in G minor.

Section 2 (measures 20–28). Here the polytonality of the first section makes its reappearance. Above and below the ostinato accompaniment phrase, G flat, B flat or F sharp, A sharp, the melody progresses on its F major and A minor road. In measures 23–24, inversion and augmentation of the melody at the same time. In measure 24, a chain of dominant seventh chords, in descending sequence; in the alto counter melody with freely inserted dissonant changing and passing notes. Such part leading is sometimes found in Bach. At measure 25, on the sixth and twelfth eighth for the right hand, the resolutions to G minor, which make the progression comprehensible, are omitted. One may also explain these omissions by imagining so faint a pianissimo that the resolution can no longer be actually heard and must be supplied by the imagination. Incidentally, this measure 25 is an admirable, masterly example of the refinements to be gained through this new technique of omitted resolutions and pauses. The left hand plays successively the arpeggios D flat major, G minor, F sharp minor, and again G minor. The upper part supplies a suitable counter melody to these arpeggios, and the middle voices fill out the intervening space with parallel fourths to the upper part, in analogy to the normally used parallel thirds (see p. 440).

In measures 26–28 the bass has the accompaniment motif in D sharp minor, against D minor in the upper part. The entire phrase is a repetition of motif (b), measures 4, 5, only complicated by the foreign bass tonality, so that now three tonalities are sounding together: D major, D minor, D sharp minor.

D flat major   G minor   F sharp minor   G minor

Section 3 (measures 29–39) contains a free fantasy on motifs (a) and (b). The soprano in measure 29 is the answer to measure 27: measure 30 is the free continuation of measure 29. The tenor melody of measures 29, 30 is related to the motif of the three quarter notes in measure 7. In the soprano, measures 31–33, there follows a capricious descending sequence on a four-note motif: B flat, G flat, F, E–A, F sharp, F, E–A flat, E, E flat, D flat, and so on, to be regarded as diminution of measure 28, which returns twice, in measures 33 and 38, and in augmentation in measures 35, 36. The curious four-note motif in sixteenth notes in measure 39 (enshrouded in a cloud of indefinable compounds of several chords) is again the diminution of the sequence motif in measure 31.

The second, smaller half of this development section begins at measures 40–43 with a slightly changed repetition of measures 16–19, transposed a fifth lower. The chain of broken chords in measures 43–44 is easily understood in its tonality if one takes each hand separately. The strange sound of both hands together is the result of canonic imitation, the left hand following the right at first a half tone, later a whole tone lower. What we see here is a canon not only of two single parts, but of two full chains of chords. Contracted into chords, the phrase would look as follows:

If one displaces the chords of the left hand at first one eighth to the left, and in the second half of the phrase one eighth to the right, the resulting chords will lose their curious aspect and will closely approach normal chord progressions. This "chord-passage" in the old sense is used as effective transition to the culmination of the piece at measures 45–47; below the high trills, motif (b) is heard fortissimo, like a fanfare of horns and trumpets. In measure 47 the trills run into a chromatically descending passage, which in measures 48 and 49 finally merges in pianissimo into that four-note motif already used in measure 39. Measures 50–54 make use of well known thematic material, pointing back to measures 28–38. The tonality of this episode is without doubt D minor. In measure 54 the bass takes up the accompaniment motif in triplets, in D minor. The soprano leaves out, as has been frequently seen in these pieces, the resolution to D, replaced by a rest, and the phrase ends abruptly on the chord F, A, E flat.

The third section, the reprise (measures 55–66), is a somewhat varied and abridged reprise of the first section, with reminiscences of the second section. Measures 55–58 contain the principal motif (a) in D flat, against the ostinato triplet motif of the accompaniment in D minor. Measures 59–60 point back to measures 16 and 18 in the development section, with the ostinato triplet motif in the bass now added. The close, measures 61–66, consists of melodic phrases originating in measures 4–8, 33–34. The ostinato triplet motif D, F, D is changed into the triad B flat, D, F by the addition of B flat in the bass. On top of this B flat major organ point the upper parts move downwards with chromatic passing tones. There cannot be any doubt as to the D minor character of the entire close, measures 59–66. But it is just as certain that never before has a D minor of so rich and choice a harmonic effect been heard, and that one is confronted here with a valuable enrichment of tonal resources.

Even the curious "atonal" close is a plain D minor, as soon as one recognizes that the final resolution into the tonic is omitted, and that the piece closes with the "next to the last," unresolved chords: [1]

drifting into the tonic
D minor

[1] Ferrucio Busoni has written a "concert version" of Schönberg's Op. 11, No. 2, in which he transcribes Schönberg's rather "abstract" music into the idiom of the piano. Though Schönberg did not approve of Busoni's arrangement, the study of this piano version will prove highly rewarding in many ways to advanced musicians. Those especially interested in the matter are advised to compare the two settings, measure for measure. Both have been published by Universal Edition, Vienna.

OPUS 11, NUMBER 3

This piece is most curious because the complications of its plan cannot be unraveled by the ear, but only by the eye. One may call it a series of variations on a rhythm. In fact, the curiosities accumulated here can only be comprehended by a rhythmical analysis.

The theme, if one may call it so, is a seven-note progression with the rhythm 6/8

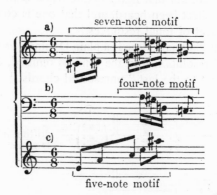

appearing in measures 1 and 2 of the alto part. At the very start this "theme" is complicated by counterpoints above and below, formed in the same rhythm, but already varied, by reduction to five and four notes, by melodic changes, by augmentation. Every variation occupies only one measure, at the most two measures, sometimes two different variations are heard simultaneously, in soprano and bass. Thus the thirty-six measures of this piece contain about thirty variations. After having comprehended the original seven-note motif in measures 1 and 2 with its reduction to four notes in the bass, with its five-note version obtained by pulling apart the intervals and doubling the note values:

one is now confronted with the problem of inspecting each measure with regard to the motifs (a), (b), (c) and their transformations.

This most laborious piece of work may be illustrated by at least a few examples. Measures 9–10, 11–12, 13–14 contain three variations of motif (c), in the soprano, in time values of quarter, eighth, and dotted eighth notes. Motif (c), originally a five-note motif, is here extended to the seven-note version of (a), and afterwards to six and eight notes.

442

Measures 23, 24 contain a double variation of the five-note motif, present in both hands, but each time in a different rhythm:

five-note motif

five-note motif

Also measures 25, 26 contain a double variation, this time of a "cantabile" character. The soprano has the seven-note motif, the bass, as counterpoint, plays the five-note motif twice, with a redundant three-note phrase:

Seven-note motif

Five-note motif   Five-note motif

Schönberg's Op. 19

Schönberg's innovations in melody are inseparable from his treatment of rhythm. To reduce his new melodic types to the old and familiar ones simply requires a demonstration of logic in the structure of the new forms which now appear ridiculous to those who do not understand or instinctively feel the as yet unformulated laws of construction governing his melody. This analysis is not of course an estimate dealing with artistic importance. Leaving open the question of the aesthetic value of Schönberg's innovations, the author is content merely to point out and explain some of Schönberg's novel technical methods. The six pieces of Op. 19 will be treated not in the succession of the printed edition, but rather progressively, taking the comparatively simple ones first.

Of these, number VI is the simplest and easiest. Its nine bars are filled out by a few chords held out for a considerable time, sounding into each other very softly, with a fragmentary melody of faintest pianissimo floating above or within the long chords. This melody leaps about in characteristic Schönbergian manner, from top to bottom, from the highest octaves to the bass register. Putting it into one plane, and making its logical coherence still clearer by a few enharmonic changes, one might present the following condensed version:

Every musician will see at a glance that it is sheer nonsense to call this "atonal." It is written in pure and simple E major, chromatically modified, and, presented in this manner, is not in the least startling or novel. In rhythm there is nothing at all remarkable in the entire little piece.

The harmony, however, calls for a few explanatory remarks. Four chords constantly repeated make up almost the entire piece. Two are dominant sevenths, with one tone omitted. The first, A–F sharp–B, is the dominant chord of E major. E–D–G sharp in the fifth bar is the dominant of A major. The other two chords show Schönberg's characteristic and novel groupings of fourths: G–C–F and C–F–B flat. Peculiar effects result from the sounding together of these chords. In the study of Schönberg's Op. 11, we were able to formulate the law governing such chord connections, a law unknown to the older theory of harmony: Any two or three chords, no matter how dissonant, which can be resolved into the same chord, may be played together. In this particular case the chords numbers 1 and 3, numbers 2 and 3, and even 1, 2, 3, and 4 (in bars 5 and 6), are correctly combined, accordingly to this law, because each one of these chords may be naturally resolved into the tonic triad E major. Schönberg omits the resolution, but in spite of his dexterous maneuver, in spite of the entire absence of the tonic triad of E major, he cannot destroy the tonality of the piece, which remains E major to anyone who really understands what happens.

How all these different chords may be resolved into the same triad of E major is shown in the following synopsis, which illustrates the combination of four different chords in bars 5 and 6, the added resolutions being placed in parenthesis:

Number II is a descendant of Chopin's famous "Raindrops" prelude. The two tones G and B, in the manner of an ostinato part, like falling drops, make their way softly but persistently through all the nine measures of the little piece, the regular succession being interrupted but once, in the sixth measure. Against this ostinato phrase there is set a brief melody of expressive sighs which shows a clearly defined tonality, occasionally clashing against the ever-repeated G–B. This tonality, belonging to the complex of E minor or B major, is veiled by the addition of a lower parallel third, and by frequent enharmonic changes of accidentals, so that the eye, glancing superficially over the page, is easily deceived as to the real tonality. The following melodic extract of the piece shows clearly that the melody is based on the scale E, F, or F sharp, G or G sharp, A, B, C, or C sharp, D or D sharp, that is, E minor, with occasional chromatic alterations such as frequently occur in Chopin's, Schumann's, or Wagner's music. A more precise statement might refer to this as the major-minor scale of E.

In the melodic sketch above, Schönberg's actual notation is frequently replaced by the enharmonic equivalent, as, for example, G sharp and D sharp for A flat and E flat, in order to demonstrate that there can be no

445

question here of atonality The construction of the little melody is quite simple: the motif (a) recurring several times, the larger motif (A) used three times in variations, bars 7–9 an inversion of bars 6 and 7.

Strange chords of Schönbergian color occur only three times, in bars 5, 6, and 9. These groupings of notes are easily understood if one realizes that many of the ultramodern chords are merely what were once known as passing or changing chords, with the distinction that they now leap over the resolutions formerly considered indispensable. Thus the chords in bar 6 and the closing chord in bar 9 might easily be reduced to an effect strictly legitimate in the sense of the older theory, by merely adding the resolution omitted by Schönberg. In both cases, the B major triad, dominant chord of the E minor scale, would thus be reached, corroborating once more the tonal character of the piece.

Number IV, a little scherzando sketch of thirteen bars, is chiefly interesting, not for harmonic effect but for melodic construction. In fact, three-quarters of the little piece is wholly without harmony, in one-part writing. The manner in which Schönberg shapes his melody here is novel. Two motifs, (a) and (b), consisting of seven and three notes respectively, are the elements of the structure. Motif (a) is used in four, motif (b) in five rhythmical variations. The ordinary principle of melodic construction consists in preserving the rhythm of the motif and varying the melodic substance, the intervals. Schönberg tries the reverse of this commonly accepted principle: he preserves the melodic substance approximately, but varies the rhythm at every new appearance of the motif. That this inverted method of melodic construction will be widely accepted seems to me questionable, but it is interesting as an experiment that opens new possibilities. The ver-

sion of the piece given below clearly reveals these melodic correspondences
and rhythmical variations.

Note, for example, that bars 3 and 4, 7 and 8, and 10 are rhythmical
variations of bars 1 and 2. Bar 10 even corresponds to bars 1, 2, and 4
together, combining in one measure both motifs, (a) and (b), in diminution. Motif (a) is characterized by the ascending third at the beginning, followed by a step downward and a wide leap downward, whereas motif (b)
is formed of three successive notes without a leap. The whole piece may
therefore be called a miniature set of variations on a double theme.

The liberty has been taken here of transposing Schönberg's melody back
to the ordinary manner of melodic structure, thus reducing, as a curious little
experiment, its unknown quantities, x and y, to familiar terms, somewhat
in the manner of an algebraic equation. In the reduction to ordinary melodic
construction, Schönberg's scherzando would run something like this:

In the fifth piece, the construction of the fifteen bars is $(3 + 3 + 2) +$ $(1) + (2 + 3 + 1) = 15$ bars, a two part construction of eight and six bars respectively, with the connecting link of a single bar after the eighth. The whole piece develops out of the first motif, comprising bars 1–3, the second part of which—bars 2, 3—is also used as a building stone. The melodic sketch below shows how the entire piece is composed exclusively of these two motifs, called here motifs (A) and (B).

In this sketch, Schönberg's "atonal" manner of notation has been re-written with enharmonic changes of equivalent sounds in order to make it obvious that the melody belongs to the tonality of the scale of B, with no more chromatic alteration than is found on any page of Chopin or of Wagner. The entire melody may be played on the organ point of the dominant seventh (B–A) sustained, which is another proof of the B tonality, as is also the resolution added at the end of the B major triad. Space forbids giving more details of Schönberg's actual harmonization, which has the tendency not to underline the B tonality of the melody, but rather to hide it, to mask it intentionally. But one illustration may be offered. The very first bars which, superficially viewed, seem remote from B major, may nevertheless be interpreted in the B tonality, as is seen from the following possible harmonization on the dominant ninth chord: B, D sharp, F sharp, A, C.

The third piece employs polytonality, that is, a different tonality for each hand. The left-hand part is easily intelligible, being written in the so-called mixolydian mode, in E flat, with D flat instead of D natural. The tonality of the right-hand part is less apparent, but, after some enharmonic changes and by allowing for a few occasional little extravagances, it may finally be reduced to the B tonality, major-minor intermixed. The question of the final effect of these two different simultaneous tonalities is interesting, but too complicated for brief treatment. In some cases polytonality gives the impression of two separate tonalities going along side by side, whereas in other cases two different tonalities heard simultaneously produce a third tonality different from either.

Hardly less interesting is the construction of the right-hand melody. Schönberg employs a rhythmical variation of a motif here, similar to the one pointed out in the discussion of number IV. This piece is a one-bar theme, followed by eight variations of a single bar's length each. The novel feature is that these many miniature variations should at the same time have the character of one coherent melody.

Number I is perhaps the most complicated piece of the whole set. It also shows a most subtle variation technique, similar to that of numbers III and IV. As a clue to comprehension of its construction, we may single out the ascending third: B–D sharp in bar 1. Following the melodic line, one will find this ascending third in almost every bar, sometimes, as in bars 4 and 5, in three or four parts in dialogue. In such places the so-called "linear counterpoint" of Schönberg becomes noticeable, an adaptation of the old tonal counterpoint to the altered demands of the new "supertonal" harmony. Note also that the top voice in bars 6–8 is answered by the bass (in the

449

right hand) of bars 9–12. The free, barless rhythms of the old Flemish music of the fifteenth and sixteenth centuries are revived; the bar lines, however, are a nuisance in such places, and the player ought to neglect them, since he is tempted otherwise to render false accents. The correspondence of the last four bars with bar 1 will easily be recognized. Less distinct is the correspondence of bar 2 with bars 6 and 7, top voice. Note also that thematic coherence is scrupulously observed in the "accompanying" parts, even in the light, quick passages of thirty-second notes, at the very beginning, in bars 2, 8, and 10. To show these and other points, a comprehensive musical sketch would be required, in which the tonality of B major–minor in the principal melody might also be revealed.

CHAPTER **XXIII**

in conclusion

At the close of an extended book, filled with structural demonstrations, aesthetic observations, and technical details, it may be welcome, though by no means necessary, to conclude with a brief methodical survey of the ideas underlying the book, a sort of finial table of contents with commentary, something comparable to the coda of a symphonic movement.

Though every single chapter is intended to be a coherent and logical unit, yet the sum total of all the chapters must necessarily, in a book of this type, be incomplete. The story to be told has no real end; it might be extended to double or more of its length, had the author thought it advisable to interpret still more works of the immense literature of music. A novel or a drama or a historical narrative needs a conclusion, a skillful presentation of the problems treated, leading to a final explosive climax or a harmonious, gentle, peaceful relaxing of the tension previously accumulated. A technical book on mathematics, chemistry, physics, or music, must, however, be satisfied with the clear presentation of its problems by selected samples of the cases involved, without necessarily aiming at a final climax, or even an exhaustive demonstration of its subject matter. It must necessarily stop at some fitting point without being able to give the impression of a real, satisfactory conclusion.

In the present treatise the author has without scruple sacrificed the related sequence of the single chapters. This means that each chapter is a unit in itself, to be studied without necessary reference to the preceding or the following chapters. Unlike a book on mathematics, a chapter here does not presuppose the study of its predecessor.

In this collection of loosely strung-together essays, the teacher is not obliged to follow the order of the chapters in the book. He may jump from a chapter in the first part to any chapter in the second part. A fairly intelligent student will understand the author's reasoning anywhere in the book, provided he has properly digested the first two chapters, the indispensable foundation of structure and form. These chapters deal with the structure of motifs and the combination of motifs in the structure of short melodies. Here the student's attention is called to the sensible shaping of plain melodies. The book does not pretend to treat this matter exhaustively. To do so one would have to write a special book devoted exclusively to the invention, structure, effect, and impressiveness of "melody" in its widest sense. Such a book does not yet exist, proof enough of the difficulty and evasiveness of the problem. Merely the basic elements of melodic structure are treated here, only so much as is needed to comprehend the structure of large melodic complexes found in whole pieces or movements by the addition of a number of melodic phrases, a chain of "periods," either in regular, normal, eight-, twelve-, sixteen-measure melodies, or in irregular three-, five-, seven-, nine-, or ten-measure phrases.

A useful help in the study of melodic structure may be found in a little book by Ernst Toch, *Melodielehre,* and in several chapters of Walter Piston's books on harmony and counterpoint. The student of this treatise will be led to study these melodic problems by his own observations in the works of the masters. He is made familiar with what the author considers the three fundamental types of melody: (1) The invented melody, the tune, in folk songs and dances, popular music. (2) The constructed melody, or "counterpoint," and (3) The declamatory melody, in recitative, psalmody, Gregorian chant. Amplification, variants, and manifold combinations and cross-relations of these three main types fill the vast literature of music.

The first two chapters in the second part are also of a general, introductory nature, whereas the remaining chapters each treat some specific topic. The chapter "Aesthetic Ideas as the Basis of Musical Styles and Forms" tries to point out to the student the importance of fundamental aesthetic ideas, which give rise to musical compositions like seeds dropped into fertile soil and growing and ripening into large plants or trees, bearing fragrant flowers and delicious fruits. The student, in his own practical experience with the art of music, its flower and fruit, is led in the reverse direction back to the roots and seeds, to the primitive ideas, whose creative powers are hardly manifest at their first crude appearance. All good melodies, whether of antique, medieval, or modern origin, whether Greek, Hebrew, Indian, Italian, German, obey the same laws of logical structure. Their form, proportions, subdivision, melodic outline, accents, rhythm, and so on, are subject to a few rather simple axioms to be formulated in a new basic theory of melody, still waiting for its convincing and comprehensive explanation. There is an abundance of material for such an investigation in the music of all great masters who have been guided by their exceptional musical instinct, their genius in finding in each case the proper cut or cast of melody, though they may not have been fully conscious of the laws governing their power of melodic invention and construction. Also in art, as in life, the power of unconscious or half-conscious activity may be proved to be great.

As regards form, the fundamental investigations of George Conus in Moscow have proved the existence of certain laws of symmetry and proportions dominating all music to such a degree that every musician is subject to them unconsciously—the more he is affected, the greater his innate talent is. We have not the power of escaping these laws, any more than we can voluntarily change the circulation of our blood stream, our heart beat, or the activity of our brain. In his analysis of Bach's fugues, Conus has demonstrated the amazing order of symmetries and proportions, as also in the songs without words by Mendelssohn, pieces by Chopin, Bizet, Tchaikovsky, Scriabin, and others. The beauty of these subconscious proportions and symmetries is quite similar to the crystalline structure of minerals. The musical talent, the organic working of the musical mind becomes manifest in its instinct for these proportions. This instinct for shaping means talent. Art adds to this subconscious activity of the mind the more precise, conscious knowledge of the laws of structure.

The second chapter, "Logic and Coherence in Music" discusses in detail the ideas and mental processes which in slow growth through the centuries have led to the amazing achievement of imparting the impression of logical structure and coherence to the fleeting air waves, the material of music.

The main body of the book, the many chapters on the specific forms, explain themselves. The method employed in them is structural analysis, and it is the author's hope that the intelligent student may learn from the book not only a number of mechanical formulas, but the proper way of inspecting an extended and complicated piece of music—a method for musical anatomy, laying bare the structure, the skeleton, its limbs, muscles, ligatures, and finding its proportions. Skill acquired in this type of structural analysis will prove of great help in the creative efforts of a serious young composer. It will enable him to inspect his own works critically, and to understand better the novel methods applied in the works of prominent masters of contemporary music.

The student may also be reminded of the difference between "form" and "the forms" mentioned on the very first pages of this book. Whenever the book deals with the term "form," pure and simple, the reader finds himself in the confines of aesthetic speculation, whereas "the forms" are classified, well defined special types, described with the help of a structural formula, different for every single type, such as the song, march, motet, fugue, rondo, sonata, and so on.

Identity, diversity, and variation are the three all-important factors of musical structure. These subjects may be subdivided as follows:

Identity equals repetition, either exact or with slight variations.

Diversity equals complete or partial contrast.

Variation equals a means of avoiding the monotony of too much repetition.

Contrast equals diversity in larger degree.

Similarity may be variation in smaller degree, partaking both of repetition and diversity, a means of bridging over the gap between repetition and diversity, and therefore convenient for transition from one complex to a different complex.

The concepts of unity and variety in their mutual relations may serve the purpose of classifying the structure of musical works of art

Form as structural concept, idea, belongs to the permanently valid, immutable fundamental properties of music. The various forms, however, are the temporal, transient application of the unchangeable idea of form. Form is related to the forms like the Platonic idea, the ideal archetype, to the real objects, the single images of the idea. Form is elemental, organic, abstract, the forms are the concrete, practical samples, shaped by artistic handicraft. The concept of form remains permanently, the specific forms change from time to time. In fact there is neither a modern nor an old-fashioned form. A piece of music should not appear to the ear as a crude formal pattern, either nailed, pasted, or sewn, but rather as grown naturally and organically. Whenever the listener is struck by vivid sound, logical development, characteristic color, true temperament, real expression, it matters little to him whether these qualities are manifest in the form of a passacaglia, a fugue, a sonata, a song, a chain of variations. And inversely the most interesting, novel form is worthless without the impression of spiritual vitality. Form might be compared to daylight, revealing the shape and nature of all objects, qualities which cannot be properly observed in nocturnal darkness.

In addition to the analytic chapters—the bulk of the book—several chapters employ what may be called the synthetic method. The chapter on

"The Accompaniment in its Formal and Stylistic Significance" deduces certain lawful observations from many isolated cases in the extended literature of music. This synthesis reveals the current methods of accompaniment for the first time. The same claim may be made for the chapter, "The Forms of Unison Music." Here the results of recent research in comparative musicology have been very helpful. European music, dominated by the concept of harmony, has only limited use for one-part, unison music, whereas the recently discovered exotic and primitive music of the orient, lacking chords and harmony, has been led from this limitation to an ingenious, impressive, and extensive use of unison.

Finally, the student should be warned against expecting too much from even a thorough study of this book. It acquires value and usefulness only in proportion to the student's constant attention to the masterpieces of musical art. A book about form can hardly be more than a guide through the structural refinements and intricacies of the scores of the great masters. Only by observing the effects produced by the masters themselves in their scores can one acquire a mastery of the laws of musical form. To help the students of composition in this difficult study is the principal aim of this book.

ERRATA

Page 29, example from Beethoven's Op. 111: the
D flat should be omitted from the key signature.

Page 276, Example III: the first note should be G.

index

457